Dakota Datebook

Dakota Datebook

North Dakota Stories from Prairie Public

Edited by
David Haeselin

The Digital Press at the University of North Dakota
Grand Forks, ND

Dakota Datebook is supported in part by Humanities North Dakota. Established in 1974, Humanities North Dakota is a nonprofit dedicated to civics education and lifelong learning in North Dakota.

Published in collaboration with Prairie Public Broadcasting, Inc.

2019. The Digital Press at the University of North Dakota

Unless otherwise indicated, all contributions to this volume appear under a Creative Commons Attribution 4.0 License:
https://creativecommons.org/licenses/by/4.0/legalcode

Cover Art: Jessie Thorson
Cover Design: William Caraher

Library of Congress Control Number: 2019946849

ISBN-13: 978-1-7328410-4-8 (ebook)
ISBN-13: 978-1-7328410-5-5 (Paperback)

Table of Contents

Acknowledgements i

Student Editors iii

Dakota Datebook Authors v

Preface vii
Bill Thomas

Introduction ix
Merrill Piepkorn

On *Dakota Datebook* xi
Brenna Gerhardt

Dakota Datebook 1

Acknowledgements
David Haeselin

I'm deeply indebted to many outstanding collaborators. First and foremost, I need to thank and applaud the student editors. This talented group went above and beyond again and again. This book is dedicated to you all.

I also need to thank those who contributed new material for the book: Brenna Gerhardt, Merrill Piepkorn, Gordon Iseminger, Bethany Andreasen, and Clay Jenkinson. Sarah Walker, Cynthia Berg, John Hallberg, and Curt Hanson all provided indispensable help finding archival materials and teaching students about permissions.

Thanks to Aaron Barth, Erik Holland, and Connor Murphy for helping us showcase our work. Additional thanks to Josh Roiland, John Harris, and Bill Thomas for visiting us and seeing our small publishing company in action.

Many thanks to my colleagues in the English department who trusted me to design and teach this course, and who helped me make it happen: Eric Wolfe, Lori Robinson, Kim Donehower, Crystal Alberts, and, especially, Kristin Ellwanger and Cheryl Misialek.

It must be said that there would not be a *Dakota Datebook* without the help of Humanities ND. Their support for the *Datebook* has been instrumental for many years, and I must also thank the board for hosting the class, allowing the students to show off their work. I believe this was the moment that the students really took ownership over the project. I'm deeply grateful for that opportunity. Likewise, I commend the State Historical Society of North Dakota for their continued support of this book, the *Datebook*, and many other noteworthy public history projects.

A huge thanks to everyone at Prairie Public, especially Bill Thomas and Marie Offutt, who have been willing and impassioned partners from the get-go. It was a great treat to work with you and to get to know you both. Special thanks go to Skip Wood for doing the hard work of editing the entries in the first place and for all his help scouring the archives and getting us what we needed to make the final book. And, of course, thank you to all the authors who contributed stories to the *Datebook* over the years. The hardest part of the process was selecting *only* 365 of these gems.

Big ups to Jessie Thorson for designing the cover and adding such much-needed whimsy to the graphic design of the book.

Thanks to Susie Caraher for her copyediting and her universally supportive attitude. I think we all know that the Digital Press would not be a thing if you were not for you.

Finally, I need to thank Sheila for listening with me and to me. If we didn't breakfast together, this, and many other projects, would have never even gotten off the ground.

Student Editors

Bailey Baesler
Katherine Byers
Ana Chisholm
Elsa Condit
Daria Ferguson
Madelyn Gentile
Allison Gorres
Sheena Hellekson
Tanner Hostetter
Savannah Kelly
Heather Nagengast
Kennedy Olson
Alexandria Stroh
Christina Walker
Brandon Weber
Morgan Young

Dakota Datebook Authors

Dan Bihrle
Alyssa Boge
Carol Butcher
Kristina Campbell
Jacob Clauson
Derek Dahlsad
Jim Davis
Jack Dura
Merry Helm
Dr. Steve Hoffbeck
Michelle Holien
Karen Horsley
Jayme L. Job
Cathy A. Langemo
Christina Perleberg
Merrill Piepkorn
Scott Nelson
Tessa Sandstrom
Dave Seifert
Steve Stark
Christina Sunwall
Lane Sunwall
Lucid Thomas
Sarah Walker
Jill Whitcomb
Carol Wilson
Maria Witham

Preface
Bill Thomas
Prairie Public Director of Radio

When I started thinking about the *Dakota Datebook* radio project, it was nothing innovative. Almanacs go back to the Babylonians. Newspapers and broadcasters have been doing "History Minutes" and "This Day…" features for a long time. But somehow it was still exciting to imagine North Dakota's own version.

My original idea was to do an almanac sort of thing — a daily rundown of interesting current and historical events. Maybe an important hearing at the Capitol, some community events and concerts, some governor's birthday, and Angie Dickinson's first movie release. Well, that was way too much. Our first writer, Merry Helm, settled down to a story per day.

Dakota Datebook stories have been very various, shaped by a changing corps of writers, and edited from the get-go by Skip Wood. But there are certain constants for which we aim. The entry should tell a good story, one that you'd want to tell someone after you heard it. It should be tied to the date, because that gives it an extra punch. The daily-ness also tells us we are getting a kind of chronological cross-section. The story should be accurate and true (thank you, State Historical Society readers). And, of course, it should be about *here*. Each entry should help us all understand better why and how this place is like it is. *Dakota Datebook* should be like the nozzle of a 3D printer, point by point, story by story, creating a fuller concept of where we live.

The idea has gone over great with our listeners. That's because public radio listeners love to know stuff. They are just as interested in Traveling Jenny, the untouchable cow/buffalo of Dunn County, as they are in the founding of the NPL. I thought this project would wrap up after a year or two after we had run through all the famous people and notable incidents. I couldn't be happier to have been wrong.

Town of Lonetree, North Dakota, is named for tree on left
Credit: John Vachon, Farm Security Administration - Office of War Information Photograph Collection (Library of Congress), 1942

Introduction
Merrill Piepkorn
The Radio Voice of Dakota Datebook

Traveling Jenny was a wild half-cow half-buffalo that roamed the badlands of western North Dakota. Many a rancher tried to lasso the beast and bring her into their herd, but never succeeded in doing so. Of the thousands of *Dakota Datebooks* I've recorded, the story of Traveling Jenny from August 6, written by Jim Davis, is still my favorite.

The *Dakota Datebook* writers are a talented bunch; their keen eyes for detail and commitment to preserving the history of this fine state that have allowed them to write the eccentric stories that you've enjoyed over the years. Recording the *Dakota Datebook* series, written by a stable of several writers since 2003, has been a highlight of my personal and professional life.

I've been interested in North Dakota lore for as long as I can remember. Maybe it's because of my early childhood growing up on a farm in northwest North Dakota, near Stanley in Mountrail County. After moving to Fargo as a nine-year-old, I returned to the family farm for several summers, living and working on the family farm, now owned by my brother. I always appreciated that rural upbringing, the neighbors of varying ethnic backgrounds, the stories of my grandparents who farmed there since 1915. I've always enjoyed poking around old stuff!

In 2000, I was extremely fortunate to land a job with Prairie Public radio hosting a daily, hour-long, statewide interview and discussion show, Hear It Now (now called Main Street). Our guests came from a wide variety of backgrounds and the topics we discussed were equally as diverse. Of course, a lot of those guests were authors, many of whom wrote about some interesting aspect of North Dakota history–stories of the pioneering days, raucous political times, Native American history, ranching, rodeo, business, and show business. You'd be hard pressed to find a topic not discussed on Hear It Now.

Shortly after the debut of Hear It Now, Bill Thomas came along with the idea for a daily snippet of history to be broadcast on Prairie Public, and *Dakota Datebook* was born. Who would have ever thought that here and now, sixteen years after that first show, *Dakota Datebook* would not only still be around, but would be a staple of the network's weekday schedule? What an amazing record.

On a personal note, my work on Hear It Now, which included broadcasts from locations all across the state, and my work on *Dakota Datebook* helped prepare me for my current job as Senator, representing north Fargo in the North Dakota Legislature. It has also made me aware of how many people listen to Prairie Public radio. I can be talking to someone in line at the Dairy Queen or the grocery store and often the person in front of me will turn around, recognizing me as the guy who does those history stories on the radio.

Bill Thomas has done a great job of building the Prairie Public radio mission and audience, but I believe his legacy of Director of Radio will be *Dakota Datebook*, whose success has exceeded all our expectations. The program is not only about North Dakota history, it will be regarded as an important part of North Dakota broadcasting history for years to come.

Much like Traveling Jenny, these selected stories refuse to settle down and become part of the herd. You are fortunate to have come into possession of this collection of 365 *Dakota Datebook* stories. Enjoy.

On *Dakota Datebook*
Brenna Gerhardt

There is a quote I scrawled on a scrap of paper years ago and keep tucked inside my writing desk: "Tell me where you are and I will tell you who you are." It reminds me that setting gives context to every character in a story. I wonder not only about the characters I create in fiction, but about the real-life characters who left their marks on this place through the years—and how my own character continues to be shaped by my time here. This is the reason I look forward to the trill of the meadowlark each morning on Prairie Public during my daily ritual of listening to NPR news. *Dakota Datebook* situates me in a place with stories cemented between the bricks of old buildings, plowed under the "progress" of cultivated fields, etched in memorial plaques, handed down by elders, deposited in libraries and family scrapbooks, and recounted in barstool mythology.

Our shared narrative is as diverse as the people who, for better or for worse, have populated our geographic space. The researchers who bring us *Dakota Datebook* rummage through the attic of our collective memory to bring to light the events and experiences, often messy and contradictory, that show us where we were, who we are, and what we aspire to be.

It reminds us that a few generations before the Dakota Access Pipeline protest at Standing Rock another reservation in North Dakota battled the federal government over land and water during the building of the Garrison Dam. And a few generations before that, the "battle" of Whitestone Hill was a massacre of the elders, women, and children who perished there. Sometimes our history takes us to ugly places, but turning our eyes away from mistakes and broken promises does nothing to erase their legacy.

We also know that before 2003—when French fries became "freedom fries" in congressional cafeterias following France's opposition to the Iraq invasion—hamburgers were called "liberty sandwiches," and the city of Bismarck considered changing its un-American German name to something more patriotic during World War I.

There are also entries in *Dakota Datebook* that remind us of the grit lining our heritage. In 1923, just three years after women won the right to vote, Minnie Craig secured a seat in the North Dakota House of Representatives, giving women a stronger voice in politics. Ten years later she became speaker of the house, the first American woman to hold this position at the state level.

Prior to this was Matilda Galpin, also known as Wambli Autepewin (Eagle-Woman-That-All-Look-At), who lived with a foot in both the Native American and white worlds and made strides to bring them together in the face of conflict. She was the only woman to sign a treaty with the United States.

Humanities North Dakota's own Ev Albers makes an appearance for his commitment to the principle that the humanities belong to every North Dakotan. Although these people may not appear in the Rough Rider Hall of Fame portraits decorating the State Capitol, their stories should remain in our public consciousness to point us toward a better future.

Of course, a good story needs to have at least a few colorful characters and outlandish scenes to keep a reader's (or listener's) attention, and *Dakota Datebook* does not fail on this front. The hair-raising Zip to Zap event or the antics of Poker Jim come readily to mind.

However, our strongest orientation to a sense of place will always come from the everyday experiences described in the diary entries of bonanza farmer Mary Dodge Woodward or in the recounted memories of German-Russian farm kids.

Thank you, *Dakota Datebook*, for telling me where, and who, I am.

Fanny Dunn Quain. First all-woman jury Bismarck, ND
Credit: State Historical Society of North Dakota (Mss 10003); State Historical Society of North Dakota (00091-0243)

JANUARY

Rustling Ring

01 JAN

Ranchers in Williston, North Dakota, anxiously anticipated the outcome of a publicized court trial on this date in history. The trial of Pat Cannon, Jud Miller, and William Coleman in Williams County District Court was viewed as the culmination of many years' work, and the "final chapter in breaking up…the famous border horse [rustling ring]."

For years, the trio, along with several other groups of horse and cattle thieves, plagued the ranchers along the border of North Dakota and Montana. Rustlers in the area grew infamous for stealing the animals, then driving them north into Canada and selling them to unsuspecting buyers. Butch Cassidy, one of the most well-known rustlers, set up a system of trails connecting Mexico to Canada. This system, known as the "Outlaw Trail," began just south of Big Beaver, Saskatchewan, north of Redstone, Montana. The trails wound south through some of the roughest and most remote parts of the country. South of Redstone, the trail connected to Miles City, Montana, then crossed the border into North Dakota, heading south again to Deadwood, South Dakota.

In the late 1890s, when the Boer War broke out in South Africa, two hundred and forty-five of Canada's Northwest Mounted Police volunteered for service and were sent there to help. That void opened the door for wave after wave of cattle and horse rustlers who headed north into Canada. Without the protection of the mounted police, Canadian ranchers were at the mercy of the outlaws for a number of years. Using the Outlaw Trail, rustlers were able to move the cattle south, to sell either in the U.S. along the trail, or head all the way to Mexico. When the war in South Africa was over, the mounted police returned to their posts, forcing the rustlers to concentrate once again on the ranches in the U.S.

Pat Cannon and Jud Miller, two of the men sentenced in Williston in 1910, each received ten years in the state penitentiary for their crimes. Their accomplice, Slim Bae, rolled over on the men, and was granted leniency for his testimony. The judge handed Slim a sentence of five to ten years, but then issued his parole immediately. It seemed that the heyday of rustling in Williams county was coming to an end.

Jayme L. Job

An Early Vote for Women

The Nineteenth amendment, granting women the right to vote, was passed in 1919. However, women in North Dakota were already able to vote in city elections under an act passed by the state legislature in 1917. In Bismarck, this created some excitement as citizens geared up for the first election that local women could vote in: an election for city commissioner at the end of that year.

One quirk of this ruling was that women had to be sworn in and vouched for. Luckily, any property holder who knew the women appeared to be enough for election officials.

Nonetheless, a few factors kept the local landmark election a small affair. According to the *Bismarck Tribune*, it had been a singularly quiet election "following a campaign in which there had been no clear-cut issues and one devoid of excitement." The two candidates were Harry Thompson, a local plumber, and John Larson, who ran a local lumber yard. The two were friendly and had kept the campaign clean.

The election day also dawned nice and cold, with a crispy morning temperature of -20 degrees. Many voters, men and women alike, did not show to take part. Most of the interest in this election stemmed from the new female voting factor, but the *Tribune* noted that by 9:00 a.m., not a single woman had voted. By noon, reportedly fewer than twelve females had cast ballots.

Nonetheless, especially with slightly warming temperatures, more men and women did turn out as the day wore on. Pro-vote women in the city were appalled to find that at least one voting location provided women with a much smaller ballot box than it did for the men. One woman complained, "You'll find before the day is over that you would have done better to switch those boxes right around and give us the larger one."

In the end, only 986 votes were cast, 287 of these from women. According to the *Tribune*, elections before women were allowed to participate had as many as 1200 citizens turning out, so overall, the numbers for this election were low.

Despite a guess by the *Tribune* that women might be more likely to vote for Thompson, a plumber, whom they might know better and work with, than Larson, who owned a lumberyard, it turned out that the woman largely voted for Larson. It was not enough to defeat the votes of the men, however, with Thompson ending up the victor.

But the election was also a win for women, and for civility, with Thompson saying, "I am particularly pleased with my election because of the caliber of my opponent [...] John Larson was one of the best men that could have been put up in Bismarck; he has always been a good friend of mine, and I know he will continue to be."

Sarah Walker

Big Bread

03 JAN

In January of 1957, the Brownee Bakery in Fargo turned out the world's largest loaf of bread. They worked on it for twelve days before getting it right, and after seventeen failures, they finally produced the perfect loaf.

Some bakers pride themselves on bread that's light as a feather; but this record breaker weighed a whopping 375 pounds. It's not clear where they got a pan or an oven big enough to handle it, but the final product was six feet long and two feet high.

Northwest Airlines flew it to Minneapolis where it was sold at an auction for $855 during a banquet honoring North Dakota. The project was a promotion cooked up by the Greater North Dakota Association, with proceeds going to charity.

375 pounds of bread… That would take a lot of baloney.

Merry Helm

Missing Evidence

An unusual case of missing evidence occurred in Cando on this day in 1904. The story begins a few weeks earlier in Bisbee, North Dakota, when the authorities broke up an illegal distillery called a blind pig operated by a father and son by the name of Gilmer. The father and son were brought to the jail in Cando until their case could be heard in the courts. While waiting for the pig case to come up on the court docket, Clerk of Court Peck, in charge of court records and evidence, requested Professor Ladd of the North Dakota Agricultural College to perform an analysis on a quart of moonshine that had been taken as evidence in the raid on the Gilmer's blind pig.

Professor Ladd conducted his analysis on the bottle and traveled to Cando at the request of Clerk Peck. The professor was to give testimony as to the alcoholic content of the beverage, but, as the court was busy with other cases, the Gilmer pig case never came up for trial. Ladd was forced to return home to take care of other business until court could be reconvened at the beginning of the new term on January 18. Since the Gilmer case would not be heard until after the winter break, Peck was in charge of holding onto the court's evidence. He placed the bottle into his office vault, and went into another room to enter the bottle and Ladd's analysis into the court's records as exhibit A.

While Peck was away, the court's janitor, Paul Gransaulky, came into his office to tidy up. Gransaulky saw the bottle sitting on a shelf in the vault and thought that, according to the *Fargo Forum and Daily Republican*, "…he'd go in and take a look at it." Moments later, Deputy Henderson walked by Peck's office and saw the janitor drinking the evidence, a tag reading "Exhibit A" still dangling from the bottle. He went into see Peck and "…asked him if he knew that the janitor was drinking that stuff in the vault." Peck, outraged, dashed to his office to find the bottle completely empty. Upon questioning, Gransaulky denied drinking the entire quart of whiskey, but when confronted by the deputy, who had seen him drinking from the bottle, he finally confessed to drinking the evidence. Fortunately for the Gilmers, since the evidence was destroyed, it could not be used in the case against them when court reconvened on January 18.

Jayme L. Job

Limpy Jack Clayton

05 JAN

Limpy Jack Clayton was in a world of hurt on this date in 1879. Clayton did it all: he was a cowboy, gambler, stagecoach driver, Sunday School teacher, and whiskey salesman at his dirt ranch on Stoney Creek, about twenty-three miles north of Jamestown.

Clayton got his nickname by double-crossing a friend; at the time, Clayton was in Duluth going by the name of Hamilton. Major Dana Wright said, "Among the assistants that Mr. Hamilton collected in Duluth was a character named Jack O'Neal and another named Dave Mullen, these missionaries of the […] Six Shooter days got themselves into some difficulties with the law and were arrested. Mr. Hamilton so far forgot himself as to testify in court against Dave so when the affair was cleared up, Dave shot Hamilton in the leg."

Hamilton moved to Jamestown after that, going by the name of Limpy Jack Clayton. Eight years later, that limp got a lot worse. It happened after Clayton did his best to ring in the New Year the night before. When he started for home the next day, he was carrying a heavy internal load of "forty rod" whiskey. The temperature was -37 degrees. Accounts differ, but all agree that Clayton fell down on the trail and his hands and feet were badly frozen.

About ten days later, Colonel Crofton, the Post Commander of Fort Totten, passed through on the stage route. Seeing Jack's condition, he ordered Clayton to be taken to the fort for treatment.

Historian August Leisch writes, "The hospital attendants cut his rags off, carried them to the stove on hot pokers and burned the outfit, bugs and all."

Henry Hale, a Ft. Totten Army Steward, later wrote to Dr. Grassick in Grand Forks, saying, "Jack entertained us for quite a while, we finally amputated part of one hand and the toes of one foot, we first tried to put him under (with) ether but it was only a good jag for Jack, during the process I remember him saying 'this is the second time the vigilantes have been after me.'"

The medical record states that Jack made it more than four months before the surgery was attempted. "Endevoured (sic) to amputate Clayton's foot," Davis wrote, "but after using 15 oz. of ether found it impossible to bring him under the influence, for just as he became insensible, he stopped breathing and the anesthetic had to be removed."

They tried it again on May 11. "2nd attempt at Clayton's foot, and though he went under ether very well, he did not reach the amputating stage tho' 25 oz. of ether were used." One week later, Col. Davis was finally successful. "With the assistance of A.A. Surg. Ruger, USA, I removed Jack Clayton's toes today. Anesthetic use – Chloroform. Reaction perfect."

And now you know how Limpy's limp got worse.

Merry Helm

Epiphany

January 6 is known by many different names. In France, it is called Three Kings Day. In England, it is called Twelfth Night, for the twelfth night after Christmas. It is also known as Epiphany. The day commemorates the arrival of the three wise men in Bethlehem, when they delivered gifts to Christ. Epiphany is a Greek word meaning revelation. It refers to the revelation of the wise men when they saw the star and followed it.

Germans from Russia brought their traditions and customs, including Epiphany, when they settled on the Great Plains. Sister Katherine Kraft wrote of celebrating Epiphany in 1948 in Strasbourg, North Dakota. She expressed her appreciation that Christmas didn't end on the 25th, being followed by a string of festive days, including a special celebration for St. John's Day on December 27. This feast honored the Apostle who sat next to Jesus at the Last Supper. Then on New Year's Eve, men went from house to house. They fired a rifle to announce the New Year and were rewarded with a glass of schnapps. Sister Katherine reported that the men grew merrier as they traveled. On Epiphany Eve, people gathered to drink the health of family and friends for the coming year. Bockbier was brewed especially for this time of year. It has a stronger taste and a higher alcohol content than other beers.

Epiphany marked the end of the Christmas season. Children dressed as the kings went from door to door singing songs, much like carolers in England. The children asked for donations for charity. They used chalk to mark the doors of the homes, writing the initials K, B, and M for the names of the three kings. In churches and homes, people did not place the figures of the wise men in their nativity scenes until Epiphany. According to tradition, the wise men brought frankincense as one of their gifts, so people burned frankincense in their homes and barns for luck.

When Epiphany was over, it was the end of the Christmas season. Decorations were taken down and Christmas trees removed. School resumed, and people settled in for the winter, warmed by the memories of Christmas.

Carole Butcher

A Football Dynasty

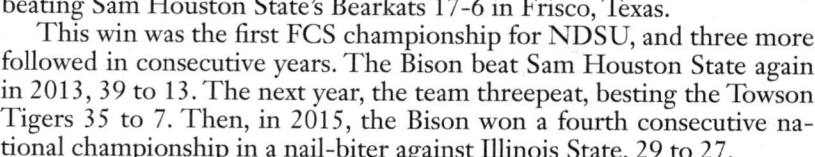

The national championship winning streak of a college football dynasty began on this date in 2012. North Dakota State University's Bison football team took home the trophy for 2011's NCAA Division I Football Championship Subdivision, beating Sam Houston State's Bearkats 17-6 in Frisco, Texas.

This win was the first FCS championship for NDSU, and three more followed in consecutive years. The Bison beat Sam Houston State again in 2013, 39 to 13. The next year, the team threepeat, besting the Towson Tigers 35 to 7. Then, in 2015, the Bison won a fourth consecutive national championship in a nail-biter against Illinois State, 29 to 27.

The consecutive wins brought much attention as the media spoke of NDSU's football dynasty. ESPN brought its "College GameDay" broadcast to downtown Fargo in 2013 and 2014. The network returned in 2015 with "SportsCenter on the Road" at the Fargodome.

A 33-game win streak also occurred during this era, until 2014 when the team fell to Northern Iowa 23 to 3 in Cedar Falls.

The repetitive wins came despite turnover at the top. Head coach Craig Bohl left the team in 2014 for the University of Wyoming. Assistant coach Chris Kleiman stepped into the shoes of the most winningest football coach at NDSU, and clinched that fourth title in his first season. Athletic director Gene Taylor also left the school, replaced by Matt Larsen.

The players also came and went, from running back Sam Ojuri to quarterback Brock Jensen to Adam Keller, a four-toed kicker. Some of those players continued in football after their time at NDSU. Former running back John Crocket plays for the Green Bay Packers. Jensen signed with the Miami Dolphins in the 2014 NFL Draft. He went on, however, to teach school in Moorhead.

The Bison's "drive for five" began in August 2015, but the team lost its opener against the University of Montana.

Jack Dura

Minnie Craig

The United Nations declared 1975 International Women's Year. The woman chosen for North Dakota's special honors was Minnie Craig, and this week marks the anniversary of that ceremony.

Minnie Davenport Craig was born in Phillips, Maine, in 1883. She was a very bright student, and after graduating from high school, she taught school, went to college, and attended the New England Conservatory of Music. She married Edward Craig, and they migrated to Esmond, North Dakota, where Edward had a financial interest in the local bank.

The couple soon became involved in the Non-Partisan League, and in 1923, Minnie decided to run for the State House of Representatives. In a state famous for its political independence and risk-taking, two women won seats that year – just three years after they'd won the right to vote.

Craig quickly earned a reputation for keeping meticulous notes, but not everybody appreciated her as a political leader. Despite this, and some male opposition, she ended up serving for six consecutive sessions. And in 1933, she made history when she was elected Speaker of the House. It was the first time in this nation's history that a woman served as the head of a legislative body.

That session was not an easy one. The first state capitol had burned down, and their temporary chambers in the Civic Auditorium were noisy and chaotic. The state was also in the midst of the worst agricultural depression in its history, and obstacles to long-lasting relief were enormous. In 1934, she left politics to work for the Federal Emergency Relief Administration, touring the state and organizing relief efforts for counties hardest hit by drought and grasshoppers.

The pioneer once gave some advice to women: "Lady, if you go into politics, leave the men alone. Don't run to them for everything you want to know. Don't swallow all they tell you. Post yourself first. Establish your own opinions. Build your own knowledge and confidence and do it by yourself.

"There's a field – a grand one for women – in politics, but women must…play politics as women and not as weak imitations of their 'lords and masters.' Men are all too inclined to 'stuff' a lady full of nonsense, treat her with not too much respect for her intellect and be far happier when she's nicely tucked away in some corner where she can do them no harm – and herself no good.

"But it doesn't have to be that way…She has certain natural talents which men don't have. Women are naturally given to detail…If they weren't, they couldn't make pies or sew dresses. Men don't like details. Because of woman's training…she's more thorough than man and right there she has a splendid opportunity for politics."

The words of Minnie Craig, of Esmond, the nation's first woman to be elected leader of a legislative body.

Merry Helm

Snowbound Ball

A series of Northern Pacific passenger trains pulled into Fargo in the early morning hours on this day in 1910. The seven east-bound trains had been scheduled to arrive in Fargo three days earlier but had been delayed. Rumors of their whereabouts had circulated through the city, as nervous friends and family members feared the worst for the train's passengers. With a blizzard raging through Montana and rumors of a horrific train wreck blocking the Northern Pacific's lines, many imagined the passengers huddling for warmth within the confines of the train cars or even worse.

As it turned out, the passengers of the trains were experiencing a much different situation. Most of the trains left from Seattle on January 3 and headed east through Montana. Familiar with January in Montana, several snow plows accompanied the trains on their journey. Near Big Timber, Montana, the trains were met with forty-mile an hour gale force winds and blowing snow. Met by three-foot high snowdrifts, train operators dispatched the snowplows to clear the blocked railway. The front snowplow began to clear the snow but was soon toppled over sideways across the tracks by the blistering winds. Others rushed to turn the plow upright, but blowing snow quickly packed the machine tightly into the snowdrifts. It quickly became apparent that it would not be possible to remove the plow until the blizzard let up. In the meantime, the passengers received the news that they would be delayed in their present position for some number of days. Undeterred to have a jolly time of their trip, passengers on Train No. 2 began planning a number of "entertainments" to be enjoyed while the blizzard continued.

The highlight of the delay was to be a fancy dress ball held in the train's dining car. Several of the men aboard the train made the short trip into nearby Big Timber and purchased material and novelties to be used for the ball's preparations. The women on the train busied themselves by creating gowns to wear to the big ball. One of the passengers, Alfred Landry, left the train in search of a musician to perform for the ball. He found a dentist in the nearby village of Pierre who happened to play the three-string violin. While friends and family in Fargo worried about the fortunes of their loved ones, one dentist from Pierre was busy enjoying such a good time that he played from 8:30 at night until 1:30 in the morning.

Jayme L. Job

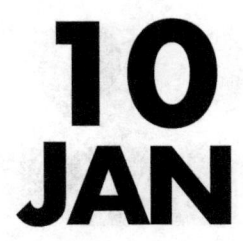

KKK Unmasked

On this day in 1923, North Dakota State Senators James McCoy and Lynn Sperry introduced a bill into the State Senate "…aimed at the Ku Klux Klan and prohibiting the wearing of a mask, regalia, or other head covering in public…" The bill—which became known as the 'Anti-Mask Bill'—was largely a response to Klan violence in southern states. News of the violence had created public outrage against the Klan, spurring North Dakota legislators to act. The senators hoped that by prohibiting Klan members' use of masks, they would lose the anonymity that enabled them to commit such atrocious crimes.

That winter, many North Dakotans were following the daily headlines of a criminal trial being prosecuted in Bastrop, Louisiana. There, members of the Klan were being investigated for the murders of Watt Daniel and Thomas Richards. Daniel and Richards were kidnapped from their homes in August of 1922, brutalized, and murdered. It became known that several of the Klan members involved were prominent citizens, and that an elaborate cover-up was staged shortly after criminal charges were filed. During the course of the trial, however, many additional crimes of the Louisiana Chapter of the Klan were made public, causing national alarm at the Klan's growing power and heinous practices. The Anti-Mask Bill, however, did face some opposition. Several members of the Non-Partisan League argued against the bill, claiming it unjustly targeted certain individuals and that there was insufficient proof that Klan members were involved in North Dakota crimes.

Senator Sperry, hoping to persuade members of the State Affairs Committee to pass the bill, requested information on the Klan from the state of Louisiana to present before the Senate. Leaguers countered by having the Reverend Halsey Ambrose of Grand Forks, a Klan member, speak to the Senate on January 23rd. Although the Reverend attempted to paint the Klan as peaceful and noble, Thomas Dixon—famed author of *The Clansman*—made national headlines condemning the actions of the Klan that same day. The next day, Nebraska passed its own Anti-Klan Bill. Two days later, charges were brought against Klan members for a physical attack on a man in Casselton, North Dakota. This created further public outcry. Opposition to the bill was flattened, and the bill quickly passed in both the Senate and House by late January.

Jayme L. Job

The Women of Hatton

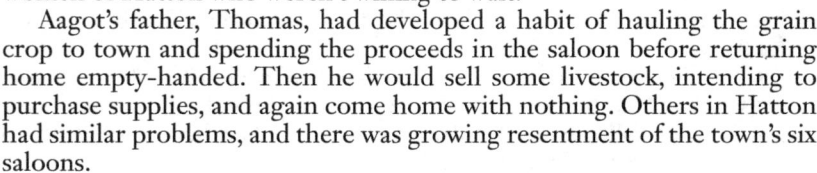

In January 1890, North Dakota was just a few months old. In voting to approve the Constitution the people also voted in favor of prohibition. Consequently, saloons would only be legal until July.

In her book, *Grass of the Earth: Immigrant Life in the Dakota Country*, teacher and author Aagot Raaen tells about the women of Hatton who weren't willing to wait.

Aagot's father, Thomas, had developed a habit of hauling the grain crop to town and spending the proceeds in the saloon before returning home empty-handed. Then he would sell some livestock, intending to purchase supplies, and again come home with nothing. Others in Hatton had similar problems, and there was growing resentment of the town's six saloons.

In that same January, Aagot's mother Ragnhild was among a dozen or so women who headed into town armed with hatchets, hammers, and long sticks. It was a busy day, with people everywhere.

Aagot Raaen writes that the first saloon was so busy, the owner hardly looked up when the door opened. "The women rushed in and madly chopped, smashed, and raked down liquor bottles so that the whole floor was soaking wet in a minute." Aagot's mother "took chairs and benches, lifted them, and hurled them at the shelves [...] windows and [...] mirrors. The crowds in the streets cheered." The women even went to the cellar and chopped at kegs and barrels until streams of liquor flowed and their shoes and long skirts were wet.

The women moved from saloon to saloon. When they got to the last one, the owner stood outside and said in Norwegian, 'Please go in.' The women complied, but were met by a cloud of burning pepper, so strong that they coughed, and gasped for breath. The trick deterred the raiders and saved the saloon.

As on most battlegrounds, there was "collateral" damage. During one of the raids, patron Peter Lomen suffered a cut on the head. That evening, he resumed his drinking and apparently failed to tend the wound. Three weeks later he was dead of an infection.

The saloonkeepers said the women caused his death. The Sheriff summoned the women to trial, and Aagot writes that her mother had a good time listening to all the funny things the witnesses said and the speeches of the lawyers and the judge. Her mother said, "We had good food and slept in good beds. I had a real vacation."

We have to assume that the women of Hatton were cleared on the merits of the case, and not because the judge was afraid to convict!

Merry Helm

Rural Delivery in Winter

The United States Postal Service has a long history stretching back over two centuries to when Benjamin Franklin became the first Postmaster General. By 1863, a door-to-door delivery was established where income could cover the cost; prior to that, a person had to pick up their mail at the post office.

That remained the case for folks in rural areas. But by 1902, after some experimentation and delays, the Post Office had finally extended rural delivery across the United States.

North Dakota's first rural routes were started in 1898, involving addresses for Wahpeton, Saint Thomas, and Mayville. Bottineau came along in 1900, followed by Kindred in 1901, and Gardner in 1902. Rural delivery allowed residents to receive their mail without running to the nearest post office. Rural carriers also sold stamps and money orders and could facilitate registered letters.

The extremes of winter brought challenges. In 1905, the *Hope Pioneer* published a notice that read: "By many it is now realized how much more difficult and trying the work of the rural letter carrier is made by having to stop at a number of places on his route, delaying and benumbing his hands with the cold at every such place, to gather up pennies from the box, left there in place of stamps for outgoing mail. Attention is called by them to this in the following: Winter means cold weather. Your mail carrier is out in the cold from five to seven hours, riding from twenty to thirty miles a day, and is in need of your consideration. With cold fingers it is hard to pick pennies out of your box. Kindly buy a supply of stamps and keep on hand to affix to your letters when mailed. Select, as far as you can, pleasant days for your money orders and registered letters, and also for the buying of your stamps. Bear in mind these suggestions and you will greatly oblige the carrier."

Sarah Walker

Bishop "Bish" Dorsey

13 JAN

The story of the first African-American baseball player in Grand Forks, a man named Bishop Dorsey, is one of great athletic glory – but marred by deep woe.

Bishop Dorsey, known as "Bish," was born in Missouri in 1876, but lived in Grand Forks from childhood. Bish Dorsey became noted for his superb baseball skills from the time he was old enough to pick up a bat and ball.

At age nineteen, in 1895, his name began to appear in newspaper stories about the local semi-professional ballclub. Sportswriters wrote that Dorsey was a "brilliant" center-fielder; as well as a "stone wall third baseman," whose "throwing to first [was] perfect."

Dorsey worked at various jobs, serving as a bellhop; as an elevator operator at the Security Building; and as a railway porter. He was a key player on the 1899 Grand Forks team that won the state championship. Bish Dorsey also got married in that championship year, and all might have been bliss. But everything changed one fateful night, on November 27th.

Dorsey was working as a bartender in Sullivan's Saloon in East Grand Forks, the wicked sister city with legalized alcohol. A fellow named John McCabe, known only as a cook for a threshing crew, and new to the area, was drinking to intoxication in Sullivan's saloon. McCabe started a verbal altercation with Bish Dorsey and McCabe verbally abused Dorsey, using a racial slur.

Dorsey punched the 55-year-old McCabe; and McCabe smashed Dorsey in the face with his beer glass, causing bloody lacerations on Dorsey's chin and neck. Barkeeper Sullivan intervened; restraining Dorsey, and telling "him not to make a fool of himself."

Dorsey immediately left the saloon; and John McCabe finished drinking and headed towards the front-door. Bish Dorsey then rushed through the saloon, brandishing a cordwood stick and "struck McCabe a vicious blow on the head," killing McCabe instantly.

Dorsey escaped to Grand Forks, but then surrendered to Minnesota authorities. The court tried Dorsey for first-degree murder; and Dorsey's lawyer used a "temporary insanity" defense. The court deemed Dorsey guilty of third-degree murder, sentencing him to twenty-one years in Stillwater State Prison.

Dorsey's friends supported him and cared for his wife, who was pregnant. On this date in 1900, Dorsey expressed his "heartfelt thanks" to his teammates for their compassion. He then wrote a farewell letter, in which he gave his best wishes to the team, asking them to remember him every time they took the field, for he feared the prison doors had closed on him forever and that he would "probably never come out alive."

Those friends provided for Dorsey's wife and child in his absence; continually sending petitions, asking Minnesota to commute his incarceration. Dorsey was a model prisoner, wanting only to come home, and finally, in 1912, after countless appeals from his stalwart friends, he was pardoned.

Bish Dorsey, ballplayer, husband, and father, returned to Grand Forks, but then disappeared from the written record, his story lost in the elusive undercurrents of history.

Dan Bihrle and Dr. Steve Hoffbeck

George Defender, Bronc Rider

14 JAN

The annual Cowboys Reunion Rodeo started out somewhat accidentally at the first Mercer County Fair in 1915. Among the exhibits was a shorthorn bull, and Frank Chase of Fort Berthold decided he wanted to ride it – which he did. The crowd was impressed and passed a hat, and Chase walked away with $30.

It was the first rodeo event in Beulah, and in the following three years, rodeos became an annual event there.

Ed Boland described how it all began: "One day during the month of August, I was mowing along the creek when A. D. Brown, the newspaper editor, and George Slowey, and area businessman, came driving across the flat in a shiny new contraption. They stated their mission flatly – 'Could we stage a rodeo at Beulah the following month?'" When they left some two hours later, the foundation had been laid for the now famous Cowboys Reunion Rodeo.

One of the riders on that first year was George Defender. He was born in South Dakota in 1891 and started working as a "rough string" rider for the DZ Cattle Company at Standing Rock when he was sixteen.

Most of George's spectacular rides never got into the record books. One of these was a first-place win in Montana at the 1914 Miles City Roundup. The Roundup was one of the biggest rodeos on the circuit, and Defender quickly earned a reputation as a top bronc rider. He competed all over the continent, including wins at Madison Square Garden and the Calgary Stampede. At one point, he was a finalist for the world championship as all-around cowboy.

George also competed in wild horse races, bulldogging, wild cow milking, bareback riding, calf roping, relay races, and buffalo riding. His ranch was on the Standing Rock Reservation, but he later worked in Arizona after contracting tuberculosis. In 1932, he was injured during a roundup in New England, North Dakota, and it was on this date in 1933 that he died at Fort Yates. He was inducted into the North Dakota Rodeo Hall of Fame in 2001.

Merry Helm

15 JAN

Wilton or Milton

Names are very important. They establish a sense of pride of who we are.

So when it was reported that on this day, in 1908, the Postmaster of the town of Wilton received a curious request—a petition, to be precise—from the town of Milton, via postal authorities at Washington, asking that Wilton might change its name, "The Wiltonites naturally (did) not take very kindly to the prospective change."

It turned out that Milton had requested this change because "the similarity of names interfered with the proper delivery of freight express and mail." Wilton admitted that these mail mix-ups happened to them, as well, but they did not find this a good reason to change their name.

Wilton took offense. The *Wilton News* stated, "If the citizens of Milton don't like the similarity of names, why don't they petition the department to change their own? Wilton is known far and wide.... The very fact that the citizens of Milton complain of their stuff going estray shows that Wilton is the best-known town of the two by railroad interests."

After receiving this letter, the people of Wilton held a town meeting, at which the *Wilton News* stated, "a discussion of the question showed that public sentiment was unanimously against it." The townspeople rallied together. Some businessmen were appointed the task of showing the statistics of business of Wilton, as well as state the businesses that bore the name of the town, and businesses were urged to write to the congressional representatives of North Dakota to protest a forced change of name.

By the following week, the Wilton newspaper was able to report, "In accordance with the outlined plan, letters were written to our representatives in congress protesting against the change. A good many were sent, and they brought about results."

From Washington, D.C., the Post Office department granted assurance that no name change would be enforced. The representatives made sure.

The story ended happily for Wilton. The *Wilton Times* had the last say: "... Wilton will continue to do business under the same old name, which is as it should be, as it would have made us much trouble and expense had a change been ordered."

After all, a rose by any other name may still smell as sweet, but it would seem sort of strange to receive a bouquet of snarfblats.

Sarah Walker

Dr. E. M. Darrow

16 JAN

Today marks the birthday of Edward M. Darrow, who was born in 1855 in Wisconsin. He was one of the earliest and most influential physicians in the Red River Valley.

In 1878, Darrow graduated from Rush Medical College in Chicago and moved to Fargo to begin a medical practice. In his very first year, he started up the first hospital in the region, the Cass County Hospital. Fifteen years later, Edward's brother, Daniel, built the Darrow Hospital across the river in Moorhead.

In 1904, Edward was on the first medical staff of St. John's Hospital, which was housed in Bishop Shanley's former residence. Their first patient was a victim of typhoid fever.

Dr. Darrow became the first superintendent of health in Dakota Territory and was given the task of issuing to physicians their license to practice. A story has been handed down through his family that he had issued five licenses when he suddenly realized that he, himself, didn't yet have a license. So he became the sixth licensed physician in Dakota Territory. He also served as Surgeon General under Governor Burke and was also a member of the "insanity board."

Much of Darrow's practice took place in surrounding towns and rural homes. It wasn't unusual for him to have to operate on patients who were stretched out on their kitchen tables. Dr. Darrow brought with him sheets, dressings, his instruments and gloves, and all had to be boiled in a wash boiler. Patients were draped with the wet sheets; then a country doctor or family member was given the job of draping – or "dropping" – a piece of gauze, laced with drops of chloroform or ether, over the patient's face so the operation could begin.

Darrow's son, Kent, later said, "I was greatly surprised, when I went to Johns Hopkins in 1909, to see ether being poured into a tight cone, which was slapped on a patient's face, practically choking him, the patient struggling violently and often turning blue. My roommate would not believe me when I told him that our patients seldom struggled when we used the open drop method."

Besides his hospitals and private practice, E. M. Darrow left another legacy: his children. His daughter, Mary, received a degree in chemistry at the North Dakota Agricultural College and married Dr. Ralph E. Weible, another long-time Fargo physician. Mary founded the first kindergarten in North Dakota and also organized a women's suffrage association. Weible Hall, a women's dormitory at NDSU, was named in her honor.

Two sons, Frank and Kent, as well as Kent's brother-in-law, and Mary's husband, Ralph E. Weible, started the Dakota Clinic in 1926. Another son, Dan, graduated from Johns Hopkins as well. He was Professor of Pediatrics at Yale University and became an authority on various pediatric diseases. E. M. Darrow died in Fargo in December 1919.

Merry Helm

17 JAN

The First Boom and Bust

When the first North Dakota oil rush began in 1951, crude oil began to flow out of the state, for there were no oil refineries within its borders. That changed quickly, for by 1954, oil companies built refineries for gasoline in Williston, closest to the source, and in Mandan.

But the first-ever gasoline refined in the state was produced by the Queen City Oil Refinery. When Amerada Petroleum Corporation struck oil near Fryburg in southwestern North Dakota, the area experienced an oil rush. Business leaders in Dickinson immediately organized a company and built the refinery in 1953 on the west side of Dickinson along U.S. Highway 10 and the Northern Pacific railroad tracks. It produced its first gasoline on May 7, 1954.

Residents of Dickinson commemorated the first gasoline refined from North Dakota crude with an "Oil Celebration Parade" on that day in May. Dickinson hoped to become "the big center" of the state's oil trade thanks to its small refinery, but the Queen City Oil Company soon ran into financial difficulties, shutting down in February 1956, despite having "issued a million dollars in stock and bonds for its operation."

The stockholders voted to sell the refinery in 1957, enduring the agonies of bankruptcy in 1958. A syndicate, made up of former stockholders, purchased the refinery for $124,000 in cash during bidding in 1959.

It was on this date in 1961 that the newly-organized Great Western Refining Company published an advertisement in the Minot daily newspaper offering stock in the refinery for North Dakota residents only. Each share was $2.75.

The Great Western Refining Company intended to produce jet fuel and asphalt, in addition to gasoline. The jet fuel would be sold to the Air Force bases and the asphalt would be used for highway and street pavements throughout the state.

Investors in Dickinson hoped to have a thriving refinery as the 1960s unfolded, and they did sell some asphalt and fuel. Unfortunately, the Great Western Refinery also failed.

Newspaper reports in 1970 wrote about hopes of the refinery being reopened, but the refinery and the first oil "boom and bust" in Dickinson faded to dust shortly thereafter.

Dr. Steve Hoffbeck

MIA's Memorial

18 JAN

A memorial service honoring four North Dakota Air National Guardsmen was reported on this day in 1970. The memorial came days after the four missing men were declared dead by the Alaska Air Command at the Elmendorf Air Force Base near Anchorage, Alaska. The guardsmen, Eddie Stewart, Ingvald Nelson, Donald Flesland, and Floyd Broadland, had been missing since August 27, when they had disappeared while on a mid-afternoon flight from Anchorage to the King Salmon Air Force Station, a flight of only two-hundred and fifty air miles. According to the *Fargo Forum*, the Elmendorf Air Force Base near Anchorage served as a temporary base for the North Dakota Air Guard "during a two-week training deployment" at this time.

The four men left the Elmendorf Air Force Base on August 27, 1969; this was the last time that anyone saw either the men or the C-54 four-engine transport plane that they flew. Flying the C-54 to the King Salmon Air Force Station near Lake Iliamna that day was part of a routine training exercise for the North Dakota Air National Guard. All four of the guardsmen had extensive military training and experience in their respective fields, so when word reached Anchorage that the men had not reached their destination, the Alaska Air Command commenced an intensive search of the area that was to last eight weeks and include air-sea rescue units from California, Michigan, Oregon, Hawaii, and Japan. After finding no evidence of either the plane or the men after four and a half months, the Alaska Air Command was compelled to change the status of the guardsmen from 'Missing in Action' to 'Declared Dead'. The command was quick to point out that "the discovery of any evidence pertaining to the aircraft...or the men, [would] reopen the formal search."

The families of the men, all of whom served within the 119th Fighter Group, elected to hold a joint memorial service in Fargo. Chaplain Major David Knecht of Bismarck presided over the service, held at Fargo's First Lutheran Church. Despite twenty below temperatures, nearly seven-hundred and fifty people, including North Dakota Governor William Guy, attended the service to pay their respects to the pilots. Major Lowell Lundberg of Fargo concluded the eulogy by saying, "These men and our comrades gave their lives in aerial flight over Alaska...while serving their state and their country. May God preserve their memories."

Jayme L. Job

19 JAN

Jazz Comes to North Dakota

In 1923, a Canadian opera singer, Eva Gauthier, made history when she included six jazz pieces in a concert of classical music at New York's Aeolian Hall. The audience was stunned to have modern composers like George Gershwin listed on the same bill as Debussy, Stravinsky and Ravel. The mezzo-soprano's accompanist was George Gershwin, and she's largely given credit for launching his career that night.

One month after that historic concert, Miss Gauthier brought her controversial repertoire to Fargo. The following day, the headline read, "Eva Gauthier's Program Sets Whole Town Buzzing: Many People Are of Two Minds Regarding Jazz Numbers – Some Reluctantly Admit That They Like Them – Others Keep Silent or Condemn Them."

Eva Gauthier was one of the most prominent singers of the first half of the twentieth century, and that New York concert set the music world on its ear. Her rebelliousness became set in 1910, when she was abruptly replaced in a London opera for having a voice too powerful. She was only 4 foot 10, but she was a dynamo of outspoken flamboyance – satin hats and yipping Pekingese dogs. Upon losing that role, she promptly gave up opera in favor of concerts and solo recitals.

The *Fargo Forum* review of her concert read:

"Not in all our experience in the theater and concert hall have we heard so much comment and argument as followed the (Gauthier) recital at the State the other night. Miss Gauthier appears to have done something to this old town of ours. It has been ticking furiously since Wednesday night, and all because she came our way and sang a group of American jazz songs."

Most of the people apparently are of two minds regarding the singer's work. Many of them reluctantly admit that they enjoyed the ragtime and the jazz, but cannot understand why they did. They believe they have sinned and should be punished. The sinning was too sweet, too joyous, and they are positive that something will be done about it. Some judgment is going to fall upon them, and they await it in fear and trembling, oblivious of the fact that they had a great time while Miss Gauthier sang 'Alexander's Ragtime Band' and 'Carolina in the Morning' and 'Do it Again.'

There are those who resented the jazz songs, who thought them an insult to them, a reflection upon their artistic temperament and knowledge and equipment. They had no intention of applauding and did not.

And, then, there are those of us who enjoyed the songs immensely, who applauded wildly and long, and who want to hear them again in concert. We sinned openly and gloriously, and today are lost souls. But we'll go into the darkness and the slough of despond with a laugh and a song upon our lips, and the song will be "Do it Again."'

Merry Helm

Dr. Fannie Dunn Quain

20 JAN

Today in 1909, the North Dakota Legislature passed a bill to establish a Tuberculosis Sanatorium at San Haven. One of the people responsible for this was twenty-nine-year-old Dr. Fannie Dunn Quain. She was North Dakota's first homegrown female doctor.

Fannie Dunn paid her way through medical school by doing bookkeeping, teaching school, working for a surveyor and as a printer's devil, and also cleaning houses. Eventually Miss Dunn ran for Burleigh County Superintendent of Schools, but the powerful McKenzie political machine rigged the ballot boxes with false bottoms stuffed with ballots for the competition. She lost the election, so she concentrated on her education. In 1898, she received her Doctor of Medicine degree from the University of Michigan.

Shortly after she came back to North Dakota, she heard one of McKenzie's men brag about how they cheated her out of the election, so she ran for the office again. This time, United States Marshals oversaw the voting process, and she won.

Life as a pioneer doctor wasn't easy. Trying to reach her patients was a significant challenge, and she used any moving object to get where she needed to go. In one instance, she got a telegram that one of her patients had been treated for acute appendicitis near Dickinson. An old country doctor had decided the man should be sent to Brainerd, Minnesota for treatment. Dr. Fannie knew it would take too long; the man would die unless she operated on him immediately.

The problem was that he was already en route by train. She would have to get from Bismarck to Mandan before the train stopped, but the only way over the Missouri River was a railroad bridge. She quickly located a railroad handcar, but the section boss would only let her use it if he was on board. She agreed, thinking he would help her pump – but he was drunk and intended to only enjoy the ride. There was no way for her to pump the four handles alone the six miles to Mandan. But three high school boys saw her problem, jumped on board and manned the other three handles. They pumped until they were within 100 feet of the oncoming train, then threw the handcar and its drunk passenger off the tracks and ran. As the last car passed, people on the back platform grabbed her hands and pulled her aboard. She located her patient on board, and when they reached Bismarck, she took him to the hospital where she operated and saved his life.

Later, after she married Dr. Eric Quain, Dr. Fannie switched her focus from active practice to the needs of children and the escalating cases of tuberculosis in the state. Ultimately, she and Dr. James Grassick lobbied the state legislature, which led to the TB Sanatorium being built in the Turtle Mountains. She also established the first baby clinic in the state.

Merry Helm

21 JAN

Prairie Children

"Every child should have mud pies, grasshoppers, water-bugs, tadpoles, frogs, mud-turtles, elderberries, wild strawberries, acorns, [...] trees to climb, brooks to wade in, water-lilies, woodchucks, bats, bees, butterflies, various animals to pet, hay-fields, pine cones, rocks to roll, sand, snakes, huckleberries, and hornets; and any child who has been deprived of these has been deprived of the best part of their education." These words were penned by Luther Burbank and were part of the Child Culture Series No. 4, which was presented by the State Normal School at Valley City on this date in 1911. Based on that, it appears the open prairies and rural lifestyle of North Dakota seemed ideal for the development of a child.

The study by Professor G. R. Davies and edited by Professor A. P. Hollis of the Normal School was to inform both parents and teachers that children needed exercise and outdoor activities before their minds could fully develop. They believed that the fine fibers of the mind did not culminate until at least twelve years of age and the first business of the child was to become a healthy animal.

Life on the farm was advantageous for learning as the variety of the chores and the physical labors that went with it were instrumental in developing the body as well as the mind. Reading fine print was not recommended for younger children as the ability to read fine text needed to be developed over time to avoid eye strain. Recommended sleep hours for a six-year-old was thirteen hours while an eighteen-year-old should get eight and a half hours of sleep.

Today, studies much like the Child Culture Series have recommended that exercise is essential to good health and is a necessity to avoid obesity in young children, but adults also need to excite and develop the mind at the same time. In 1911 it was believed that children needed to first develop their physical attributes and then good mental development would result. It is interesting that Professors Hollis and Davies chose the writing of Luther Burbank to document their study for Mr. Burbank was a horticulturist, better known for developing the Burbank Russet potato. In horticultural terms, Mr. Burbank summed up his study in this way: "We do not look for fruit from orchard trees until after a long period of growth; so with the child." It appears that this 1911 study shows that North Dakota prairies are as good for children as they are for potatoes.

Jim Davis

Milking It

22 JAN

Prior to the Great Depression, the 1920s roared by; many Americans experienced an economic boom like none before. However, such was not the case for many farmers and ranchers, who dealt with dropping prices and instability throughout the decade.

For many dairy farmers, January of 1929 was tumultuous. Many of them went on strike in Illinois and Wisconsin, and Indiana soon joined their ranks. They wanted to get $2.85 per hundredweight, instead of the $2.50 they received from Chicago distributers. Some became violent, carrying weapons, kidnapping truck drivers delivering milk, and dumping milk wherever they could, even mixing in chemicals such as kerosene to pollute it. As a result, milk was getting difficult to come by in Chicago.

On this date, the *Bismarck Tribune* reported on a ripple effect of the strike, with Burleigh County sheriff, Rollin Welch, saying the price of milk and cream is going up in Bismarck just as fast or faster than it is in Chicago.

That tongue in cheek remark referred to farmer Carl Bjorstrom of Menoken, who recently sold some milk and cream, receiving checks for $7 and $8, but he took the liberty of adding some zeroes to the checks, cashing them for $700 and $800 dollars!

Afterward, he took off for Chicago, the site of all the dairy action. He was arrested by the East Chicago chief of police, where he was collected and brought back to Bismarck to face charges.

This strike added to the unfolding economic drama of 1929. As the year ticked on, more troubles would loom on the horizon, culminating in the crash of the stock market that fall, which pushed America into the Great Depression. The farmers and other businesses in the country would see a great deal of pain before stability returned.

Sarah Walker

23 JAN

Inconvenient Capitol

Anyone passing through Bismarck today is able to go to the seventeenth floor of the Capitol building, the observation deck, and view the landscape of the city from above. Tiny people, cars, trees, and buildings can be seen in every direction. There weren't seventeen floors in the original Capitol, but at the time it was built, there was much less to look at. The building was quite some distance north of the developing city.

A Capitol "bus," drawn by horse, carted visitors and officials back and forth across this divide. In 1905, a trolley car was put into service, originally to haul coal up the hill to the Capitol, but the car also hauled people and was faster than the horse-drawn bus.

January of 1907 wasn't necessarily one of the most memorable winters, though the *Ward County Independent* reported that one man from Ryder, Peter Ramstad, rode forty-five miles "with a fierce northeaster staring him in the face." He reported the worst ride he ever experienced in his twenty years living there.

However, on this date, news of the winter and one of its storms was spreading. As the *Grand Forks Evening Times* reported: "The disadvantages of having the Capitol located so far from the residence portion of the city was doubly apparent [...] when the blizzard which was raging over this portion of the state put the street car line out of commission and made it next to impossible to reach the building."

Drifting snow had forced the street car into suspension early on in the day – a hardship for the legislators attending the session. But those who had business at the Capitol still found a way, as carriages and bobsleds were "called into requisition," but the round trip cost $1 as opposed to 10 cents on the street car.

Sarah Walker

Sacred Medicine Bundle

24 JAN

On this date in 1938, three Hidatsa men were celebrating the rescue of important relics that they believed would end the drought, dust, and depression that were ravaging the North Dakota prairies. One of these men was Arthur Mandan, who, later that year, became the first chairman of the Three Affiliated Tribes. The other two men were 75-year-old Drags Wolf and 84-year-old Foolish Bear, both of the Hidatsa Water Buster Clan.

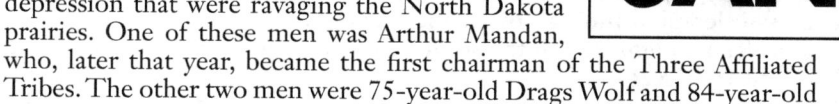

An important aspect of Native American oral traditions involves sacred bundles of relics that help storytellers remember the tribes' stories and histories. According to newspaper reports from the 1930s, certain members of the Hidatsa's Water Buster Clan were responsible for praying for rain and also for safeguarding a sacred medicine bundle that contained two ancient human skulls wrapped in a buffalo robe. The skulls represented two huge eagles that had turned into human beings; they were Thunder Birds, sky spirits that could send rain. At some point, the keeper of the bundle, Small Ankle, unexpectedly died without passing along his knowledge of the rituals and ceremonies needed for bringing rain. Small Ankle's son, Wolf Chief, was not eligible to take over, because he was not a member of the Water Buster Clan – membership is passed down through the mother. Wolf Chief was also a converted Christian. Still, he had physical possession of the bundle and sold it to a Presbyterian missionary for $30. Later, in 1927, the Heye Foundation in New York bought it for its American Indian museum. When the drought and dust of the Great Depression hit the prairies, the Water Buster Clan believed it was because the medicine bundle had not been properly kept. So, in 1933 they began the very difficult task of raising $400 to send a delegation to New York to get the bundle back. Unfortunately, the Heye Foundation was not willing to part with it, even when the elders offered them $250 for just the two skulls. A letter from the Foundation illustrates its insensitivity: "Do you think a copy of (the bundle) would be acceptable?" they asked. "Some of the older members of the clan might be able to work 'medicine' on it. If that won't be acceptable, would it be possible for you to use photographs? It might be possible that they would rub the original over the copy of the photographs and that might have some effect with the old timers."

The Water Busters' spokesman was Arthur Mandan. He too was not a member of the Clan, but he came on tribal business council and was known for his powers of persuasion. His children say that Mandan went so far as to get the issue before Congress, but it was when the newspapers picked up the story that the Foundation finally consented to trade the bundle for an equal artifact.

The clan hastily put together a roughed-up stone hammer and a sun-bleached bison horn stuffed with sage. In New York, Drags Wolf, Foolish Bear, and Mandan were given the red-carpet treatment, including a dinner at the home of Joseph Kennedy and a meeting with President Franklin Roosevelt. On January 23, 1938, the exchange was taking place at the museum when a staff member began to open the medicine bundle for the press. Foolish Bear and Drags Wolf rushed forward to shield the contents from photographers and headed home.

When the medicine bundle was safely back in North Dakota, the Hidatsa celebrated through the night. They say the clouds burned red for a day and a night, and in the spring, the rains came back and turned the prairies green again.

Merry Helm

Streeter Libel Law

25 JAN

The North Dakota State Legislature passed the Streeter Libel Law in 1905. The law was named for its sponsor, Darwin Streeter, a member of the House of Representatives.

In spite of the fact that Streeter was a newspaperman who founded the Emmons County Record in Linton, newspapers across the state were quick to condemn the move. W.C. Taylor, editor of the *LaMoure Chronicle*, expressed the sentiments of many when he called the law the most questionable act of the legislature. He said legislators who voted for the law "fairly tumbled over each other in their mad haste to muzzle the press."

The new law provided a very broad definition of libel. It included any material in writing, print, signage, picture, or effigy that exposed a person to contempt or ridicule. Taylor observed that there were politicians in the state whose public records couldn't help but to expose them to contempt or ridicule. Taylor noted that hiding a politician's official record would not change the facts. In such a case, it was the politician's own actions that exposed him to contempt or ridicule. Taylor concluded his editorial by saying, "The truth is never libelous."

It did not take long for a libel case to arrive in court. In 1906, the *Hope Pioneer* reported on a case in Devils Lake. John H. Bloom was the first person arrested and charged under the Streeter Libel Law. The case revolved around a story Bloom wrote for the *Devils Lake Journal*. He reported that a deputy sheriff of Ramsey County charged surrounding counties for the use of the Ramsey County Jail and pocketed the money. Bloom observed that the county should be reimbursed for housing prisoners from outside the county, but the money should not enrich the deputy sheriff.

Chief Deputy Herman Stenseth claimed to be the person referenced in the article, but the defense pointed out that there were numerous deputy sheriffs throughout the county, and the person in question had never been named. The jury felt Stenseth's argument was weak. They deliberated for all of five minutes before returning a verdict of "not guilty."

As for the Streeter Libel Law, it remains on the books to this day.

Carole Butcher

26 JAN

Widows Go West

Horace Greeley encouraged more than just young men to go west. "Young men! Poor men! Widows!" he said. "Resolve to have a home of your own! If you are able to buy and pay for one in the East, very well; if not, make one in the broad and fertile West!"

In her book, *Land in Her Own Name*, NDSU Professor of Sociology Elaine Lindgren describes hundreds of women who followed Greeley's calling by staking claims in North Dakota. Here is a small sampling of those who came as widows.

Norwegian immigrant Kari Skredsvig became a widow when she was only thirty-eight years old. Left with seven children between the ages of two and ten, she was destitute. A friend urged her to put her children in an orphanage so she could go out to find work, but instead, Skredsvig moved to North Dakota to file a claim in Burke County.

Breaking the land for the first time was a grueling job, and many homesteaders hired the job out. Kari didn't have the means for that, so with a team of horses, she and her 10-year-old son broke their first ten acres by themselves. To supplement what she could make from her land, she washed clothes for others, cared for the sick, cleaned and cooked ducks for hunters and also became a mail carrier. Sadly, being a widow further lowered her status in the community; when her children tried to bring in money doing odd jobs, they were paid less because they "were the widow's kids." Kari managed to prove up, however, and she lived on her 160-acres for forty-two years until her death.

Anne Furnberg came from Norway with her husband in 1869. Two years later, he died shortly after their first child was born, so Anne went to North Dakota. Her first home was a log cabin west of Fargo. To support her young son, Christian, she kept a cow and some chickens so that she could sell butter and eggs – but her market was across the Sheyenne River, which she had to cross by crawling on a log. When she was 38, Anne filed on eighty acres south of Fargo. While she did the farming, her 11-year-old nephew, Ole, cared for little Christian and cooked the meals.

In Towner County, a family of four women each filed their own claims. Karen Olsen Storberget, a 64-year-old widow, homesteaded in Grainfield Township. On nearby claims were her daughter, Karen, a 36-year-old widow, and two other daughters who were yet single, 22-year-old Bertha and 23-year-old Maren. Between them, they all proved up.

Not many people realize how many women filed claims in North Dakota. Lindgren's research sampled only nine of the state's fifty-three counties, but in these nine counties alone, more than 4,400 women filed for *Land in Her Own Name*.

Merry Helm

From Sheep to Shawl

27 JAN

North Dakota is known for a variety of agricultural products. The state leads the country in honey and sunflowers, among other crops. Corn, wheat, and cattle are high on the list. Very few people would think of sheep.

On this date in 1936, The North Dakota Wool Pool announced that their annual convention would be held on February 11 in Devils Lake. The purpose of the organization was to boost North Dakota sheep production for both meat and wool. They had their work cut out for them. According to The North Dakota Sheep Industry Newsletter, the state's sheep business went into decline during the 1940s. That was partially due to a labor shortage during World War II. In addition, American GIs came back from the war with a poor opinion of mutton, which they ate while stationed in Europe.

In 1954, the Federal government passed the National Wool Act. The Act was a price support measure for wool and mohair. This sustained the domestic sheep industry for twenty years, but during the 1970s, domestic lamb consumption fell even further out of favor with the American public. Production decreased from almost 700 million pounds in 1970 to about 325 million pounds by 1980, this despite some nutritional advantages. The North Dakota State University Extension Service points out that lamb is similar to beef and pork, but with lower fat, sodium, and potassium, and a calorie content about the same as chicken and tilapia.

After Congress ended price support for wool in 1993, the industry continued to decline, but the wool from North Dakota sheep still has its fans. The North Dakota Handspinners promote the use of the wool. With several hundred members, they hold an annual conference, offer presentations, and teach classes on spinning, knitting, and crochet. Some clean the fleece themselves, card it, and even dye it using natural dyes like tea and onion skins. The number of these handcrafters is growing, and with grass-fed meat gaining in the marketplace, the North Dakota sheep industry is confident that the decline is a thing of the past.

Carole Butcher

28 JAN — The White Way

Darkness ruled the night on city streets until streetlights illuminated avenues with kindly light. On this date in 1914, the *Grand Forks Herald* published an article proclaiming that the town of Cando had completed a new "White Way" of electric streetlights.

The "White Way" terminology came from Broadway in New York City, which had a "Great White Way" of tungsten-filament electric streetlights and illuminated signs on storefronts. Broadway's Great White Way was considered the most talked about street in "North and South America and the most prosperous avenue in the world."

A "White Way" lit up downtown streets so that shoppers would flock to the blazing lights, just like moths. Even a small town like Cando, in Towner County, wanted to have a white way to show that its downtown business district was a thriving place. Cando's boosters boasted about twenty-eight newly-installed streetlamps that made "everything bright" with a "new radiance" along the town's two main business blocks. The article reported that "pedestrians smiled in a pleased sort of way" at the "bright zone" of light in their progressive little city.

The White Way system was part of the "City Beautiful Movement" from 1900 through the 1920s, in which communities worked to improve all aspects of city life. The rapid growth of American cities after the Civil War had created haphazard development of business and industrial areas, plagued by poor sewerage and sanitation, with muddy streets polluted by horse manure and uncollected garbage. The City Beautiful Movement brought paved avenues, manicured parks and boulevards, as well as municipal sewer, electric, and water works.

The White Way brought new light and life to downtown businesses across the face of North Dakota by promoting extended shopping hours in the evening; while its brilliant beams also deterred crime. Grand Forks led the White Way movement in the state, installing tungsten lights in 1911. Underground wiring eliminated the ugly overhead wires from earlier arc lights; ornamental lampposts with white-glass globes brought beauty to it downtown avenues.

Other towns built their own white ways – Hatton, Dickinson, and Ray in 1912; Kenmare, Minot, Wahpeton, and Devils Lake in 1913. And on this date in 1914, it was Cando's turn, with the White Way of streetlights showing the town's spirit of "civic pride, prosperity [...] safety [... and] enterprise."

Dr. Steve Hoffbeck

Last Illegal Execution

29 JAN

The last illegal execution in North Dakota happened in Schaefer on this date in 1931 when a mob seized a prisoner named Charles Bannon and lynched him a half mile from the jail.

About a year earlier, in February, people had begun to notice that they hadn't seen the Albert Haven family around. Twenty-two-year-old Bannon had just started working on the Haven farm, and when people asked him about the family, he said the Havens had gone to Oregon and that he was now renting the place. By October, neighbors became suspicious when Bannon started selling off the family's property. Bannon's father, who had been helping his son take care of the farm, left about that time, saying that he was going to try to find the Haven family. On December 2, James Bannon wrote to his son from Oregon, saying he couldn't find the family, and he advised Charles to be careful and "do what is right."

Soon thereafter, authorities jailed young Charles for grand larceny and realized there was more to the story. Over the next few days, Charles broke down and, through three conflicting confessions, admitted that he had killed the family nine months before. On about February 10, the boys had been out milking cows when he and twenty-year-old Daniel Haven got into a teasing match. He pointed his gun at Daniel and, he said, accidentally shot him. He got scared and then killed fourteen-year-old Leland, too. When their parents came out to investigate, Charles also ended up shooting them, as well as two-month-old Mary and two-year-old Charles.

Rumors flew, including one that Charles stabbed Mrs. Haven fifteen times and then cut her in pieces in order to get her out of the house. It was also reported that the two-year-old was named after Bannon. It's difficult to determine the truth, because Charles never went to trial. Bannon maintained that he acted alone and that his father knew nothing about the killings. Nevertheless, authorities found James and put him in custody.

The father and son were moved to Schaefer, five miles from Watford City, the night of January 28; arraignment was planned for the next morning. Sometime after midnight, approximately seventy-five men in masks broke into the jail and overpowered Deputy Sheriff Pete Hallan. Sheriff Thompson came out to investigate but was too late. The mob battered open Charles Bannon's cell door, dragged him out and locked the two lawmen into a cell with the elder Bannon and another prisoner.

The plan was to lynch Bannon on the farm where the family died, but a caretaker chased them off. They hanged him from the Cherry Creek Bridge a half mile from the jail instead.

Bannon's father swore that he had no knowledge of the murders – just like his son had said – but he received life in prison. He was pardoned nineteen years later.

Merry Helm

30 JAN

Planning a Peace Garden

January is a crucial month for a gardener. Like a blank canvas to a painter, a gardener's imagination allows the frosty white rectangle beyond the window to explode with green growth and bright colors. By the end of the month, seed catalogs are dog-eared, orders are penciled in, and colorful dreams and schemes begin to solidify into a plan.

So it was on this day in 1932, when a group of North Dakota and Manitoba gardeners—and dreamers—went public with their plans for a new garden in the Turtle Mountains that would span the 49th parallel between Dunseith, North Dakota and Boissevain, Manitoba. Not a vegetable garden, mind you—but a 3,000-acre plot containing hills and trees and lakes to be dedicated as a natural monument to peace.

The sponsors announced, "The site will be known as the International Peace Garden. Free of commercialism, and the land, half in the United States and half in Canada will be a shrine to peace."

For several years, people had been gathering in the "shady recesses of the Turtle Mountains" for annual "peace picnics" that celebrated the long history of peaceful relations between the two nations. It was out of these peace picnics, which were attended by as many as five thousand people, that the dream of a permanent memorial was born.

The founders envisioned a natural landscape complemented by the work of "leading gardeners and landscape artists" of both nations. Their vision excluded any commercial development. They were seeking legislation that would disallow any "gasoline stations, road houses, dance pavilions and other resorts" within five miles of the park—providing a "protected zone" in all directions.

No small thinkers, they asked for $5 million in support, right in the middle of America's Great Depression—over $70 million in today's dollars. One-fifth would be used for "direct improvements of the park," and the remaining four-fifths would be set aside as a permanent endowment to assure proper maintenance down through the years.

The organizers targeted "the nickels and dimes of American and Canadian school children," as well as adults, service clubs and state and provincial governments for support. They did not ask for federal support.

Perhaps the financial bleakness of the 1930s, and the fears and uncertainties of those years between the two World Wars, helped fuel the imaginations of the peace garden planners.

The plans of January looked forward to July of the same year, when citizens and officials would gather for the formal dedication of this unique enduring garden at the center of North America—the International Peace Garden.

Merry Helm

Lights, Camera, Fargo

31 JAN

Filming was just underway on this date in 1995 for Joel and Ethan Coen's movie *Fargo*. The crime drama released in 1996 is often pointed to as Fargo and North Dakota's first pop culture reference even though the film's story had little to do with the city.

A stammering car salesman hires two crooks from Fargo to kidnap his wife for ransom money to be paid by her wealthy father. The plan goes badly wrong as bodies pile up and a pregnant police chief closes in on the criminals.

Despite a story based in Minnesota, several scenes were shot near Bathgate in northeastern North Dakota. This was necessary due to a lack of snow, with Minnesota experiencing its second mildest winter on record. The film crew came to North Dakota "at the eleventh hour," wrote a Coen Brothers biographer. They erected a Brainerd welcome sign and a 25-foot Paul Bunyan statue on Pembina County Road 1.

As Joel Coen explained, "The landscape up there is even flatter and more bleak than it is around Minneapolis. So, in a sense we got more interesting exteriors than we might have otherwise."

Fargo became a cult classic with its characters' outrageous accents and darkly humorous story. Actress Frances McDormand won the Oscar for Best Actress, and the film was entered into the National Film Registry in 2006. And the wood chipper in the film's well-known body disposal scene? It's on display at the Fargo-Moorhead Convention and Visitors Bureau.

Fargo fervor has continued, twenty years after the film's debut, with writer Noah Hawley creating a same-name crime drama for FX. In its first two seasons, the series featured more unlikely murders and crime sprees, including a 22-person massacre in downtown Fargo.

Jack Dura

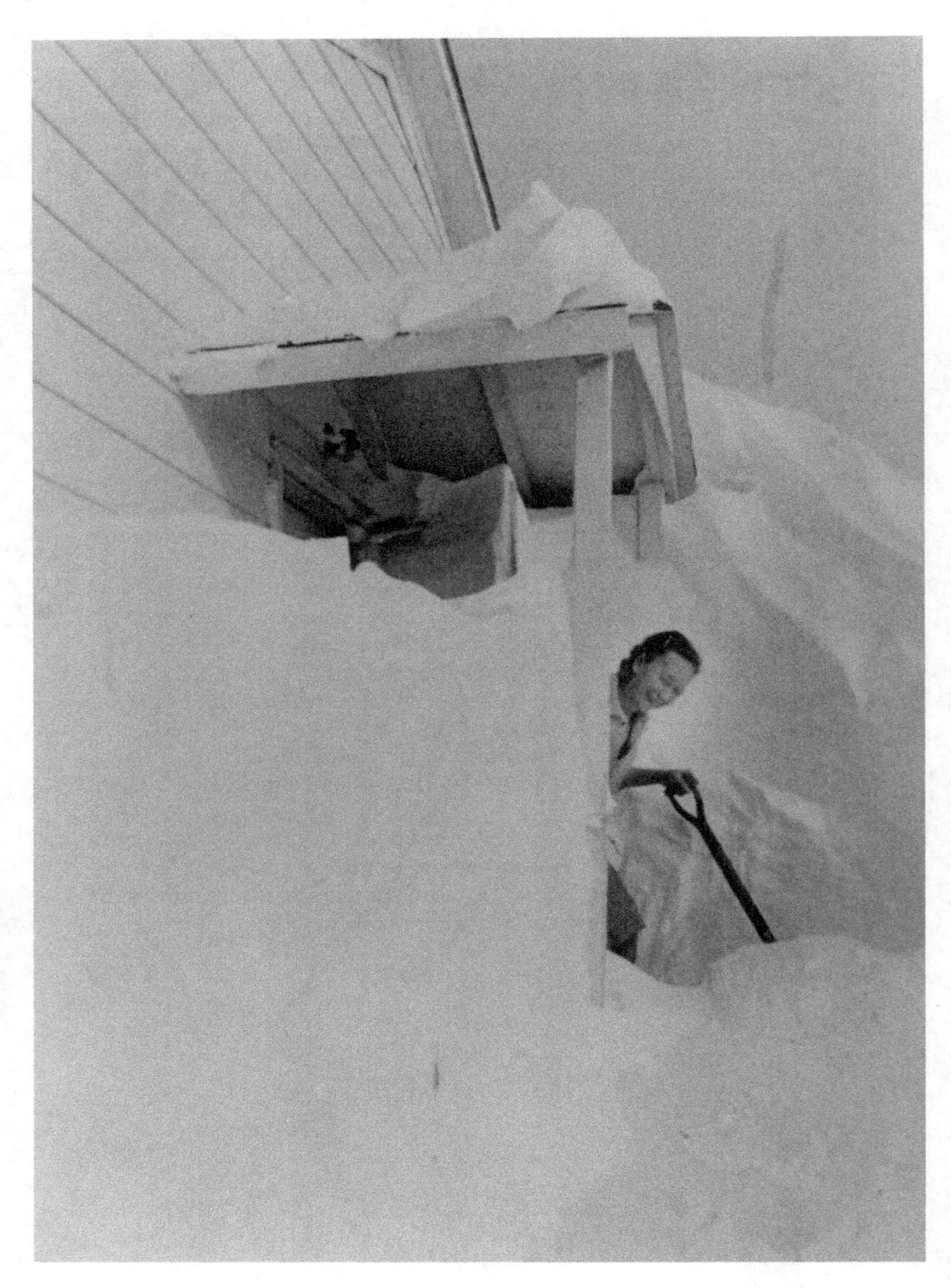

Too Much Snow
Credit: Fargo Public Library Photograph Collection, NDIRS-NDSU (2065.30.3).

FEBRUARY

FEBRUARY

Standing Pat

01 FEB

In 1918, when the U.S. was fighting Germany in World War I, there were some U.S. citizens who allowed war fever to rage too hot. Some fervent patriots thought all things German were un-American, changing the name of "hamburgers" to "Liberty sandwiches;" dachshunds to "Liberty pups," and sauerkraut to "Liberty cabbage." That turmoil also affected cities with names associated with Germany. North Dakota's capital, Bismarck, endured wartime pressure to change its venerable name.

Originally called Edwinton in 1872 for railway man Edwin F. Johnson, the Northern Pacific stockholders changed the name to Bismarck in 1873 in honor of Otto von Bismarck, the unifier of Germany, in an effort to encourage German capitalists to invest in U.S. railway bonds.

Controversy surfaced in early 1918, when Fargo's Women's Relief Corps petitioned North Dakota Governor Lynn Frazier, asking him to change the name of the capital city to one that sounded English or more American.

Governor Frazier responded to the petition by saying "it would not be advisable to change the name of the state capital," and that Bismarck would keep its name intact.

Frazier pointed out that Otto von Bismarck had died way back in 1898 and that, obviously, the deceased former-chancellor had been out of German politics for some time. Bismarck, being dead, had "nothing to do with the present trouble in the world."

Others agreed. The editor of the *Devils Lake World* wrote that changing Bismarck's name would be a "foolish action," defying history and denigrating common sense.

It was on this date in 1918, that the *Bismarck Tribune's* editors chimed in, stating definitively: "Bismarck stands pat on its name. Bismarck stands pat on its destiny.... YOU BET!!!"

Other towns in the U.S. did not stand strong, bending to hysterical name-changing demands. In Minnesota, the village of New Germany changed its name to "Motordale." In Missouri, Potsdam turned into "Pershing," honoring World War I General John J. Pershing. In Ohio, New Berlin became "North Canton." Similarly, Berlin, Michigan, was renamed "Marne," commemorating U.S. soldiers who perished in the Battle of the Marne. And Tennessee's Germantown temporarily became "Neshoba," meaning "wolf."

Wartime controversy over Bismarck's name did not disappear immediately. Some suggestions for a new name included Edwinton, Capital City, and Roosevelt. The *Mandan Pioneer* jokingly wanted to overtake Bismarck and call it "East Mandan."

Dr. Steve Hoffbeck

02 FEB

7 Months, 4 Governors

In 1932, "Wild Bill" Langer of Casselton was elected governor, giving the Non-Partisan League complete control over state government. He was a rough and tumble sort of guy, and many immigrant settlers – who distrusted slicker-looking politicians – liked Langer for his boisterous opposition to taxes, nepotism and corporate corruption.

A financial crisis was making people desperate, so one of the first things Langer did was put a moratorium on foreclosures. And with the state treasury empty, he took dramatic moves to raise the price of wheat and lower the salaries and funding of government departments. He cleaned house and appointed persons loyal to himself. He started a party newspaper and asked his appointees to buy subscriptions equal to 5% of their salaries, with the proceeds going toward campaign financing. Langer also made enemies, and they used this fundraising scheme to bring him down.

Langer was brought before the courts on conspiracy charges, and the state Supreme Court suspended him from office. On July 17, 1934, Republican Lieutenant Governor Ole Olson of New Rockford took the top seat while crowds outside shouted, "We want Langer!"

Ole Olson's tenure was short-lived, however, as Democrat Thomas Moodie of Williston won the election for governor that fall. He took over on January 7, 1935.

Bill Langer, meanwhile, discovered that Moodie had voted in Minneapolis in 1930. State law demanded that a governor "shall have resided in the state for five consecutive years preceding the election," which shouldn't have been a problem for Moodie – he had been living in North Dakota for more than thirty-five years, except for a stint between August 1929 and April 1931 when he worked for the *Minneapolis Tribune* as an editorial writer. On this date in 1935, after only five weeks in office, Thomas Moodie had to step down after the state Supreme Court declared him ineligible.

Next in line was Lieutenant Governor Walter Welford, a Leaguer from Pembina – the state's fourth governor in seven months.

And what happened to Langer? After a grueling number of trials, he was acquitted of all charges and again ran for governor. It was a three-way battle with Governor Welford, now running as a Republican, and Hazen Democrat John Moses, who campaigned in English, German, and Norwegian. Welford and Moses were both conservative, which split Langer's opponents, and Wild Bill won the race with only 36% of the vote. He was North Dakota's seventeenth and twenty-first governor.

Merry Helm

The Day the Music Died

03 FEB

A small plane on its way to Fargo, North Dakota crashed near Clear Lake, Iowa on this date in 1959. Carrying three of America's most promising rock and roll performers, Buddy Holly, Ritchie Valens, and J. P. Richardson, the single-engine plane was originally chartered by the musicians to their next gig in Moorhead, Minnesota. The day remains memorialized in Don McLean's iconic song "American Pie," where it's referred to as "the day the music died."

The musicians were together as part of "The Winter Dance Party Tour," planned and organized by Holly. Waylon Jennings and Tommy Allsup came along as Holly's bandmates, and Dion and the Belmonts rounded out the tour, which was to cover twenty-four Midwestern cities in three weeks. Given the tight schedule, a series of mishaps and inconveniences had already occurred by the night of February 2. The heater in the group's large tour bus had broken a few days earlier. Holly's drummer actually suffered from frostbite while traveling on the bus and had to be hospitalized. No performances were scheduled for February 2, which would have given the group time to rest and travel to Moorhead. However, promoters called the Surf Ballroom in Clear Lake and booked the show at the last minute. Holly, frustrated with the freezing conditions on the bus and a lack of clean laundry, decided to book a charter plane to Fargo's Hector Airport to save time and give his bandmates a rest.

Jennings offered his seat to Richardson at the last minute, knowing the singer was coming down with a fever. Richardson, known by his stage name "The Big Bopper," gladly accepted. The other seat was reserved for Allsup, but Valens, having never flown on a small plane, asked Allsup for his spot. Allsup and Valens flipped a coin and Valens won, securing him a seat on the ill-fated flight. The three musicians took off from the Clear Lake airfield just before 1 a.m. on the morning of February 3. Fargo's airport contacted authorities around 3:30 a.m. to report the missing plane.

A pilot discovered the crash in a cornfield the following morning, only five miles from the departure airport. All three musicians and the young pilot were killed. The pilot's inexperience combined with the blinding weather conditions are believed to have led to the tragedy.

Jayme L. Job

04 FEB

Bismarck Lyceum

For middle-aged adults, the word "lyceum" might conjure memories of a guest speaker deliver a lecture in the public school auditorium. But in the 1800s, the term referred to a form of community education in which neighbors shared their personal expertise in literature, fine arts, and music; or it could feature a debate or readings and recitations. The lyceum meetings served as social events, too, as a pleasurable way to gather together on a regular basis.

The citizens of Bismarck, seeking to uplift, educate and entertain each other organized a lyceum group in the early 1880s, looking for a way to enliven winter evenings, providing a night full of "entertainment, instruction, amusement, hilarity, fun, frolic and joy."

On this date in 1881 the *Bismarck Tribune* declared that the local Lyceum Association was "an established fact," for the group's leadership had set up programs and committees and were ready to draft a constitution and establish their by-laws.

The Bismarck organization used the local Methodist Church, and one of the first debate topics pondered whether "the statesman or the warrior" was most beneficial to the U.S., with the judges deciding in favor of the statesman.

No lyceums were held that summer, for there were plenty of other things to do, but weekly lyceum meetings began again that autumn. A November topic was particularly fascinating, exploring whether "intemperance is more destructive than war." The debate ensued over alcoholism versus battlefield casualties, with the verdict that alcoholism was worse.

Month by month, local debaters examined questions such as: Should the telegraph system of the U.S. be under the control of the government? And which has done the most good for the nation – the printing press or the steam engine?

All of the lyceum meetings were exciting and entertaining because of the opinions expressed and the colorful personalities who did the speaking. Colonel Thompson was said to deliver "eloquent and stirring speeches." The school principal, Mr. Logan, was inspirational while reciting "Curfew Shall Not Ring Tonight."

The meetings were so enjoyable, partly because "music was interspersed" with the readings and debates. Songs and laughter echoed throughout the Lyceum Nights, bringing cultural refinement to the rough-and-tumble railroad town of Bismarck in 1881.

Dr. Steve Hoffbeck

A Real Blizzard

05 FEB

On February 5, 1949, the North Dakota Air National Guard was called to drop feed for stranded starving animals in the western part of the state, where a storm had dumped sixteen inches on top of the fourteen that were already on the ground.

North Dakota is often accused of having the worst winter in the lower forty-eight, but, surprisingly, many of our records are surpassed by other states. In terms of duration, the worst blizzard on record blasted the entire upper plains from March 2 – 5, 1966. In Broken Bow, Nebraska, wind gusted to more than 100 miles per hour, leaving snow drifts forty feet high. In Bismarck, visibility was zero for forty-two consecutive hours, and a new record for single storm snowfall was set at 22.4 inches.

The deadliest blizzard in North Dakota's modern history hit on March 15, 1941, killing seventy-nine people. Winds gusted to 85 miles per hour at Grand Forks, and snow drifts reached 12 feet in north central Minnesota.

The term "blizzard" was used for the first time in 1870 by an Iowa newspaper, the *Estherville Vindicator*, to describe a severe snowstorm that hit Minnesota and Iowa. Early settlers were particularly vulnerable to these storms. Agatha Jerel immigrated with her family from Switzerland when she was fifteen. She married Lorenz Arms in 1883, and they homesteaded near Wimbledon. In her memoirs, Agatha described a "real blizzard" during the winter of 1889:

"One morning the sun was shining, but it was twenty or twenty-five degrees below zero […] Just before noon everything seemed to change; the air turned hazy and smoky; the sun disappeared from out of sight; and before anyone realized what had happened the storm was here…

Being greatly worried over me who was home alone, [my husband Lorenz] started on foot across the field. The storm grew worse and facing that terrific wind that was coming directly from the north made matters all the worse. Lorenz hurried, but it was hard plowing through the snow. He was growing very stiff and cold; the fine powdery snow was switching in his eyes, nose, and mouth. He was sure he was going the right direction and kept on plowing through drift after drift.

Glancing across the field, he could see a little light, which he followed for about a mile. Soon, he came closer and closer and hazily saw a house. He walked to the door and pounded; the door flew open, and he fell to the floor. When he woke up, he was lying on a bed, not in his own home but exactly ten miles north of the farm. Several people froze to death during that blizzard. Many bodies were not found until the snow melted in the spring."

Merry Helm

Adapted from *The Way it Was: The North Dakota Frontier Experience, Book 1, The Sod-Busters*. Edited by D. Jerome Tweton and Everett C. Albers.

06 FEB

Mid-Winter Suffragettes

On this date in 1914, citizens of Devils Lake were eagerly looking forward to the Mid-Winter Fair to be held the following week. The *Devils Lake Weekly World* announced that the arrangements for the fair were complete, with the Fair Committee promising a greater number of exhibits than ever before. Several talks were scheduled, including "Developing the Live Stock Industry in the Lake Region," "The Country Church as a Social Center, Modern Conveniences in the Country Home," and "Evil Effects and the Ways to Avoid Them." Immigration was a major topic with several programs scheduled to discuss it. Classes in dairying and hog raising were available, along with judging of grains, grasses, corn, vegetables, livestock, and poultry.

The newspaper asked local women to make a good showing in the embroidery, art, needlework, and sewing categories. In order to be eligible for prizes, the work had to be created in the Lake Region and could not have won a prize previously at Lake Region fairs.

But of special interest to ladies was a Women's Suffrage booth. The movement was nothing new, with the first women's rights convention being held over sixty-five years earlier in Seneca Falls, New York. That convention had passed a resolution in favor of women's right to vote. In 1869, Susan B. Anthony established a national suffrage organization and Elizabeth Cady Stanton formed a competing group. They finally merged in 1890 as the National American Woman Suffrage Association. Anthony emerged as the leading force. Women repeatedly attempted to vote and were arrested, with the Supreme Court ruling against them each time.

The Nineteenth Amendment, which granted women the right to vote, became part of the Constitution on August 26, 1920, six years after the Mid-Winter Fair in Devils Lake. Women in the United States finally exercised their right to vote in a national election in the fall of that year.

Carole Butcher

Bad Lands *Cow Boy*

07 FEB

Arthur Packard established the *Bad Lands Cow Boy* newspaper at Medora on this date in 1884. As Medora's first newspaper, the *Cow Boy* recorded the town's earliest history. A journalist with a fascination for cowboys, Packard headed west soon after his graduation from the University of Michigan. He became managing editor of the *Bismarck Tribune*, although the stint proved short due to his notorious temper; Packard resigned after throwing sundries at local critics. He moved across the river and worked on the *Mandan Pioneer*, but soon continued west to Medora. After converting a blacksmith shop into a makeshift printing office, Packard released the *Cow Boy*'s first issue. The owner, writer, editor, and manager of the paper, Packard once wrote, "The *Cow Boy* is not published for fun, but for $2 a year."

Today, Packard and his paper are best known for recording much of Theodore Roosevelt's life in the Badlands, as well as forecasting correctly young Roosevelt's future presidency. Roosevelt became close friends with the young editor, and spent many hours telling stories and arguing politics in the *Cow Boy*'s office. The future president claimed that he preferred the newspaper office to the town's many saloons, saying he avoided the "…booze joints, because he liked chatting with the men who liked the smell of printer's ink to feel civilized." He believed that the "…saloons were the cowboy's nemesis," while Packard was, according to him, "…a good fellow, a college graduate, and a first-class baseball player." The Marquis de Mores also spent many hours in Packard's office. When locals accused the editor of bias favoring the Marquis, Packard replied that the Marquis was the paper's best advertising customer, but he never let his friendship with the powerful de Mores affect his editorial instincts. In the *Cow Boy*'s third issue, he wrote, "We are not the tool of nor are we beholden in any way to any man or set of men…" Of course, the fact that Packard dined most nights in the Marquis's chateau did not help matters.

Unfortunately, Medora's boom lasted only as long as the paper itself; a devastating fire in January of 1887 destroyed Packard's office. Along with most of the city's residents, Packard left Medora after that brutal winter, making the *Cow Boy*'s December 23rd issue its last.

Jayme L. Job

08 FEB

Zeronia

Winter in North Dakota is not for the faint of heart, and its frosty air has sometimes been a discouragement for those who considered moving into the state.

When North Dakota gained statehood in 1889, prominent citizens and the state's "booster press" boasted about the state's climate, people and prospects, but the cold reputation persisted, and outsiders were wary about these faraway hinterlands.

A writer named P.F. McClure, writing in *Harper's Magazine* in 1889, judged there were "really but two seasons in Dakota, summer and winter," and he noted that January temperatures "occasionally" registered at "40 degrees or more below zero."

McClure described blizzards as "most disagreeable storms," with "strong winds blowing almost a hurricane," but acknowledged that terrible winter storms were actually fairly rare and of short duration. However, the "most disastrous" blizzard "on record . . . swept over the Territory on the 12th of January, 1888." It horrified the nation, in part because of "woeful exaggerations and distortions" in the newspapers in other parts of the U.S.

These headlines really scared off potential settlers.

The *St. Louis Post-Dispatch* read: "Fearfully Fatal; Western Prairies Strewn With The Frozen Dead."

"Hundreds Frozen," wrote the *Newton Daily Republican* in Kansas.

"Smothered In The Snow," headlined the *Chicago Tribune*.

"A Thousand Lives Reported Lost In Dakota," yelped the *Butler Citizen* in Pennsylvania.

"Terrible Effects of Dakota's Fatal Blizzard," squawked Nashville's *Tennessean*.

"The Worst Blizzard Ever Known Sweeps Dakota and Minnesota," said the *New York Sun*.

"Arctic Temperatures Reported in Dakota," *Chicago Inter Ocean*.

Even an official weather report admitted that the average temperature for that deadly month of January 1888 had been a shivering "14 below zero." Published on this date in 1889, it contributed to the negative coverage of Dakota's climate.

When decision-time came concerning an "appropriate name" for "blizzardous" northern Dakota, the *Chicago Tribune* "zeroed" in on the future state's below-zero temperatures, cold-heartedly recommended "Zeronia."

Another suggestion was "No-Man's Land." More kindly-hearted authorities suggested "Wheatland," for the prodigious Bonanza farm harvests.

But the territorial name "Dakota," was still considered the best choice for the new states. The territorial citizens had become attached to the name and entering the Union as South Dakota and North Dakota seemed right, these strong names becoming forever *frozen* in time. And they both sound better than Zeronia, or MegaKota, for that matter.

Dr. Steve Hoffbeck

09 FEB

A Town Returned

On this date in 1966, word came from Bismarck that a North Dakota town was going to be given back to Montana. At the time, Westby was a town of about 300 people. The residents were used to thinking they were from Montana, but between 1963 and 1966, the official state map of North Dakota showed it as belonging to North Dakota. Montana, however, maintained that Westby folks were still part of Big Sky country, and no emergency meetings were held.

The problem stemmed from out east – Minneapolis to be exact. An official state "base map" is made for North Dakota about every four years. The firm that held the map-making contract was out of Valley City, but they subletted the contract to a firm in you-know-where.

Douglas Walby, the chief draftsman for the North Dakota Highway Department, acknowledged the mistake, but said Westby wouldn't be given back to Montana until 1967 when a new base map was made.

When State Travel Director, James Hawley, was asked about the seizure of the poor little town, he said, "We think Montana people are fine individuals. We'd like to add them to our population since we're such a sparsely settled state, but we intend to give the town back to Montana next year."

The town actually did begin as a North Dakota town – on July 1, 1910, to be precise. But then the railroad – also from out east – came along in 1913 and ran the rail line two miles outside of town.

That didn't make sense, so almost everybody moved closer to the tracks, and suddenly Westby was in Montana. Now, one needs to remember that the town was named *West*by. West because it was so far west in the state. By all rights, if Montana intended to keep the town, they should have done the proper thing and renamed it *East*by. But Westby kept its name, and the old townsite became known as Old Westby.

As it turns out, the town actually belongs to both states. Some folks built their homes on the right side of the tracks – that would be the North Dakota side – and those residents are actually North Dakotans. But the post office is on the wrong side of the tracks, so everybody's official address is Montana.

Merry Helm

Recruitment Order

10 FEB

Dakota Territory was wilder than ever on this date in 1863 when acting governor John Hutchinson issued a recruitment order in response to the U.S.-Dakota War.

Hutchinson sought to recruit men to Company C of the Dakota Cavalry for protection of settlers. Over 600 white civilians and soldiers had been killed in the uprising in Minnesota the previous year (Dakota death counts are uncertain). At the time, Company A was the only unit of troops in the territory outside of Fort Randall, assigned to patrol the frontier from the Big Sioux River to Chouteau Creek.

The "extreme urgency" for government troops on the Dakota frontier was hard to meet. Hutchinson was unable to bring in outside troops owing to the ongoing Civil War. Territorial officials feared Dakota's farming population would leave as the Sioux involved in the Minnesota actions moved into Dakota. Hutchinson's predecessor had called for volunteers the previous fall, but he accepted none of the militias formed in the "slow and discouraging" recruitment process.

Recruiting the number of soldiers officials called for appeared impossible. Company B of the Dakota Cavalry had been thrown together at Sioux City, Iowa in December 1862, and that same month, the previous governor had created a consolidated Company C, but a need remained, and Hutchinson's new recruitment order proved ineffective. Generals Alfred Sully and Henry Hastings Sibley eventually led their punitive expeditions with cavalries from Iowa, Minnesota, and Nebraska.

Companies A and B of the Dakota Cavalry did play a small role, however. In 1864 they traveled as a bodyguard for Sully for a rendezvous near present-day Pierre, South Dakota, prior to the Battle of Tahkahokuty Mountain, also known as the Battle of Killdeer Mountain, the largest armed conflict between the U.S. Army and Plains Indians.

Jack Dura

11 FEB

The Silk Train

Silk has a natural beauty, unmatched by lesser fibers. Silk ranks among the strongest of fibers and most lustrous and shiniest materials on earth while remaining the softest to the touch. Nothing holds the color of dye more deeply than silk.

Spun by silkworms into cocoons, silk has always been a luxurious commodity. From 1900 to the late 1930s, silk cargoes, originating in Japan, passed through North Dakota from Seattle on special "silk trains," in order to get raw silk across the continent to manufacturers in New York City.

On this date, in 1915, the *Bismarck Tribune* published a news report revealing that a "silk train valued at a million and a half dollars" passed through Grand Forks "on train 28 on the Great Northern" Railway. Four railcars were "packed end to end with bales of the finest silk," destined for elite clothiers.

The Great Northern Railway competed for prestige with the Northern Pacific and the Union Pacific to be the leading cross-country transporters of the precious silk cargoes. The price of the valuable commodity fluctuated rapidly, so manufacturers wanted shipments delivered on time. Furthermore, raw silk was delicate and vulnerable to damage by heat, noxious fumes, excessive moisture or by puncture, so speed was essential. Great Northern silk trains set new transcontinental records by sending special trains on dedicated tracks.

Insuring silk cargoes was expensive, for fear of damage or theft. If stolen, it was nearly impossible to track down, being raw and unmarked. Therefore, silk trains were not often sidetracked, thus reducing exposure to robbery.

The silk trains were highly profitable for the Great Northern and other railways. "Pound for pound, silk earned more for the railway than any other product," wrote UND historian Gordon Iseminger, in his masterful account of silk train history. After gold and silver, silk was the most-expensive product shipped by railroads, though it was far lighter in weight.

Many trainloads of silk passed through Grand Forks from 1910 until February, 1937, when the Great Northern Railway ran its last silk train. Demand for silk had declined as rayon and nylon took market share, and shipments slowed as Japanese – U.S. relations deteriorated.

So ended the era of fabulously-fast silk trains passing through North Dakota.

Dr. Steve Hoffbeck

Who was FPG?

12 FEB

This week marks the birth of Felix Paul Greve, a mysterious writer born in Germany in 1879. Greve was only twenty-one when his first known work was published. He soon became renowned for his translations, poetry, fiction and plays in Europe.

In October, 1902, Greve was staging Oscar Wilde comedies in Berlin when he became friends with August Endell, an up and coming architect. Greve became attracted to Endell's wife, Else, and they became involved.

A year later and deeply in debt, Greve was sentenced to one year in prison for defrauding a friend for an enormous amount of money. After he got out, he eloped with Else to Zurich, where he began writing novels and translating works into German.

In 1909, something happened to prompt Greve to stage his own suicide. He left Europe for Montreal under the name Frederick Philip Grove. Within the year, Else joined him in Pittsburgh. From there, the couple moved around. There are stories of Greve working as a waiter in Toronto, living as a hobo in New York, taking part in a book-selling scam in Pittsburgh and farming in Sparta, Kentucky. Much of it is unsubstantiated, but we do know that Greve left Else and her hot temper behind in Kentucky.

For the next ten years, Greve hid his whereabouts, including a move to North Dakota in 1912, where he worked on a Bonanza Farm. He also started writing again, with much of his fiction based on true stories of his life. But he didn't start publishing again until he learned Else had moved back to Europe. His works were no longer signed either Greve or Grove; he was going by his initials, FPG.

In 1927, he published a novel, *A Search for America*, a fictionalized biography. North Dakota was never named — but he slyly inserted clues by describing the wealthy owners of a huge Bonanza farm. He placed the town of Amenia in New York and Sharon about five miles away in Connecticut.

After working in North Dakota, Greve moved to Canada and married, claiming he was born in Moscow and was a widower. In 1946 he published *A Search for Myself*, which was regarded as the "real" autobiography of Frederick Philip Grove. He won the Canadian Governor-General's Award for Non-Fiction for that book in 1947, and the following year, he went to his death with his secrets intact.

In 1971, his true identity was discovered, but it wasn't until the 1990s that scholars finally realized his earlier works were biographical. One of the tipoffs? The 1996 discovery that Grove's fictional bonanza farm actually existed in real-life North Dakota.

Merry Helm

13 FEB

Death and Taxes

On this date in 1983, there was a shootout between Federal Marshals, Gordon Kahl and other members of the Posse Comitatus on a road east of Medina, North Dakota.

Kahl was born in 1920, the oldest of five kids. He is described as being musical, loving to hunt, a practical joker and an excellent mechanic. He was a teenager when World War II broke out, and was anxious to join up. He became a tail-gunner and flight engineer on a bomber. He flew fifty-seven missions and received nineteen medals, including the Presidential Unit Citation.

After the war, he and his new bride, Joan, settled down on 160 acres near Heaton. Kahl tried college and farming, but became disillusioned with government farm programs. In 1968, he sent a letter to the IRS saying he would no longer pay Federal Income Tax, and he became the state coordinator for the anti-tax group, the Posse Comitatus.

Two years later he was brought up on tax evasion charges and spent nine months in prison. He was given five years probation but still refused to pay his taxes, so the IRS filed a lien on eighty acres of his land and prepared to serve a warrant on Kahl if he showed up for the auction sale. The sale was uneventful, but matters got sticky after a subsequent series of arrest attempts failed.

The only place Kahl went without his gun was the grocery store, and it was proposed that this be the way to take Kahl without casualties. But lawmen instead tried a rural roadblock. Kahl was tipped off, and a shootout commenced. It's still not clear who shot first, but when all was said and done, two marshals were dead and three others were wounded. Kahl became a fugitive.

On June 3, 1983, Gordon Kahl was killed in a final shootout in Arkansas. His story was later made into a TV movie, and a Prairie Public documentary called *Altered Lives*.

Merry Helm

Flour Mill Fire

14 FEB

A terrible fire destroyed the Krem Roller Mill on this date in 1906. Although little remains of the town today, Krem was once the "largest and most progressive" town in Mercer County. Much of the town's commercial success, however, was the result of its large flour mill. Losing the mill was the beginning of the end for the North Dakotan prairie town.

In the 1880s, immigrants flooded into Mercer County, eager to take advantage of the Homestead Act; three out of every four were of German heritage, coming from the areas of southern Russia. The majority of these Germans from Russia took up farming, but found it difficult to transport farm products to the Missouri River for sale and transport. They also found it difficult to file papers and conduct business in Stanton, the county seat, which was located on the far eastern edge of the county. Some county residents were forced to travel as long as two or three days to reach the far-flung county seat.

In order to alleviate the burden, many settlers proposed the creation of a central market and seat of government. In 1888, Carl Semmler established a new townsite near his farm north of Hazen. Centrally-located, Semmler named the town Krem after the Crimean homeland of many of the area's settlers. Semmler was able to lure investors to build a large flour mill on the site, enabling local farmers to bring their wheat directly to the mill. Mill owners also hoped that the future rail-line from Mandan to Killdeer would run through Krem, giving their newly-ground flour a way to reach larger markets.

The large four-story roller mill could grind fifty bushels a day, powered by steam produced from local lignite coal. With its 24-hour schedule, however, the mill frequently ran out of fuel and was forced to use straw instead, although straw created sparks. In February of 1906, straw sparks led to a fire that quickly burned the mill to the ground. Although quickly rebuilt, the cost created a strain on the mill's owners. When the railroad decided to lay its line through Hazen rather than Krem seven years later, most of the town's businesses and residents relocated. By 1940, the town of Krem was one more prairie ghost town.

Jayme L. Job

15 FEB

Self-Defense

On this date in 1901, the *Oakes Republican* reported that Coroner T.W. Millham and Sheriff Thompson had been summoned to investigate the death of Charles Brucker. The first report was that Brucker had been killed when his wife shot him with a shotgun. Mrs. Brucker was the daughter of Ferdinand Kosanke, a prominent member in the Germans from Russia community. She was only with husband Charles a short time before they quarreled and split up. Mrs. Brucker returned to her family. One evening, Brucker arrived at the Kosanke home threatening to kill his wife and the entire family.

The Kosanke sons overwhelmed the man and tied him up. Then they went to get their father who was visiting at a neighbor's house, intending to return with their father and call for the sheriff. They left Mrs. Brucker, armed with a loaded shotgun, to guard Charles. Before the men could return, Brucker was able to free one of his arms. Mrs. Brucker told him if he tried to get up she would shoot him. He ignored her threat and continued his efforts to free himself. As he tried to stand, his wife shot him, killing him instantly.

Upon completing his inquest, the coroner determined that Mrs. Brucker's account was accurate. The coroner's jury absolved the woman of all blame. They concluded she had acted in self-defense, and it was assumed the matter was settled.

But that was not the end of the story. Three months later authorities decided to prosecute Mrs. Brucker for the murder of her husband. Some of her neighbors had become suspicious of her story. It came to their attention that Mr. Brucker carried a $2,000 life insurance policy. His wife was the beneficiary and she was attempting to collect. The neighbors thought it was suspicious that her brothers left her alone to guard Charles rather than guarding him themselves and sending their sister to find their father. As a result of the neighbors' concerns, a warrant was issued for her arrest.

However, the result was the same. A second investigation determined that Brucker's death was indeed a result of self-defense. Charges against Mrs. Brucker were dropped, and she eventually did collect on the $2,000 insurance policy.

Carole Butcher

Gold in North Dakota

16 FEB

On this date in 1876, a party of thirteen men left Grand Forks, following the Northern Pacific Railroad. They reached Bismarck on March 2 and rested for the next three weeks. When they forged on, their group had swelled to fifty, including a woman, seven children and a destitute sourdough prospector from California named "Rattlesnake Jack."

The group's goal was the same as it was for many others – get to the Black Hills to prospect for gold. Their mission was dangerous and for a good reason. The 1868 Sherman Treaty had guaranteed the Great Sioux Reservation full, undisputed rights to the land west of the Missouri River, including their favorite meeting grounds, the Black Hills. Then, in July 1874, Custer and his men were in the Black Hills when gold was discovered in French Creek. Custer immediately sent "Lonesome Charley" Reynolds to Ft. Laramie to announce the discovery to the world.

Historian Erling Rolfsrud writes, "The Indians who saw the ruts cut by Yellow Hair's 110 wagons called his route the 'Trail of the Thieves'... Despite Army warnings that the Black Hills were forbidden to whites, mining expeditions organized to go there. Sioux City and Yankton newspapers (advertised) Black Hills prospector outfits. By the summer of 1875 about 800 men had eluded the military patrol(s), coming into the Hills from Bismarck, Laramie, and Sioux City."

Meanwhile, several tribal leaders were invited to Washington, where General Grant's request to either sell or lease the Black Hills was flatly turned down. The Sioux had no intention of opening their beloved Black Hills to white settlers.

By the time the Grand Forks prospectors approached the Black Hills the following spring, some 25,000 gold seekers had already infiltrated the area. So it was that when the Grand Forks party bedded down near Meadow City that Indians crept into their camp and ran off five of their horses and about 20 head of cattle. The cows belonged to a Bismarck man named Collins, who was going to start a dairy for the prospectors. The next day, about twelve men trailed their missing livestock to a gully about fourteen miles away, but when they went in to round them up, they found about fifty Indians waiting for them.

Grand Forks insurance salesman, D. M. Holmes, told a reporter they had to kill some of their stock to crouch behind and that the battle lasted until nightfall. A Bismarck man named Ward was killed, and two others – Jim Williams of East Grand Forks and a Mr. Collins of Bismarck – received arrow wounds to their legs. Holmes, presided over Ward's burial the following day but later learned the body was dug up and scalped soon after they left.

A 1922 *Fargo Forum* story recounted the results of the expedition: "Most of the prospectors were working for placer gold, yet Rattlesnake

Jack discovered a vein of quartz. He received $25,000 for his rights to the property, and thereupon entered an orgy of gambling and drinking that did not stop until [he] was broke… One by one some of the Grand Forks prospectors straggled home. Some of them never did return. Mr. Holmes was away about four months. He spent about $1,000 and found about $2.50 worth of gold."

Ironically, the Rattlesnake Jack mine was still operating as late as 1922.

Merry Helm

The 16th Amendment

17 FEB

The Industrial Revolution began in the middle of the eighteenth century and swept the world like a storm. Following a time when human and animal labor were the main sources of production, inventions like the steam engine and electricity improved the living conditions of many people. However, these improvements did not come without cost. As time went on, a few select persons were amassing large amounts of money as a result of industrialization. By the end of the nineteenth century in America, a few people at the top controlled financial and manufacturing assets that were being missed by national taxation. It was clear a new system was needed.

Thus, Congress proposed the 16th amendment in 1909 to establishing an income tax, no matter the source of the income. This bill was largely supported by the lower working classes, who felt they were being disproportionately affected by the rise in the cost of living and in tariffs, which were the main source of government funds. On this date in 1911, North Dakota chose to ratify the 16th amendment. However, the amendment's ratification has been a source of debate ever since its conception.

Secretary of State Philander Know, declared the amendment law on February 25th, 1913, after hearing that thirty-eight states had approved it. But after a closer examination of the processes used, it is revealed that many states did not follow correct procedure. In some states, the wording of the bill was changed so the people did not truly ratify the amendment exactly as written, and in others they never returned a properly certified bill. North Dakota had a properly worded amendment, but it was one of thirteen states that violated a rule requiring the bill to be read on three separate days before the state legislature voted. The rule allows for a cooling off period; it enables members who may be absent for one reading to be present for another; and it allows for a better familiarity with the measure.

A notable critic of the 16th amendment is William Benson, who wrote a book on the subject called *The Law that Never Was*. His arguments, however, have not allowed his tax evasion attempts to succeed, so think twice before skipping your taxes.

Lucid Thomas

18 FEB

Otto Bremer

Otto Bremer and his brother Adolph immigrated to Minnesota in 1886 and within a few years Otto had entered into the banking business as a bookkeeper. He then decided to make a run at politics as a candidate for the City Treasurer for St. Paul, an office he held from 1900 to 1910. In 1903, Bremer became a charter member of the American National Bank in St. Paul and served on the board of directors. He joined his brother Adolph in the Jacob Schmidt Brewing Company as secretary-treasurer in 1910 while retaining his position at the bank.

The farm economy saw a general upswing the years prior to World War I. Supported by the Non-Partisan League, with their own state-owned bank and flour mill, North Dakota farmers deemed the prosperous times as a good time to expand and buy new equipment. In 1920 there were 898 banks in North Dakota, most with insufficient capital, which were willing to take a chance on extending credit based on the mortgage value of the land but with inflation, drought and low grain prices the end of prosperity came quickly.

The American National Bank under Bremer and his associates had practiced tighter control in the lending practices and it was to them that many banks in North Dakota would look for help. As early as 1914 Bremer had purchased the bank in Powers Lake and had also begun obtaining controlling interest in many other banks in the Midwestern states. By 1933 Bremer's banking empire had control of fifty-five banks. Conditions were such that 573 banks had failed in North Dakota alone. It was during this time in dealing with small-town banks that Otto Bremer developed his deep commitment to the rural communities.

The early 1930s were eventful in another way for him. At the Democratic Convention in 1932, Bremer, along with James Farley, brought the nomination of Franklin Roosevelt to the floor which resulted in Roosevelt's first term. Also Edward Bremer, his nephew, was kidnapped and held for $200,000 ransom by the notorious Ma Baker-Alvin Karpis gang in 1934. The nephew was released unharmed.

In 1944, Otto Bremer founded the Otto Bremer Foundation to aid educational, religious, scientific and charitable organizations. The aim of the foundation was not to build buildings but to aid organizations which provided help to enhance the lives of the average person who, like himself, were mostly immigrants or the sons and daughters of immigrants. Otto Bremer died on this date in 1951. He was a powerful, self-made man who, it appears, never lost sight of his roots.

Jim Davis

Dying for Keeps

19 FEB

On this date in 1904, the citizens of Linton, North Dakota were furious with Mr. Porter, the Secretary of State. The subject of the dispute was a proposed cemetery. A town meeting had been held to discuss establishing a cemetery for the town. After a favorable vote, a proposal was sent to Bismarck. Land had been chosen and the plan seemed to be well thought out. All the citizens of the area were in agreement. To everyone's surprise, Secretary of State Porter rejected the proposal. He responded that the request seemed to be for a permanent facility, but state statute had a limit of twenty years. He said a new proposal was needed, one that adhered to the twenty-year time limit.

Lintonites were not the least bit pleased. The newspaper printed a scathing editorial, pointing out that limiting the cemetery to a period of twenty years was not at all practical. The editorial stated; "We may be hayseeds down here, but we know our rights." It went on to point out that people in the Linton area were entitled to the same privileges as those who lived in Bismarck. After all, people in Bismarck were entitled to stay dead for longer than twenty years. In fact, they were allowed to stay dead as long as they pleased. The people of Linton demanded the same consideration. Linton was described as a growing town, but new people would not relocate there if they knew they would not be allowed to *stay dead*.

The newspaper promised dire consequences. Refusing to allow people to stay dead for keeps could drive Emmons County to the Democrats! It was such a serious issue it could even deliver the entire state to the Democrats!

Just as the paper was about to go to press, a new response arrived from Bismarck. It seemed that Mr. Porter had misread the original proposal. Instead of a cemetery, he thought Linton was proposing to build a creamery. The time limit for creamery charters was twenty years. The cemetery was approved, and all was forgiven.

Carole Butcher

20 FEB

The Diary of Mary Dodge Woodward

"Oh, the dreary winter, how the storm has raged all day!" So penned Mary Dodge Woodward during a North Dakota blizzard, on this day in 1884.

Mary Dodge Woodward was born on June 27 in 1826, far from the Dakota prairies in Vermont. She later settled in Wisconsin with her husband and raised five children. After the death of her husband, Mary moved with three of her children to the Red River Valley at the age of fifty-six.

Mary and her family arrived in Dakota Territory and worked over two sections, or about 1,500 acres of wheat. What makes Mary Dodge Woodward stand out among the many settlers who braved the Dakota prairies was her journal. Her daily entries provide an important source of information detailing the life, weather and dangers of Dakota Territory. Here, a few excerpts from her diary:

May 23, 1885. "The wind blows all the time, so hard that one can scarcely stand before it…About four o'clock the sky looked fearful, we heard a distant roar, and soon the storm was upon us. The hailstones were as large as nutmegs and oh, how they did kill things![...]Our wheat that looked so green has disappeared and the fields are bare."

May 31, 1885. "The wheat is rising out of the ground. The day is very beautiful and I have been out nearly all of it picking posies. The air is soft and cool. I think there is something fascinating about gathering wild flowers, strolling along, not knowing what you will find."

August 6, 1886. "A beautiful day. The men are all harvesting[…]They have been cutting sixty acres a day with all five harvesters running[…] The reapers are flying all about us, stretching out their long white arms and grasping the grain. They remind me of sea gulls as they glisten in the sunshine."

January 24, 1888. "The wind came up last night and by twelve another blizzard was upon us. This morning I could only now and then see the buildings[…]Except for the cold winters, I should like this place very much indeed."

The Woodwards eventually left their Dakota farm in 1889 and returned to Wisconsin. Although Mary died just over one year later, the writings she left behind provide a clear picture of the struggles and joys of those who braved the plains of North Dakota over a century ago.

Lane Sunwall

Mr. Hockey, Fido Purpur

21 FEB

Between 1934 and 1945, North Dakota hockey legend Clifford "Fido" Purpur played for the St. Louis Eagles, St. Louis Flyers, Chicago Blackhawks, Detroit Red Wings, and the St. Paul Saints. When Purpur was awarded the North Dakota Roughrider Award, it was said the state had become a hockey hotspot because of him.

The U.S. Hockey Hall of Fame states: "When Fido Purpur stepped on the ice with the St. Louis Eagles in 1934 he had become North Dakota's first native son to play in the National Hockey League. Purpur made the NHL when he was just 20-years-old, and when the Eagles folded after the 1935 season, he signed with the American Hockey Association's St. Louis Flyers. He stayed with the Flyers until 1942 when he returned to the NHL with the Chicago Blackhawks. His best year of many good years in St. Louis was 1939, when he scored 35 goals and 43 assists in the regular season and three goals and three assists in the playoffs as St. Louis won the Harry F. Sinclair Trophy, which was emblematic of the league championship."

In a 1999 story for the *Forum*, Jeff Kolpack wrote, "Purpur got his nickname (Fido) because he skated so close to the ice. He has about 200 stitches from the neck up, a tribute to his toughness." St. Louis fans idolized "little" Fido Purpur because of his gutsy moves and terrific speed, not to mention his four 20-goal seasons with the Flyers. They also liked that Purpur took the time to talk with them and sign autographs for the kids. He, himself, starting skating as a young kid, using skates his brother bought for five cents.

When the Chicago Blackhawks signed Fido, it was to team him on a line with Max and Doug Bentley, and also to shadow the legendary Montreal player, Maurice "Rocket" Richard. "I followed him everywhere," Purpur said. Purpur played in every one of the Blackhawks' fifty games in 1943, scoring 13 goals and 16 assists.

Around this time, Fido developed a puzzling ailment that elevated this body temperature. He was able to keep playing, but after a few years, it started to sap his strength.

He finished his professional career in 1947 and went back to his hometown, Grand Forks. But the Purpur legend wasn't finished, it was growing. In 1949, Fido became UND's hockey coach, a post he held for seven years. During that time, he coached a standout center, who went on to play in the 1956 Olympics. That player was Fido's brother, Ken. Then, there were Fido's six sons, all of whom played the game. Purpur's great-nephew, UND standout Jeff Panzer, signed with the St. Louis Blues in 2001.

Purpur died on this date in 2001 at the age of 88. The funeral took place in Grand Forks, and the procession to the cemetery was led by the Zamboni machine from the Fido Purpur Arena.

Merry Helm

22 FEB

The Evils of Hoarding

Banks in North Dakota were in big trouble in the 1920s and early 1930s as the farm economy turned sour. Of 898 banks in 1920, 573 went bankrupt by 1933 – an appalling sixty-three-percent!

In those days, when a bank failed, those with savings accounts struggled to get deposits back, getting only one-fourth to one-half of their money, because there was no Federal Deposit Insurance Corporation.

Fear of banks and bankers intensified, and some North Dakotans withdrew their money, oftentimes demanding $20 gold pieces instead of paper money. Those who kept the coins in teapots, mattresses, closets, attics, or in safety-deposit boxes, were denounced as 'hoarders' by bankers and government officials who worked to revive the economy. There had always been a class of people who mistrusted banks and had habits of burying or hiding their wealth, but treasure-hoarding became more widespread in 1930 and grew in frequency over the next three years.

On this date in 1932, Fargo hosted the Seventeenth Annual Northwest Credit Conference, where financier E.B. Moran decried the "evils of hoarding," launching a "stinging attack on the hoarder" who squirreled away money in fear, thus denying those funds for loans and investments. Nationally, President Herbert Hoover instigated an anti-hoarding campaign, urging citizens to put money back into the banks.

Fear overrode patriotism, helping Franklin Roosevelt win the presidency. In Roosevelt's first presidential action, in March 1933, he declared a bank emergency, shutting down all banks for one week.

FDR ordered every American to stop hoarding, commanding citizens to bring gold coins and gold certificates to a local bank, exchanging those for paper money. Each person could keep $100 in gold, but any coins above $100 had to be surrendered. Violating this Executive Order was punishable by a $10,000 fine or ten years in prison, or both.

In Bismarck, fear of punishment made many fearful hoarders bring their gold coins to the city's newly-reopened banks. Most of these were five-dollar gold pieces.

However, not all hoarders gave up their coins, keeping them in secret hidden places. If you have an old house, someday you might unearth a stash of coins, carefully stacked in a jar and buried underneath your front-porch. Who knows what treasures you might find?

Dr. Steve Hoffbeck

The Oblong Box

23 FEB

On this date in 1905, the *Courier Democrat* of Cavalier County ran a story about a spooked paymaster. Willard Bugbee had withdrawn $12,000 from the bank to pay railroad workers. He then went to catch the train to Drayton, in Pembina County. At the station, he noticed a fellow passenger, a squinty-eyed man he had seen at the bank. He also noticed a large oblong box about the size of a coffin being loaded onto a freight car.

Bugbee arrived in Drayton about six that evening, locked his money in the office safe, went to the hotel and had supper. He then went back to the station where he used the office as a counting room. He took out the cash and sat down to work.

He could see into the dimly lit freight room where, among barrels, packages and crates was the oblong box standing up on end. Half an hour later Bugbee noticed that the box had moved about two feet! He got scared, thinking his mind – or perhaps ghosts – were playing tricks on him.

He went back to work, but then heard a crash. He picked up a pistol and leaned to have a look and the oblong box was gone. He picked up his lamp, cocked his revolver and tiptoed into the freight room.

The oblong box had tipped over. He pried it open far enough to see a man inside. A live one.

With Bugbee's gun on him, the man squeezed his way out of the box and admitted that he was there to relieve Bugbee of his moneybags. The box cover had been designed to open from the inside, but it had been set up on end, with the cover against another crate. The guy had squeezed his hand out and pushed on the adjoining crate bit by bit, easing the box out of Bugbee's sightline, but the box had toppled over, trapping him inside. The robber explained he was supposed to throw something over Bugbee and then let his partner in.

Bugbee locked the robber in the freight room, dimmed his lamp, went to the door and whistled. When the partner came in, Bugbee threw a cover over him and called for help. The partner turned out to be – who else – the squinty-eyed man from the bank.

Merry Helm

24 FEB

Poker Jim

Not to be confused with Fargo State Representative Jim Kasper, an advocate for North Dakota becoming a haven for online poker, the original Poker Jim is a legendary North Dakota Badlands cowboy who lies buried in a cemetery that bears his name in McKenzie county, near the North Unit of Theodore Roosevelt National Park.

Poker Jim, whose real name remains a mystery (likely by his own choice), may have loved the game, but his last act before his fellow cowboys laid him to rest was to break up a game, sending cards, cash, and cowboys flying through the air. No doubt the colorful cowboy's story has been told around many a Badlands campfire over the years. Our source is Leonard Lund, reporting from Squaw Gap, as published in the *Minot Daily News* on this day in 1973.

Poker Jim was probably an outlaw who came into the area with a cattle drive from the south. He was employed by the Frenchman Pierre Wibaux of the enormous W Bar Ranch. Wibaux was a contemporary of the Marquis de Mores and Theodore Roosevelt. Unlike his contemporaries, Wibaux's ranch was a profitable operation, and became the largest cattle operation of the time.

Lund writes, "During the winter of 1894, Poker Jim [...] and a companion, Cash Lantis, were stationed at the line camp at the mouth of Hay Draw near the Little Missouri. By February their food supply had gotten so low that Poker Jim was delegated to ride to Glendive, Montana, at least 65 miles away," for provisions.

"But he never made it back. About a week later cowboys found his frozen body propped against a huge scoria rock along a small frozen creek about 10 miles from the cow camp. Poker Jim's horse, tied to a tree, had eaten off the bark. Burned matches about the corpse were evidence that Poker Jim had tried to build a fire."

"Harlowe (Tough) Bentley reported that Poker Jim, whose love for gambling was exceeded only by his fondness for whisky, had seemed a little sick from drinking when he left the Smith Creek line camp that last morning."

"After staying overnight with Bentley at the horse camp, Poker Jim began the 16-mile ride back to his camp on Hay Draw. Those who found Poker Jim's frozen body carried it into a small shack and placed it across the rafters, in cold storage."

"Later another group of men gathered at the shack for a poker game. They heated the building and the body gradually thawed. Finally if fell right onto the poker table directly below. According to the tale, no poker game ever broke up so fast."

"Poker Jim was laid to rest beside his old friend, Sid Tarbell, the first person to be buried on the hill overlooking the cow camp." Several others have been buried there over the years, but the cemetery bears the name of one unforgettable nineteenth century cowboy – Poker Jim.

Merry Helm

A Man of Many Firsts

25 FEB

A man present for many North Dakota firsts died on this date in 1910. Frank J. Thompson came to Fargo, Dakota Territory from Michigan in 1878 to practice law. Thompson wore many hats prior to coming to Dakota; he was a machinist, taught music and later studied law. He formed a partnership in Fargo with Henry Krogh in law and real estate that lasted eleven years until 1892. Thompson married in 1882 and had two children with his wife Elmodine. In 1892, he became grand secretary of the Grand Lodge of Ancient Free and Accepted Masons of North Dakota. Until his death, he worked to improve the organization.

Thompson was also a member of the state's first legislature as a Republican, though he was only partially affiliated with the party. He served as Judiciary Committee chair and worked closely with his friend, William Mitchell, the first superintendent of public instruction. Thompson also served as state assistant attorney general from 1891 to 1893.

Thompson's greatest legacy is rooted in the Fargo Public Library. He was the library's first director and organized its founding through the Grand Lodge in 1900. For two years, the library was housed in the Masonic Temple. An assistant librarian was hired for $3 a week. Fargo Mayor John Johnson supported the library founding and solicited donations, which brought in "several hundred volumes."

In 1902, library promoters turned to industrialist Andrew Carnegie, who donated $20,000 for a brick building, which opened in 1903. Thompson was also a founder of the North Dakota Library Association and was its first president. He championed education, a privilege he did not have as a young man. He served on the Fargo school board and sought to improve educational opportunities all around.

Thompson lived in Fargo for over 30 years. His death came as a surprise as a result of a heart condition.

Jack Dura

26 FEB

Schools at War

As the United States entered World War II, everyone on the home front was called upon to help. The Schools at War program was organized on September 25, 1942 by the War Savings Staff of the Treasury Department and the U.S. Office of Education. The program was set up to attract the interest and participation of students in public and private schools, grades kindergarten through twelve. Students were asked to save, serve and conserve by giving money through the purchase of war stamps and bonds, conserving money and materials for the war effort, and by saving for personal security.

On this date in Griggs County, Agnes Evenson, county superintendent, who was serving as a member of the "Schools at War" Committee, reported that students were deeply engaged in the program. Also on the committee was Superintendent E.V. Estensen of Cooperstown, and Miss Minnie Anderson of Hannaford.

Among their activities, the Griggs County students were collecting metal, hosiery, and fat. Evenson said that during the spring and summer months, many of them would assume more elaborate tasks, like the raising of victory gardens and taking the place of full-grown men who left important farm jobs to serve in the military.

The youth had helped in the fall with this sort of farm work, and Evenson said it was not unusual to see teenagers driving farm tractors and doing other tasks that "are considered to require adult strength and experience."

Across the country, the students recorded their "Schools at War" activities in scrapbooks. The Griggs county scrapbooks would be shown at the Griggs county North Dakota Education Association. From there, the best books would be sent to a state exhibit, and from there, to a national exhibition.

It was a way to include everyone and to offer them some incentive and reward, outside of the stress and worry about what was going on "over there."

Sarah Walker

The Official Stray Newspaper

27 FEB

By 1906, the days of the Wild West were over. Barbed wire closed off much of the open range. Cowboys no longer guided vast herds of cattle up the well-known trails. But there were still echoes of the past. On this date in 1906, the *Bismarck Daily Tribune* published a clarification about the "North Dakota Herd and Estray Law."

No one was allowed to take possession of a stray between November and March unless the animal was on the person's property. Anyone taking in a stray was required to make an effort to find the owner. The finder had to take out a newspaper ad describing the animal and within ten days had to send notification by registered mail to the commissioner of agriculture in Bismarck. The receipt for the registered mail and a copy of the newspaper ad had to be sent to the county auditor as proof that the law had been followed. A person failing to follow these rules would be guilty of a misdemeanor and liable to the owner of the stray for any damages.

The *Washburn Leader* was designated as the "official stray newspaper." Newspapers had to forward all stray notices to the *Leader*. An editor who failed to do so was also guilty of a misdemeanor. The *Leader* would then send copies to each state auditor.

In order to recover a stray, the owner had to appear before a justice of the peace and sign an affidavit asserting ownership. The owner had to pay the finder for any expenses. If the finder had used the stray for work – for example, using a mule to plow a field – there was no compensation.

If no one claimed the animal after a year, the finder became legal owner. It was more complicated if the animal was worth more than twenty-five dollars. In that case, the animal was sold at auction. If the owner came forward after the sale, he or she would receive the money. If not, the money would be turned over to the county school fund.

Livestock was allowed to range free from December through April, although counties were permitted to pass fence laws. The stray laws applied to stray "horses, mares, colts, donkeys, mules, cattle, sheep, hogs, and goats."

Carole Butcher

28 FEB

Maxwell Anderson

Today marks the anniversary of the death of playwright Maxwell Anderson, who died in 1959. He was one of the most important American playwrights of the twentieth century.

Born in 1888, Anderson spent his first three years on a farm near Atlantic, Pennsylvania. The family moved to Jamestown in 1907, where Anderson graduated from high school. He then attended UND where he joined nearly every club related to writing and drama. For money, he waited tables and worked the night copy desk of the *Grand Forks Herald*.

After taking his B.A. in English Literature, Anderson moved to Minnewaukan, where he was the high school principal and an English teacher. He was an avowed pacifist, and two years later he was fired for protesting World War I in front of his students. Later he moved to Palo Alto, California, to get his Master's degree from Stanford University. He eventually became chair of the English Department at Whittier College near Los Angeles, but was fired again for making public statements on behalf of a student seeking conscientious objector status.

Anderson decided it was time to get into a different business – newspaper reporting. He worked for several papers in San Francisco and New York, and then began a different calling – he penned his first play, *White Desert*. It enjoyed only twelve performances, but it won the attention of Laurence Stallings, a reviewer for the New York *World*, and the two collaborated on a war comedy, *What Price Glory?* It was a giant hit and had a run of more than 430 performances. Anderson quit the newspaper business and went into writing plays full-time.

In the next few years Anderson wrote, among many others, *Elizabeth the Queen*, *Mary of Scotland*, *Key Largo* and *Anne of a Thousand Days*. In 1933, his play, *Both Your Houses*, won the Pulitzer Prize. He also won the First Annual New York Critics Circle Award for *Winterset* in 1935 and again for *High Tor* in 1936. He also wrote radio shows and collaborated on screenplays for movies like *All Quiet on the Western Front* and *Death Takes a Holiday*.

During the 75th anniversary of the founding of UND in 1958, Anderson was conferred as a Doctor of Humanities. He was too ill to attend, but he wrote a letter saying the university had been there for him when he needed it, saying "If I hadn't gone to the university, I might have been an unhappy and mediocre banker, farmer, or store-keeper. I'd have gone no farther."

Maxwell Anderson died the following year after having a stroke. He may have lost jobs because of his words, but his words have forever inked his place in history.

Merry Helm

Votes for Women League tent at Bottineau County Fair
Credit: State Historical Society of North Dakota (10204-00005)

MARCH

Washburn's Ag College

01 MAR

The citizens of Washburn reported their desire to procure the North Dakota Agricultural College for their own city on this day in 1916. Community members had held a mass meeting in order to form the Agricultural College Removal Association in the hopes of taking the college from its present location in Fargo. The activities were the direct result of an attack on the school launched by John Alman of Walsh County. Alman, a member of the constitutional convention, called on the state's Attorney General to "dig up his crowbar, come to bar and pry the college loose from its present site."

Alman's insistence was fueled by a small misnomer concerning the land on which the college rested. According to him, the college was granted the land inappropriately from the state common school fund under a federal grant; the land should have been acquired by public institution funds. Since the same board administered the public school fund and the public institution fund, the mistake appeared as a minor technical error made by the members of the board. Alman argued that the state pay the common school fund for the value of the property, or the Agricultural College be removed from its site in Fargo. Several cities jumped at the chance to acquire the school, including the hopeful citizens of Washburn. The city's Agricultural College Removal Association raised over $10,000 in a campaign to relocate the school. Large contributions came from Washburn's businessmen and farmers, and the city hoped to raise an additional $15,000 in the coming weeks. The association also began a massive circulation of initiative petitions across the state.

Meanwhile, the citizens of Fargo fought back, calling the accusations "mere piffle." Fargoans saw the technical error as "a matter that [could] be readily adjusted–and certainly without the necessity of dumping the Agricultural College off the lot." The college's president, E. F. Ladd looked "on the whole affair as being without foundation." As time has told, the school was never relocated to Washburn, but with the help of a little corrective legislation, was allowed to remain firmly rooted to its original location.

Jayme L. Job

02 MAR

The Creation of Dakota Territory

During most of the 1850s, the modern-day region of North Dakota belonged to two different territories. Land west of the Missouri River was part of Nebraska Territory; the region east of the Missouri belonged to Minnesota Territory. When Minnesota was granted statehood in 1858, land east of the Missouri was left unorganized while the west remained a part of Nebraska Territory.

Three years later, on this day in 1861, an act of Congress, signed by President James Buchanan established the Territory of Dakota. When initially created, Dakota Territory consisted of present-day states North Dakota, South Dakota and most of Montana and Wyoming. Two years later, the size of the territory was reduced to the current region of North and South Dakota.

Christina Sunwall

The Liner Dakota

03 MAR

On this date in 1907, the Liner Dakota was on her seventh voyage on a clear bright afternoon when she struck a reef off the coast of Japan and sank. The liner was launched only three years before on February 6, 1904, at New London, Connecticut. Christening the bow with champagne was seventeen-year-old Mary Belle Flemington from Ellendale, North Dakota. Mary Belle stood 6 foot 3 and had been voted the prettiest girl in North Dakota by her fellow UND students. The New York press called her the "Diana of the Prairies."

Mary Belle was given a tour of the sights in New York, but she wasn't that impressed. After six days, she headed home, saying, "I wouldn't give my little garden in Ellendale [...] with its broad vista of the prairie, for all the palaces on Fifth Avenue."

Mary Belle's christening of the Dakota held more responsibility than one might think. She had to break the champagne over the bow only after the ship started sliding from its braces into the water, but before it was out of reach. The luck of the ship was at risk, and the more the bottle shattered, the better luck. If she missed entirely, sailors would possibly refuse to board. In the case of the Dakota, the ship should have had great luck, as Mary Belle's aim was true.

The Dakota's twin cargo-passenger ship was the Minnesota, both of which were part of the Great Northern Steamship Company owned by railroad magnate James J. Hill. The ships had accommodations for two-hundred first-class passengers, with room for at least 1,800 in steerage class.

The Dakota and Minnesota were the largest steamers in the world flying the American flag. Hill believed the liners' cargo capacity would lower operating costs, attract more business, and make his shipping venture profitable. But, the maximum speed was only thirteen knots – pretty slow for a passenger liner.

The Dakota departed on her first voyage from Seattle to the Far East on September 20, 1905. On her seventh voyage, the Dakota was about forty miles south of Yokohama, Japan, when Captain Emil Francke steered her into what Japanese fishermen called the Devil's Sea. The area was well charted and widely avoided by mariners because of its treacherous reefs, and that day, the sea lived up to its name.

Captain Francke later said he realized his mistake and tried to change course, but it was too late to avoid steaming onto a reef. Thankfully, the ship was close enough to shore to avoid loss of life; all the passengers were safely evacuated, and a third of the cargo was salvaged before the vessel broke apart and sank.

Maybe they should've used better champagne at the christening.

Merry Helm

04 MAR

The Great McEwen

A traveling hypnotist came to Grand Forks in March of 1897 and mesmerized his audiences night after night in seven performances. The hypnotist, known as the "Great McEwen" or as "Professor McEwen," had a wonderful stage show in which he entertained large audiences with startling feats of mind control and suggestion, all done with care and good humor towards the subjects who volunteered.

Professor McEwen's performance was publicized in the *Grand Forks Herald* on this date, explaining how the hypnotist had been performing as a "mesmerist" across the nation for the past five years, and that he had recently been in Fargo for a week of performances, where he earned praise for his "amusement making powers."

McEwen lived up to the hype. He induced two young men into a trance and had them imitate heavyweights in a boxing match with one foot fastened to the floor. The hypnotist then put a strong young fellow into a deep trance, commanding him to become stiff and then placed him in a position where five men sat upon him like a park-bench. After awakening, the man said he felt fine.

Professor McEwen also hypnotized a dozen men and had them assume a rigid position. He then stacked them like cordwood, crisscross, in a human woodpile.

Another night, the hypnotist induced a willing subject to pantomime that he was fishing. The audience howled as the angler pretended to bait his hook, cast, and catch imaginary fish.

The Great McEwen gave the hypnotic suggestion to a "score" of young men and boys to play a baseball game on the stage, pitching, catching, and fielding an imaginary baseball. One participant attempted to steal a base and got so enthused that he slid clear over the edge of the stage headfirst into an audience that went "nearly wild," because the "fun was so funny."

McEwen also put a volunteer into a deep sleep one night, put him on display in a store window *all the next day*. He awakened him the following evening.

We do not know if Professor McEwen used the classic hypnotic inducement of "you are getting sleepy, very sleepy." But we do know, from old newspaper stories, that it was a "week of wonder," when Mesmerist McEwen mystified, surprised and entranced his audiences in Grand Forks with his skill and showmanship.

Dr. Steve Hoffbeck

Der Kaiser's Goat

05 MAR

In 1918, a goat traveled around Fargo, quickly going from one owner to the next. "Get the Kaiser's Goat" was a unique method for encouraging the sale of War Thrift Stamps.

Consisting of a large portrait of an evil-looking billy goat with the inscription "Der Kaiser's Goat," the package included a book in which the names of the Goat Getters were recorded as it was passed from one person to the next. Before the goat could be passed on, the holder had to promise a subscription of War Thrift Stamps ranging from 25¢ to $10 a month for the rest of the year. New members also called in to the committee to record their pledge and track the progress of the goat.

The idea originated by the *Fargo Forum* and was further developed by Walter Cushing and Joe Pierce of the War Saving Stamps Committee of Cass County. The initial drive began at noon March 2 when A. W. Cupler, chairman of the Cass County committee, sent the goat on its journey. The Order of the Goat Getters was so successful that it garnered twenty-seven members in the first hour, raising over $200 in pledges. To ensure that the pledges were honored, the committee collected them at the end of each month.

An additional element of fun was implemented in which the individual who was in possession of the goat at noon each day was declared "Grand Goat of the Day" and he who had the goat at sunset was declared "Supreme Goat of the Night."

So successful was the campaign that Fargo collected over $1,500 in pledges for each month through the end of the year. Other cities in North Dakota soon followed Fargo's lead and established corrals. Within weeks, the novel idea had spread across the United States. Orders for the Kaiser's Goat came in from across the nation within days after an Associated Press article on Fargo's success hit the newspapers. Many developed their own ideas using goat replicas instead of the portrait, and in Fargo and other communities, more than one goat made the rounds. It was a simple, fun idea and by the end of the first month it was estimated to have generated $100,000 nationally in the sales of Thrift Stamps per month. One Indiana newspaper proclaimed that Kaiser's Goat was the "Goat that made Fargo Famous."

Jim Davis

06 MAR

A Very Special Egg

During a visit to Europe in 1881, famed Civil War nurse Clara Barton learned of the Red Cross. When she returned home, she was instrumental in establishing Red Cross in America. Barton led the American Red Cross for twenty-three years. It supported American troops in the Spanish-American War and assisted in both domestic and overseas relief efforts. The Red Cross mission includes supporting members of the American Armed Forces and providing relief in disasters.

When World War I broke out, the organization experienced unprecedented growth. From 107 chapters in 1914 the Red Cross grew to 3,864 chapters by 1918. In that time membership grew from 17,000 to over twenty million adult and eleven million junior members. The Red Cross staffed hospitals and ambulances and recruited 20,000 nurses to serve the military.

North Dakotans supported the organization with enthusiasm. On this date in 1918, the *Hope Pioneer* reported the results of local fundraisers. The Luverne chapter had held an auction followed by a dinner and a dance. Farmers donated livestock, grains, and produce. Not to be outdone, businessmen donated various products and services. The event raised $2,265.75. The Luverne chapter also donated finished products to the Red Cross. The knitted socks were especially appreciated by the soldiers on the front lines.

The Hope chapter held a lunch and an auction. Some items were displayed in a store window prior to the sale, with farm machinery outside and livestock for viewing in the local livery stable. The auction began at 1:30 p.m. and didn't conclude until ten o'clock that night. Once an item was sold, the buyer often donated it back. A red and white heifer sold four times for a total of $152. A King Plymouth Rock Rooster sold twice. A silver dollar sold four times for $6, and the last buyer returned it to the original owner. The Hope fundraiser brought in $3,907.82.

One of the most notable sales of the day came when a five-year-old boy gave the auctioneer an egg he found in a poultry crate. The first time it was auctioned, it sold for $10. It was repeatedly auctioned and donated back. The egg brought a total of $41 – one very special egg for a very special cause.

Carole Butcher

Fish and Wildlife Service

07 MAR

From the stubble fields of fall farmland to the grass-lined pools of water dotting the state's prairie, North Dakota is widely recognized for its excellent hunting and fishing opportunities. The abundance of deer, pheasants, grouse, ducks, geese, and even the occasional mountain lion, serve as a testament to the state's natural bounty. The federal organization dedicated to the preservation of these North Dakota natural wonders is the U.S. Fish and Wildlife Service.

The history of the Fish and Wildlife Service stretches back to two separate government programs created in the latter half of the Nineteenth century. The first, the U.S. Commission on Fish and Fisheries, was created in 1871 by Congress inside the Department of Commerce to investigate the declining numbers of fish numbers in U.S. waters. Fourteen years later, in 1885, the Division of Economic Ornithology and Mammalogy, later known as the Bureau of Biological Survey, was established within the Department of Agriculture to study the effects birds had in controlling pests and also to document the geographical distribution of plants and animals throughout the United States. In 1903, the Bureau was given another task by former North Dakota resident Theodore Roosevelt – the preservation of the first national wildlife refuge, Pelican Island, Florida.

From 1939 through 1940, the U.S. Commission on Fish and Fisheries and the Bureau of Biological Survey were combined under the Department of the Interior into one program, the Fish and Wildlife Service. Along with state and local organizations, the Service began addressing the decline in wildlife in states like North Dakota, where hunting excess and pervasive drought in previous decades had damaged their numbers. The Fish and Wildlife Service reported on the initial success of their programs in an official announcement released on this day in 1941. The number and habitat of many animals and game birds, such as pheasants, sharp-tail grouse, and water-fowl, were rebounding. Today the Fish and Wildlife Service manages sixty-two National Wildlife Refuges in North Dakota, the highest number in any state, as well as the twelve Wetland Management Districts. In sum, these refuges and wetland districts protect over 1.3 million acres of North Dakotan beauty.

Besides the preservation of North Dakota's ecology, the Fish and Wildlife Service is important to the state's economy. It has over twenty offices scattered throughout the state, employing nearly 250 people. Federal aid, important for the operation and protection of North Dakota's natural beauty, contributes nearly $200 million to the state's wildlife infrastructure. Furthermore, the wildlife refuges and wetland districts attract nearly 500,000 hunters and tourists each year. North Dakota and the Federal Fish and Wildlife Service continue to work together to ensure that North Dakota retains both its scenic beauty and its plentiful gaming opportunities that are a source of enjoyment to so many throughout the year.

Lane Sunwall

08 MAR

The Biggest Spectator Sport in the Country

On this date in 1974, the front page of the *Bismarck Tribune* sported a startling photo of young people leaping about naked. The headline explained that the day before, streakers frolicked by the thousands on college campuses throughout the country. University of Georgia streakers claimed the record after as many as 1,000 students participated. But students at the University of Colorado claimed that over 1,200 streakers had dashed about their campus. Streakers ran, walked, biked, and danced. Some even jumped out of an airplane over the University of Illinois wearing only parachutes. In neighboring Minnesota, streakers dashed across the court during a basketball game at St. Olaf College in Northfield. It happened so quickly that the game was not interrupted. Most of the players did not even notice the event.

North Dakota was not left out of the festivities, although the numbers were not very impressive. At Jamestown, eight men streaked through the women's dorm, and there were only about a dozen participants in the entire state. The chilly weather may have been a factor. Police said there were no arrests in any of the incidents.

That tolerant attitude has not continued into the Twenty-first century. On November 19, 2011, three pledges from Delta Tau Delta ran streaking through the UND campus just after midnight. All three were caught. They were charged with disorderly conduct, refusal to halt, and minor possessing or consuming alcohol. Police reported that after being spotted, the three ran to a fraternity house where they were arrested. The following year, a streaking event known as the Anchor Run led to the interfraternity council approving an alcohol ban in fraternity houses. The council said any fraternity violating the policy could lose privileges.

Streaking seems to have largely fallen out of favor. It may be the result of attracting arrest rather than smiles. The times have changed since the day the *Bismarck Tribune* called the nationwide streaking event "The Biggest Spectator Sport in the Country."

Carole Butcher

Drought and Depression

09 MAR

The entire economic system of the United States began to break down following the Stock Market Crash of 1929. Unemployment swept across the nation, and North Dakota suffered even more than most of the country because of a devastating drought. Production was down and so were prices. In 1933, the per capita personal income in the United States was $375. But in North Dakota, it was only $145. Thousands lost their farms. There was a mass migration out of the state. Over one third of the remaining population lived on relief.

North Dakotans were not united in how the government should respond to the crisis. They tended to be extremely independent. Farmers did not want the government to tell them to change their farming methods, and the residents in general were reluctant to live on charity handed out by Washington, considering it a loss of independence and freedom. In spite of efforts by a Democratic Administration to get the country back on its feet, North Dakotans remained staunchly Republican.

Franklin D. Roosevelt was elected in 1932 and inaugurated on March 4, 1933. More than thirteen million Americans were out of work. There was no time to lose. He had to act, and he had to act fast. On this date in 1933, the Emergency Banking Act was introduced in a special joint session of Congress. The sense of crisis was so great that there was only one written copy of the Act available, and it was read aloud before Congress. It passed that evening. Roosevelt immediately signed it into law. The Act expanded the powers of the President to respond to a banking crisis, allowing him to regulate virtually all banking functions.

Roosevelt told Americans that "it is safer to keep your money in a reopened bank than under the mattress." His immediate action had the desired effect. Within two weeks, Americans deposited more than half the funds they had withdrawn from banks. The Stock Market began a slow recovery.

The Great Depression was by no means over. North Dakotans continued to suffer. People drifted off the farms into towns, where they were no better off. Governor Langer believed it was crucial to increase farm prices to save the state. He declared a moratorium on farm foreclosures. With measures instituted by both Washington and Bismarck, North Dakota slowly emerged from the Great Depression.

Carole Butcher

10 MAR

Breach of Promise Suit

Spring is the season of love, and that can mean all kinds of trouble. This was true for Mrs. Sybil Kleity from North Dakota, who found love in a most unexpected place, public transportation.

Mrs. Kleity was a beautician who moved from Minot to Fargo in 1936 after leaving her husband, Raymond Kleity of Minot. En route from Grand Forks to Fargo she met Mr. Frank G. Lansing of Minneapolis, an employee of the Overland Transportation Company.

However, this love was as fleeting as the paper her one-way ticket was printed on. Even though Mr. Lansing proposed to Mrs. Kleity in July of 1938 with a sparkling ring in the presence of fifteen witnesses, Mrs. Kleity found herself duped. The man was not only in a relationship with another woman in Minneapolis, he was already married and had four children.

This caused Mrs. Kleity much anger, $25,000 worth according to the *Minot Daily News* of 1939. Mrs. Kleity took Mr. Lansing to court for misconduct of the heart, formally called a "Breach of Promise Suit." Mrs. Kleity cited "great physical and mental anguish [...] and embarrassment."

These "Breach of Promise Suits" have a deep history. Originating in medieval times, they occurred well into the early twentieth century. In many cases, the man's promise of engagement was considered a legally binding contract and when "breached" could result in litigation and damages. This contract of engagement to be married created liability for men, but not often for women, reflecting the differing social expectations of men and women throughout most of history. In the early part of the Twenteith century in the United States, many "yellow journalists" covered these cases with tabloid-like enthusiasm, as many of the lawsuits involved attractive, young society women and wealthy older men.

On this day in 1939, Mrs. Kleity won in her suit when District Judge M. J. Englert ordered a default judgment of $2,000. The amount is a little shy of the compensation sought, but there was no doubt satisfaction in her justification of heartbreak.

Certainly, the unusually steep cost for breaking this particular heart is a little upsetting and comical. However, it has been said, "Caring and trust is the cost of the ticket on the bus of love."

Maria Witham

Champagne Music

11 MAR

The world-famous musician, band leader, and showman Lawrence Welk was born on this date in 1903 near Strasburg, North Dakota.

In his book, *Wunnerful, Wunnerful*, Welk recounts the discovery of his famous music style. When his announcer showed him a pile of fan letters, they found that many added descriptions of how the music sounded "sparkling," "light," "effervescent," "happy," and "bubbly."

"'You know what these letters are saying, don't you?' Welk's announcer demanded. 'They're saying that dancing to your music is like sipping champagne. Lawrence, you've got yourself some Champagne Music!'"

"With our new title came a real flash of inspiration," Welk wrote. "I dug out the song I had written years before to celebrate Shirley's birth, 'You're My Home Sweet Home.' Originally, I had written it as a slow, sweet legato ballad, a kind of hymn to my daughter, but now I began to play the same tune at a much faster tempo, with a few added runs and frills. The result was a light, frothy piece which seemed to suit our musical style perfectly, and I began to use it as our theme song. When people asked me what the name of it was, 'You're My Home Sweet Home' just didn't sound right to them, and so one day I decided to have a contest to give the song a new name...Within a matter of days we had found the name we wanted – 'Bubbles in the Wine'."

"But," Welk continued, "we had trouble trying to get the sound of a champagne cork exploding out of the bottle, which we needed to go along with our new theme. At first we tried opening a real bottle, but we never got the same effect twice, and it was almost impossible to get it opened at the exact moment required in the song. I finally solved the whole thing by sticking my finger in my mouth and popping it out with a 'whoosh' – something I still do today and something the boys tell me I have developed into a real art form. I may not play the accordion as well as Myron Floren," Welk wrote, "but I play a champagne bottle much better than he does."

Merry Helm

Adapted from Welk's autobiography *Wunnerful, Wunnerful*. New Jersey: Prentice-Hall, 1971

12 MAR

Spirit Lake Massacre

The 1850s were a time of increasing conflict between the Dakota and settlers who were steadily moving west. The encroachment on traditional hunting grounds left the Dakota frustrated. Relations between the two groups were tense, with sporadic violence. Then came the shocking massacre at Spirit Lake, Iowa. Suffering from cold and hunger, Inkpaduta was angry. He led his band in an attack on the settlers, killing about thirty. They crossed into Minnesota where they killed seven more. On this date in 1857, they killed one more before riding west.

News of the killings spurred Minnesota settlers to form militias. They demanded that the marauders be punished, and they attacked any Dakota they could find, even the innocent. The hard feelings remained after the fighting died down.

Five years later came the Dakota Uprising, with both the settlers and Dakota suffering casualties. The uprising was short-lived, lasting only two months, but led to an ongoing conflict in Dakota Territory.

General Henry Hastings Sibley and General Alfred Sully were tasked with following the Dakota and putting an end to the threat they posed. Sibley and Sully led expeditions to do just that in the summer of 1863, but without much success. The summer culminated in Sully's attack on a large gathering at Whitestone Hill. Twenty soldiers were killed in the fighting, with Dakota losses estimated at 300 – most of them women and children.

Sully tried again the following year. He met Inkpaduta at Killdeer Mountain. Inkpaduta was joined by noted chiefs Sitting Bull and Gall. Sully seemed to be getting the worst of the fighting until he opened fire with artillery. Once again, women and children were killed. Inkpaduta and his followers decamped and rode for the Badlands.

The fighting continued across the Dakotas. In 1876, General Custer rode out of Fort Abraham Lincoln for his last battle at Little Big Horn. The Spirit Lake Massacre happened in Iowa. But over the next several decades, the incident continued to have repercussions in Dakota Territory.

Carole Butcher

Campus Protests

13 MAR

There's no doubt that many stood against "the man," whatever form he took, in the 1960s. Doing so often took the form of protest, and campus revolts made headlines across the United States.

On this date in 1969, Governor William Guy signed a bill into law that was supposed to help maintain order on the campuses of North Dakota state colleges and universities. The bill stated that "persons will be ejected from the campuses in disturbances and action will be taken to expel the students."

This bill, however, was contested. Some said it repeated statutes already in existence. Others said the bill was intended to scare off trouble before it started. Also, according to Representative Aamoth - who was a prime sponsor of the measure - the bill was supposed to "take care of nonstudents who come in from outside the school to create trouble."

However, Senator Meschke - who was against the bill - said "personally, I prefer to respect our North Dakota young people and students, rather than insult them for something that they have not done."

Yet the college protest movement was prevalent around the country, and college students were not the only ones to find reason for revolt. The National Association of Secondary School Principals conducted a survey with 1,000 principals in public and private schools. They found that 56 percent of junior high schools and 59 percent of senior high schools reported some kind of protest activity. Heading the list were restrictions placed on the personal appearance of the students; one third of the principals reported objections to school dress codes, and one fourth reported objections to regulations governing hair length and style.

Students also protested smoking rules, cafeterias, assembly programs, censorship and regulation of school papers, and the scheduling of sports and social events. Only ten percent of the principals cited difficulties between races.

The protestation of younger students seemed to follow and echo that of the college revolts, and principals thought that the protests were really against "society in general," or "the system," and reported that "not only kids, but their parents, their teachers and various community groups are getting in on it."

In what must be the understatement of the decade, one school head observed: "To be a principal in times like these is not for the fainthearted.'"

Sarah Walker

14 MAR

Candy Cigarettes

"Light me up!" On this date in 1953 no longer could kids in North Dakota expect to buy a pack of cigarettes—candy cigarettes, that is.

Senate Bill 153, prohibiting the sale of any candy or confectionary which was designed to imitate packages of cigarettes or other tobacco items, was signed into law. Jack Hagerty, working for the United Press in Bismarck, had been ordered to look for any offbeat legislative item by the UP headquarters in New York and he stumbled across the candy cigarette issue that had been all but ignored by the rest of the press. The New York editors were intrigued by Jack's story, which made it onto many front pages all around the country, and they requested additional information. At this point the Associated Press also picked up the story and the North Dakota Legislature became a point of national ridicule. Such a furor was created that the candy cigarette issue overshadowed almost all legislation from the 1953 Session. At one point some senators rose and demanded that the *Bismarck Tribune* apologize for the scathing criticism.

Looking back on it twenty-five years later in his "That Reminds Me" column written for the *Grand Forks Herald*, Jack wrote, "If the measure had not attracted so much attention, it is quite possible it would have been allowed to die quietly." But the legislators weren't going to kill the bill because of the ridicule so the bill making it unlawful to sell, exchange, transport, possess, display or offer for sale candy cigarettes made it through the session with only minor changes.

In the mid 1950s Jack Hagerty joined the *Grand Forks Herald*, later becoming senior editor. As to his part in breaking the candy cigarette story, he stated that he disagreed with the charge that "the media not only decides what is news, that they help make it."

What effect the candy cigarette law had is difficult to say. The 1950s saw the rise of James Dean, Elvis, and other teen idols. Black leather jackets were in and so was the word "cool"; most of the "cool kids" smoked. Many kids tried the real thing behind the barn or in the back alley and ragweed, pipe stem, and other plants were poor substitutes for candy cigarettes.

The candy cigarette law remained on the books until 1967 when a revision of Chapter 19 of the Century Code omitted this section of the code and no effort was made to revive it. Modern legislative sessions have dealt with the elimination of tobacco products and, it is interesting to note, that the children of the 1950s, now grandparents, in carrying on a tradition, often pass out candy cigars to announce the birth of a grandchild in place of the real ones. Although candy cigars were never part of the candy cigarette bill, they are now preferable so that their friends don't say, "Light me up!"

Jim Davis

The Blizzard with No Warning

15 MAR

On this day in 1941, an intense and fast-moving "Alberta Clipper" hit North Dakota. Originating in Northern Canada as a result of an unsettling pattern of high and low pressure systems, the storm didn't last long or produce an unusually high amount of snowfall, but winds of 50 to 80 miles an hour blew with deadly force across the plains.

The day began very mild. Mrs. Lawrence Ramsey and her sisters were ice skating on a pond in front of their farm house near Crystal, ND, but had to quit when the ice began to melt. Warm afternoon temperatures caused melting and puddling in the farm yards across the region causing farmers to take advantage of the mild weather, hastily doing their morning chores so they could get to town and enjoy the day. Many of them were trapped in town or were injured or even died as they tried to race back home ahead of the fast-moving storm later that day.

Weather forecasting has always been an inexact science, and in 1941, people just did not have advance warning of the rapidly moving blizzard. One story exemplifies the tragedy of this violent spring storm. Mr. and Mrs. Warren Taylor farmed just four miles southeast of Dazey. The evening of March 15, Leo, 17, and Donald, 15, took their twin ten-year-old brothers, Dickie and Robert, roller skating in town. After skating they left for home in their car. Their car stalled and they began to walk home. When the boys didn't show up on time, Mr. and Mrs. Taylor got worried. News of possible danger spread quickly, and neighbors began searching for the boys. Ralph Bender and Beaumont Stowman from Dazey started out at midnight, walking about fifteen miles in the storm looking for the boys. At 7:45 a.m., the morning of the 16th, the older boys, Leo and Donald were found frozen to death. Vernon Jacobson, another neighbor out searching, saw the feeble wave of an arm, and began digging. Vernon uncovered Dickie, who would die just a few minutes later, but his twin, Robert was alive and taken to the hospital in Valley City. Robert would be the only one of the four brothers to survive the storm that night.

Hundreds of stranded travelers survived the blizzard by staying with their cars although some of them did experience severe frostbite. A few of those who left their cars got lucky and struggled their way through the storm to safety. Of course, the storm was also tough on wildlife and farm animals, but two lucky turkeys emerged from a snow bank after being buried in the snow for twenty-three days on the Robert Grindler farm near Rogers and a live sheep was uncovered at the Fred Schroeder farm near Valley City seventeen days after the storm.

When it was all said and done, the March 15th, 1941 blizzard caused seventy-one deaths in North Dakota and Minnesota.

Merrill Piepkorn

16 MAR

Legendary Slogans

John F. McGrann was completing a week-long circuit of the state of North Dakota on this day in 1924. Mr. McGrann, as the vice-president and business manager of the newly formed North Dakota Automobile Association, was making his rounds in an attempt to promote his novel idea for increasing tourism to the state.

McGrann claimed that the only thing necessary to increase the state's tourism was a catchy slogan. He urged "the businessman, newspaperman, banker, professional, school teacher, and all he [came] in contact with to practice simple courtesy toward the tourist who visits the state" by saying "Hope you like North Dakota." He viewed the friendliness of the people of North Dakota as the state's greatest asset for bringing in tourists.

Although McGrann's idea for an official slogan never caught on, and "Hope you like North Dakota" has been forgotten over time, a number of slogans have been used in the state in an effort to encourage tourism. In the 1980s, North Dakota's Department of Tourism attempted a more humorous approach to advertising the state. Signs along the eastern end of the state proclaimed, "Welcome to North Dakota, Mountain Removal Project Completed," while on the western end they read boldly, "Stay in North Dakota: Custer Was Healthy When He Left."

Jayme L. Job

Historic Preservation Act

17 MAR

On this date in 1966, Senator Edward Muskie, with the support of Senator Mike Mansfield of Montana, Senator Edward Kennedy of Massachusetts, and Senator Wayne Morse of Oregon, introduced two bills that would profoundly affect the ability to preserve and record significant historic places. The Senate bill provided financial and other aid to encourage and assist in the preservation and maintenance of historic structures. The legislation promoted and coordinated historic preservation activities of the Federal, State, and local governments, and other public bodies, private organizations, and individuals.

On introducing the legislation, Senator Muskie stated, "Many of our buildings and sites, which are rich in American history, architecture, archeology, and culture, are threatened by bulldozers or neglect. Already, half of our most historically significant structures have been destroyed. If we wait another five years, there may be no need for this legislation. By then, most of the structures, which could and should have been saved, may have fallen."

The mid-1960s were a time of rapid change, socially and politically, including the arrival of the Baby Boomer generation into the workplace. Cities were expanding into suburbs and inner cities were being revitalized. Old landmarks were giving way to modern structures. Senator Muskie further noted that, "Our landmarks lend stability to our lives. They are a point of orientation. They help establish values of time and place and belonging."

One purpose of the legislation was to find, survey, and register significant structures. The selection of worthy sites would be governed by an advisory council. Grants and loans would be provided for the acquisition and restoration of registered buildings. Architects and technicians would be trained to fill the critical shortage of professional personnel in the field. It was the triumph of more than a century of struggle by a grassroots movement of committed preservationists. The resources of both private and public organizations would be marshaled to save the nation's heritage of stone and mortar.

Old landmarks would be revitalized and become a viable part of the landscape. More importantly, as Senator Muskie pointed out, the legislation "will help us save for the future the best of what we have inherited from the past." North Dakota has a total of 440 sites as of this writing – many counties have one, two, or three sites. Grand Forks County has the most with sixty-eight.

Jim Davis

18 MAR

From the Wheatfield to the Battlefield

In the fall of 1914, Ray Crandall ran away from everything he knew to seek the adventure of his life. Twenty-one years old, Crandall was a farmhand threshing wheat near New Salem when he seemingly disappeared. Ray's father, Mr. H.A. Crandall, who had a farm a mile north of Zap in Mercer County, had no word from his son and began a long search. Half a year passed before the story of the mysterious disappearance finally became known to Ray's father.

On this date in 1915, the *Ward County Independent* published a story that traced Ray Crandall's path from North Dakota. "I'm with the Canadian soldiers on the battle field in France," wrote Crandall in a letter that explained his motivations for leaving. "Farm life was too dull," he wrote. He and a fellow worker named William Falk of Glen Ullin had "left the threshing fields of New Salem" and headed to the Canadian border at Portal. There the authorities refused entry to the young men and sent them away.

After a stop in Minot, Crandall and Falk tried again to cross the border at another location. Once again, they were sent away, ending up in Grand Forks. Refusing to give up, the two men crept to the border after nightfall and finally crossed into Manitoba. They "hiked to Winnipeg" and joined the Canadian Army.

Their regiment was eventually sent to France, where Crandall and Falk fought under the flag of Great Britain. Transferred from France to the Dardanelles combat zone in Turkey, where the two men were caught in the thickest fighting. William Falk was killed and Ray Crandall was shot through his right shoulder.

Ater recovering in England, Crandall rejoined his regiment in France and was again "severely wounded" in a "shower of sniping by the Germans." When he healed, Crandall began training as an aviator and served as a pilot through the end of the war.

Coming back to America, Crandall made his home in Vancouver, British Columbia, venturing into business there. In 1921, he quietly returned to his home state to visit old friends, sharing many "interesting tales" of his "combat days."

The man who disappeared from the Dakota wheatfields had finally reappeared, having found excitement and harrowing adventures on the battlefields of World War I.

Dr. Steve Hoffbeck

The Marmarth Mummified Dinosaur

19 MAR

It's not often that Marmarth, North Dakota makes national news. For years the tiny town of 140 has sat comfortably in its anonymity – just one of many small towns in North Dakota. But that was all before it became the site of one of the rarest and most important dinosaur finds in a generation.

In 1999, Tyler Lyson was visiting his uncle's ranch in the Badlands outside Marmarth. Interested in fossils, the teen went hunting for dinosaurs. His hard work scouring the countryside was soon rewarded when he discovered some remains. What exactly was buried beneath the hard sandstone and rubble wasn't clear, but at first glance, the find seemed to be just another Edmontosaur; a herbivore of the late Cretaceous period.

Like the bison of the old American West, but scaly and weighing three and a half tons, *Edmontosaurus* was an incredibly successful animal. Millions of years ago, huge herds of the massive dinosaur migrated throughout the American continent searching for food, and at times serving as prey for the fearsome *Tyrannosaurus rex*. As the Edmontosaur was such a common prehistoric animal, thousands of their skeletons have been uncovered. Tyler Lyson's find was personally exciting, but it wasn't exactly earth shattering to the world of paleontology; that was before Lyson really began to dig.

As the years rolled by, and Lyson steadfastly picked away at the rock and debris, he began to realize the importance of his find. Lyson wasn't just unearthing an Edmontosaur skeleton, he was digging up a sixty-seven million year old mummy; complete with skin, tendons, and bones. Only a handful of these dinosaur mummies have ever been discovered, and Lyson's Edmontosaur eventually proved to be one of the best preserved.

What makes Tyler Lyson's Edmontosaur, nicknamed Dakota, so incredibly rare is the way the animal was preserved. While the vast majority of most dinosaurs decompose before they're buried and fossilized, Dakota was buried shortly after death. Kept away from most decomposing bacteria, Dakota's soft tissues survived long enough for the fossilization process to preserve the parts rarely seen by scientists. These "soft" tissues, which are now rock hard, give researches a much clearer idea of what dinosaurs looked like, how they moved and how their bodies were put together.

The media quickly gained wind of the historic find from the North Dakota Badlands. It was on this date in 2008 that newspapers from around the nation informed the country of Dakota, the sixty-seven million year old *Edmontosaurus* from the small town of Marmarth, North Dakota. And Tyler Lyson? His interest in dinosaurs continued, as he went on to Yale to earn his doctorate in paleontology.

Lane Sunwall

20 MAR

State Scientific School Opens its Doors

The North Dakota State College of Science in Wahpeton, which opened as the State Scientific School, has its beginnings around 1903. Today, it is one of the oldest public two-year colleges in the United States.

Reports of ongoing events at the local school were often published in the *Wahpeton Times*, but visitors were not allowed to wander around unsupervised. So it was of particular interest when, on this date in 1914, the school extended an invitation to the general public to visit the school for an open house. The event took place on a Thursday evening from 8:00-9:30.

Many residents took advantage of the opportunity, and they were abuzz with what they had learned. Many students and staff took part, stationing themselves in the labs and shops. Others acted as ushers, helping guests find their way. The staff and students presented some of their lessons and research in ways that resonated with the visitors.

In the biological laboratory, guests could view slides of animal and plant life via compound microscopes. In the agricultural department, students showed the method and results of the Babcock test of milk, for the purpose of determining the fat content; other students demonstrated seed testing and other matters "of interest to the prospective farmer."

Students in the physics lab were using a hand dynamo machine that generated electricity, giving shocks "to any party who wanted to try the sensation." They also had an X-ray machine, allowing visitors to look at the bones in their own hands.

In the electrical laboratory across the hall, one of the professors explained how a wireless telegraph worked. Visitors could even try on the head harness of the machine and listen for signals.

In the domestic science rooms, both men and women sat in on sewing demonstrations. They also enjoyed refreshments in the kitchen, an area where visitors were typically barred.

There was a lot going on, and the *Wahpeton Times* proudly reported, "Every visitor is loud in the praises of the school in what they saw and learned," feeling a "renewed interest in this worthy institution." The appreciation shown by guests also left the members of the school feeling "highly repaid for the time and trouble."

Sarah Walker

Mandan Flood

21 MAR

Ice blocking the Heart River near Mandan caused extensive flooding on this date in 1948. The flooding eventually overtook the southern half of the city and cut off transportation between Bismarck and Mandan. Although the flood was primarily due to the build-up of ice floes, the majority of the damage was confined to the lowland area where the Heart flowed into the Missouri.

On the evening of March 20, dozens of volunteers began adding sandbags to the dikes surrounding the city. A haphazard dike was also thrown up across US Highway 10, the main thoroughfare connecting Mandan to Bismarck. Later that night, five families were forced to evacuate their homes as the water continued to rise. As residents of Mandan prepared for bed that night, the river flowed only two to three feet below the city's emergency dikes. City officials warned that the water was likely to pour over the dikes by morning. The Mandan Memorial building was opened to house evacuees.

Overnight, a giant ice jam formed upriver, easing the flow. The flood water even receded somewhat, but the reprieve proved temporary. Mandan residents waited, watching the giant blocks of ice. Movements of the jam were tracked by planes above the city.

On March 23, the upstream ice jam gave away and flood waters rushed over the dikes. The hundreds of volunteers, drawn from local high schools and area businessmen, were forced to give up and watch helplessly as water engulfed the entire southern half of the city. Icy chunks floating downriver stripped the bark off trees, snapped telephone poles, and even took out a steel bridge. Hundreds were evacuated, and the army dispatched an amphibious boat from Bismarck loaded with blankets and cots, but the icy waters were too much for the seven-ton vehicle, which was forced to turn back. The aid was instead shipped by railcar.

Spring flooding was not uncommon for Mandan residents, but the following year, construction on the Heart Butte Dam was completed, helping tame the once-violent river.

Jayme L. Job

22 MAR

Louis L'Amour

Today is the birthday of Louis L'Amour, one of the most prolific writers of the twentieth century. His father was a large-animal veterinarian who had moved to Dakota Territory in 1882, and it was in Jamestown that Louis was born in 1908, the last of seven children.

Louis' grandfather, Abraham Dearborn, lived in a little house behind the LaMoore's, and he sparked Louis' imagination with adventure stories based on his days as a soldier in the Civil War and then in the Indian wars. Louis was soon devouring the fiction of Robert Louis Stevenson, Jack London, and Edgar Rice Burroughs – anything with adventure.

When Louis was fifteen, everything changed. Louis' son, Beau, writes, "After a series of bank failures ruined the economy of the upper Midwest, Dr. LaMoore, his wife Emily, and their sons Louis and John took their fortunes on the road. They traveled across the country in an often-desperate seven-year odyssey."

During that time, Louis met hundreds of people who would later become inspirations for his adventure and western novels – cowboys, desperados, military men and, yes, even gunfighters. He also started boxing, sometimes making enough money to buy gas for the family to move on. Several times, he won enough prize money to allow him to box full time in gyms all across the west, where he met fighters, managers, gangsters, and gamblers who later surfaced in his books.

L'Amour began writing – and changed the spelling of his name. His career was just taking off when he was inducted into the army in 1942. He trained as a Tank Destroyer, but because he was almost thirty-five, he was ruled too old for combat. Instead, he was sent to England and then to Europe where he commanded a platoon of gas tankers. Again, he soaked in everything for later use in his books.

When he got back from the war, L'Amour found that the market for his adventure novels had all but dried up; now everybody wanted mysteries and westerns. He chose westerns and his output became tremendous. During one year he sold almost a story a week, in addition to writing others that didn't sell. Louis' average income per short story was less than $100, however, and it was his novels that finally brought him significant success, especially his series on the Sacketts.

L'Amour went on to write a total of 116 western novels. He won award after award, including the ND Roughrider Award, but it wasn't until he was sixty-five that he felt financially secure enough to slow down.

In the fall of 1987, L'Amour was diagnosed with lung cancer. The following June, he was editing his long-postponed memoir, *Education of a Wandering Man*, when he died in his bedroom office. Only days before, he had been notified that sales of his books had topped two hundred million.

Merry Helm

Escaping the Draft

23 MAR

A military draft was instituted during the American Civil War. It proved to be very unpopular, and was abolished when the war was over. But when World War I broke out, the draft was reintroduced with the Selective Service Act of 1917. All men ages of 21 to 30 had to register. This was later expanded to ages 18 to 45. Some exemptions were granted. Men who had dependent families, necessary jobs, or physical disabilities were excused. Members of pacifist organizations like the Quakers were granted conscientious objector status, but they had to perform service that did not require fighting. By the end of World War I, almost three million men had been inducted into the military.

The country's involvement in World War I was not popular in North Dakota. Some say that was because of the high population of Germans. To be fair, residents of the state had been equally reluctant to get involved in the Spanish American War. But, just as with that earlier conflict, North Dakotans were determined to support the country. When war was declared, the state did its part. Company E of the 164th Infantry was reorganized in October, 1917, and served as an element of the 41st Infantry Division. The unit served with distinction.

However, not all North Dakotans were anxious to serve their country. On this date in 1918, the *Fargo Forum and Daily Republican* reported on a man who went to great lengths to avoid service. Louis Steiber claimed he was too old to be drafted. At the time, the upper age was 30. An indictment said Steiber presented a false document to the draft board. An altered date on a forged baptismal certificate made it appear that he was 31. In the process, he also got a friend in trouble. A.F. Marquetie, the owner of the Bismarck steam laundry, was arrested by a U.S. Deputy Marshal and charged with conspiracy for helping Steiber.

An article in the *American Legion Weekly* estimated that there were almost half a million draft dodgers during World War I. It stated that the War Department was determined to prosecute them all.

Carole Butcher

24 MAR

An Equine Threat

In the early part of the twentieth century, horses still provided most of the horsepower. In 1915 there were over twenty-six million horses in the United States. Now, there's just over nine million.

For most people, horses have completely disappeared from day-to-day life. But back in the day, horses were everywhere. If you wanted to ride a streetcar, buy produce shipped in from a farm, or purchase ice from the ice man, you used horses.

On this date in 1915, W.F. Crewe of the North Dakota Live Stock Sanitary Board announced an effort to eradicate a threat to the state's horses. It was dourine, a fatal venereal disease that affects horses, donkeys, and mules. Even today, there is no vaccine for the disease, and treatment remains far from certain. Dourine used to be widespread, found in countries around the world. By 1915 it was less common. But the state still had some cases.

Mr. Crewe announced a program, an ambitious one, to inspect all of the horses that had been inspected the previous year and that way, they'd determine if the disease had made any progress. He said other horses would also be inspected, and he thought the disease would be wiped out by summer. Veterinarians were supposed to report all cases. New horses should be quarantined until known to be disease free, said Mr. Crewe. He also noted that native ponies tended to be of hardier stock and they seemed more resistant to dourine – which, remember, often killed. A few horses recovered, but the mortality rate was estimated to be 75%. Some experts put it even higher.

In order to prevent the spread of dourine, any horses showing symptoms had to be put down. The fatality rate was 100% in detected cases. You could see why ranchers, farmers, and others who depended on horses were concerned. Crewe assured them that they would be compensated, with the state and federal governments splitting the cost.

Crewe was right to be optimistic. By that summer in 1915, there were very few cases of dourine in North Dakota. It continues to be a concern worldwide, but a small one around here, and they repealed the chapter about it that was in the North Dakota Century Code in 1965.

Carole Butcher

The Hotel Brown Opens for Business

25 MAR

William H. Brown helped develop land across the state of North Dakota. Among other jobs, Brown established The William H. Brown Land Company, one of the largest such companies west of the Missouri River. He also platted and founded several townsites, including Flasher, Haynes, and, in 1904, Mott.

In March of 1911, a hotel built by William H. Brown opened in Mott. In celebration of the new Hotel Brown, the Mott Commercial Club joined the hotel staff in organizing a grand opening. Invitations were issued to local commercial clubs across the state. George Welch, president of the Bismarck Commercial Club, and General E. A. Williams, president of the Bismarck City Commission, served as delegates from Bismarck. Other businessmen from the capital city also attended.

The opening featured a banquet at 9 in the evening. Places were set for approximately 200 individuals, and the White City Orchestra of Mott was hired to perform. Extra help and additional silverware were located, and plenteous cut flowers were everywhere.

After dinner, speakers from all across the state addressed the crowd. General Williams spoke of living in the area during the territorial days. W. E. GIllespie of Fargo spoke on behalf of Fargo Mayor Lovell. C. L. Timmercan of Mandan talked about his early experiences in the area. Secretary of State P.D. Norton also spoke.

On this date, the *Bismarck Tribune* reported on the success of the event, stating, "The palatial Hotel Brown, which is a monument to its builder, Wm. H. Brown, was opened here [...] with a dedication banquet that was attended by representatives from most of the commercial clubs throughout the Slope country." It was "luxuriantly furnished," described as having "apartments similar to those of an eastern hotel." $50,000 was invested in the building.

Coincidentally, William H. Brown was unable to attend due to "the stress of business," but the Mott Commercial Club and the hotel management received telegrams of congratulations from him and from another absent invitee – Howard Elliot of Chicago, the president of the Northern Pacific Railway.

Yet, the *Tribune* reported, "The affair was a decided success in every particular and many words of praise were expressed on all sides for the efficiency displayed by the several committees in charge. It was simply another evidence of the unprecedented enterprise of the citizens of Mott, the spot."

Alas, the grand Hotel Brown no longer stands.

Sarah Walker

26 MAR

Gerrymandering

Gerrymandering is a practice by which a political party attempts to manipulate voting district boundaries for political advantage. The party in power has control of the process, so the party out of power regularly accuses the other of gerrymandering. The term was coined on this date in 1812. It appeared in a political cartoon in the *Boston Gazette*. Governor Elbridge Gerry signed a bill into law that would benefit his party by redistricting. One of the new districts was said to resemble a salamander. The cartoonist combined that description with the governor's last name to invent a new word. "Gerrymander" has been in use ever since.

North Dakota has previously been dominated by the Republican Party. Whenever the subject of redistricting comes up, accusations of gerrymandering tend to arise. In 2010, a committee redrew district lines. It was approved by the legislature and signed into law by Governor Jack Dalrymple. Democrats accused the committee of gerrymandering to maintain control of the state. They pointed out that the committee was controlled by Republicans. The Republicans responded that the Democrats win so few elections that they do not get many seats on committees. They also noted that the Republicans gained two seats in the house, but the Democrats gained two in the Senate, so it evened out.

Voting districts in North Dakota are redrawn every ten years. Burleigh County Auditor Kevin Glatt said that gerrymandering does not promote a positive voting experience. The district lines sometimes run through backyards, and divide neighborhoods. He said voters have a negative attitude, as they have the impression that the districts are manipulated for political purpose. The League of Women Voters agree that gerrymandering should be opposed. They point to some oddly shaped districts as evidence of the partisan intent.

A survey from 2015 showed that North Dakotans seemed to agree, preferring that a non-partisan commission be in charge of redistricting. Participants in the survey felt that gerrymandering did indeed give an advantage to the party in power.

The populations of Grand Forks and Fargo are growing as of 2015, and that might help Democrats. But new immigrants to western North Dakota are expected to be more Republican. It was, and still is now, difficult to determine just how the political winds are blowing in North Dakota.

Carole Butcher

Colonel Lounsberry

27 MAR

By 1864, the Union army under General Ulysses S. Grant had been forced to abandon their plans to capture the Confederate capital of Richmond, VA by direct assault. But twenty-five miles south of Richmond lay Petersburg, an important supply center to the capital city. Boasting several railroad lines and key roads, both Grant and Confederate General Robert E. Lee understood that if these were cut, Petersburg could no longer provide Richmond with much needed supplies.

For nearly ten months, Union troops encircled Petersburg, gradually cutting each supply line. By April 1, 1865 Union General Phillip Sheridan successfully captured the last rail connection into Petersburg. The next morning, Grant ordered attacks all along the siege line. By nightfall the VI Corps had broken through to the west of the city and the Army of Northern Virginia began evacuating Petersburg as well as Richmond. General Lee's final surrender at Appomattox Courthouse was only a week away.

Perhaps you're wondering what this has to do with North Dakota? The Michigan troops who were the first to advance into Petersburg and hoist their flags on the Courthouse and Customs House were led by Colonel Clement A. Lounsberry, the founder of the *Bismarck Tribune*. Lounsberry conducted the advance and personally accepted the surrender of Petersburg, from its mayor.

Clement A. Lounsberry, born on this day, March 27, 1843, enlisted as a private in the First Michigan Volunteers at the outbreak of the Civil War in 1861. Wounded and captured at the first Battle of Bull Run he was taken to Richmond where he spent nearly a year in a Confederate prison camp before being released in a prisoner exchange.

Reenlisting one month after his release from prison, Lounsberry mustered into service as first sergeant of Company I, Twentieth Michigan. Over the following three years, he received several wounds and spent another three weeks in a Confederate prison camp. General B. M. Cutcheon later wrote, "Colonel Lounsberry served under me as a private, a sergeant, a second lieutenant, a captain, as aide, and as assistant adjutant general and chief of my staff, and finally succeeded me as colonel, and I feel that I can say that I think he was the bravest man I ever knew."

In the decades following the Civil War, Col. Lounsberry moved to Dakota Territory where among other services, he established the *Bismarck Tribune*, served as the first president of the North Dakota Historical Society board of directors, and published a three-volume book on the history and people of North Dakota.

Christina Sunwall

28 MAR

Ev Albers

On this date, during "the Great Blizzard of 1942," Ev Albers was born in Oliver County. Dakota Datebook probably wouldn't exist if it weren't for Albers, because he, as executive director of the ND Humanities Council, made sure we received the necessary funding.

Albers grew up on a dairy farm near Hannover, graduated from Dickinson State in 1966, and received an MA in English at Colorado State University, Fort Collins. He was also a Lutheran seminary student, a Peace Corps trainee, a medical student, briefly an ROTC cadet, and a construction worker.

Ev married Leslie Rae Kubik in 1975 and they raised two children, Gretchen and Albert, in Bismarck. Besides nurturing the Humanities Council into existence in 1973, Albers also founded a modern-day Chautauqua movement that focuses on first-person characterizations of historical writers and thinkers. Among these was – and still is – Clay Jenkinson, who portrays Thomas Jefferson in the popular radio program "The Jefferson Hour."

Ev was diagnosed with cancer in 2002 and was given three months to live, but he lived and worked for another eighteen months, while writing a daily online journal. In his first journal entry he acknowledged his terminal pancreatic cancer.

Six months later, he wrote, "I'm quite happy to be alive today – which I wasn't at all, yesterday morning, for the weest bit. I take the great changing weather of Dakota as an omen, this 28th day of March, the day I was born in the other great Bismarck health facility a block or two away from me. The snow came in earnest sixty-one years ago… I've decided that every time it snows on my birthday, I'm going to be around for another year – and because it rained and thundered, I'm not just going to be vegetating – I'm going to be working and writing and loving – in fact, I've decided that what I need is the weest bit more piss and vinegar in my life."

A year later he wrote, "…I've made (it) to age sixty-two – at least a year beyond the time that I'm supposed to be ambulatory and reasonably alive here in this middle world… So I'm gonna play this day for all it's worth – rather shamelessly, I fear – ain't gonna move unless I feel like; gonna drift off to a nap whenever I wish, (and) read if I feel like it…"

Ev Albers passed away the following month, on April 24, 2004.

Merry Helm

The Sensational Rolf Harmsen

29 MAR

Rolf Harmsen was deaf, so he couldn't hear the gun, the hard breathing or the pounding steps of his competition on the track. But the Hazen native was also quick, so chances are he wouldn't have heard them anyway as he strode far ahead of his competition, despite his disability. Unlike the other boys who reacted to the sound of the gun, Rolf had to wait for his competitors to move. This put Rolf at a split-second disadvantage—a split-second that could mean the difference between first or second place. But the disadvantage was easily overcome as he became known as the "North Dakota Flier," and on this day in 1968, earned a place in the American Athletic Association of the Deaf Hall of Fame.

Rolf claimed his first state title in the 100-yard dash as a junior at the Devils Lake School for the Deaf in 1921, but his track career reached new heights the following year. Far out-classing the other runners, Rolf had no one to beat but the state record-holders of 1910. In a race against the clock, Rolf sprinted for record-breaking times in the preliminaries for both the 100-yard dash and the 220-yard low hurdles. If this wasn't enough, he knocked another fifth of a second off his day-old 100-meter dash record in the final race. Before the meet was over, Rolf had also picked up a third gold medal for the 220-yard dash, and he and another record-breaker, Mike Mueller claimed fourth for the School for the Deaf in the half-mile relay.

That track meet, Rolf proved himself a "wonder," and the newspapers couldn't get enough of this sensational athlete. What really caught their attention was when he took a trial jump in the running board jump and leapt 21 feet. Rolf was not able to compete in the running board jump because he was already in too many events, but had he been able to, he would have also claimed first in this event by one foot. The North Dakota *Banner* reported on Rolf's all-around performance: "There is no question but if the Deaf School athlete were allowed to enter in all the events he wanted to, he could win the meet alone. He is one of the most powerful runners seen on the university track since the days of Claud Runyon, or Boyd of Langdon in most recent days." The School for the Deaf placed third in the overall track meet, and Rolf was the overall point winner with his total of 15 points.

Rolf went on to compete for Gallaudet College and improved his time in the 100-yard dash by a half a second—without starting blocks or a hard track. He was considered a good bet for the 1923 Paris World Olympics. Unfortunately, the Olympics committee ruled a club could not sponsor its own athlete, and Rolf was not able to show his prowess on the international level. After college, he returned to North Dakota and became a printer for the *Bismarck Tribune*.

Tessa Sandstrom

30 MAR

Japanese Bomb Balloon

An unmanned, Japanese, bomb balloon landed in the Minto-Warsaw area of Walsh County on this date in 1945, but the incident was kept secret until World War II ended five months later. That August, the *Fargo Forum* reported that several balloons were sighted and reported to army authorities at Fargo, Park River, and Mandan. The Walsh County balloon had been dismantled and taken to Fort Snelling.

It was later learned that the Japanese released approximately 9,000 balloons, expecting 10% would survive the trip to explode and start fires in the U.S. The balloons were made of layered rice paper strengthened with a type of waxy sizing that made them waterproof. Inflated with hydrogen, each carried five bombs, four fire-starters and a thirty-three-pound fragmentation-type anti-personnel bomb. It took three to four days for them to cross the Pacific, and they were timed to explode after that timeframe. On May 5, one balloon exploded in Oregon, killing six civilians.

The balloon in Walsh County was lodged in the top of a tree and was estimated to have been thirty-five feet across and ninety feet tall. Some of the fire cartridges had already exploded, but a number of unfired fuse plugs still remained.

The *Forum* article reported that the balloon attacks had been kept secret to prevent the enemy from learning the results. By that July nearly 230 of the balloons or their remnants had been recovered and more were being discovered in isolated areas, where unexploded bombs still posed a danger.

Captain Vernon Scott was commandant of an army air base in Fargo and had been involved when the first Japanese balloon was found. It was discovered while he was stationed in Montana. "We searched for them by plane," he said. "Our instructions were to get over them and shoot them down [...] before they reached urban areas."

Japanese propaganda announced great fires and a panicked American public, but the people killed in Oregon were the only casualties. The blackout on information about the balloons was lifted in order to warn the public, but it came five months after the deaths in Oregon.

The wife and daughter of Harry Drews, one of the *Forum* newspaper printers, had spotted a bomb balloon above Fargo in June. They told the *Forum* it was at about 2,000 feet as they watched it float over town, across the NDSU campus and over Hector Airport. But it was a story the newspaper couldn't tell until August.

Merry Helm

Grand Forks' Mayor Recalls the Civil War

31 MAR

When the Civil War ripped the U.S. in two in 1861, William H. Brown was working in a hardware store in Massachusetts. He immediately enlisted in the 10th Massachusetts Regiment, joining 1,000 other "strong, young business men," who gave up their usual pay of $100 dollars a month for the paltry $11-per-month of a soldier.

W.H. Brown endured all the way through the war's conclusion in 1865. After the war, he went west to St. Paul, Minnesota, where he was a hardware man until moving to Grand Forks with his family in 1877. Mr. Brown established a hardware store and served as the city's first mayor in 1881.

It was on this date, in 1887, when W.H. Brown gave a talk at the Y.M.C.A. about his Civil War experiences. Brown spoke of "marches, charges, bivouacs, retreats, and triumphs," not with flowery oratory, but with the simple, powerful words of a soldier. He described the "good times" the 10th regiment had on the way to Washington, D.C., but said they loaded their guns in Baltimore after the 6th Massachusetts had been stoned there, with "orders to burn the town if they were assailed."

Brown spoke of guard-duty escapades near Washington when he mistook a "farmer's cow one dark night for a rebel spy." He also told of the Peninsular Campaign, in Virginia, when "it rained for weeks, nearly every day" so that the "mules almost disappeared in . . . mud" and he helped pull cannons through "mud almost knee deep."

His fighting commenced at the Chickahominy River, when 60,000 rebels surrounded the 10th. A desperate, bloody battle ensued. Brown spoke of "his first excitement under fire, loading and firing . . . and how his whole past . . . flashed before him" as bullets fearfully whizzed nearby. He said that no man could fully "illustrate the horrors of battle [...] the groans and moans of the wounded and dying, and the crack of the cannon and musketry." Sadly, when the regiment's enlistment expired, "only 286 of the 1,000 [men] marched home." Brown later enlisted in the 61st Massachusetts and rose in rank to First Lieutenant.

As part of the program in 1887, when Brown spoke, everyone sang a lively song entitled "Sherman's Dashing Yankee Boys." And after Brown concluded his talk, the large audience gave him patriotic thanks for his Civil War recollections on an unforgettable night of wartime remembrance.

Dr. Steve Hoffbeck

German Russian women and children in front of sod house, Dunn County, N.D.
Credit: State Historical Society of North Dakota (00433-0022)

APRIL

April Fools' Time

01 APR

For many people, April Fools' Day is a time for mischief and tomfoolery. However, on this date in 1943, mischievous time itself fooled many North Dakotans.

"If you did not sleep an hour later this morning, you gypped yourself," lamented the *Oakes Times* in Dickey County, "because all clocks were set back an hour to conform with Mountain time, and we now join the area west of Bismarck and Montana in the hour of getting up and when we should go to bed."

The time change came about when the North Dakota legislature passed the Standard War Time act on March 17 of that year, stating "the standard war time of this state shall coincide with that known and described as United States Mountain War Time, until the present War Time Proclamation of the President of the United States is no longer in effect."

The President's emergency act was similar to and inspired by one passed in 1918 during World War I, which was to provide a standard time throughout the country. During World War II, this act was developed under FDR's campaign to "promote the national security and defense by establishing daylight savings time." Passed in January, 1942, it was to expire six months after the end of the war or at an earlier date, as the U.S. Congress saw fit.

In North Dakota, farm groups and farm members of the Senate and house pushed the legislation through. Though he opposed the bill, Governor Moses signed it, because it was the desire of the majority.

It didn't make the time shift any easier, though. To top it off, railroads, the great proponent of time zones, still followed their own schedule. So did other specially timed events, such as radio shows.

Newspapers cautioned, "Greatest confusion will come in meeting train schedules, for all railroads continue to operate under the old time. To board the N. P. east bound train at 11:40 a.m., we must remember it will be 10:40 by our time; knock off an hour and beat it for the depot[...] In all your calculations beginning with today, be sure to reckon with the old time as regards radio and train schedules."

There were plenty of fools on that April Fools' Day.

Sarah Walker

02 APR

Stormy Weather

A tragic shooting rocked the small town of Zap, North Dakota, in April of 1941. The shooter, a local farmer and father of eight, was considered a hard-working husband and family man before financial trouble and a minor dispute pushed him over the edge.

Early in 1941, Fred Sinirius was evicted from his farm near Zap by the Bank of North Dakota. The Sinirius family moved to a nearby farmstead, but the elderly farmer later returned to the foreclosed property to remove the home's storm windows and screens. Sinirius claimed he had purchased them himself and wanted to use them on his new home. The bank, however, claimed the windows were part of the original property, and therefore belonged to them.

On April 1, the bank sent field agent Val Wolf from Mandan to collect the windows from Sinirius and return them to the original farmstead. Wolf was met by Deputy Sheriff Joseph Runions at the Sinirius farm. The two men met Mr. Sinirius outside his home and explained the reason behind their visit. Enraged by the intrusion, Sinirius demanded that the men leave his property. He ran inside and emerged with a shotgun, taking aim at Runion and Wolf. He shot at the two men, but, believing the shotgun's aim inadequate, quickly exchanged it for a rifle. Runion later claimed that the sixty-year old Sinerius chased him and Wolf as they ran to their vehicles.

The farmer continued shooting until both men had fallen. Although Sinirius believed them both dead, Runion survived and managed to drag himself to the highway and flag down a passing vehicle. He was rushed to the hospital at Stanton and later transferred to Bismarck's critical care unit. Mercer County Sheriff Otto Poschadel arrived at the farm and arrested Sinirius later that evening; he offered no resistance and confessed immediately. Deputy Runion lost sight in one eye, and Wolf, a father of four, lost his life to the argument over those storm windows. Sinirius was arraigned for the murder of Wolf and the attempted murder of Runion on this date in 1941.

Jayme L. Job

Jefferson Kidder

03 APR

Few North Dakotans have likely heard of Jefferson Kidder, although most have heard of Kidder County, which was named for the nineteenth century North Dakotan. Kidder's many and varied roles ranged from Lieutenant Governor to State Senator, and ran from his native Vermont to the wilds of Minnesota and Dakota Territory. His son was killed in action under Custer, and his grandson went on to become one of the greatest lawmen of the Old West, but Kidder himself made his name in politics.

Born in 1815, Kidder is remembered today as one of Braintree, Vermont's most famous sons. He graduated from the Norwich Military Academy in nearby Northfield and went on to study law in Montpelier. He was admitted to the Vermont bar in 1839. Only four years later, Kidder became a member of the Vermont constitutional convention. At only twenty-eight, he was named Vermont's State Attorney. He served two years as a State Senator, and was named Lieutenant Governor in 1853. He was afterward sent as a delegate to the Democratic National Convention, but shortly after moved to St. Paul and became a Republican member of the Minnesota House of Representatives.

In February of 1865, President Lincoln appointed Kidder to the Dakota Territory Supreme Court. Kidder moved to Vermillion to serve as an Associate Justice. While serving on the court in Vermillion, three important things happened to Kidder. The first was that his son, Lyman, was killed by a Sioux and Cheyenne war party in what became known as the Kidder Massacre in Kansas. The second was that Kidder County was created in Dakota Territory and named for the judge, and the third was that his grandson, also named Jefferson, was born in Vermillion. The younger Jefferson became an Arizona Ranger and was killed in one of the most memorable shoot-outs in the history of the Old West in 1908.

The elder Kidder was reappointed to the court on this date in 1869 by President Grant. He went on to become the territory's delegate to Congress. After two terms, he returned to the Territorial Court in Vermillion, where he served until his death in 1883.

Jayme L. Job

04 APR

A Shocking Flood

Floods are a regular springtime worry in North Dakota, and almost a season by themselves during some years. In the east, the Red has flooded many times, with the 1826 flood believed to be the largest in recorded history. It washed trappers and natives off the land, resulting in deaths from drowning and starvation.

In 2011, the Souris River flooded, thereby devastating Minot. The Sheyenne has hit Valley City several times.

Another major flood was foretold on this date in 1969 when the Heart River overflowed. The river flooded parts of Mandan following warm temperatures and rapidly melting snow. In the days to come, the Heart would hit its ninth highest recorded crest – over twenty and a half feet. The river was the first in North Dakota to flood that spring, a harbinger for Minot, one hundred miles to the north.

The sunny skies and highs in the 60s swelled the Souris and Des Lacs rivers three days after the Heart flooded Mandan. Sandbagging and evacuations began almost immediately. Thousands of homes were evacuated in what city officials said was the second most damaging flood in city history.

Minoters worked around the clock to fight the floodwater. The Souris River overflowed the Lake Darling spillway, chopping Minot in two, as one headline put it. The National Guard and Minot Air Force Base were called in to help. The stress of the flood fight even caused an elk and an emu to die from shock as the Roosevelt Park Zoo scrambled to save its animals from the water. Some peacocks even got loose, prompting the zoo to ask Minot residents to feed them if they could.

Rumors flew, including stories about ice chunks threatening to rip apart the Lake Darling Dam. Eventually, over 10,000 Magic City residents were displaced and more than half of the homes had water on the main floor before April was over.

Jack Dura

Bagg Bonanza Farm

05 APR

The National Historic Preservation Act was created to help preserve the diverse archaeological and architectural treasures of America. Among those treasures were the bonanza farms with their images of agricultural abundance that helped promote the huge influx of settlers to Dakota Territory. Railroad land grants included every other section in a corridor extending forty miles to either side of the railroad line. Eastern Syndicates purchased this land and created vast farming operations, many in the Red River Valley. Known as bonanza farms, they encompassed thousands of acres of land and were overseen by managers hired by the syndicates.

J. W. Downing, a wealthy attorney from Erie, Pennsylvania, established the 5,000 acre Downing Farm in Richland County in the mid-1880s with headquarters at Mooreton. Beginning in the 1890s, it was managed by Frederich A. Bagg, Downing's thirty-year-old nephew, who came to Dakota Territory in 1888. Frederich Bagg proved to be an efficient manager, and as part of his compensation he was given land along with a salary.

When J. W. Downing died in 1913, the land was divided among his heirs. With land acquired from Downing, as well as land he had accumulated privately, Frederich Bagg moved his center of operations one mile west of the Downing Farm in 1915. The Bagg Bonanza Farm included thousands of acres.

The site chosen for the new headquarters consisted of only three buildings – the foreman's house, a cattle barn, and a granary. Bagg modified his farming operations and expanded the farm infrastructure. Many of the buildings at the Downing farm were moved to the Bagg site, including a large mule barn, the foreman's house, four machine sheds, the bunk house and a small grain elevator. By 1930, over twenty-six buildings occupied the new site and more building were purchased and moved to the farm. As tractors replaced mules, the mule barns were converted to machine sheds. Other new structures included chicken coops, hog barns, sheep sheds and a power house.

The bunk house from the Downing farm, at 84 by 30 feet, became the main residence for the Bagg family and also housed the staff and a communal dining area. The rest of the buildings were arranged in an orderly, functional approach with residential buildings painted white clustered on the north side of the complex and the red utility buildings for livestock, machinery and storage to the south. The eleven acre parcel, containing over thirty of the original buildings, was accepted as a National Historic Landmark on this date in 2005.

Jim Davis

06 APR

Army Day

Today is Army Day. Well, it used to be Army Day. A *Bismarck Tribune* article stated President Franklin Roosevelt was proclaiming this day in 1943 to be Army Day as a way to honor "the men of the United States Army who have carried the flag of the United States and its ideals which it represents to every part of the earth, and who with their brothers-in-arms from the nations united with us are offering their lives for the future of America and the world."

Actually, Army Day was first observed in a rather obscure manner in 1924. Rather than celebrating the Army, the day was actually an observance of Defense Testing. The day was observed that way again the following year, but after that, Congress disallowed further observances under the title of Army Day.

Three years later, in 1928, Colonel Thatcher Luquer, of the Military Order of the World War, successfully established a new Army Day, which was held May 1. May Day was chosen as a way to counter-balance communists who used that date to celebrate Workers' Day.

The date was shifted the following year to April 6, the anniversary of America's entry into World War I. Emphasis was placed on the Nation's need for military preparedness. According to the Department of Defense, we needed to head off "the failure to make adequate preparation for the inevitable struggle, the consequent suffering from disease and death entailed upon the armies which were hastily raised, the prolongation of the conflict far beyond the time which sufficient and equipped forces would have required for victory, and the heavy costs of reconstruction."

President Roosevelt made it official on April 4, 1936, when he proclaimed April 6 should be observed nationwide as Army Day; Congress passed a subsequent resolution the following year. But Army Day was observed for only a dozen years before its discontinuation in 1949.

Merry Helm

Andy Hampsten

07 APR

Today is the birthday of cycling great, Andy Hampsten, who was born in 1962. Andy grew up in Grand Forks, where his parents taught English at UND. They gave him his first road bike when he turned twelve, and he was smitten for life.

U.S. television paid little attention to cycling, so Andy turned to the library, where he found articles in foreign newspapers. In 1977, he started competing and soon joined the American Cycling Federation. His first race as a junior was in Milwaukee in 1979, which he won.

In 1985, Andy turned pro, signing with the newly founded American team, 7-Eleven. When they went to the Giro de Italia that year, the Europeans didn't take them seriously. But Andy and his team silenced them with wins in two stages, including a solo victory by Andy on a mountain-top finish.

The following year, Andy was the first American to win the Tour de Switzerland. His next major race was the Tour de France, where he claimed the Best-Rookie Jersey, and he shared a first place team award for his role in helping Greg LeMond to victory. The following year, Andy again won the Tour of Switzerland – the only American to win it twice.

Hampsten's career highlight came in 1988 during the Giro de Italia "on a day," as one cyclist put it, "when strong men cry." During a legendary stage over in the Dolomite Mountains, Hampsten got caught in a blizzard. Followed by a long line of cars struggling to make it through a mountain pass, Andy wouldn't give up. With bare legs and arms, he pushed on in what has now become one of the most legendary cycling stages of all time. Hampsten persevered and took home the coveted prize, the Maglia Rosa. Although he was the first cyclist from North America to win the Giro, U.S. television still wasn't interested.

Hampsten's next goal was to win the Tour de France. By then, he had twice placed in the top-four. Now, he wanted the yellow jersey – signifying first place.

Hampsten's great strength was climbing, but in time trials, he didn't do as well, so he tried to improve this weakness by changing his training. Unfortunately, the change came at the expense of his climbing, and the Tour de France victory never materialized. The disappointment was partially overcome when he retrained for climbing and won many other victories before retiring in 1996.

When asked by an interviewer about his worst moment in cycling, Andy replied: "eight years old and hitting that parked car in front of my house at five miles per hour that I knew was there."

Now that's a true champion.

Merry Helm

08 APR

H-T Ranch

Arthur Clark Huidekoper was a rancher and cowboy of great renown around the turn of the century in North Dakota. Originally from Pennsylvania, he was enticed out to the western portion of North Dakota, where he set up a ranch and business alongside the famed rancher Marquis de Mores.

Huidekoper and Sidney Tarbell established the H-T Ranch, named after themselves, about ten miles west of Amidon in Slope County. In 1883, Huidekoper also established the Little Missouri Cattle Company. In 1887, he turned from cattle to horses, forming the Little Missouri Horse Company. He started with 600 horses. In 1889, he expanded to include show horses. By 1900, he had 4,000 horses, and he sold them to farmers and to cities for use in conveying street cars. The ranching operations were at their peak in the 1890s, but eventually, the ranch corporation dissolved.

On this date in 1906, residents of the area were surprised to learn that the ranch had transferred over to Fred Pabst, a millionaire brewer out of Milwaukee, owner of the Pabst Brewing Company. The brewing company was already considered one of the world's largest, and Pabst was always looking for new ways in business. His company added artificial ice machines in 1880, incandescent light in 1882, and was one of the first breweries to open for tours.

Pabst's acquisition of the ranch was one of the largest land purchases in North Dakota at that time – $300,000 dollars for 65,000 acres, the buildings, and equipment.

Although Mr. Pabst was "an enthusiastic horseman" and would be importing Russian Orloff trotters, purebred Percherons, and other stock, the land did not stay long in his hands, and was parceled out and sold by a land holding company, reducing the ranch's land to 5,000 acres.

Today, the H-T Ranch is on the National Register of Historic Places, serving as a testament to an industry that helped shape the history of western North Dakota.

Sarah Walker

Saving UND

09 APR

The University of North Dakota in Grand Forks has survived much since it first opened its doors in 1884. In 1887, a tornado demolished most of the university. In 1919, the institution was among the hardest hit in the country a deadly flu epidemic, and in 1970, it was the site of some of North Dakota's largest protests after the Kent State shootings. Flooding has also been problematic, with the Red River inundating portions of the campus in 1997. Most recently, the university faced the controversy over the Fighting Sioux logo. Despite these obstacles, the greatest challenge to the university came in the form of budget cuts in 1895, stemming from the panic of 1893 – the most serious depression the country had seen to that time. Railroads went bankrupt, crops were poor, farm prices were low, and tax revenue subsequently plummeted.

Faced with tough decisions, North Dakota Governor Roger Allin vetoed the educational appropriations made by the state legislature. The move was unprecedented and cut the funding to each of the state's schools by up to 80%. At UND, the $63,000 two-year appropriation was cut to less than $16,000. This was just enough to pay the operational costs of the current semester, meaning the university would have to close in a matter of months.

After Allin's announcement, university students, officials, and Grand Forks citizens held a meeting on this date in 1895 to discuss the future of the school. They created a statement to help solicit private funds that read, "Shall the University of North Dakota be closed? This is the question which confronts the people of the state. The closing of the university would be a calamity in many ways. It would advertise to the world that North Dakota is either unwilling or unable to maintain for her sons and daughters an institution of higher learning."

In a show of great support and generosity, the Grand Forks community came together and raised nearly $10,000 for the school. Faculty members donated a quarter of their own salaries, and contributions from private citizens elsewhere brought the total raised to nearly $26,000 within a month. The episode represented the closest instance that the university had come to closing its doors, but also served to bind the school and the Grand Forks community together in the face of adversity.

Jayme L. Job

10 APR

Black Stallion

On this date in 1980, the Academy Awards ceremony took place. *The Black Stallion*, was nominated for best picture and best supporting actor. A sequel, *The Return of the Black Stallion* immediately went into development, and Corky Randall, the head trainer on *The Black Stallion*, was searching for a new black Arab for the starring role.

Sometime earlier, Susan Smestad was teaching school in Michigan when she started investing in her passion – horses. She bought a number of Arab mares for breeding but was hesitant about owning a stallion until her husband, Richard, persuaded her to buy one named Diamond Night.

Writer Merrie Sue Holton later interviewed the Smestads, who had by then permanently located outside Harvey, ND. Susan told Holton that her prospective stallion turned out to be a "pussycat – more afraid of me than I was of him."

Unfortunately, there came a day when a new blood line was needed, and Diamond Night was put up for sale in *Arabian Horse World* magazine. Corky Randall spotted the ad and went to the Smestad farm for a look.

United Artists wanted only black purebred Arabians for the film – no easy matter. Susan explained that true blacks are determined by noting: A) the color of the horse itself; B) the color of the parents; and C) the color of the offspring. Ironically, a true black isn't born black, and even true blacks produce black offspring only 50% of the time.

Corky Randall knew his stuff. In fact, he trained Trigger for Roy Rogers, Silver for the *Lone Ranger*, and all the horses in the chariot-race scene in *Ben-Hur*. For the *Black Stallion* project, though, he needed something special: a horse gentle enough for a child and intelligent enough to train. He also needed a stallion that could be turned loose with mares and foals. Unlike "box-stall" stallions, 5-year-old Diamond Night had rounded up mares in the field. Corky liked what he saw, and the following February, the Smestads delivered the stallion to new owners in California.

Unfortunately, Diamond Night's acting career was short. During a training session on June 29, he reared, lost his footing, and ended up collapsing onto his right shoulder. Onlookers said they heard what sounded like a rifle shot, and when the stallion got up, his front left leg was dangling from several bad fractures. Typically, a horse with these kinds of injuries would be put down. Veterinarian James Bullock said "most horses will not tolerate a sling. [But] Diamond Night is an extremely intelligent horse and did very well."

The following day, the stallion went through a five-hour operation in which horizontal pins were inserted through the leg bones. These were held in place with an assembly of external vertical pins inspired by the Kirschner-Ebner device, an appliance previously used only for smaller animals. It took a while, but the horse did recover; he lived a full life and died at the age of eighteen.

Merry Helm

Calamity Jane

11 APR

Traveling alone, a woman stepped off the train in Oakes, North Dakota on her way to Jamestown. Her name was Mary Jane Canary, better known as Calamity Jane. In 1902, the *Oakes Republican* reported on her unexpected visit.

Calamity Jane was a celebrity and a most unusual woman. She was described as being able to shoot like a cowboy and drink like a fish. Born in Missouri in 1852, she loved the outdoors and became an accomplished horsewoman. Her family traveled to Virginia City on a wagon train. She spent her time on the journey riding and hunting. She proved herself to be fearless and was a crack shot.

Calamity Jane drove a stagecoach, drove mule and bull teams, was a Pony Express rider between Deadwood and Custer, kept a saloon, performed in Buffalo Bill's Wild West, and always dressed like a man. She even claimed to have signed on as a scout with George Custer in 1870.

She was just shy of her fiftieth birthday when she stopped in Oakes. The newspaper reported that the morning after her arrival, Jane went to one of the hotels for breakfast. She returned to the depot where she spent most of the day reclining on a couch in the men's waiting room, calmly smoking a cigar. Unfortunately, she was in no condition for an interview. Before arriving in Oakes she had spent $30 in an Aberdeen saloon where, as the paper put it, she made "a good fellow of herself." She offered to buy rounds in Oakes if anyone could show her where that could be had, but with North Dakota being a dry state, the best she could do was the cigar. She remarked that Oakes was not the town she thought it was—where "a decent woman could not buy all she was willing to pay for." Calamity Jane left Oakes on the midnight train.

The following year, on August 3, Calamity Jane passed away in Terry, South Dakota. She's buried in Deadwood's Mount Moriah Cemetery next to Wild Bill Hickok.

Carole Butcher

12 APR

Matchmaker, J.D.

William Murray of Minot was a renowned judge in Ward County. He started off in railroad work, but studied law on the side, and in 1906, he passed the exam at Grand Forks and was admitted to the state bar. In a biography on him, Clement A. Lounsberry wrote he had "an excellent record as a jurist, being not only well informed as to the law, but also possessing the necessary qualities of an impartial and an unbiased mind."

Perhaps he proved this the year after passing his exam, in 1907, when he unwittingly set up a small matchmaking business on the side. According to the *Minot Daily Reporter*, it all started when a young man discovered he might lose some of his property unless he either reached the age of adulthood or married by a certain date—neither of which appeared to be viable. Out of options, the man turned to Judge Murray.

Murray told the young man if he intended to take a marriage seriously, they could manage it. He told the man to appear before him at four o'clock with his guardian, so he had permission to marry. In the meantime, Murray himself found the bride and prepared the license.

Everything went as planned, and the *Minot Daily Reporter* announced, "as they walked out of the judge's office, to face the world as man and wife, there was not one in the room who witnessed the ceremony, that did not feel that while the cyclone manner of the joining of these two hearts was away out of the ordinary, the pair were not mismatched by any means, and all predicted that they would go down life's pathway, hand in hand."

The story didn't stop there as other newspapers picked up on the item. And on this date, one bachelor farmer from Donnybrook trekked to Minot to solicit help from the judge. Murray said he would keep him in mind – and he was not the only one, to the great amusement of the community. As one newspaper proclaimed, "If you want to get married and can't find a wife, just apply to Judge William Murray of Minot […] He has found wives for other people, and the Minot supply is not yet entirely exhausted. It is not a bad idea to get your application in early anyway, for the principle of first come, first served, will be observed."

Sarah Walker

Titanic Survivor

13 APR

On this date in 1912, twenty-seven-year-old Oskar Hedman was coming back to North Dakota after conducting business and visiting family in Sweden. Known to his friends as "Happy," Oskar was a smallish man with "a Jimmy Durante face." He had lived around Bowman for six years, farming, selling land and working as a settlement recruiter.

On this trip, Hedman and at least fifteen prospective settlers were traveling in third class steerage on a new ocean liner, the Titanic. The following is based on newspaper accounts posted on the website, "Encyclopedia Titanica."

On the evening of the 14th, Oskar was sleeping in a berth he shared with twenty-five-year-old Carl Jonsson, a laborer described as a "giant Swede." They woke to an unusual jolt. Oskar said they probably would've paid no attention, except for the commotion that began minutes later.

He and Jonsson headed for the front of the ship through water that soon reached their armpits. Hedman said, "we found great heaps of ice [...] the life boats were being lowered [...] but they were already roped off, and officers with guns ordered us to stand back for the women and children.

Then distress flares went up, and Jonsson realized they were going down. They decided to jump. Both were expert swimmers, but although the water was calm, it was deadly cold.

"My friend grabbed something that floated by and told me to hold onto it," Hedman said. "It proved to be a dead man inside a life preserver. I climbed on and rode like I was on horseback." Meanwhile, Jonsson grabbed at an overturned life raft but was pushed away. They'd been in the water for thirty minutes already, and Jonsson went under.

Hedman neared a lifeboat filled with forty women and children when one of the four men fell overboard and was lost. Someone yelled out to Hedman, asking if he could row. He lied, saying he was an expert rower. They pulled him in, and they rowed away from the sinking ship just minutes before the boiler exploded. It was 2 a.m. when the deck caved in the middle and untold numbers of people fell to the bottom of the hold to be swallowed by the ocean. Hedman said the sight was too awful to put into words, saying only that he thought again and again of watching grain being sucked into the hopper on his farm.

Hedman was on Lifeboat 15, the last one launched before the Titanic sunk. In an unexpected twist, Jonsson was found alive on a floating door six hours later. The two men arrived in New York four days later. Penniless, Oskar wired a former St. Paul employer for money, which he split with Jonsson and an eighteen-year-old Finnish girl so they could all reach their destinations.

Merry Helm

14 APR

Land of Opportunity

The 1890s were not kind to North Dakota. The price of wheat declined by 70%. High railroad rates hurt farmers. State tax receipts decreased, and the state had difficulty paying its bills.

That changed, however as the period from 1898 to 1915 brought North Dakota's second boom. Railroads almost doubled in size, increasing from 2,662 miles of track, to 5,226. Where the railroads went, people followed. The population of the young state increased by 135 per cent. Towns blossomed into cities. Bismarck grew from 2,100 residents to 5,400. Minot exploded from a population of 2,100 to 6,100.

On this date in 1910, the *Ward County Independent* printed an editorial that highlighted the important role of newspapers in attracting people to North Dakota. The *Independent* announced in an editorial that the newspaper had attracted many young men by publicizing the opportunities in the state. In the spring of 1910, dozens of young men arrived, lured by the promise of good employment.

This was illustrated by a man who arrived at the office of the *Independent* and presented a letter of introduction from a subscriber living in Chicago. The writer of the letter stated that he believed North Dakota was a land of opportunity and had encouraged his friend to make a new start there. The writer of the letter described the man as honest and hardworking, and hoped the newspaper could help him get a job. The letter stated that anything the editor of the newspaper could do to help would be greatly appreciated.

The editorial stated that while many new people had arrived in the state looking for work, it was far from enough. The farmers still needed more help, and jobs were to be had for anyone wanting work. The editor was quickly able to arrange work for the young man with farmer just north of Minot. The job paid $35 a month, with all expenses paid. The editor was confident that if the new North Dakotan carefully saved his money, he would soon own a farm of his own. That was something he could not hope for had he stayed in Illinois. The editor closed by urging young men to "Come west and grow up with the country!"

Carole Butcher

Horses and Mules

15 APR

In the early 1900s, horsepower was provided by, well, horses. They were commonly used in cities as well the country. In 1879, the first streetcars in Fargo were pulled by horses. This began to change when an electric system was established in 1904, but horses remained in use for many years. Postcards and photos from the early 1900s show horses sharing downtowns with trains, streetcars, and foot traffic.

But not everyone agreed that horses were the most efficient and cost-effective means of transportation. In 1904, a controversy about horses was sparked by an article appearing in the *Fargo Forum and Daily Republican* that claimed mules were superior to horses. On this date the paper printed an anonymous response. The writer said he had no wish to start a "horse-mule" controversy, but in all good conscience he could not let the previous article pass without comment.

In the March article, author E.S. Delancy of Valley City stated that large cities had gone to the use of mules almost exclusively. He said mules could stand up to the work on the hard streets better than horses. The responding author took exception, saying when he last visited large cities eight months before, he saw many splendid teams of draft horses. In fact, he said there were 300 teams of draft horses for every team of mules. He doubted that a large number of horses had been replaced by mules over the course of a few months, noting that such a development had not been mentioned in any of the newspapers.

One major difference between horses and mules was the price. A mule colt sold for $80, while a draft horse colt might cost $1,500. Nevertheless, many people in the hauling trade preferred horses. This was at least in part because of temperament. Horses can generally be coaxed into performing while mules can be stubborn, and it can be difficult to convince them to change their minds.

The anonymous author of the April letter stated he did not want to discourage people from using mules. He only wanted to point out that horses had advantages of their own. He also took issue with Delancy's statement that "No man will lose money in the mule business."

Carole Butcher

16 APR

A Bright Idea

Thomas Neary, a well-known attorney from Minot, had a marvelous invention to improve rifle gunsights, back in the year 1909. He was going to "revolutionize modern warfare" *and* make big-game hunting easier with a new idea.

Mr. Neary's great notion was to place two tiny electric light bulbs on a rifle to help the shooter fire more accurately in low-light conditions. He installed one bulb just behind the front gunsight and another behind the rear gunsight so that a soldier or hunter could clearly see the sights at dawn or in the sunset gloaming or even at night.

Thomas Neary had been at work on his invention for years, making modification after modification until he patented it. He connected the lights to a battery installed in the stock. A small push-button on the gun barrel at the point where the left hand grasped the barrel allowed the rifleman to turn on the lights without moving his hand. The tiny bulbs were so well-protected that they could not be dislodged, even in the roughest conditions.

Mr. Neary contacted the U.S. Army and the officials gave him an opportunity to test his invention in late 1908. Placed on a standard U.S. Springfield Army rifle, the innovation performed brilliantly at an Army testing range. Neary brought his own marksman, who shot five shots at a target 200 yards away, after sunset, when the target was barely discernible, and the shooter hit five bullseyes. The officers then subjected the device to every conceivable endurance test, and the bulbs and wires remained intact.

Inventor Neary got several letters from Washington, D.C. that were "most encouraging," but his gunsight lights had to pass muster with West Point Army leaders and arsenal directors.

Mr. Neary was very pleased when he received a request from the Springfield Rifle Company asking for permission to equip two hunting rifles with his lights so ex-President Theodore Roosevelt could take those guns on an African safari.

So how did it work out for Thomas Neary? Well, his invention was overshadowed by World War I, which began in 1914. The night-fighting in that war was terrible, and had no place for Neary's tiny rifle-lights. Instead the enemies illuminated the night-skies by means of flares, searchlights, and "star-shells," lighting up the battlefields as brightly as midday.

Dr. Steve Hoffbeck

Dr. John E. Engstad

17 APR

X-rays were so named because this radiant energy was of unknown origin. The "X" in "X-ray" was a scientific symbol for "the unknown." Discovered by Wilhelm Roentgen in 1895, X-rays were immediately put into practical medical use the following year.

The new technology came to Grand Forks in 1896, when Dr. John E. Engstad secured an X-ray machine, using it that December to conduct successful wrist surgery.

On this date in 1898, the *Grand Forks Herald* printed a small advertisement for Dr. Engstad and his fellow surgeon, Dr. A.A. Westeen. Engstad, who had been born in Norway in 1858 and who immigrated to the U.S. with his parents that same year, had been practicing medicine in Grand Forks since 1885. Dr. Engstad became nationally known for founding St. Luke's Hospital in 1892, the first hospital in the U.S. built and owned by a Scandinavian.

It was in 1898 that Dr. Engstad made headlines for an X-ray operation noted as a "peculiar case." A man named William Dodge had accidently stepped on a large sewing needle in his home in the nearby village of Inkster. Involuntarily jumping up in pain, Mr. Dodge somehow broke the needle into two, with one end stuck in his right foot and the other half embedded in his left ankle.

In pain, Mr. Dodge visited his local doctor, who quickly plucked out the visible part of the needle, but the doctor could not locate the other half. The doctor sent Dodge to see Dr. Engstad, who "used his large X-Ray machine to locate the needle point." The "X-Ray photograph plainly showed the needle entirely hidden between […] two bones […] at the ankle." Having determined the needle's exact location, Dr. Engstad easily removed it.

The X-ray machine proved its worth, and in 1917 Dr. Engstad bought a more powerful machine, said to be an "exact duplicate" of one at the Mayo Clinic.

Dr. John Engstad had a long medical career, passing away in 1937, at age 78, having been one of the revered "pioneer physicians" of Grand Forks.

Dr. Steve Hoffbeck

18 APR

Anti-Spitting Law

In North Dakota's bygone days, people were free to spit outdoors wherever they pleased, as long as they did not hit others. The practice was even permissible indoors, if they used spittoons.

The liberty to freely spit ended in Grand Forks in 1901, when the city council passed an ordinance "prohibiting spitting on sidewalks, in the entrances to public buildings . . . and in any public place or building." The main purpose of the anti-spitting law was to limit the spread of tuberculosis germs, but it was also intended to discourage the spitting of tobacco juice in public.

On this date in 1908, Dr. G.F. Ruediger delivered a lecture entitled "Tuberculosis and Its Prevention" at the University of North Dakota; he told his audience practical ways to limit the spread of this terrible lung disease, known then as "consumption." Dr. Ruediger, a UND instructor, spoke of the hazards posed by TB germs in saliva. When a consumptive coughed or sneezed or spit out saliva, other people could catch TB germs by breathing the air or by breathing in dust from spittle that had dried on a sidewalk and then was lifted by the wind. Dr. Ruediger urged all to beware of consumptives who would "expectorate whenever and wherever the desire comes upon them."

The 1901 anti-spitting law in Grand Forks could help prevent TB, but the law was not strictly enforced. However, in July 1908, a man by the name of Hans Evenson was spitting tobacco juice – "snoose" – on the sidewalk at the corner of Third Street and DeMers Avenue. A policeman told Evenson to stop; Evenson answered by telling the officer "that he figured he could spit where he pleased," whereupon the policeman placed Mr. Evenson under arrest.

In court, the policeman said to the judge: "Your honor, this man is accused of spitting on the sidewalk." The judge looked in his city lawbook and found the anti-spitting ordinance called for a "fine of not less than $5 or more than $25." Mr. Evenson paid the five-dollar fine, and his arrest was noted by the *Grand Forks Herald* as the first arrest "to be made under the ordinance."

Thus the anti-spitting law made an example of Mr. Evenson to make citizens more aware of germs, spitting and spittoons – and prevention of the terrible disease called tuberculosis.

Dr. Steve Hoffbeck

Theodore Roosevelt Rough Rider Award

19 APR

Today in 1897, Theodore Roosevelt was appointed Assistant Secretary of the Navy. Serving in the position for one year, Roosevelt was instrumental in preparing for war with Spain by planning naval strategies and ensuring George Dewey was named commander of the Asiatic Squadron.

Once war had been declared, Roosevelt resigned. He wrote, "I had preached, with all the fervor and zeal I possessed, our duty to intervene in Cuba [...] and from the beginning I had determined that, if a war came [...] I was going to the front."

In spring of 1898, Roosevelt became Lieutenant-Colonel of the 1st U.S. Volunteer Cavalry Regiment; better known as the "Rough Riders."

In remembrance of Roosevelt, an honorary rank of Colonel in the North Dakota Theodore Roosevelt Rough Riders was created during the 1961 Dakota Territory Centennial to acknowledge other North Dakotans who had achieved national recognition in their field.

Christina Sunwall

20 APR

German-Russian Farm Kids Remember: Flying Dog

William Adam Merkel, Jr.
Interviewed: Eureka, SD, 17 May 2008
Born: McPherson County, SD, 11 October 1925

The thing that I remember a lot about is cleaning the barn, an old horse barn and cows. Horses were in the barn, cows were in the barn, as soon as it got a little cold they were put in the barn. That was the older barn; we have a newer barn out there now. During the winter months, every three days we had to haul hay. There was a hay stack put up on the north side of the farm. We had to haul it on the hay wagon.

Dad had made made a big door on the west side of that old barn and we could only roll up 2-3 loads at a time. One time, I can remember that I always unhitched the horses and went to the other side. The hay slinger was four ropes with cross ropes on them and two ropes that came out of the barn and hooked onto the other side of the hay sling. Steel cable came across the top and hooked it on the front end of the hay rack and they rolled the hay up. I usually unhooked the horses and brought them around to the other side and those horses already knew that they were going to be pulling. One time, I took off with them and looked around and here the dog was going about fifteen feet up in the air (laughter). He was standing across the table and had it quickly tightened up and just threw the dog in the air. I still remember that very vividly. Then we took them off and pulled rope cable out back again and took the sling and filled it up again and did that about every three days. One time I remember, my two older brothers were in the service then and it was just too cold to haul hay into the hay barn. So, we just got one load and took it on the other side of the barn and there was just a small door, Dad forked it in, and I had to fork it away just for a few days anyways.

German-Russian Farm Kids Remember: First Rubber Tire Tractor

21 APR

Wilfred Jacob Boechler
Interviewed: Allan, SK, 23 July 2006
Born: Allan, SK, 14 February 1926

It was the first rubber-tire tractor around here. It was a little Case tractor and it was in 1940 when he bought it. It had something to do with my grandfather passing away and my grandfather was what you would call a wealthy man. My mother got some money and my dad bought the Chevy car for $1,400. It was a Special Deluxe and it didn't have a heater, (soft chuckling) didn't have a radio, but it was a Special Deluxe in those days. It was a beautiful car.

He also bought that little Case rubber-tire tractor. Whenever we would be out in the field working with it, the neighbors would drive by and stop and walk in when we came in and want a ride on that tractor. Sometimes we had to unhook it and show them how it went into high gear, it went about 10 mph and "Oh man, could we whip around in those field with that thing." It was quite something to have a rubber tire, and everyone thought that the rubber was going to wear out so quick that you are going to have to buy new tires every year. It didn't work that way, they were good. Then, of course, different people started buying tractors. There was a big concern over that. Some people were very opposed to it, because, they felt that they could raise their own power and they could have their horses, they would have colts and have their own power. These rubber-tire tractors, when they ran out, you would have to go and buy new ones and those kinds of things. Like progress, it went on, we moved into bigger ones and bigger ones, and finally the air-conditioned ones and so on.

22 APR

German-Russian Farm Kids Remember: A New Car

Elda (Schultz) Rasch
Interviewed: Bismarck, ND, 25 July 2007
Born: Fredonia, ND, 20 September 1928

Well, I hauled grain for some of them, and I hauled that with a wagon and horses, you know, and then they had a truck. I did drive that truck. We had an older truck and so that one I could handle, it wasn't so big. Well, then my Uncle bought a new Chevrolet, I don't know if that's on here or not, so anyway, that one day they sent me to town with that truck and then my Dad showed me how to shift it, you know, and he said "now shift it in low not higher than medium when you get on the highway ok." So, I did. Well it drove so good. So I shifted it into high and when I got down to town, to Fredonia. You know where the grain elevators in Fredonia are now? I got to that corner where you need to turn and coming from the North, I did that alright. I came around the corner, and funny I didn't flip it, and I got to the elevator, and I didn't know what to do. They had called in and told the elevator man that I was coming, and he should watch for me. So, he was outside, and the pit was shut, and I went right through the elevator and if the pit would have been open, I would have killed myself. He kept saying "STOP, STOP, step on the brake!" Well, finally I stepped on the brake and I jack-knifed the whole thing, but I didn't tip. That was the end of my truck driving, yup, (laughter) horses after that and no more trucks. I suppose I was about 13 or 14, what time, that was when that war was, when was that, I suppose about 14 or 15 that's about all I was, and you know I wasn't very strong, you know my arms, I was frail. Oh, I was scared. I shook forever, I got a scolding, he said "You could have killed yourself and look what you have done to Uncle Garret's truck, it was brand new and I told you." Well I cried, and that was all the good that did. I didn't get a licking or anything. I think they were so glad that I was alive that they didn't really care (laughter). Oh, that was something. But that's what you did.

Clara Darrow and Votes for Women

23 APR

Elizabeth Cady Stanton once confided to her journal, "we are sowing winter wheat, which the coming spring will see sprout, and other hands than ours will reap and enjoy."

Stanton spoke not only for herself, but for the thousands of women who dedicated their hearts and souls to the cause of women's suffrage yet would not live to see their dream fully realized – women like North Dakota's Clara Darrow.

Women's suffrage had first taken root in North Dakota as early as the 1889 Constitutional Convention. But several failed attempts sapped the energy of the movement. By the first decade of the twentieth century, organized suffrage activity was virtually non-existent in the state. By 1912, that began to change.

Clara Darrow, the wife of a prominent Fargo doctor, made it her mission to rally the state's women in the cause for suffrage. She invited the internationally-renowned suffragette Sylvia Pankhurst to Fargo to help organize a statewide suffrage movement. In early February of 1912, Darrow, Pankhurst, and other local supporters met at the home of Clara's daughter, Mary Darrow Weible. Out of that meeting, the Votes for Women League of North Dakota was born. At the first statewide conference, members elected Mrs. Darrow as president. Her daughters, Mary and Elizabeth, accepted positions as vice-president and campaign manager. The Darrow women and other dedicated workers blazed a trail, forming local chapters across the state to garner support for women's suffrage. They organized Chautauquas, fairs, meetings, lobbied the press and politicians and even brought in special speakers like Dr. Anna Howard Shaw, president of the National American Woman Suffrage Association.

Clara was not one to simply sit back and delegate duties. She accompanied Dr. Shaw through her entire Dakota campaign. As Shaw later wrote, Clara took "every burden from my shoulders so efficiently that I had nothing to do but make speeches." Her talents extended beyond organizational skills. In 1914, Clara penned a pamphlet entitled "I Want to Vote," delivered at the Grand Theater in Fargo. It garnered so much attention it was later presented at the national suffrage conference in Nashville, TN.

Darrow's work and dedication laid an important foundation that would eventually lead the movement to victory, but like Elizabeth Cady Stanton's prophetic words, it was not a victory she would personally enjoy. Clara Darrow died on this date in 1915, before North Dakota women had gained the right to vote. But her two daughters, Mary and Elizabeth, continued the fight begun by their mother. When Governor Frazier signed the North Dakota women's suffrage bill two years later, both of Clara's daughters witnessed the historic event.

Christina Sunwall

24 APR

Adams County

This week is National County Government Week; fittingly, the county government of Adams County in southwestern North Dakota was organized on this day in 1907. The county itself was created from the southern portion of Hettinger County by proclamation of Governor John Burke on April 17, 1907. This explains why the location of the city of Hettinger, North Dakota is in Adams County, rather than its namesake county to the north. The creation of Adams County actually deprived Hettinger County of nearly one thousand square miles of land, in addition to its largest city. Hettinger became the county seat of the newly formed county, and remains so to this day, whereas Hettinger County named the nearby city of Mott as its own county seat.

Adams County was named for John Quincy Adams, but not the sixth United States president of the same name. This John Quincy Adams, although a distant relative to the sixth president, was in fact the General Land and Townsite Agent for Chicago, Milwaukee, and St. Paul Railroads. This railroad's main line west was built through southwestern North Dakota in 1907, and the residents of Adams County believed that the county's success was a direct result of the railroad's placement. Area newspapers echoed the sentiments of the county's citizens: at the time, the *Adams County Record* reported that "One force has been more largely responsible for the peopling of the fertile prairies here than any other [...] the Chicago, Milwaukee, and St. Paul Railway." Residents showed their appreciation by naming the county for the railroad agent. Today, Adams County is home to nearly 2,600 North Dakotans.

Jayme L. Job

Bismarck Booze Bust

25 APR

During its early years, Bismarck was right on the heels of Deadwood in terms lawlessness, violence, and the selling of liquor. But, by the early 1900s, some Bismarck residents felt it was time to actually enforce prohibition. Saloons that carried on in secret were called "blind pigs," and their beverages were either illegally produced locally or brought in from Canada by "runners."

On this date in 1907, a *Bismarck Tribune* headline read: "Thousand Dollars Worth of Booze Found in a Cave," because Chief Carr found an 'Unusual Quantity' of 'Joyful Water' under a hill near Fifth Street. He and Temperance Commissioner Murray found a door reinforced with iron bars, so Carr got a shovel and burrowed under it. Inside, they found a 10 x 16 room "filled to the roof with about every kind of intoxicating liquor consumed in this neck of the woods…"

Commissioner Murray posted guards, and at dawn they packed the booze into five wagons and took it to the capitol. The paper reported the cave was "the house of a thousand bottles." The next day, the paper gave a detailed inventory and reported, "…amid watering mouths and downcast eyes the stuff was taken into vaults and locked up to await the judicial verdict that shall consign it to mother earth or send it up in vapors to lead the birds to new song and agitate the leaves of the trees with an unwonted glee."

Officials opened each container and tested the contents of each to determine "whether or not they were in the nature of an intoxicating liquor." They were. The judge declared all should be destroyed.

On May 18, 1907, the *Tribune* reporter waxed elegiac:

Not a drum was heard or a funeral note
as the booze to the rampart was hurried;
not a toper fired a farewell shot, o'er the grave
where the bottles were buried.
They burned it swiftly at 2 o'clock,
when the shadows were eastward falling,
and many a mourner near died from shock
at the tragedy so appalling.
Hundreds of bottles of Blatz and Schlitz
that made Milwaukee famous
were flattened and shattered to little bits
when bitterness overcame us.
Barrels of whiskey with heads in caved
were rolled over hill and hollow
and earth, so thirsty was drenched and laved
till no one was left to swallow.

Barrels and bottles and casks and jugs
were opened and gently flowing
a mingled stream of stuff sought the bugs,
and up from the fresh earth blowing
came incense sweet as the breath of morn,
or fields in the Junetime splendid
when loosened spirits of rye and corn
in a perfume sweet were blended.

And Oh but the sight was sweet and sad –
this pouring of free libation
and Oh but the crashing was much and mad,
and would tickle Carrie Nation;
for such is the stuff that is full of woe
and trouble and fret and worry
and such is the cure that the stuff must know –
the cure whose first name is Murray…

Merry Helm

End of the Track Gang

26 APR

On this date in 1877, Bismarck saloonkeeper, Peter Branigan, was scheduled to be executed. He had killed a soldier named Massengale in his saloon on Christmas and was almost lynched by angry soldiers that night. Branigan was found guilty in February, escaped from jail in March, and was caught in Audubon, MN, a few weeks later.

Bismarck was considered one of the toughest towns in America in the 1870s. But, northern Dakota Territory was referred to as the Northwest back then, and much of its history never made it into the history of the Wild West. Bismarck's most lawless era began in 1870, when hundreds of railroad workers began advancing the Northern Pacific from Duluth. As the workers moved west, so did those who entertained them and took their money, including prostitutes, gamblers, saloonkeepers and drug dealers. Collectively, they were called the "End of the Track Gang." When railroad construction stalled in Bismarck, these "people of bad character" settled in for the duration. Two spots became particularly dangerous – Whiskey Point, opposite the Missouri River from Fort Abraham Lincoln, and "Bloody Fourth Street."

Two of the gang's worst were Dave Mullen and Jack O'Neil, former partners of Limpy Jack Clayton. In fact, Limpy got his nickname after Mullen shot him in the leg for testifying against him in Duluth. All three moved on to what was becoming Jamestown, and then Mullen and O'Neil split off and went to Bismarck to open a saloon. No love was lost between the fort's soldiers and the End of the Track Gang. Even though soldiers were Mullen and O'Neil's bread and butter, Mullen said he never "missed a good opportunity to shoot or rob a soldier."

One October night in 1873, a gambler named "Spotty" Whalen shot and killed a soldier out at Whiskey Point. The civilian authorities didn't do anything about it, so a group of soldiers decided to take matters into their own hands. In what became known as the "Battle of Mullen's Corner," the soldiers tracked Whalen to Mullen and O'Neil's saloon. Mullen answered their knock by opening the door and shooting a soldier named Dalton to death. The others returned fire and Mullen quickly passed into the next life.

It was in this same time period that Branigan killed Massengale in his saloon. Unfortunately for him, nobody was interested in the details. A *Bismarck Tribune* article later explained: "He was convicted because public sentiment demanded a sacrifice. No matter what evidence might have been brought in his favor to show that the killing was done in self defense, there was a disposition to convict in order to stop the shooting scrapes which were then common incidents at Bismarck."

Branigan's case marked the end of Bismarck's most violent era. Gold was discovered in the Black Hills that year, and "end of the trackers" who came to Bismarck were now catching the stagecoach to Deadwood – the "next" toughest town in America.

Merry Helm

27 APR

Buechner and Orth

From the late 1880s to around 1925, architecture took a turn towards the opulent. The Beaux Arts style was in full swing throughout America.

Beaux Arts, which simply means fine art in French, had its roots in the Ecole des Beaux Arts in Paris. Many American architects studied at the Parisian school and brought what they had learned back to America. Beaux Arts architecture is known for its formal design, elaborate details, and symmetry. It is a combination of classical Greek and Roman architecture, with a bit of the Renaissance thrown in. The architectural style was most often used for museums, libraries, and courthouses.

Charles Buechner and Henry Orth were one of the most successful architectural teams in their day. Their firm specialized in movie theatres and courthouses throughout the upper Midwest. Norway- born Henry Orth made his way to America in 1866, and eventually settled in St. Paul, Minnesota. Charles Buechner, who was born on this day in 1859, hailed from Darmstadt, Germany. Buechner was educated in Switzerland, France, and Germany. After making his way to America and meeting Henry Orth in St. Paul, the Beaux Arts Dream Team was born.

From one corner of North Dakota to the other, you'll find twelve courthouses designed by Buechner and Orth:

The Pierce County courthouse in Rubgy is one creation by the Dream Team. Its massive copper front doors open wide, giving way to marble flooring inlaid with cube mosaic. Stained glass ceilings decorate the twenty-foot rotunda. Inside the large silver dome atop the roof, intricate paintings depict local prairie scenes: buffalo grazing, settlers homesteading in covered wagons, and farmers plowing with "new-fangled" traction engines.

The Grand Forks County courthouse is another Buechner and Orth design. A statue of Themis, Goddess of Justice, has been perched upon the massive courthouse dome for over ninety years. Themis has been a symbol of truth and justice for centuries, revered by ancient Egyptians and Greeks alike. Arm proudly raised high, her hand gripped around a set of scales, Themis and her courthouse are an architectural "must-see" for locals and visitors to the Forks area.

From Wahpeton to Crosby, Grafton to Mandan, North Dakotans can find a bit of Beaux Arts architecture in their own home towns thanks to Charles Buechner and Henry Orth.

Jill Whitcomb

Marble Mania

28 APR

All across North Dakota in 1937, boys and girls age fourteen or younger were preparing to go head to head in a great marble tournament.

Depending on size of the community, schools held tournaments first; then cities held their own tournaments, waiting for the best player to shoot his or her way to the top. Next, county tournaments separated, and then, tri-county tournaments. For example, Emmons, Logan, and McIntosh counties were to face off against each other. Finally, the top shooters were sent to Grand Forks to compete for district and state championships.

Marble Champs were "out for blood" in Bismarck. There were reports of expected "kibitzing" from the grade-schoolers. "If the excitement of the school tournaments last Saturday is any indication, police squads will have to be called out [...] to quell the inter-school riots as fans root for their champs," the *Bismarck Capital* reported.

It was a big deal in Ashley, too. It was on this day that Ashley hosted a vicious, county play-off against Wishek. Wishek won; then the problems began.

Some of those involved in the tournament found that it was unfair: "Members of the committee, consisting of four boys [...] protested on the grounds that the county marble tournament was not satisfactory, and because of the cold weather, should never have been played."

Indeed, the weather was particularly bad that week, and papers across the state reported roaring gales that carried sleet, snow and dust with them to different parts of the state. Whether or not that affected the outcome of the tournament was debatable—but it was debatable enough that they decided to leave all decisions about the tournament's outcome up to the county supervisor.

It didn't matter in the end, though. The big game in Grand Forks—and, in fact, every game he played there—was won by eleven-year-old William Stroh, from Mandan. He beat Howard Moen, a thirteen-year-old from Mayville, by 3-1 in the final match. Third place went to Cornet Haroldson of Aneta, fourth to Dale Butterfield of Stanley, and fifth to the "southpaw" Bob Odney of Grand Forks.

In this case, one tournament caused the whole state to lose its marbles.

Sarah Walker

29 APR

Axis Grinder

Today's story is about Lt. Col. James Buzick, a Fargo man who started his military career in World War II. Buzick was an original member of the 577th Squadron of the 392nd bomb group, which flew its first combat mission in September 1943. He was a ball turret gunner on a B-24H S/N 42-7495, the first ever equipped with nose-turrets.

April 29, 1944, was a deadly day for the 392nd – the second heaviest in its combat history. They were to lose eight of their eighteen planes and suffer seventy-seven aircrew casualties that day. Their target was Berlin. Buzick and the rest of the crew were aboard the Axis Grinder when the bombers ran into trouble. For about five minutes, they lost their fighter escort planes, and some fifty German fighters took advantage by attacking the American bomber formation two abreast, in a double line.

The Axis Grinder was hit with five 20mm shells, which injured the navigator and the right waist gunner and took out the plane's number 3-engine. The shell that wounded the right waist gunner also hit one of Buzick's guns and hot shrapnel set off some of his 50-caliber ammunition leaving the ball turret inoperative. Luckily, Jim was not injured; he was able to get the guns pointed down and retreat back up into the plane.

Buzick found Sgt. Walter Kolczynsky bloody but still manning his waist gunner position. When Buzick tried to take over for him, Kolczynwky refused, saying, "No damn German is going to shoot me and get away with it."

Concerned about his wounded men, 1st Lt. Floyd Slipp radioed from the cockpit to his crew. Should they head for Sweden or aim for England, which was farther away? At this point, two ME 109s spotted them all alone and made a pass at them. Slipp dove down into the safety of heavy clouds and, in agreement with his crew, headed for England.

After some time of flying blind, the Axis Grinder pulled up out of the clouds only to be jumped by more ME-109s. This happened every time they came into the open, and Lt. Slipp figured German radar had a lock on them. He aimed downwards, hoping to fly below the clouds.

Buzick said when they emerged they were in Holland and so close to the ground he had to look up to see the top of a windmill they were passing – a windmill with German troops shooting at them.

As they crossed the English Channel, the missing third engine became a more serious problem; at times they were only fifteen feet above the water. As they neared the cliffs on the British coastline, Buzick said they threw everything out of the plane that wasn't bolted down. The Axis Grinder cleared the cliffs and successfully made it to base in Wendling.

Merry Helm

Mosasaurs

30 APR

Today we'll be bringing you a glimpse of what our state was like before humans came. On this date, seventy-five million years ago, the area around Cooperstown was under salt water.

Actually, a shallow, sub-tropical sea covered almost the entire state. The Pierre Sea was part of the Western Interior Seaway, which divided the North American continent right down the center, connecting the Arctic Ocean with the Gulf of Mexico.

But back to Cooperstown seventy-five million years ago. On a typical day, sand tiger sharks, dogfish sharks, and two types of cow sharks were trying to "out-lunch" each other. The water in that area was only about 100 yards deep, and the sharks' entrees included numerous types of bony fish. Down on the seabed, coral, and seaweed sheltered snails, tusk shells, clams, starfish, sea urchins, shrimp, crabs and lobsters.

There were also creatures like the octopus, squid and the chambered nautilus. On the sea's surface were turtles and hesperornithids — a seabird that couldn't fly. At six feet tall, it had powerful legs and teeth.

Now we get to one of the creepier predators: the mosasaur. These marine reptiles lived during time of dinosaurs, but they're in a different classification more closely related to monitor lizards, like the Komodo dragons of Indonesia. Mosasaurs had powerful toothy jaws like alligators, but they didn't have legs. They had flippers, and they propelled through coastal waters much like a snake.

Mike Hanson and Dennis Halvorson of Cooperstown found the jaw of a mosasaur in the Sheyenne River valley around 1993. John Hoganson of the North Dakota Geological Survey came out to investigate. To make a long story short, at least twelve mosasaurs have now been found in that area. Two separate species were identified, but one stood out.

The unusual one was found on Beverly and Orville Tranby's property, and it was almost completely intact. They donated it to the State Fossil Collection for further study. The entire skeleton turned out to be twenty-three feet long, with the skull alone reaching three feet. The large size and unique bone structure revealed it to be a new species not found anywhere else in the world. Some of its bones had tooth marks, and thousands of dogfish shark teeth found with the skeleton paint a pretty clear picture of the lizard's last moments: sharks lose a lot of teeth when they're attacking and feeding.

This one-of-a-kind mosasaur is now displayed in the Underwater World section of the Adaptation Gallery at the Heritage Center in Bismarck.

Merry Helm

Hope second baseball team, Hope, N.D.
Credit: Institute for Regional Studies, NDSU, Fargo (Folio 102.SpB73.1)

MAY

The History of North Dakota Lives On

01 MAY

For many years there has been a key "go to" print source for information about North Dakota's past. North Dakotans, with either a casual or intense curiosity about the heritage and historical perspective of their state, have benefited from Dr. Elwyn B. Robinson's *The History of North Dakota* since its publication in 1966.

Robinson was a professor in the UND history department and served for a time as director of the State Historical Society of North Dakota. His work on the book took many years, and it became the standard historical text for the thirty-ninth state, which was carved from Dakota Territory.

In his preface, Robinson wrote: "I have sought to view North Dakota's history in broad perspective, relating it to major events in the history of the Western world, and to demonstrate how the conditions of existence shaped the character of the men and women who settled the state. For it is my conviction that an adequate knowledge of North Dakota's past provides the best foundation for making public decisions which will determine its future."

The book fell out of print, but was re-published on this date in 1988, making it easily available to new readers. With its clear style, the book starts with the history of the land before human life and takes the reader well into the twentieth century.

The 1988 edition's postscript was written by Dr. David Danbom, well-known and recently retired NDSU history professor. Danbom captures an optimistic and thoughtful observation about the land and its people. This is part of what he writes: "North Dakotans continue to be part of the 'commonwealth' political tradition. They take their responsibilities as citizens seriously and they vote in large numbers (65 percent or better in most presidential contests). They are civil to one another and distrust the negative, sound-biting campaigning that plays such an important role in contemporary politics in the United States [...] North Dakotans continue to expect their elected officials will be honest, forthcoming and accessible. North Dakota leads the nation in elected officials per capita [...] it can be interpreted as showing the willingness of some North Dakotans to serve their communities and the desire of others to have accessible and responsible government."

In celebration of the fiftieth anniversary of the book's original publication, the Chester Fritz Library at UND released a digital version of this pathbreaking work through the generous support of the Northern Plains Heritage Foundation, the North Dakota legislature, the North Dakota University System, and the family of Elwyn B. Robinson.

Steve Stark

02 MAY

Erik Ramstad

In 1883, Erik and Oline Ramstad set out from Grafton in Dakota Territory to become the first settlers of present-day Minot, ND. Three years later, Erik Ramstad's land sale to the railroad companies would set into motion the creation of the city of Minot. Ramstad would profit handsomely from these sales, and he became not only a bank and lumber company president, but a father of the Magic City.

Erik Ramstad did not begin life with expectations for such success on the Dakota frontier. He was born in Sigdal, Norway, to the family of a poor landless farmer. Erik's father, Reier Pedersen, had the infamous reputation of being both the town brawler and drunkard. Due to his father's poor reputation Erik forsook the family name of "Reier" for that of his employer Stener N. Ramstad. Seeking to further distance himself from his family connections, and for a chance at inexpensive land, Erik Ramstad immigrated first to a large Scandinavian community in southern Minnesota in 1880. He was too late to claim the cheap land of a frontier community in Minnesota, so he spent two years earning money felling trees and wrestling men for money. The money Erik Ramstad earned forcing trees and men to the ground was not enough to start a farm in Minnesota. It was, however, enough to start one in Dakota Territory. Hearing of the inexpensive land on the Dakota frontier, Ramstad moved to Grafton, Dakota Territory in 1882. At year's end, Erik Ramstad was unable to find any land that suited him. However, he did manage to find a wife, Ingeborg Oline Gullson, and by the beginning of 1883 they were wed.

In May 1883, the Ramstad's packed up their belongings into a single covered wagon and made their way 200 west miles to the Mouse River Valley. After a month of traveling, Mr. Ramstad and his wife found a quiet wooded valley, and began to build their home. Three years later, Ramstad agreed to sell sections of his homestead to James J. Hill's railroad company that was building through the area. The railroad company founded the present-day city Minot on the forty acres of land that it originally had bought from Eric Ramstad for $1000. In later years, Ramstad continued to sell and give away acres of land. Today, elementary schools, cemeteries, churches, and Minot State University are all located on land originally donated by Eric Ramstad, a man who left Grafton this month in 1883 a poor Norwegian immigrant and became one of Minot's most celebrated forefathers.

Lane Sunwall

Broste Rock Museum

03 MAY

In Paul Broste's book, *The Proem*, we find the words of wisdom that drove him: "The time to quit is when you are dead and buried." The day Mr. Broste "quit" was on this day in 1975.

Broste was the nucleus around which the nationally acclaimed Broste Rock Museum was built. He was an unassuming bachelor farmer whose passion showed up early. It involved his pants pockets, which were always so jammed with rocks that his suspenders broke.

In 1940, he began what was to become a very fine collection of mineral specimens. This didn't satisfy his creative needs, so he bought some machinery and learned the art of lapidary so he could cut and polish his own stones. He soon became fascinated with making polished stone spheres.

By 1950, he had more than 300 spheres – some as small as golf balls and other as big as bowling balls. He wanted a way to display some of them at a national mineralogical show in Milwaukee, so he and his nephew created a six-foot iron "tree" with graceful curved branches that held the spheres like peaches sitting in saucers. His display got him media attention, and he was soon surprised to learn he had the largest collection of stone spheres in the world.

People started flocking to Broste's farm to have a look, and within three years, he had more than 2,000 names in his visitors' book. In the early 1960s, the people of Parshall built a museum for Broste and his work, made almost entirely by volunteers. The building is constructed of native granite with walls five-feet thick at the base tapering to a "boulder's width" at the top; the floor is of Mexican onyx tiles cut and polished by Broste. A special hexagonal room was included for a twisting, swirling vortex of spheres reflected on all sides by floor-to-ceiling mirrors. This is called the Infinity Room, but Paul called it his "Astronomical Cavalcade."

The museum opened in 1966, but Broste didn't want to be seen as looking for attention. "I did not paint for the matter of getting fame," he wrote. "I did not cut rocks for the matter of making 370 spheres; I did not publish a book for the matter of publishing a book… (it's like) when you are thirsty you want to drink, when you are hungry, you want to eat."

When Broste died, the museum was turned over to the town of Parshall. The building fell into disrepair and was closed in 1997. Thankfully, it has since been renovated. Geologists have inventoried Broste's collections, which they term "spectacular." They found almost 600 spheres, as well as many Smithsonian-quality mineral specimens that are so rare they can't be found anywhere else in the world.

Merry Helm

04 MAY

Upright Sleeper

We've all heard about talking in your sleep – and many of us do. And then there's sleep walking, which afflicted pilot Carl Ben Eielson the night before he'd set out on any new adventure. But today's story is about something far more unusual.

On this date in 1905, the *Fargo Forum and Daily Republican* published a story titled "Aged Negress Slept Standing Twenty Years." The story was about a woman named Mary Dickerson, who was called Aunt Dickie by most people. She lived with Mrs. B. H. Smoot in north Fargo.

There were few background details on Aunt Dickie, but the story said she was "so old that she herself doesn't know her age." She knew only that she was born into slavery in Mississippi somewhere between 1825 and 1835. No one knows how Dickerson ended up in Fargo. Mrs. Smoot said only that Aunt Dickie was sprightly, did her share of the housework and regularly went to church. She had also been using morphine for fifty years; how she got started on it wasn't explained.

Aunt Dickie had fought her morphine addiction for many years without success, and doctors were unable to help her kick her habit. "A brown, wrinkled arm, punctured by a myriad of pricks of the hypodermic needle, tells the life story of Aunt Dickie," the story read.

Mrs. Smoot said, "…she'd be crazy at times and would go to extremes to get the drug." Then, on Christmas morning, 1904, Aunt Dickie had an abrupt recovery while attending church at the Christian and Missionary Alliance. "…the god (sic) Lord has saved me from this awful shame," she told the reporter. "He has made me whole."

Mrs. Smoot confirmed Aunt Dickie's recovery, saying, "Now she is able to work and is at peace with the world." But there was still one thing Aunt Dickie couldn't do. She couldn't sleep lying down.

Dr. E. L. Siegelstein said, "I attended her several months ago when she was slightly ill. I told her she must go to bed for a few days. Her answer startled me. 'I can't go to bed,' she said. "I haven't been to bed for twenty years.'" Dr. Siegelstein assumed she slept in a chair, but he was wrong. Aunt Dickie slept standing up.

"I didn't believe her at the time," he said. "But sometime later I visited the house again and found her asleep. She was leaning against the wall and was sound asleep as though she had been in the softest bed. I was greatly interested and questioned her. She gave a novel but plausible reason, but I have failed to find a parallel case in medicine."

"It's this way," Aunt Dickie explained. "When I took the dope, I had the most terrible dreams. The more morphine I took, the worse the dreams got. I found that when I took the dope and went to bed, I would dream of falling into hell's fire or going through the worst tortures. I just couldn't stand it and I'd have to get up and take more dope.

"I just couldn't afford that," she said. "I had just money enough to buy a little of the stuff at a time and couldn't afford to take it day and night. So, I started to sleep in a chair. That was better. But the dreams still came and so I started to sleep standing up. Then I had no bad dreams and I've kept it up ever since. I couldn't sleep in a bed now if I wanted to."

Merry Helm

05 MAY

The Chewing Gum Craze

Some people like to chew gum. Some don't. This basic truism has been around for a long time.

In Jamestown, back on this date in 1882, the local newspaper editor noted that a "mania for chewing gum" had "struck some of our young ladies," for he had observed three women "chewing" that week.

In those days, there were several kinds of chewing gum. Spruce gum proliferated as an established favorite, for this gummy ooze from spruce-trees had been sold in lumps since the early 1800s. Around 1850, sweetened paraffin wax became popular, soon surpassing the old spruce gum. In the early 1860s, juice from chicle trees in Central America came to America, and gum made from chicle dominated the market by the 1880s.

Numerous critics thought gum chewing was a nasty habit. A scientist warned young women that too much chewing excessively exercised the facial muscles, creating "hollow-cheeked," un-ladylike looks. Professor Eliot Norton of Harvard University thought women who chewed gum were "vulgar" and that gum chewing was "barbarism." Other naysayers believed chewing gum was unnatural. All that chewing might be good for cows who were supposed to chew their cuds, but the gum-chewing jaw motion over-stimulated the salivary glands, they said, causing the saliva to become over-churned with air, creating great discomfort in the stomach.

Some fear-mongers claimed that people who swallowed their gum got wads stuck in the appendix, causing appendicitis. And one critic of the gummy habit thought it was awfully expensive – for if a person chewed "three pieces a week" the habit would cost $1.56 a year, or, in 67 years, a shocking total of $104.52.

Others defended gum chewing as a positive good. One physician said that all that chewing made people thinner and healthier *by channeling more saliva into the stomach*, thereby stimulating *improved* digestion. And some thought chewing gum was far better than chewing tobacco – a prevalent vice back then.

A sentimental source contended that "gum chewing . . . [was] not so bad," for some of his most pleasant memories were associated with times when he was chewing gum – while fishing, playing baseball, or just whiling away youthful hours.

One headline promoted "gum chewing as an art." Likely an exaggeration, it became a reality for creative North Dakotans in the twentieth century after Frank Fleer breathed new life into the gum business with the invention of Blibber-Blabber bubble gum.

Dr. Steve Hoffbeck

Preserving Our Heritage

06 MAY

The land of North Dakota has quite a history, and no place has done as much to keep that history alive as the North Dakota Heritage Center. They maintain archives, present exhibits, preserve artifacts, and tend fifty-six historic sites. There are even programs to provide children hands-on learning experiences. For many years the center sought to expand. Their first efforts began over thirty years ago, but it wasn't until this date in 2009 that Governor John Hoeven signed legislation appropriating almost $40 million, contingent on another $12 million from private sources.

The funding made it possible to build a 97,000 square-foot addition for new exhibits. The displays include dinosaurs, early residents, agriculture, and even the recent oil boom. The additions have been quite a success.

Over 4,400 people attended the opening on November 2, 2014. This was more than expected, which pleased the staff, and it showed how much the people of North Dakota enjoy their history.

The mission of North Dakota Heritage Center is "to identify, preserve, interpret, and promote the heritage of North Dakota and its people." Understanding the roots of North Dakota and how it began keeps our growing history alive[…] and from the dinosaurs to the first people to walk this land, the Heritage Center helps remember them.

You can learn more about the Heritage Center's collections and history by reading the entries in this volume from March 19, April 30, May 22, August 15, and December 3.

Lucid Thomas

07 MAY

Summertime Heat

The first Saturday in May marks the date for the running of the Kentucky Derby at the Churchill Downs in Louisville, Kentucky. As the most celebrated horse race in America, the race brings thoroughbred horses from across the globe to compete for the "crown of roses."

The derby might be "The Most Exciting Two Minutes In Sports," but it takes hours, days, years, and even decades of training and know-how to produce a champion. Part of that know-how is feed, which brings us to Alan Woodbury of Woody's Feed and Grain in Dickinson, who's been feeding champions for decades.

Woodbury "grew up in the agriculture industry" and attended North Dakota State University, where he received a degree in animal science and agricultural economics. After graduating he moved to Dickinson and took a job as salesman for a local feed mill. A little over a decade later, Woodbury purchased the mill, beginning Woody's Feed and Grain.

Woodbury did not start out feeding horses, but rather cows. It wasn't until prompted by his brother, a horse trainer on the West Coast, that Woody delved into horse feed. His special blends soon caught on in the racing community. Most notable among Woodbury's winners is Nyquist, the champion of the 2016 Kentucky Derby. Nyquist's trainer noted that Woodbury's "Summer Heat" blend was an essential part of Nyquist's regimen.

Instead of the usual oats, "Summer Heat" uses beet pulp, a bi-product of the sugar industry. Along with high-fat soy oil, the beet fiber allows for slower digestion, which improves nutrient absorption. This is particularly important for racehorses, which need energy-dense foods and lots of nutrients. It doesn't hurt that beets are a prominent crop in North Dakota, which makes for a plentiful supply.

Alan Woodbury retired in 2015. Although Scranton Equity bought the company, it is still run by Alan's son. Today, Woody's Feed and Grain continues the tradition of creating great feed for champion horses.

As the saying goes, "If you can't *beet* them, join them."

Maria Witham

Prison Riot

08 MAY

On this date in 1957, newspapers across the country were reporting a prison riot at the State Penitentiary in Bismarck that had occurred the day prior. The trouble started late in the morning, when 220 prisoners refused to go back to work in the binder-twine factory. The convicts complained of poor food, the actions of a particularly hated guard, and inadequate time for recreation. The inmates went back to their cellblock but refused to enter their cells. The situation escalated about two hours later, when they barricaded themselves inside and began smashing things.

Four prison guards hid in the boiler room and the hospital, where they were able to call for assistance using a telephone. Warden Nygaard, who was in Jamestown, told them to remain hidden; he didn't want the rioters to take them hostage. State patrolmen, Bismarck policemen and two firetrucks soon surrounded the prison.

A United Press reporter managed to climb a ladder and talk with five of the strike leaders through the bars of a window. The men said prison guards were stealing money and valuables from them. They also told of an abusive guard who would go into Bismarck and then come back and taunt the prisoners with tantalizing stories about their wives and sweethearts.

A reporter for the Associated Press was told the trouble actually started when a prisoner got thrown into solitary confinement. Guard Tom Wrangum confirmed he threw an inmate into the hole the previous day, but he refused to elaborate.

The prisoners demanded to see Governor John Davis, Attorney General Leslie Burgum, or Warden O. J. Nygaard. Nygaard hurried back to Bismarck, where he told reporters he had a pretty good idea of who was leading the revolt—about seven or eight chronic troublemakers.

Matters came to an abrupt head late that afternoon. A "flying wedge" of prison guards charged the rioters with rifles and shotguns firing above their heads. The *Fargo Forum* reported, "what threatened to become a full-blown riot [...] folded up like an accordion after a tense five hours when officers used tear gas on 220 convicts."

Three prisoners were reported wounded, and the four hidden guards were freed. The men went to bed without supper that night because food in the kitchen was contaminated by disinfectant broken open during the smashing spree.

When asked how he was going to proceed in the aftermath, Warden Nygaard said he was going to ignore the convicts' charges, saying they were "cooked up" accusations.

Merry Helm

09 MAY

USS Robalo

Construction began on the USS Robalo on October 24 in 1942, when its keel was laid down in Manitowoc, Wisconsin. A Gato-class submarine commissioned by the U.S. Navy for patrols in the Pacific, the Robalo was launched on May 9, 1943. It sunk less than fifteen months later, in July of 1944. In 1960, the Robalo was adopted by the state of North Dakota as a move to honor and remember the fifty-two submarines lost by the United States during World War II.

Like many of its sister ships, the Robalo's naval career was tragically short. The submarine began its first patrol out of Pearl Harbor during the early months of 1944, commanded by Stephen Ambruster. The crew spent two months hunting Japanese ships west of the Philippines. In March of 1944, Manning Kimmel took command, and the Robalo began a patrol of the South China Sea. Assigned to intercept Japanese traffic between Vietnam and the Philippines, the Robalo's second patrol proved more aggressive; the crew engaged in four different attacks and suffered a direct hit by a Japanese bomber. The submarine returned to dock at Fremantle in Western Australia for repairs. Before setting out on her third patrol, Commander Kimmel offered leave to several men, and some accepted. It would prove a fortunate decision for those lucky few.

The Robalo struck a mine north of Borneo on July 26 and sunk. Seventy-seven of the ship's crew drowned, and the remaining four survivors swam to shore. Picked up by Japanese forces, these men were placed in a Philippine prison camp, but were never heard from again. It is believed that they were put on a Japanese destroyer that was later sunk.

During the 1960 meeting of the Submarine Veteran's of World War II, each U.S. state adopted a lost submarine to honor. North Dakota chose the Robalo, and in 2005 a memorial commemorating the crew was dedicated at Fargo's Lindenwood Park. In 2009, David Zier was honored at the memorial by local leaders and veterans. Visiting from his home in Maryland, Zier was one of those crewmen who remained behind in Australia during the ship's final mission. Standing in front of the memorial, engraved with the names of his lost shipmates, Zier expressed his gratitude to the state for honoring the lost ship and her crew.

Jayme L. Job

Zip to Zap

10 MAY

Today is the anniversary of the only official riot in state history. In the spring of 1969, NDSU student body president, Chuck Stroup, couldn't afford to go to Florida for spring break. So, he came up with a cheap alternative – a gathering near his hometown of Hazen called "Zip to Zap." He took the idea to NDSU's school paper, the *Spectrum*, placing a classified ad.

The idea prompted a front-page article that praised the beauty of the Knife River and stated that the people of Zap were welcoming the idea. The article also predicted that people from all over the Midwest would come to the "Lauderdale of the North." UND picked up on the idea, and within weeks, Zip to Zap was being promoted nationwide as a "Grand Festival of Light and Love."

Unprepared for such a huge response, the student organizers quickly got permission from Zap landowners to allow camping in their vacant fields. They also hired some regional bands to keep the audience entertained.

Meanwhile, Zap's citizens were guardedly optimistic. The café started working on "Zapburgers," and the town's two bars stocked up on beer. Since there was no way to predict how many would attend, Governor Guy talked with the Highway Patrol about controlling traffic, and the National Guard boned up on procedures for crowd control.

By Friday evening, May 9, 2,000 people descended on Zap. The bars were overwhelmed and raised their prices, upsetting the students. Pretty soon, it didn't matter – the beer was all gone, and the café had to close. Students vomited and urinated in the open – others passed out in the street. Temperatures fell below freezing, and wood from a demolished building was used for a bonfire on Main Street. Pretty soon, the townspeople asked the crowd to break up and go home. Some complied, but others didn't. The party atmosphere disappeared, the security was overwhelmed, and the café and one bar were broken into and trashed.

By dawn, 500 National Guardsman surrounded the town. Two hundred of them moved in, facing about 200 students who were still carrying on, and another 1,000 sleeping wherever they had landed during the night. Their wake-up call was at the point of a fixed bayonet. Cold, hungry, and hung-over, there was little resistance, and the crowd dispersed in front of reporters who had arrived on the scene. That evening, the Zip to Zap fiasco was the lead story on the CBS Evening News.

Damage from the riot was assessed at more than $25,000. A lot of fingers were pointed, but the student governments of UND and NDSU were handed the bill – which they paid.

Merry Helm

11 MAY

Oscar Coen, Eagle Squadron

Oscar Coen was born on this date in 1917 at Walum, just a few miles south of Hannaford, North Dakota. Oscar graduated from high school, went to college and became a teacher. In 1940 he joined the Army Air Corp to become a pilot. The Army had other plans however and slotted Coen to be an Aviation Navigator. When Oscar found out, he abruptly resigned his commission, high-tailed it for Canada, and was welcomed into the Royal Canadian Air Force for pilot training.

When Coen got his wings, he was sent to England where he joined the Royal Air Force and was assigned to number 71 Eagle Squadron. The Eagle Squadrons were made up of American pilots who volunteered to fly for the British before the US entered the war. Coen first flew Hurricanes, then later Spitfires. On October 20, 1941, Coen was strafing a German munitions train when it blew up, damaging his Spit, and causing him to crash land in occupied France. Oscar was rescued by the French resistance and was able to get back to England by way of Spain. He returned to his Squadron on Christmas day, 1941.

In April, 1942, Coen shot down three Focke Wulf 190 German fighters, and in August he downed two more German planes during the unsuccessful Dieppe landings. Oscar often flew wing with his close friend Michael McPharlin.

When the US became fully involved in the war, Coen was welcomed back into the fold of the Army Air Force, transferred to the 4th Fighter Group as Squadron leader, and started flying P-47 Thunderbolts. While flying his P-47 near Alconbury, the engine exploded causing Oscar to execute a high-speed bailout, breaking and dislocating his shoulder in the process. After several months' recuperation, Coen returned to duty, and in April of 1944 transferred to the 356th Fighter Group as Deputy Group Commander.

On June 6, 1944, Oscar's friend, Mike McPharlin, had engine trouble during a mission and was lost while trying to return to base. After the war, Oscar married McPharlin's widow, Virginia, and raised Michael's daughter as his own.

Oscar Coen has the distinction of being one of North Dakota's combat Aces. He made a career of the Air Force and retired in 1962 with the rank of Colonel. He passed away in 2004.

Scott Nelson

Oil Boom Jobs

12 MAY

The history of oil in North Dakota can best be described as episodic. From the early 1900s to more recent times, the search for oil has added an exciting chapter in the history of the state. While drilling wells in search of water, early homesteaders found trace evidence of oil or natural gas, giving rise to a belief of vast deposits beneath our feet. Geologists, speculators and even schemers sought ways to extract the oil with various results. It was not until April 4, 1951, that the first major-paying well came in – the Clarence Iverson #1 Well near Tioga.

The news of the find spread across the country. Post-World War II production was winding down, and war veterans were finding jobs difficult to acquire in the Eastern states. In the next few years, a flood of workers began looking toward the North Dakota oil fields and the related surge in the economy of state's western communities. Prior to this, the state had been predominately agricultural, with a seasonal influx of migrant farm workers, but a declining population overall. So, shortly after the announcement, came the speculators wanting to cash in on the prosperity, the workers seeking good-paying jobs, and merchants and craftsmen hoping to find a niche in the booming economy.

On this date in 1954, the *Bismarck Tribune* stated that the city had been flooded with job hunters. The flow of workers came from as far away as New York and Oklahoma and consisted of mostly skilled workers. According to L. M. Bechtel, Bismarck district manager at the North Dakota Unemployment Service, workers were arriving at the rate of 200 to 300 per day. There was also an average of sixty additional requests being received each day by mail and telephone. Some found work at the refineries in Mandan and Williston, some at the Garrison Dam as it neared completion, but when offered farms jobs, most moved on westward.

According to an oil field character named Blackie Davidson, this was too bad because a farm is a good place to find oil. When asked why they always chose the best field of wheat to drill their wells, Blackie responded, "Oh, we always look for a good wheat field," he drawled. "That's the easiest way to find oil. You can always find oil under a good wheat field. I guess it's the gas pressure that pushes up that there wheat!"

Jim Davis

13 MAY

Over There

World War I was one of the bloodiest conflicts in human history. Sixty-four million people served in the war, and about nine million soldiers died. The United States entered World War I in 1917 as President Woodrow Wilson called on Americans to "make the world safe for Democracy." Mobilization for the war included a military draft and Uncle Sam posters declaring "I Want You" for the U.S. Army. The mobilization of the mind included propaganda against warlike Germans and fear of encroaching spies within our borders.

Patriotism sprang forth, too, with songs that inspired loyalty to America's war-crusade. Foremost among the war-songs was the tune entitled "Over There," written by George M. Cohan, and it was on this date in 1918, that a movie called *Over There*, named after Cohan's song, premiered at the Royal Theater in Grand Forks.

The film was advertised as the most enthralling war film ever made. The advertisements promised "*Actual* Trench Scenes, *Actual* War Scenes," and "Thrills! Thrills! Thrills!" As a special added attraction, "Over There" and a selection of other patriotic songs were sung by well-known Minneapolis tenor Harry Kessell. The *Grand Forks Herald* reported that the singing of Kessell was the best feature of the night as Kessell gave a "fine interpretation of Cohan's famous song." The lyrics urged: "Johnny get your gun, get your gun," and "Take it on the run" "Send the word, send the word over there, that the Yanks are coming, the Yanks are coming, over there."

George M. Cohan's song became the most inspirational patriotic song since the Civil War. North Dakotans heard, and answered the call for a total of 31,269 serving in the military during the conflict. Many went "over there" to the trenches in France, and they were proud when victory had been won, that they *had* made the world "safe for democracy." But many never came back, with 117,000 Americans dying in that most terrible war. And among that total were 1,305 North Dakotans, whose mothers and fathers plaintively mourned their deaths, with sad hymns and with bugles playing "Taps."

Dr. Steve Hoffbeck

German-Russian Farm Kids Remember a "Typical Day"

14 MAY

Clarence Meidinger
Born: Lehr, ND, 15 May 1929
Interviewed: Edgeley, ND, 14 July 2007

The first time when he got up you know, they had milking to do. Well, we milked about a dozen and a half cows at least maybe fifteen to eighteen, and that was the first year. In those days they used to separate by hand, and so that took time, and they pail fed the calves and fed the pigs. I would say they probably got up at six o'clock and didn't get into the fields until at least eight or after. And then they would take off for dinner. And a lot of times, I think all the times, and I don't think they just had an hour noon. I think they had a longer noon hour than an hour, and then they'd go back, they'd go back to the field and I suppose they'd be back in around 6 or 6:30 to do the chores and that, so I don't think they had much of a seven or eight-hour day with the horses. With the tractor it was a little different. With the tractors they went a lot and some went 'til midnight.

15 MAY

Johnson versus Stenehjem Baseball

In May of 1981, reporter B.J. Phillips said in an article for *Time* magazine, "In the beginning, there was no baseball. But ever since, there have been few beginnings as good as the start of a new baseball season [...] the national pastime arrives with spring."

This has been true in North Dakota, even if our spring comes a little later than in other areas of the country. Baseball has ushered in spring in North Dakota for over 150 years, beginning in the 1870s with soldiers at the military forts creating teams to pass the time. As more and more settlers came west with the expansion of the railroad, so did baseball. As the population grew in Dakota Territory, so did the sport's popularity.

By the time North Dakota became a state in 1889, teams were organizing in every city across the state. However, a town did not need a proper league to assemble a team. All that was necessary for a wholesome good time was an open field, a bat, a ball, and nine team members.

Sometimes those nine all came from the same family. As The *Jamestown Record* reported May in 1914, a team from Ray, North Dakota had "the most unique baseball team in United States," with all team members carrying the last name "Johnson." The Johnson ball team had tied in their first game of the season, but manager Gilbert Johnson predicted that they were on their way to win against any semi-pro team in the state.

However, the Johnsons were not the only family-oriented team. On June 25, the *Jamestown Record* reported that the Stenehjems of Arnegard were organized and ready to play. The team consisted of nine brothers and their manager, A.A. Stenehjem. The Stenehjems challenged the Johnsons to a game, with bragging rights at stake.

The outcome of the Johnson-Stenehjem game appears to be undocumented. However, for many avid baseball fans happily filling bleachers and suiting up for games this spring, a shared love of the game brings its own kind of family.

Maria Witham

Garrison Dam Deaths

16 MAY

Over two miles long, the Garrison Dam is one of the largest rolled earth dams on the planet. Its construction brought degrees of misery for many of those involved. The Three Affiliated Tribes lost the rich Missouri river bottomland of the Fort Berthold Reservation. The Mandan, Hidatsa and Arikara people had cultivated these lands for generations. The flooding forced them to higher ground and poorer soil.

The dam took seven years to build. It was constructed for flood control and hydroelectric power. Damming the Missouri was by no means an easy task – fifteen men died during the construction. One of those deaths occurred on this date in 1952 when carpenter and foreman John Hoffman fell from the dam's intake structure. He was twenty-nine years old and a World War II veteran. His death was the first in over three and a half years at the site.

Most of the deaths took place after the project was well over halfway done; with eleven deaths in the last three years. Early on, the project had logged 16 million consecutive man hours without a fatal accident. However, numerous non-fatal accidents did occur: from vehicle accidents, equipment problems, and falls. Contractors received a number of letters advocating safer practices.

Some workers also died from heart attacks, which might also have been linked to the work. But despite the deaths and injuries, the Garrison Dam project was reportedly considered the safest project of its kind in the twentieth century. Signs remembering those who died are on display at Garrison Dam Park.

Jack Dura

17 MAY

The Only Studio Car in the World

A traveling photo studio managed by a famous photographer might seem to be an innovative idea even in contemporary times. With that in mind, just imagine its attraction in 1886 Dakota Territory.

Frontier photographer F. Jay Haynes created such an enterprise to record the life and times of prairie pioneers. After a trip to La Moure, he headed to his next town, which happened to be located near the James River. On this date in 1886, his Haynes palace studio car was parked in Jamestown for a six-day stay. The car was a former Pullman coach and the location was a Northern Pacific Railroad sidetrack.

Haynes' arrival had been preceded throughout Jamestown by posters (or bills, as they were then called) announcing that the Haynes Palace studio car would be in town May 15 to May 20, "offering residents of this city an opportunity of […] strictly first-class photography."

People in the region had heard of Haynes. The official photographer for the Northern Pacific had made an admired name for himself. In fact, his photographic abilities had helped him earn the respectful title of "Professor Haynes", a title bestowed upon him for his achieved artistry rather than any earned degree.

Photography at the time was still new, expensive, and complicated. The professor's traveling business was a brilliant combination of studio, office, and gallery. The light in the side windows highlighted the hundreds of framed works of photographic art that extended from floor to vaulted ceiling. Mirrors strategically placed helped reflect the carpeted parlor. The beautifully paneled wood interior was decorated with frills and ornamentation worthy of abundant praise. Colorful rugs led its users through decorated rooms that were eye-catching and awe-inspiring.

Billed as "the only studio car in the world", Haynes sought to create an irresistible invitation to the curious. An editor from the Fargo newspaper wrote: "the palace car is glittering. No gilt-encircled, gold emblazoned circus car can compare with this paragon of brilliant beauty, this novelty of modern art." Haynes' remodeled Pullman had caught the fancy of photographers across the nation. *Scientific American* printed the description of the interior, and the *Photographic Times* chronicled it as well.

Haynes travelled from the Red River Valley all the way to the Cascade Mountains capturing pictures of expansive vistas, pioneer families, burgeoning frontier businesses, and railroad activity. On this date in 1886, though, he was in Jamestown capturing families and individuals with the magic of his camera.

Steve Stark

First Prison Rodeo

18 MAY

North Dakota's first annual prison rodeo began on this day in 1974. The two-day affair featured fifty-four inmates from the North Dakota State Penitentiary in Bismarck. The inmates competed in sixteen events, including bull riding, wild horse racing, steer wrestling, bareback and bronco riding, the 'hard money chase,' and a mad bull scramble. In the 'hard money chase' event, a $50 bill was attached to a bull's horns. The bull was set loose in the arena, and the first inmate to snatch the $50 got to keep it. In the mad bull scramble, several bull-riders were set loose into the arena at once; the inmate who remained atop his bull the longest was declared the champion.

The rodeo was the brainchild of prison inmate Ervin Plentychief, who served as the chairman of the event. Plentychief had been an active rodeo participant since the 1930s, so it was natural for him to suggest the idea to prison officials in 1963. Officials at the time were not so open with the idea, and threatened Plentychief "with a week in the 'hole' for suggesting such an outlandish idea." As time passed, officials warmed to the idea. Several other states, including South Dakota, Wyoming, Texas, and Louisiana, had held prison rodeos for quite some time, so it was not an unusual event by the 1970s. Finally, in 1973 Plentychild was granted permission to hold the rodeo in the penitentiary.

Two months before the rodeo was to be held, the North Dakota Prison Rodeo Association was incorporated to help pull the event together. The inmates made North Dakota Governor Arthur Link honorary chairman of the association, and Andrew Anderson honorary vice-chairman. Anderson, incarcerated since 1919, was the longest-serving inmate in the state's history at the time. Although the inmates were practicing for the event since October, the famed steer-wrestling champion Jack Chase held a rodeo clinic for participants a month before the rodeo to ensure that the men were prepared for the event. North Dakota rodeo legends J. C. Stevenson and Emerson Chase were in charge of bringing in livestock for the event. Stevenson succeeded in securing the bull Yellow Jacket, touted as the "meanest critter in North Dakota."

A rowdy crowd of one thousand spectators attended the first day of the rodeo. Despite the fact that the second day was rained out, the rodeo was considered a great success by both participants and officials.

Jayme L. Job

19 MAY

Finding the Shining Mountains

The first recorded visit of a non-native person in what is now North Dakota was by Pierre de la Verendrye when George Washington was just six years old. While working at a trading post north of Lake Superior, local native people told Verendrye about a westward flowing river that reached the Shining Mountains; and, beyond those mountains lay a great salty sea.

Verendrye went to the governor of New France, in the Quebec region, and asked for permission to find this river and to claim it for France. The governor granted permission and promised to reward Verendrye with a fur trading franchise if he succeeded; but, Verendrye would have to raise the money himself.

Verendrye convinced a number of Montreal merchants to give him supplies in exchange for furs he would send back. Then, in June 1731, his expedition of fifty men began paddling their canoes west. Verendrye took along three of his sons, Jean, Pierre and Francois, as well as his nephew.

Historian Erling Rolfsrud writes, "For seven grueling years Verendrye struggled slowly westward. Several times he or a part of his men had to return to Montreal to replenish supplies or to placate the Montreal merchants when furs sent them were not adequate to meet their demands. The men mutinied when they had to live on boiled roots and strips of moccasin leather. The nephew died. Indians killed the eldest son, Jean." Verendrye established small trading posts and supply depots along the way; the last was Ft. La Reine, which is now Portage la Prairie, Manitoba. There, the Assiniboine Indians told Verendrye there was a tribe to the south that knew how to find the Shining Mountains and the sea beyond. Even though winter was quickly approaching, Verendrye immediately set off to find this tribe.

Four weeks later, the expedition, along with about 600 Assiniboine, arrived at a stockaded village believed to have been somewhere near Minot. This earthlodge tribe is generally thought to have been Mandans; they gave the party a friendly reception and insisted on carrying Verendrye into their village. One chief was concerned about the cost of hosting the 600 Assiniboine, so he leaked a rumor that the Sioux were on their way to attack; the Assiniboine promptly left, along with Verendrye's bag of gifts and his Cree interpreter.

Verendrye and his men stayed with the tribe long enough to realize none of their hosts had been to the Shining Mountains or the sea beyond. Verendrye left two men with the tribe to learn their language and, despite being quite ill, headed back through deep snow and blizzards to Ft. La Reine, which they reached in February.

Verendrye's Montreal backers refused to advance him any more money, but his sons didn't give up the search. On this date in 1742, Francois and Louis de la Verendrye again visited the Mandans, who offered to guide them west to the "Horse" Indians. The young men made contact with a number of tribes and partially climbed what many think was a mountain in the Bighorns on January 12, 1743. They went far enough south to meet the Teton Sioux, and on March 30, they inscribed and buried a lead plate, which a group of children found near present-day Pierre in 1913. But the sea beyond the Shining Mountains wasn't to be theirs.

Merry Helm

Adapted from Erling Rolfsrud, *The Story of North Dakota*, Lantern Books, 1963.

20 MAY

Poker Alice

Among the more notorious women of western Dakota Territory was Alice Ivers, known as Poker Alice. Alice was born in 1853 and educated in England and then moved with her family to Colorado. There, she eventually married her first love, a mining engineer named Frank Duffield. It was Duffield who taught Alice how to play poker, a game at which she proved particularly lucky.

When Duffield was killed in a mining accident, the young widow turned to gambling to support herself. Her youthful beauty proved a great strength against the men she played, and soon she was known not only for her card-playing skills, but also for her charm, her fine wardrobe, and her New York spending sprees.

One of Alice's gambling adversaries was Warren G. Tubbs. Unlike Alice, Tubbs wasn't lucky. But he made a decent living as a house painter, and Alice married him. They raised seven kids, who Alice helped support with her card playing. She was so good she'd sometimes gloat and challenge all comers – of which there was no shortage. On a good night, she could make $6,000.

Although her husband's bad luck irritated her, Alice always defended Tubbs, sometimes with the .38 revolver she carried. At some point, the couple had settled in Deadwood, where Tubbs eventually succumbed to tuberculosis.

After Tubbs died, Alice moved around the Black Hills a bit. She eventually landed in Sturgis, where she married an admirer named George Huckert. Unfortunately, the marriage was brief, and for the third time, Alice was a widow.

By this point, the blush of her youthful beauty was gone, as was her stylish wardrobe. She adopted a costume of a khaki skirt, a man's shirt, and an old frayed hat. The allure of poker had stalled. She smoked cigars and became a bootlegger until prohibition brought that to a halt. Then, since Sturgis was near Fort Meade, she opened her own place, named Poker Alice, and catered to the earthly desires of soldiers.

On this date in 1913, the *Bismarck Daily Tribune* reported Alice shot and killed one of her customers. Pvt. Bennie Kotzell was dead from a bullet to his head, and another soldier, Pvt. Joseph Minor was in critical condition from a bullet to his left side.

"The trouble is alleged to have started between a member of Troop M and 'Poker Alice' about ten or eleven days ago," the *Tribune* reported. "It is said to have been renewed again the latter part of last week and again last night. Minor and Kortzell [sic] were standing a distance outside of the building when the electric wires were cut, and the resort left in darkness. Almost immediately a volley of stones and rocks were hurled at the house, breaking nearly every window. The rocks were replied to by several shots thought to have been fired by 'Poker Alice' herself.

"After the affair had quieted down," the story continued, "Sheriff Collins and States Attorney Gray arrived, placing 'Poker Alice' under arrest along with several women found in the house. A Winchester rifle was found just outside of the door of the building and a magazine from the gun was found lying on the woman's bed."

We're not sure what happened as a result of her arrest, but we do know Poker Alice remained on earth for another seventeen years. It was more likely her cigars finally brought her down. She died in 1930, ten days after her 77th birthday, and was laid to rest in St. Aloysius Cemetery in Sturgis.

Merry Helm

21 MAY

Buffalo Wolves

Rueben Humes was a young Dickinson sheepherder whose flocks were often threatened by predators like coyotes and bobcats. One day in 1900, Rueben went hunting for prairie chickens near the Heart River. His shotgun kept misfiring, but he finally shot a chicken, which dropped onto the opposite riverbank. As he forded the river to get it, he saw something.

"It looked like a big black sheep," he said. "It was gray and had a huge mane of hair. I was so surprised I just stopped and looked […] it was the largest wolf I had ever seen." Rueben fired, but his gun misfired, and the wolf took off. Back at camp, the men told Rueben he had seen a buffalo wolf, which is a sub-species of the gray wolf.

Lewis and Clark discovered the buffalo wolf, *canis lupus nubilus*, in 1804. Lewis wrote, "We scarely see a gang of buffaloe without observing a pack of those faithfull shepherds on their skirts in readiness to take care of the maimed wounded. The large wolf never barks, but howls as those of the atlantic states do."

At first, the Corps of Discovery had lumped the wild canines into two groups: coyotes were referred to as "prairie wolves," and gray wolves were called "large wolves." When they discovered the buffalo wolf subspecies, Lewis made detailed observations of how a pack would isolate an antelope from the herd so they could chase it down. He wrote they "are very numerous, they are of a light colr. & has long hair with Coarse fur."

By 1926, buffalo wolves were extinct, as were all wolf species within the state. Recent studies, however, indicate there may still be buffalo wolves in northern Minnesota, Wisconsin, and Upper Michigan. Wolves may also be re-colonizing some of their former habitat here in North Dakota.

Merry Helm

Johnsrud's Fossils

22 MAY

Today's story has its roots—so to speak—in the subtropics that covered most of North Dakota 60-million years ago. It was the Paleocene Epoch, during which time palm trees, redwood trees, sycamores, magnolia and bald cypress trees provided habitat for turtles, crocodiles, champsosaurs, alligators and many other exotic animals.

Fast-forward to modern-day North Dakota. For several years, a sugar beet farmer living near Williston had been escalating a hobby into a consuming passion. In 1981, the *Bismarck Tribune* reported, "[Sixty-five year old Clarence] Johnsrud had been a farmer all his life, but had since 1978 switched from working the land to working in the land. About 16 miles southwest of Williston, Johnsrud walked down the road to his neighbors' hill every morning and began digging. The neighbors, the Gibbins, claimed, 'This hill is Clarence's.' In three years, Johnsrud had found 34 varieties of fossilized plant life [including a] petrified redwood tree."

Six years after that story ran, a road construction crew was rebuilding a rural road running between Williston and Fort Buford on the old Lewis and Clark trail. As bulldozers dug into what's known as the Sentinel Butte Formation, they excavated a substantial deposit of hard, cream-colored mudstone. When fossils were discovered, someone contacted Johnsrud.

Johnsrud drove over to have a look and quickly convinced the road-construction supervisor to hold up and allow him to haul away the mudstone so it wouldn't get reburied beneath the new road in what would thereafter be known as the Trenton Hill fossil site.

For the next several days Johnsrud used a farm loader and truck to deposit several tons of rocks into his barn. Hand-splitting the rocks with a hammer and chisel, his efforts soon began yielding what would become some of the finest plant fossil specimens in the world.

Some thirteen years later, Johnsrud estimated he had cracked opened some twenty tons of stone, exposing several hundred exquisite fossils. Not one to keep his discoveries to himself, Johnsrud donated some of his pieces to UND, Williston State College and Minot State. He also donated several specimens to the Denver Museum of Natural History and the Florida Natural History Museum.

It was about this time in 2000 that Johnsrud donated the bulk of his collection to the North Dakota Geological Survey State Fossil Collection at the North Dakota Heritage Center. He and his family also included a gift of $200,000 to create a permanent exhibit for the fossils and to help renovate the Geological Survey's paleontology lab at the Center. The North Dakota Geological Survey thereafter named the modernized facility the Johnsrud Paleontology Laboratory.

Merry Helm

23 MAY

King of the Whiskerinos

On this date in 1922, the city of Sacramento, California opened the week-long "Days of '49" celebration with a "longest beard in the United States" competition. The title of "King of the Whiskerinos" went to Hans Langseth, of Barney, North Dakota, who won the contest easily with his seventeen-foot-long beard.

Hans was born in Norway in 1846, and settled in Kensett, Iowa after immigrating to the United States with his wife, Anne. In 1875, Hans shaved for the last time and started growing his famous beard. The couple had six children in Iowa, but after Anne passed away in the 1880s Hans and his family moved first to Glyndon, Minnesota, and then to Barney, North Dakota, where Hans lived for the rest of his life.

Hans had gained attention for his extensive beard well before his visit to Sacramento. He appeared in circus sideshows and even one movie, allowing people to see, and even feel with their own hands, that his beard wasn't fake. When not on display, Hans kept his beard wrapped up and tucked in a pocket or inside his shirt, to protect it from damage.

There were few challengers even approaching the length of Hans Langseth's beard in Sacramento in 1922. The lengthy beard of Zachary Wilcox of Carson City, Nevada was the closest threat. Wilcox's beard came in at an official length of fourteen feet, as measured by the "Chief Whiskerino of the Golden West," who officiated the event. As runner-up, Wilcox was dubbed "Crown Prince of the Whiskerinos," and Hans Langseth, their King, was awarded an engraved gold medal from the Governor of California.

Hans returned to North Dakota a champion, and no person has ever grown a longer beard since. On his death in 1927, a portion of his beard was sent to the Smithsonian Museum, where it remains in their collection today. At the time of his death, the beard of Hans Langseth was over eighteen feet, six inches long. The portion in the Smithsonian's collection measures only seventeen feet, six inches. The Langseth family left one foot of record-setting beard on his chin, because it wouldn't be right to send Hans Langseth to his grave clean-shaven.

Derek Dahlsad

McLeod's One-Room School House

24 MAY

In 1986, *People* magazine ran a story titled, "Lowest Paid Teacher in America." Janice Herbranson taught kindergarten through sixth grade at the one-room school in McLeod, North Dakota. Her salary was only $6,800 a year.

At the time, there were fourteen one-room schoolhouses still operating in the state, and McLeod's was closing its doors. Of the three students still attending, two would be moving on to 7th grade, and there was no way to keep the school running for the remaining child.

The *People* story was ten pages long. It was the first time the magazine's lead story was told only through photographs and captions. Photographer Barry Staver considered the assignment one of his most personally rewarding. He recalled visiting the classroom in February – it was 18 below when the kids went outside for recess.

In addition to teaching, Herbranson also prepared two hot meals a day. Arriving early, she cooked a hot breakfast, and throughout the morning, she would periodically check the lunch simmering on the stove. After school was out for the day, she also cleaned, swept and had often worked on paperwork for grants to keep the school open. The only thing that allowed her to work at such a low salary was her income from co-owning of the Sand Dune Saloon in McLeod.

On this date in 1986, the school let out for the last time. In an article for the *Fargo Forum*, Kevin Murphy wrote, "As each student left Friday, clutching paper bags to protect just-made scrapbooks from a light spring rain, Herbranson handed them their report cards and an ice cream bar."

Herbranson was quoted in the paper saying, "In a way, it was a blessing to have the media here. If we were all alone, we'd have to dwell on this being the last day. This is a day the kids will remember. I don't want them to remember it with tears." Two preschoolers who attended the school two afternoons a week joined the three students for a picture in front of their desks.

Herbranson took college courses the following year, then spent a year teaching kindergarten in Texas. In 1988, the McLeod school board elected to reopen the school and gave Herbranson a call. She came back to McLeod to pick up where she left off – and yes, she did get a raise. But in 2002, the school closed again, this time for good. The Ransom County Historical Society now owns the building.

Merry Helm

25 MAY

Memorial Day in Jamestown

Originally, Memorial Day was known as Decoration Day, a day that the graves of those who died on the battlefields of the War of the Rebellion were decorated with flowers. In 1882, in Jamestown, there were no soldiers' graves to decorate. Dakota Territory was far away from the bloodied battlefields where thousands of Union and Confederate soldiers lost their lives. Although the tide of land seekers to the new territory had included many soldiers, the war had ended only seventeen years earlier. Most veterans living in Dakota Territory were still in the prime of their lives. So, on this date in 1882, the members of the Methodist Church in Jamestown met on the church lawn to plant trees, not only to commemorate this national day of remembrance, but to add beauty to the landscape.

In 1887, only five years later, the graves of four Civil War veterans at Hillside Cemetery were garnished with wreaths, and over forty members of the Grand Army of the Republic marched in the Memorial Day parade. Over each successive year, time claimed more veterans, and by the turn of the century the ranks had thinned significantly. In January of 1897, the GAR requested that Congress change the name of the day to Memorial Day to honor all fallen soldiers. Within a year, the Spanish American War and the Philippine Insurrection would claim many more lives, including soldiers from North Dakota.

On Memorial Day in 1903, the ranks of the Civil War veterans in Jamestown were joined by the North Dakota boys returning from the Philippines who were honoring their war dead from Company H of the First North Dakota Militia. F. G. Kneeland, a Jamestown attorney, addressed the gathered crowd at the services, stating: "May the American citizens guard well their precious heritage, transmitting it unimpaired to future generations. On Memorial Day, especially, may they recall the lessons and achievements of the past. And may they resolve that this shall continue to be a land of the free [...] where men shall be equal before the law; and that the American flag shall ever be as it was [...] saved by the men who fought beneath its folds—beautiful and glorious, with every stripe untarnished and every star undimmed."

During Memorial Day we need to remember that the past was secured with the lives of our soldiers, but the responsibility for the present and the future rests with us.

Jim Davis

Bison Latifrons

26 MAY

On this date in 1998, North Dakota paleontologist John Hoganson received a telephone call from Kent Pelton, a teacher in Watford City. While fishing on Lake Sakakawea near New Town, Pelton had discovered what he thought were two mammoth tusks. Hoganson was excited, because very few remains of mammoths have ever been discovered here.

A few days later, Hoganson traveled to Watford City to take a look. After a few minutes, he realized the long curved pieces weren't tusks; they were horn cores of a giant extinct ice age mammal called Bison latifrons.

Hoganson says this was an even more exciting and scientifically important discovery than mammoth remains. Only one other specimen of this type of bison had been found in N.D. – a horn core discovered in 1918.

Hoganson, Pelton, and several others immediately went by boat to the site where the bones were found. There, Hoganson located several more pieces of the skull and some other fragments.

The remains were on land administered by the U.S. Army Corps of Engineers within the borders of the Fort Berthold Reservation. After several months of discussion, it was decided the Corps of Engineers would provide the funding to restore the bison skull for exhibit at the State Heritage Center in Bismarck. They also agreed to make several cast replicas for other exhibits.

Tests revealed that Pelton's specimen was more than 47,500 years old. The animal was about 25-50% larger than modern-day bison, and its horns were dramatically different. Whereas today's bison has a horn-span of about two feet, the latifrons – or "longhorn" – has a span of up to seven feet.

Hoganson says the longhorn bison lived a bit differently than today's bison. It appears it wasn't as social. Rather than traveling in herds, the latifrons' habits more closely resembled those of the modern-day moose, travelling alone or in small groups. Most paleontologists also believe longhorn bison were browser-grazers living in woodlands or in forest openings, rather than on open grasslands.

The first ice age mammal discovered in the state was a mammoth found on a ridge that once existed as the beach of Lake Agassiz. A geologist named Warren Upham discovered it in Cass County in 1895 while mapping Agassiz's former boundaries. While discoveries of ice age mammals have been relatively scarce in North Dakota, paleontologists have found remains of staghorn moose, mastodons, horses, and the giant ground sloth, like the one in the movie *Ice Age*.

Merry Helm

27 MAY

The Free Air of Dakota

The issue of slavery and its expansion into new territories erupted as the great political debate of the mid-nineteenth century, eventually leading to secession and civil war. Slaveholders insisted any ban on slavery in the western territories was a discrimination against their peculiar form of property; it would undercut their economic and social stability as well as their national political dominance. Free state residents generally sought to halt the advance of slavery; some for moral reasons, others as a threat to free labor. Thus any region seeking territorial status and eventually statehood during these turbulent years became embroiled in this bitter debate.

Although a large slave population in the present-day region of North Dakota was unlikely to develop, the area nonetheless found itself at the very center of this controversy. Despite growing pressure from settlers and land companies, Congress moved slowly, still reeling from the violence that erupted after the creation of Kansas Territory. Thus a number of efforts to establish Dakota Territory were derailed as Southern Democrats objected to the entry of a territory explicitly excluding slavery. But in January of 1861, opposition receded as one Southern state after another left the Union. Congress immediately took advantage of the South's absence and established the territories of Dakota, Nevada and Colorado. Congress assumed Dakota would remain a free territory, and with good reason, but it was ultimately left up to territorial citizens to define their free status.

The battle-cry was taken up by Dakota's first territorial governor, Dr. William Jayne. A close friend of Abraham Lincoln and a staunch abolitionist, he was inaugurated on this date in 1861. In his first annual address to the Dakota Territorial Legislature, Governor Jayne insisted the legislators pass a law forever forbidding slavery within its borders. "I hope," he said, "that the free air of Dakota may never be polluted or the fair, virgin soil pressed by the footprints of a slave." He called for the legislators to take a stand against slavery by unanimously passing a territorial law banning the practice.

Unfortunately, the territorial legislators were too wrapped up in the controversy surrounding the location of the first territorial capitol to give much attention to the issue of slavery. Governor Jayne's plea went unheeded, but by 1865 it no longer mattered as the thirteenth amendment to the U.S. Constitution formally abolished slavery within the United States.

Christina Sunwall

Red Scare

28 MAY

Charges of Communist activity at North Dakota Agricultural College in Fargo surfaced in the spring of 1935. In an address to the Fargo Kiwanis Club, attorney Eli Weston accused groups at the school of demonstrating "all the earmarks and resemblances of communism." He said a recent local strike was controlled by communists, and faculty members had advised and supported the strikers. Weston said communism was being spread by faculty and students at North Dakota schools.

The faculty of the college pointed out that there were very few true Communists in the United States, and most of them were in New York City. That left a small number for the rest of the country, and certainly not very many for North Dakota. The faculty countered the accusations by saying that their accusers were motivated by fear of open discussions and criticism of the old order on college campuses. One staff member said he called Weston and asked for a definition of communism, but did not get one.

In May, E.D. Lum, publisher of the *Richland County Farmer-Globe* in Wahpeton, repeated Weston's accusations at a meeting of the Sons of the American Revolution. He said that fully half the faculty of the Iowa State Agricultural College were Communists. He said conditions at the North Dakota Agricultural College were very similar, calling the school a "hotbed of communist activity." Lum's newspaper was joined by others across the state demanding a full investigation.

John Shepperd, president of the school, refuted the accusations. He called Lum's announcement "irresponsible." John West, president of UND, agreed. West said that there were absolutely no facts to bolster accusations of communism at either North Dakota school.

On this date in 1935, it was announced that the North Dakota Board of Administration had opened an official investigation into the rumors of communism at state schools. This was in response to the outcry of newspaper editorials. None of the accusations were confirmed.

The country was distracted from the issue a few years later by World War II, but the accusations of communist activity at the Ag College and the University arose again during the Red Scare of the 1950s. Once again, none of the accusations were confirmed.

Carole Butcher

29 MAY

Blowed Away

North Dakotans are familiar with the danger posed by tornados. The state ranks nineteenth in the number of tornados and twenty-sixth in the number of deaths. June and July are the primary months for tornadoes. The earliest in North Dakota was March 26, 2006 and the latest was November 1, 2000.

On this date in 1953, an F5 tornado struck Fort Rice. It hit at eight o'clock p.m. with little warning, and people had very little time to take shelter. A road construction crew took cover in one of their trailers, but they said it just blew up. They were lucky to suffer only minor injuries. A farmer hid in his creamery, but was sucked out of it and felt lucky to be alive. An elderly couple went out on their porch to look at the strange clouds. The tornado hit almost instantly. The man was badly injured, and his wife was one of the two fatalities.

One resident described the town as being "blowed away." In addition to the two deaths, twenty people were injured. Almost every building in Fort Rice was flattened, including the Catholic Church, grain elevators and the school. The owner of the mercantile had to run his business out of a basement until he could rebuild.

Rescue efforts were complicated by the lateness of the hour, with workers combing the wreckage in the dark. Heavy rain turned dirt roads to mud, and it was hard for emergency personnel to reach the scene. Shortly after the storm, residents flagged down a Northern Pacific passenger train. The train transported the injured to Mandan and Bismarck hospitals.

The Fort Rice tornado was 600 yards wide and was on the ground for over 14 miles. It was estimated to be an F5, the strongest category. The only other F5 to hit North Dakota was the deadly tornado that struck Fargo in 1957.

Today the Weather Service uses radar and trained spotters to give as much warning as possible for severe weather. With sirens, radios, a 24-hour weather channel, and telephone apps, a tornado is much less likely to take people by surprise.

Carole Butcher

Peculiar Train Accident

30 MAY

A "peculiar accident" was reported by the *Fargo Forum* on this day in 1902. The incident occurred two days before near Glasgow, Montana, and concerned the Chamberlain family of Forest River, North Dakota. The family was returning home by train from their annual winter stay in Seattle, Washington when the irregular event occurred.

According to Mr. and Mrs. Chamberlain, the family was sitting down to lunch in their train car when Mrs. Chamberlain gave her oldest son an empty glass bottle to toss out of the car's open window. This was obviously a time before litter laws were in place, as throwing trash from train cars was a common practice of the day. Anyhow, the five-year old boy took the bottle from his mother and proceeded to the opposite side of the car to toss it out. The boy threw the bottle with all his might from the car, and then, in his excitement, leaned over the edge of the window's sill to get a good look at the bottle's landing. As he peered after the bottle, the boy lost his balance and fell completely out of the open window. The Chamberlains rushed to the window to see what had become of their son and saw that he had hit the ground a ways back and had rolled to the edge of the ditch alongside the locomotive's tracks.

Mrs. Chamberlain sounded the car's alarm and brought the steam engine to a halt. The worried parents ran to inform the conductor, who immediately reversed the train an eighth of a mile to where the boy lay. Miraculously, the family found the boy conscious and, despite some minor cuts and bruises, relatively unharmed. Mr. and Mrs. Chamberlain had their son looked after by a doctor upon their arrival in Grand Forks. The doctor believed that the boy had suffered a concussion in the fall, but could find no physical maladies besides a small cut on the boy's knee. The train had been moving at full speed when the boy fell from the car, but the small five-year old had managed to walk away from the incident relatively unscathed. The *Fargo Forum* added that the same accident would normally prove fatal to any adult, little less a small boy.

Jayme L. Job

31 MAY

Fort Lincoln Internment Camp

Ft. Lincoln was built south of Bismarck around 1898 and is now owned by the United Tribes Technical College. It served various military purposes until 1941, when the U.S. Justice Department turned it into an Internment Camp for people the government deemed enemy aliens.

The fort's new purpose came as a shock when it was announced in April 1941, that it and several other military posts would be housing foreign seamen who were taken from their ships and detained as belligerents in World War II – even though the U.S. was still neutral at this point.

Historian Frank Vyzralek states, "Despite protests, a detachment of Border Patrol officers and immigrant inspectors arrived in Bismarck to begin preparing the proposed detention camp. They did most of the work themselves, the local WPA administrator proving to be totally hostile to the establishment of a detention camp."

The detainment camp was designed to house 2,000 people. Twenty wood-frame buildings were purchased and shipped up from Alabama; each could house forty-two people, but none had insulation. Cots, mattresses and bedding came from federal agencies.

Ten-foot high cyclone fence topped with barbed wire was used to enclose an area measuring 500 feet by 1300 feet. To discourage tunneling, 3 foot long steel rods were driven into the ground every six inches under the fence. Seven steel guard towers with weapons and flood lights ringed the fenced enclosure, and a control center was equipped with gas bombs, Remington automatic rifles, gas masks, 12-gauge riot guns, gas guns, four machine guns, and gas billies. Three German shepherds and three saddle horses were kept on the hand for chasing escapees.

The first prisoners were to be Italian seamen. Despite the high population of local Germans and German Russians, many thought Italians would be preferable to German prisoners, because the news portrayed Hitler's men as nastier and more violent. But the train cars loaded with Italians didn't stop – they continued west to Fort Missoula. On May 28, the *Bismarck Tribune* announced the camp's first prisoners would instead be Germans.

On this day in 1941, 220 German seamen got off the train at Bismarck's Northern Pacific depot at about 7 p.m. that evening. When they arrived at the detention camp, the fence enclosure wasn't finished, and INS inspectors had to guard the opening throughout the night.

The Border Patrolmen were pleased at how smoothly everybody settled in, but it wasn't to last. Two weeks later, a ship's young third officer, 23-year old Johann Marquenie, used a broken shovel to dig his way under the fence at a point where it crossed a shallow ditch. He disappeared across the Missouri River bottom lands, stole a boat and headed south. The next day, the patrolmen acted on a tip and tracked him to the Huff neighborhood, where they found him resting in some brush. Marquenie said he simply wanted to be "out alone."

Soon, thirty-seven more seamen arrived, and the camp's population was about 280 until December when Pearl Harbor plunged the U.S. into WWII. Over the next five years, the camp's population expanded to 3,600, most of whom were U.S. citizens of Japanese and German descent.

Merry Helm

John Frederick of Grant County, North Dakota, shows how high his wheat would grow if there were no drought
Credit: Arthur Rothstein, Farm Security Administration - Office of War Information Photograph Collection (Library of Congress), 1936.

JUNE

Blue Laws

01 JUN

Blue laws are state or local laws that prohibit commercial activity on Sundays. It is difficult to trace the origin of the term. In his 1781 book *A General History of Connecticut*, the Reverend Samuel Peters described what he called "blue laws." Peters stated that early decrees restricting Sunday sales were called "blue laws" by the colonists, but he did not explain why. Some people thought the name originated because the laws were printed on blue paper, but there is no evidence to back up that claim. In fact, there is no evidence of the term being used prior to Peters' book, and it is possible he made it up himself. However the name came about, the regulations are still called blue laws today.

On this date in 1914, the *Fargo Forum and Daily Republican* reported a controversy in Hankinson relating to blue laws. The previous week, a Hankinson merchant was tried for failing to observe the Sunday closing laws. The jury returned a verdict of not guilty. Merchants who liked the blue laws decided to make a point. On Sunday, May 31 virtually every business in Hankinson was closed. It was usual for bars and liquor stores to be closed on Sundays. But even the ice cream parlor and candy store were closed. Drivers were unable to buy gas for their cars. Housewives who had put off shopping on Saturday were surprised to find they could not purchase groceries on Sunday. It was unclear if the merchants intended to close again the following Sunday.

North Dakota instituted blue laws upon statehood. They were loosened slightly in 1966, after a blizzard on a Saturday left people needing goods and services on Sunday. In 1981, state legislator Charles Reiten referred to a proposal to repeal blue laws as "the final nail in the coffin of rural North Dakota." He said if stores were open on Sunday, people would leave rural areas and move to cities. While the effort failed that year, the laws were loosened in 1991, but there are still some restrictions. Most stores can't do business before noon, and some businesses, including car dealerships, are not allowed to open on Sundays at all. In 2013, the House of Representatives voted down two attempts to relax the state's blue laws even more.

As of 2019, North Dakota is the only state with the ban. In January 2019, the N.D. House approved a measure to repeal the Sunday closing law. The measure will now go to the State Senate.

Carole Butcher

02 JUN

First American Mosque

A few miles west of Stanley, North Dakota, is Ross, which technically existed as a town site as far back as 1887. It was really just a Great Northern stopping point back then, consisting of a siding and a water tank. Then, around the turn of the century, development began, and on this date in 1902, a post office was established.

Ross has a couple claims to fame; it was the hometown of Ruth Olson Meiers, who was the state's first female Lieutenant Governor. Historians state the Ross community also had the oldest known Muslim group for organized prayer in America.

The primary ethnic group in that area came from Syria, starting with a pioneer named Hassen Juma, who settled on 160 acres in 1899. Nearby was Sam Omar, and by 1902, twenty other families had followed their path from Bire (Berrie) and Rafid, Syria.

These families ran into problems, because the U.S. objected to their naturalization, but in 1909, the government withdrew the ban, and Syrians were able to apply for citizenship. As the Ottoman Empire blurred territorial boundaries in the Middle East, Arab settlers were variously called Turks, Syrians or Lebanese, depending on what country presently claimed their homeland. While as many as 90% of the Syrians who emigrated to this country were Christians, the group at Ross were Islamic; their North Dakota neighbors called them Muhammadans.

To give a little background, Muslims believe in a chain of prophets starting with Adam and leading up through Noah, Abraham, Ishmael, Issac, Jacob, Joseph, Job, Moses, Aaron, David, Solomon, Elias, Jonah, John the Baptist, and Jesus. Muslims diverge from Christians at this point, believing God reconfirmed his message through one more prophet – Muhammad – who began receiving revelations from the angel Gabriel in the (Christian) year 610.

The Muslims in Ross prayed five times a day and gathered in each other's homes for Jumah – a prayer service held on Fridays. The leaders for these meetings were educated laymen, as there was no imam – or Muslim prayer leader – in the community.

In 1929, the residents built a Jumah mosque which is said to be the Nation's first. Accounts differ, but it's generally agreed that other Muslims around the country organized their mosques in rented spaces. The mosque at Ross is said to be the first built specifically as a house of worship.

The building itself was not an attractive one. It was long and low, sunk into the ground. There's a reason for this; it was intended to be the basement of a structure yet to come. Unfortunately, the depression hit soon after it was built, and the transformation never happened. The building was used as late as the 1960s – by then, intermarriage had led many to join Christian churches.

In 1983, author Francie Berg wrote: "The potential significance (of the building) went unknown for many years. However, a few years ago, the North Dakota Historical Society began some research into the mosque, intending to submit it for inclusion on the National Register of Historic Places, in order to preserve it. Researchers soon were disappointed to find out the building had been torn down a year or two earlier."

While the mosque is gone, the Arabic cemetery remains. You can spot it by its arched gate adorned with a crescent and star.

Merry Helm

03 JUN

Teddy Bear Craze

Who could ever resist loving Teddy Bears? We commemorate Teddy Bears, because on this date in 1911, a newspaper story in the *Grand Forks Herald* made mention of a piano recital where a student named Mildred Johnson played a song entitled "March of the Teddy Bears," a tribute to the lovable, fuzzy, furry stuffed toys.

Teddy Bears were the stuff of legend, arising from the legendary president, Theodore Roosevelt. The story went like this – while President Theodore Roosevelt was bear hunting in the state of Mississippi in 1902, his hunting guides tracked a black bear, surrounded it by dogs, rendered the bear unconscious, and tied the old bear to a tree, waiting for Roosevelt to arrive and shoot it.

When the President came upon the scene, he refused to shoot the old mother bear, believing it was unsportsmanlike and unmanly. Instead, he asked a hunting guide to put the bear out of its misery.

Word spread nationally through newspaper stories that the President had compassion for the bear. A political cartoonist named Clifford Berryman drew up a cartoon featuring Teddy Roosevelt and the bear in the *Washington Post*, with Roosevelt refusing to shoot it, showing a kinder and gentler side of the manly, big-game hunter who aspired to "speak softly, but carry a big stick." As the bear was re-drawn several times, the old mother bear became smaller and cuter, finally appearing as a bear cub.

The story of Roosevelt's bear hunting episode inspired businessman Morris Michtom, and his wife Rose, to manufacture stuffed bear toys in honor of the President who refused to shoot a bear. They called it "Teddy's Bear." After obtaining Roosevelt's permission to use the nickname, Michtom made thousands of the toy bears in 1903. Word of the Teddy Bears spread throughout the land and little children began to hug them and adore them in an effervescent flow of love that flooded the nation. It became known as the "Teddy Bear craze," and it took several years for the phenomenon to get to the Upper Midwest.

According to the *Grand Forks Herald*, Teddy Bears arrived in the region in 1906 and over the following year, stores could barely keep ahead of the demand. Almost every child wanted one. By 1907, the "Teddy Bear fad" began to fade, and critics lauded its apparent demise, but Teddy Bears never went away, as stores continually promoted the universal fascination Teddy Bears held over infants who were amused and quieted by the fuzzy toys. "Nothing will please the children like a Teddy Bear," advised a storeowner.

Even though the Teddy Bear craze subsided, the little bears, having been fully loved, can often be found in old toy boxes, tattered and with the fur worn nearly off, with button eyes fully satisfied, as a testimony of having been simply irresistible.

Dr. Steve Hoffbeck

The Interstate

04 JUN

The U.S. Interstate Highway System is the biggest civil-engineering project in world history – 46,876 miles in length. It was funded with gasoline taxes and cost about $129 billion dollars. Construction began in the late 1950s and continued through 1977. The system linked Americans from coast-to-coast and cut the cost of shipping goods. North Dakotans have zipped along its two interstate highways daily for over fifty years.

Every state is supposed to have an east-west interstate and a north-south interstate. In North Dakota, it's Interstate 94 from Fargo to the Montana line, and Interstate 29 from Pembina to South Dakota.

The design requirements were simple – being able to handle speeds of 50 to 70 miles per hour; a minimum of two lanes in each direction; 12-foot-wide lanes with a 10-foot-wide right paved shoulder, and 4-foot-wide left paved shoulder. The key element, however, was requiring these highways to be limited-access roads. With few entrance and exit points, they proved far safer than highways with intersections and rail crossings.

The arrival of interstate highways brought major changes. North Dakotans became increasingly dependent upon their cars, pickup trucks and semi-truck trailers, which led to a decline in railway passenger traffic. The quick transportation helped give rise to shopping malls and suburbs.

These changes came especially to Fargo, where I-94 and I-29 cross. Bypassing the central business district caused downtown Fargo to lose business. The West Acres shopping area, which is near the intersection, gained prominence. And West Fargo grew as a sort-of-suburb along the I-94 corridor.

It was in this week in 1967 that the *Grand Forks Herald* noted that I-94 had become the "heaviest traveled of N.D. roads," with the "stretch of Interstate 94 which links Bismarck and Fargo" rated as the state's busiest highway.

As the Fargo-Moorhead metro area has grown in the past twenty years, to nearly 240 thousand people, Interstate 94's traffic has proliferated. Both I-94 and I-29 now have three lanes in each direction.

Who knows? As Fargo expands maybe terms like "gridlock" and "traffic jams" and four-lanes in both directions may happen – someday.

Dr. Steve Hoffbeck

05 JUN

Draft Registration Day

It was a critical day for many young men on this date in 1917. America had entered World War I, but it was lacking the manpower to sustain the type of warfare that had evolved in the trenches of Europe. While many believed America's entrance into the conflict would bring a quick end to the war, the current military strength was not enough. With the enlistment rate inadequate, a draft was initiated.

Each state had a quota based upon population, and North Dakota was expected to register 77,000 men. June 5 was registration day for all men 21 to 30 years of age. There was only one day set aside for registration, and anyone who failed to register would be imprisoned. Those who attempted to falsify answers on the registration form faced a more severe penalty, being sent to a prison camp for training before assignment to the front lines. With Canada already in the war, draft evaders who fled across the border to avoid registration found little sympathy and were quickly arrested and placed in detention camps.

But on this day, patriotism ran high. At 7:00 a.m. church bells chimed, factory whistles blew and sirens sounded as draft registration got underway. Fargo registered over 1,500 men by mid-afternoon with a final registration of 2,100. Khaki armbands were provided for the 800 registrants in Bismarck who then led a parade when registration ended at 9:00 p.m. In Langdon an impromptu patriotic celebration ensued when the marching bands from Milton and Munich joined with a local band. Registrants, Red Cross workers, school children, war veterans, and Highland dancers marched in a parade to the opera house for patriotic speeches.

For some communities in North Dakota, draft registration was a mere formality. In Mott almost every man had already signed up for military service – so much so that the town was forced to abandon its baseball team.

All across the state registration went smoothly. Citizens and noncitizens alike registered. Single and married men of all nationalities and races, and from all occupations, filled out the forms. Even those with physical disabilities were required to register. Exemptions would be determined later.

Nationally, ten million men were registered on that day. So significant was the number that it led the War Department to issue a statement that read in part, "The manhood of the nation volunteered in mass […] it remains but to select the men who are to go to the front."

Jim Davis

Julian Eltinge

06 JUN

Around this date in 1918, the Bismarck Theater featured a performer "hailed by women as the most beautiful example of their sex." However, Julian Eltinge was not a woman, but a "female impersonator," and one of the most celebrated and highest paid performers in the United States.

Eltinge was born William Dalton in Massachusetts in 1881. As a boy, he showed an affinity for performance, and was fond of dressing up in ladies' clothing. Dalton's affinity was encouraged by his mother, but prohibited by his father. In the 1890s, the Dalton family moved to Butte, Montana, a booming mining town where several saloons and vaudeville houses sprang up. As a teenager, Dalton performed as a dancer in the saloons, dressed as a woman. This practice was not uncommon in the rough railroad and mining towns, due to the fact that the incoming population was predominately male, and a "respectable" young woman would not have been found near a saloon.

Dalton's employment in the saloons was short-lived. When his father found out, Dalton was swiftly sent back to Boston to work as a store clerk. Yet his love of theater persisted. He studied dance and became active in amateur theater. It was during this time that the female alter ego of "Julian Eltinge" was born. In 1904, he made his New York Broadway debut in *Mr. Wix of Wickham*, which rocketed him to worldwide acclaim.

By 1912, Eltinge, a.k.a. Billy Dalton, was not only a Broadway headliner; a theater was named in his honor—The Eltinge 42nd Street Theater in Manhattan. However, a lesser-known theater was also named in his honor… in Bismarck, North Dakota!

In 1919, E. A. Hughes announced that his newly planned vaudeville and movie house would be named The Eltinge. According to the *Grand Forks Herald*, "the fair Julian" was "an old friend of the Hughes family." Apart from the social ties, the air of glamour that accompanied Eltinge's name likely figured into Hughes' business decision. In 1920, The Eltinge Theater opened on 3rd Street in Bismarck.

Eltinge's career straddled the era of vaudeville and motion pictures. Throughout the 1920s he starred in several films, while still performing in vaudeville tours. However, by the late 1930s, cultural tastes changed, and the trend of female impersonation was no longer regarded as light-hearted entertainment. Some cities even enacted laws against drag performances. Eltinge's career declined, and 1941 he passed away after a performance in Manhattan.

The old theater building in Bismarck went through a couple of name changes and was eventually demolished. However, Eltinge's legacy lives on in the preserved cinema productions. As for the original Eltinge Theater in Manhattan, it's now a movie theater.

Maria Witham

07 JUN

A New Fargo

On this date in 1893, the growing development of Fargo was struck by a terrible fire. It started on what was then Front Street – now called Main Avenue. Strong winds spread the fire, burning away most of the downtown area. Forty-two city blocks were destroyed, an estimated $3 million in damage. However, the people of Fargo did not let this disaster bring them down, and within the next year, they had already constructed 246 new buildings, thereby revitalizing the area.

In 1913, Fargo observed the twentieth anniversary of the fire with a mammoth parade featuring floats, trade displays, civic organizations and military groups. The anniversary coincided with a big Masonic homecoming week and Shrine Jubilee, which the *Weekly Times-Record* out of Valley City called "the greatest Masonic Event in recent years." It enticed many former Fargoans who had been involved with the Masonic Temple to make a return visit. As the *Times-Record* reported, "the first week in June will be a memorable one, not only to the Masonic fraternity, but the citizens of Fargo as every effort possible will be urged to bring back 'ye old timers.'" The week-long Masonic celebration ended with a large parade of its own [...] one of three huge parades within two days. And many of those visiting Masons stayed to observe the fire festival anniversary. Notable participants in that parade were the surviving members of four early-day volunteer firemen's organizations. Some were noted as being in their seventies.

The *Bismarck Tribune* reported of the festival, "Unlike most other cities, Fargoans do not regard the fire of a score of years ago today as having been a calamity. In fact, they view it rather as a blessing in disguise as it marked the birth of a new Fargo."

And the parades received nationwide attention, thanks to film companies that recorded the events. That footage was shown throughout the United States.

Sarah Walker

The Antiquities Act

08 JUN

In the early 1900s, there was a growing concern about protecting prehistoric Indian ruins and artifacts. These were primarily located in the west. Private collectors were removing artifacts at an alarming rate. John F. Lacey, Iowa Congressman and chair of the House Committee on Public Lands, traveled to the southwest in 1902 to see the situation for himself. He came to the conclusion that these valuable cultural resources needed immediate protection.

On this date in 1906, President Theodore Roosevelt signed the Antiquities Act into law. On September 24th of that year, Roosevelt named Devil's Tower in Wyoming as the first National Monument. He went on to designate seventeen more National Monuments, including the Grand Canyon.

The Antiquities Act gives the President the sole authority to designate public lands as "National Monuments" and to set them aside as protected areas. National Monuments are different from National Parks because the parks require Congressional approval. The Act also requires a Federal Antiquities Permit for any excavation at a National Monument.

The Verendrye National Monument was established at Crow Flies High Butte in North Dakota in 1917. It commemorated the Verendrye expedition that explored the northern Great Plains. It was located on the site used as an observation point by the sons of Verendrye during their exploration of the area. However, it was later determined that the site was not accurate. It was withdrawn as a National Monument in 1956 and the land was transferred to the State. Ironically, new research indicates that the site may indeed be where the explorers viewed the Missouri River in 1742. North Dakota does not currently have any National Monuments.

The Antiquities Act is not without controversy. Some feel it gives the President too much authority. These critics say current use of the Act goes beyond the original intent. Designating land as a National Monument takes it out of the hands of citizens. Those opposed to the Act say that it should be a matter for Congress, not for the President alone. Contemporary Presidents still designate National Monuments. George W. Bush named five and President Obama named three. Halfway through his first term, Donald J. Trump has named only one, and his cabinet has dismissed such monuments' significance for tourism and archaeology.

Carole Butcher

09 JUN

Northrup's Steamboat

On this date in 1859, Anson Northrup's steamboat arrived at Fort Garry, in present-day Manitoba, and residents celebrated with both thanksgiving and gunpowder. It was the first time a boat had successfully navigated the Red River, and commerce there would be changed forever.

In his book, *The Challenge of the Prairie*, Erling Rolfsrud writes, "No real progress could be forecast for a region as remote as the Red River Valley until some form of transportation was perfected."

Beginning with the Panic of 1857, St. Paul businesses were suffering from an economic depression. The Red River carts that transported goods between them and the Hudson Bay Company were very slow, and the businessmen dreamed of finding a way to move their wares by water instead.

In late 1858, the St. Paul Chamber of Commerce offered $1000 to the first person who launched a steamboat on the "Ruby Red" by the following spring. Anson Northrup, who had a steamboat on the Mississippi River, agreed to try for the prize, but only if it was increased to $2000. He set out to navigate west on the Crow Wing River.

By late February, they could sail no further; they had to dismantle the boat in order to move it overland the next 150 miles. Northrup had his men load the boat's machinery, cabin and lumber onto sleighs. Historian Elwyn Robinson states that Northrup used thirty-two teams of oxen and sixty men, while historian Erling Rolfsrud states that he used thirteen yoke of oxen, seventeen teams of horses, and had only thirty-one men. Either way, the party headed due west without a guide.

On March 5, one of Fargo-Moorhead's earliest citizens, R.M. Probstfield, found part of the Northrup expedition floundering in the snow near what is now Detroit Lakes. He later wrote, "Another part of the expedition had gone ahead to build a bridge across the Otter Tail River at one of the upper crossings, as the river was not frozen over. The snow was deep, some sixteen or eighteen inches. The bridge was built for the boiler and other heavy machinery."

By the 1st of April, the Northrup crew arrived at the Red River, across from where the Sheyenne joins it north of Fargo. The men spent six weeks reassembling the boat and cutting oak trees for planking a new hull. Before launching it, they re-christened it the "Anson Northrup."

On June 5, the journey north finally began. The spring thaw had raised the Red River's water level, and the voyage to Ft. Garry took only four days. Three days later, Northrup headed back south to Fort Abercrombie with twenty passengers aboard. Then, leaving his boat behind, he hurried back to St. Paul to claim his prize. Soon after, he sold the Northrup for $8,000, and the new owners again sent it north. By then, however, the water level had dropped, and the crew had to tie up for the winter at Indian River, short of their Fort Garry destination.

Merry Helm

Fatal Car Bombing

10 JUN

This date in 1939 was not a typical day in Fargo-Moorhead. The Crown Prince and Princess of Norway were winding up a three day visit to the area, when early that morning they heard an explosion from the east side of the river.

It was 6 a.m., and 28 year-old J. Milton Lee was on his way to work at his father's Moorhead business, the Northwest Bakery. A graduate of Fargo's Agricultural College, Lee had just returned from bakery school in Chicago. He would not make it to work that day, nor any other.

Papers reported, "So terrific was the blast that. . .the hood was blown through the roof of the garage, the radiator and fenders were torn loose, [and] part of the motor was blown into the body of the car." Investigators later determined sticks of dynamite were rigged to the car's ignition.

Milton's father, John Lee, told authorities that members of the local bakers' union had been trying to get him to join. Recently, he had told an anonymous caller he'd been treated unfairly and wasn't interested in joining. The caller replied, "Then I'm serving notice on you right now that we'll get you."

Roland Tougas, the president of the local bakers' union, was arrested without charge. He admitted he had notified John Lee that his bakery was going to be added to the list of unfair bakeries, but he denied any knowledge of the car bombing plot.

Meanwhile, investigators found, in the wreckage, a tattered piece of filing card on which was written, "Just a warning Lee. Keep to your own sales or else." Milton's young fiancée confirmed that Milton had been worried, but he hadn't confided his reasons.

Two days after the fatal blast, Clay County attorney James Garrity announced, "From our investigation thus far, I am firmly convinced that no labor union as an organization is involved."

Garrity suspected the bombing was instead the work of an individual member, or former member, of the union, and he released Tougas.

Early in 1941, authorities charged Louis Anderson, a Fargo truck driver, with 1st degree murder. The arrest was based on an accusation by his friend and roommate, James Wood. Several weeks later, Wood changed his story, saying Anderson was innocent. Soon after, Wood switched his story again, saying he was with Anderson when he rigged the car bomb in 1939.

On April 17, 1941, a grand jury determined there wasn't enough evidence to put either man on trial for Milton Lee's murder. The case appears to remain unsolved.

Merry Helm

11 JUN

Wolfology

Ben Corbin (1835-1912) was known as the "champion wolf hunter of the Northwest." Others called him "Ben, the Boss Wolf Hunter." Some referred to him as a "wolf charmer," but there was nothing charming or disarming about how Ben Corbin sought to exterminate all wolves in North Dakota. In his lifetime, he claimed to "have caught and killed over 4,000 wolves."

It was on this date in 1900 that Ben Corbin's book on "wolfology" was ready to be released. The title revealed its content: *Corbin's Advice; or the Wolf Hunter's Guide*. The cloth-bound pocket edition sold for $1 and, in it, Corbin told "how to locate, catch, and kill wolves wherever found." As the *Bismarck Tribune* tartly commented: "No author on the [Missouri] Slope ever published such an interesting book before. Corbin knows all about wolves and he *tells more than he knows* in his book . . . any hunter who has a copy of this book in his pocket can stop a wolf."

Corbin had "made wolves a life study," and reportedly knew "things not supposed to be known outside of their hole in the ground." He insisted that governments pay a "generous bounty" to wolf hunters and trappers in order to limit the predator's numbers. When there was no bounty or low bounties, wolves proliferated.

Corbin, who lived in the village of Glencoe in Emmons County, near Linton, lobbied the legislature constantly concerning wolf-bounties. The definition of wolves at that time included coyotes, called "prairie wolves," and larger gray wolves, including "buffalo wolves," that had once lived on bison. After the passing of the bison, in 1883, the wolves preyed on livestock.

To prevent losses of calves, lambs, colts, pigs and poultry, Ben Corbin made it his mission to eliminate the "ravenous beasts." His *Wolf Hunter's Guide* revealed his secret methods, shocking to modern sensibilities, for he caught wolves with bait and hooks on steel lines. Disdaining poison, Corbin also told how to best use guns and traps to kill the cunning predators.

Corbin died in 1912, at age 77, in obscurity. But, because Corbin published his 1900 book, this plain blunt man of little formal learning, has been reviled in later history books as a wolf exterminator. Others, however, acknowledged the "champion wolf hunter" to have been "one of the most remarkable characters" in North Dakota's history.

Dr. Steve Hoffbeck

Resisting World War I

12 JUN

On this date in 1917, draft registration was over and North Dakota fell slightly short of its goal; but with many already enlisted, Registration Day was deemed a success. Most registrants did not seek exemptions, however, there were some North Dakotans who came up with original excuses. First, there was the man engaged to a girl who was a conscientious objector, and he could not go to war against her wishes. Another fellow stated that he had already been dismissed by the army because of health reasons, but upon questioning, it was learned that the army in question was the *Salvation* Army. One gentleman wished to be excused because blood made him sick, and another had a numb trigger finger. Several stated their church forbid it, but failed to name the church.

Then there was the man who needed to remain home because he was the only barber in town. Possibly the most original was the Fargo man who could not go to war because he had planted a victory garden that only he could maintain. Upon inspection it was learned the so-called garden consisted of several stalks of beans, a few radishes and a couple of onions.

The echoes of the patriotic celebrations of Registration Day had barely faded away, when Arthur Townley, the founder of the Non-Partisan League, proclaimed that the "Flower of the nation was going to die for the profit of the rich." He said farmers were willing and able to increase crop production tenfold, but he condemned the middlemen who bought the grain at $1.50 a bushel and sold it for $5.00. Townley warned farmers that they should think of themselves and not increase production unless they were handled fairly, arguing that it was not the farmer who benefited from the high price of wheat.

Lewis Crawford, President of the State Board of Regents, called Townley's word treasonous and stated, "All of our enemies are not in Germany." Townley countered that war profiteers will saddle the country with a huge debt which the soldiers, returning without arms, legs or eyes, would have to face – a debt that could keep them slaves for decades. He believed big business, supported by corrupt government officials, were responsible.

Traveling with Townley, Governor Lynn Frazier, in a prophetic statement, advocated for the recall of government officials who did not do their duty as their constituents believed they should. Frazier himself, would be the subject of a recall only five years later.

Jim Davis

13 JUN

Restroom

On this date in 1914, the ladies of the local Woman's Civic League in New England, ND, were waiting to hear back from their city council as to whether they could establish a special room for the ladies of the country: a restroom.

They asked the council to turn over a part of city hall for this purpose and to furnish two or three couches and other articles of furniture. They also intended to place a "competent" lady in charge of the rooms, to provide care and comfort.

No definite answer had been given, but it was reported to be an idea to their credit, which "hundreds of people in the New England territory" would appreciate, and so they were already 'flush' with success.

Sarah Walker

The Drunkometer

14 JUN

In 1931, chemistry professor Roland Harger invented a device called "the drunkometer." It was the first practical device to measure whether people had imbibed too much. Harger deliberately made it very easy to use so judges and juries would understand how it worked. In 1938, he served on a subcommittee of the National Safety Council. He helped draft an act that would legalize the use of evidence from such chemical tests and to set the legal alcohol levels for drivers. The act was incorporated into drunken driving laws nationwide.

The drunkometer was first used on New Year's Eve, 1938, in Indianapolis. To use the invention, a person suspected of being legally drunk breathed into a balloon. The air from the balloon was passed through a chemical solution. If the solution did not change color, there was no alcohol. But if the solution changed color, it meant there was alcohol. The greater the color change, the more alcohol was present. Indianapolis police reported that, with the end of Prohibition and a boom in car sales, drunk driving was becoming a serious danger. They were confident that the drunkometer would help them put a stop to the fast-growing problem.

But the results of the drunkometer were not consistently accepted in court. During this week in 1954, Casper Hanson of Minot was appealing his conviction on a charge of driving under the influence. His conviction was based on drunkometer results.

During the appeal, Judge Eugene A. Burdick allowed assistant city attorney Paul Campbell to demonstrate the drunkometer in court, but he did not permit additional testimony about the results of the tests. He felt this would give the city a better basis on which the evidence could be tested further in the courts. City attorney Campbell said if he lost in District Court, he would take the case to the State Supreme Court, but he need not have worried. Hanson lost his appeal.

The drunkometer had a relatively short lifespan. It was replaced by the breathalyzer in 1954. The breathalyzer was invented by Robert Borkenstein, another Indiana chemistry professor. It is much smaller, more portable, and easier to use than the drunkometer, and it is still in use today.

Carole Butcher

15 JUN

Where Valor Sleeps

Arlington National Cemetery is considered America's most hallowed ground. It is located on land that was once belonged to George Custis, adopted son of George Washington. Custis built a house where he kept many of Washington's prized possessions. He left the property to his daughter. When she married a promising young West Point graduate named Robert E. Lee, the house became known as the Custis-Lee Mansion. It was their home until the outbreak of the Civil War.

The Federal government seized the land in 1862. On this date in 1864, Arlington was established as a National Cemetery for war dead. As the fighting raged, the dead were brought from the battlefields for burial at Arlington. Most were Union soldiers, but a few Confederates were buried there as well. Arlington now covers 612 acres. It is the final resting place for 250,000 veterans and their families, including two presidents, dozens of famous generals, and a few astronauts.

But Arlington is not big enough to accommodate all military burials. And some families want their loved ones closer to home. Consequently, there are 147 national cemeteries in the United States, reserved for veterans and their spouses. In addition, there are also state veterans' cemeteries.

There are no national cemeteries in North Dakota, but there is a state cemetery. The North Dakota Veterans' Cemetery was established by the Legislative Assembly in 1989, but the Legislature did not provide funding. The project was completed with the use of private donations, and the National Guard did most of the construction. It is located near Mandan in the southwest corner of Fort Abraham Lincoln State Park. The completed cemetery includes paved roads, a parking lot, and a meditation plaza. The first burials took place in 1992.

The cemetery at Mandan is dedicated to all the men and women who served our state and our country. It honors them by providing an appropriate location for their final resting place where they will always be honored and remembered. Like many other state cemeteries, North Dakota's is reaching capacity, and there is a push for the federal government to approve new national sites.

Carole Butcher

Grand Forks Cyclone

16 JUN

Grand Forks witnessed one of the worst storms in the history of North Dakota on this date in 1887. The storm came quickly as two weather systems collided over the city. Shortly after 3:00 p.m., rain and hail began to fall and winds increased to 70 miles per hour. Half an hour later, the city was in ruins. The storm was so ferocious, newspapers labeled it a cyclone.

The Fargo *Daily Argus* reported that "Houses were blown down, unroofed, or torn from their foundations, while the ears were deafened by the crash of falling houses and the terrific roar of the storm. Teams broke loose, and tore wildly through the streets; the air was filled with flying timber and no element of confusion was missing from the scene." Eight people died in the storm.

Afterwards, it was difficult for people to find where the fairgrounds had been; nothing was left but wooden planks strewn on the ground. The two upper stories of UND's west wing were in complete ruin. Luckily, summer vacation had commenced the previous day, and no students were injured, but the University's museum was hit hard. One story read, "Prof. Montgomery's magnificent collections are all destroyed [...] At one fell sweep of the wind he lost what cost years of faithful work and diligence."

Most of the city's residential areas were devastated, and "houses that were not blown down outright, were so badly damaged as to be uninhabitable." St. Michael's Church was also destroyed, and the roof of the Grand Forks roller mill was torn off, ruining equipment and sacks of flour stored inside.

One story read, "May Cambell attempted to hold a door shut, but the wind was too strong and she was carried with terrible force out of the house and over the prairie for about forty yards. Her shoulder was slightly hurt, but she had a most thrilling experience and was nearly crushed by a falling building."

Another report said, "A barn belonging to W H Vosberg was lifted up, inverted and dropped, driving the roof into the ground."

A southbound passenger train near Pierson was blown into a ditch; with most of the passengers sustaining injuries.

But was the storm a tornado? Interestingly, there was reluctance to call it that in the late 1800s, a time when towns were seeking to attract residents. Grand Forks leaders were known to advertise that the city didn't have tornados. But researchers, almost 120 years later, determined that the 1887 storm was indeed a tornado — an EF3, and possibly even an EF4, with winds reaching 148 to 210 miles per hour.

Merry Helm

17 JUN

Theodore Roosevelt's Reclamation Act of 1902

Although Theodore Roosevelt's time in Dakota was short, the territory nonetheless left a distinct mark on the future president. His vigorous life in Dakota taught the sickly easterner the value of a hard day's work and the inherent worth of even a common laborer. Roosevelt's experiences in the Dakota Badlands did more than undermine the social elitism of his wealthy East Coast past – it dramatized the beauty of the American West and the need to care for and preserve the land.

Of principle concern was the maintenance of the region's resources, which meant acknowledging the land's limitations. As early as the 1880s, Roosevelt saw that local cattlemen were overstocking the prairie. The parched semi-arid land simply could not support intensive ranching or farming. In 1889, Roosevelt's fears were echoed by Maj. John Wesley Powell who warned the delegates to North Dakota's Constitutional Convention of the dangers posed by plowing up the western and central portions of the state without secure water sources.

While Roosevelt and others rightly feared the consequences of pushing the land beyond its natural limits, he was ever hopeful of the improvements possible through the latest in irrigation technology. Many more shared in these sentiments, including Senator Henry Hansbrough of North Dakota. Hansbrough proved instrumental in pushing through the Reclamation Act signed by Theodore Roosevelt on this date in 1902. The resulting irrigation projects served as a cornerstone to Roosevelt's national conservation program.

Among the twenty-four irrigation projects designated in the act was the Lower Yellowstone Project in the Mon-Dak region of western North Dakota and eastern Montana. First authorized in 1904 and operational by 1909, the irrigation project's sixty-two miles of main canal transformed over 40,000 acres of prairie on the west bank of the Yellowstone River into prime farmland, breathing new life into the nearby farming communities and stabilizing local farm production.

Today some 160,000 acres of North Dakota farmland are maintained by irrigation systems. They provide farmers greater crop selection, higher yields and security from recurrent drought. Perhaps even more importantly, the canals confirm the foresight of President Roosevelt. Farming in North Dakota must be conducted with great planning and care, respecting the limits of the land, while finding new ways to push those limits even farther than before.

Lane Sunwall

Nettie Roberts, Frontier Survivor

18 JUN

Women homesteaders who were single or widowed had much to contend with while proving up. In her book, *Land in Her Own Name*, North Dakota author, Elaine Lindgren writes, "For those who had grown up on their parents' farms, the skills needed for living on their own claims came as second nature, but young women from the city had a lot to learn. But it was much more difficult for some than for others. On this date in 1908, Grant County's *Carson Press* published the following letter to the editor:

"The *Carson Press* said something about a woman 70 years old having the pluck to take up residence on her claim. We have a woman (Mrs. Nettie Roberts) in the vicinity of Stebbins who has even more pluck or nerve, which ever you may call it. She had the misfortune to have (a) runaway and got all her ribs broken on the left side, her back broken, one toe broken, and was paralyzed from hips down. She only stayed in the hospital two months and returned home with paralyzed bowels and had to be cauterized twice a day."

"She had bed sores about the size of goose eggs," the letter continued, "which ran to the back bone. She was unable to turn or lift herself with no nurse or doctor. She boarded the switch at Bismarck and was carried to and from the backs at Mandan, then put into a buggy and driven sixty-five miles to her homestead, knowing all the care she would get was what Mr. Roberts and his ten-year old daughter could give her."

The writer went on to say that Mr. Roberts was the young widow's brother-in-law. The letter stated, "Of course his being a veterinary surgeon and understanding how to treat sores was a great help, but they got no outside help. Talk about pluck! She has some. She has suffered now for eight months in which time she has never walked a step."

"She was given up by five doctors," the writer continued, "and made her will while at Bismarck. She called a priest and was christened by Father Henry at the age of 22 years.

When she was interviewed, Nettie said, "I was preparing to die but did not think I would die [...] I must say I am getting better. I can creep on all fours like a babe, but I am very lonely and wish my neighbors would come in and see me. Some of the busybodies said I didn't seem to like anyone to come in and see me. This is a sad mistake. I wish all to come. It is a pleasure to me to see you come – big and little – even if you can't help me."

Merry Helm

19 JUN

The Jamestown Asylum

As we grow older, we see more clearly how fragile human life can be. Perhaps nowhere is this fragility more readily apparent than in the realm of mental health.

Emotional and behavioral disorders have been known by many names. What we now call "mental illnesses" might have once been called "insanity" or "madness." Dakota Territory built a Hospital for the Insane in Jamestown in 1885, and by then, a movement to establish mental hospitals had swept the nation. The 1889 North Dakota Constitution mandated Jamestown to be the permanent location for the state's Insane Asylum. On this date in 1900, the *Grand Forks Herald* reported that there were 344 patients in the hospital. This statistic from the U.S. Census Bureau would not seem to be controversial, but the newspaper explained that 251 of the 344 patients were of "foreign birth."

The author of the article claimed that "officials of foreign countries" had deliberately "unloaded" mentally ill people on the United States, sending them "west as immigrants" so that their governments would not have to care for their own mentally-ill patients. On its face, the idea that two-thirds of the patients in the Jamestown mental hospital were foreigners might seem startling. However, a closer examination of North Dakota's population data can make sense of what was happening. According to the census data, in 1900, the state had a total population of almost 320,000 with over a third foreign-born, and almost a third more of "foreign parentage." So, sixty-seven percent were considered "foreign."

Therefore, it was logical that two-thirds of the mentally-ill patients in Jamestown were said to be foreigners, because two-thirds of North Dakota's population were of foreign birth or of foreign parentage.

The largest ethnic group among those immigrants were the Norwegians, who made up about twenty percent of the population, followed closely by Germans, who made up another twenty percent. At Jamestown's mental hospital, twenty-eight percent were of Norwegian extraction, while Germans made up about nine percent.

While Emma Lazarus's famous poem, as engraved on the Statue of Liberty, encouraged the nations of the world to send their "huddled masses yearning to breathe free;" their "wretched refuse," and "homeless" people and those 'tempest-tossed,' to the United States, federal immigration laws established barriers. The First General Federal Immigration Law of 1882 excluded as immigrants "any convict, lunatic [...] or any person unable to take care of himself or herself without becoming a public charge." Any such immigrants, including the mentally ill, were to be sent back to their homeland.

The care of those who fall into mental illness, including senile dementia and schizophrenia and other maladies, remains an obligation of North Dakotans today through the many private and public agencies, including the Jamestown State Hospital.

Dr. Steve Hoffbeck

100-Year Rain in Fargo

20 JUN

The city of Fargo may have kept the high floodwater of 2009 at bay, but in the summer of 2000, a 100-year rain soaked the city. Seven inches fell in seven hours overnight. And on this date, when it was all said and done, half the city's homes had taken on water. The damage estimates hit almost $100 million.

The North Dakota State University Library was heavily damaged. Two feet of water had already pooled in the basement when the windows burst, adding another two feet of water. The library tossed out 10,000 periodicals and journals and sent microfilm records to Chicago for freeze-drying and preservation. Other journals were moved to temporary safe spots in town. Pamela Drayson had been the library's director for barely three days when the rainwater racked up $4 million in losses.

Nearly every building on campus had water in its basement. Phone and internet service was lost. NDSU had $18 million in water damage plus $21 million in losses to crops and research.

The Fargodome didn't fare well either. The arena flooded with six feet of water. The water had swept in from loading docks, utility tunnels, and overhead doors. The turf field floated off the floor. It took two days to pump out 52 million gallons of water. The damage total was about $10 million.

Vehicles stalled in the streets as Fargo's major routes flooded. Power went out across the city and the sewer backed up. Some residents had to battle water coming in through toilets and bathtubs. Some residents in basement-level apartments had six feet of water in their homes, losing everything. Mayor Bruce Furness declared a state of emergency. Dennis Walaker, who was then Fargo's operations director, called the storm a 100-year rain event. Fargo gets about twenty inches of rain a year. On this occasion, it got seven inches in one night.

Jack Dura

21 JUN

Dorothy Stickney

It was on this date in 1896 that Dorothy Hayes Stickney was born in Dickinson, North Dakota. She was the daughter of Victor Hugo Stickney, also known as the "cowboy doctor."

Even before she was one year old, it appeared she was having vision problems. Her parents took her to a specialist in St. Paul, who immediately performed the first of seven operations for ulcers on her corneas. Vision problems plagued Dorothy until she finally healed at age eigthteen.

After high school, Dorothy went to New York to pursue a career as an actress. During the first years, she got bit parts in second-rate Vaudeville shows and also performed in summer stock in Maine, where she was directed by her future husband, Howard Lindsay. During this time, she happened upon a Maureen Watkins' manuscript for a new play called *Chicago*, which later became the basis for the Oscar winning movie of the same name.

There was a character in the play named Crazy Liz, a foul-mouthed, slovenly hag who was jailed for murder. Pretty, blue-eyed Dorothy Stickney wanted the part, and she obtained a promise to let her try out if the play ever went into production.

Meanwhile, Stickney was cast as a sweet young thing in the 1926 hit, *The Squall*. But when she heard that *Chicago* was finally headed for the stage, she used makeup and costuming to transform herself into Crazy Liz and reminded Sam Harris, the producer, about his promise. The part was already taken by that time, but when the actress playing Crazy Liz didn't show up that day, Dorothy tried out. By the time she finished the first scene, Harris gave her a three-year contract. She was a hit.

Shortly thereafter, Stickney learned that her father back in Dickinson had inoperable cancer, and she left the show to be with him. After he died in July 1927, Dorothy went back to New York, married Howard Lindsay and continued acting.

Although the couple could have had their pick of film projects in Hollywood by now, they opted instead to borrow money so Howard could finish writing a play called, *Life with Father*. The two of them were to play the roles of the mother and father. Unfortunately, everyone turned down the finished play, so they staged it themselves in summer stock.

Finally, on November 8, 1939, they brought it to the Empire Theater on Broadway, where their faith in the play paid off big time. It ran for seven years – with 3,224 performances. It's the longest running non-musical to ever play on Broadway.

Howard died in 1968 in New York, but Dorothy lived another 30 years, reaching 101.

Merry Helm

Pint-Sized Prophet

22 JUN

On June 17, 1921, a terrible flashflood struck the Badlands near Medora, North Dakota. Three section men working for the railroad had been out checking the rail line when the storm struck, and they did not return home. For three days, search parties attempted to locate the missing men. On this day in 1921, authorities in Dickinson reported that the 11-year-old son of one of the missing men, Tom Everetts, was able to lead searchers to his father's body, which was trapped underwater near a washout. Apparently, the young boy had awoken from a dream in which he learned of his father's location. Years earlier, the boy had also foretold the death of an aunt hours before a telegram confirmed the prophecy.

Jayme L. Job

23 JUN

Lots of Bread

Food prices spiraled upwards in 1972. There were many reasons, including the devaluation of the dollar, a decline in world grain production, and an increase in the demand for meat in developing countries. But those reasons offered no comfort to American consumers.

An article in the *Bismarck Tribune* on this date in 1972 noted that the price for a one-pound loaf of bread averaged of 24.5 cents. That was close to the all-time high of 25 cents, reached the previous year. Of that cost, farmers received only 3.5 cents. That was the same amount they received in 1947.

A newspaper column suggested that consumers should shop for lower-priced bread and take advantage of specials. They were urged to buy day-old bread on sale. It was also noted that whole grain breads are more nutritious than white bread, and consumers should consider making the switch.

Prices were on the minds of government officials as well. The Price Commission planned to hold an unusual Sunday meeting. President Nixon considered lifting meat import quotas to slow the rise of food prices. He ordered a study of the impact. Nixon acknowledged that the move would not bring immediate relief. It would take some time before it had any effect.

The news was of particular interest to North Dakotans. Representative Arthur A. Link said the Federal Price Commission should not even consider price controls at the farm level. He said it was totally unfair to blame the farmer for inflation when the farmers were actually the victims of that inflation. He said farmers received grossly inadequate prices. Link noted that farm prices for food had risen by six percent while overall consumer prices had risen by forty-three percent. He also said that farm output was increasing twice as fast as manufacturing output. There was no evidence, he said, that price controls should be placed on raw agricultural products.

President Nixon had created the Cost of Living Council to oversee wage and price controls. The Council was considering a recommendation by the Price Commission that the exemption of raw agricultural products from controls be ended. The Price Commission said that "firm and immediate action" had to be taken to bring food prices under control.

Even today, in the age of $5 hipster toast, the farmer isn't doing a whole lot better, getting just a dime or two for every loaf.

Moving Robe Woman

24 JUN

On this date in 1876, Custer and the 7th Cavalry were one day away from their fate at the Little Big Horn River. Among the warriors who fought the following day was Tashna Mani or Moving Robe Woman. The following is an abridged version of her account of what happened:

"Several of us young Indian women were digging wild turnips when I saw a cloud of dust rise beyond a ridge of bluffs in the east. We looked towards camp and saw a warrior ride swiftly, shouting that the soldiers were only a few miles away, and that the women and children and old men should run for the hills in the opposite direction. I dropped the pointed ash stick, which I had used in digging turnips and ran toward my tipi. I saw my father running toward the horses... in a few moments we saw soldiers on horseback on a bluff just across the (river).

"[...] I saw my father preparing to go to the battle. I sang a death song for my young brother, One Hawk, who had been killed. I ran to a nearby thicket and got my black horse. I painted my face with crimson and braided my black hair. I was mourning. I was a woman, but I was not afraid.

"By this time the soldiers were forming a battle line in the bottom about a half mile away. In another moment I heard a volley of carbines. The bullets shattered tipi poles. Women and children were running away from the gunfire. In the tumult I heard old men and women singing death songs for their warriors who were now ready to attack the soldiers. The songs made me brave[...] Father led my horse to me and [...] we galloped toward the soldiers. Other warriors joined in with us.

"When we were nearing the fringe of the woods, an order was given by Hawk Man to charge... The troopers were all on foot. They shot straight, because I saw Hawk Man killed... The charge was so stubborn that the soldiers ran to their horses and[...] rode swiftly toward the river where the horses had to swim to get across. Some of the warriors rode into the water and killed some of the soldiers and unhorsed some of them. The warriors chased the soldiers across the river and up over a bluff, then they returned to where the battle took place and sang a victory song.

"Someone said that another body of soldiers was attacking the lower end of the village. I heard afterwards that these soldiers were under the command of Pehin Hanska (Hair Long)[...] I rode in that direction holding my brother's war staff over my head. Rain in the Face shouted, "Behold, there is among us a young woman! Let no young man ride behind her garment!"

"We crossed the Greasy Grass below a beaver dam where the water is not so deep, and came upon many horses. One soldier was holding the reins of eight or ten horses. An Indian waved his blanket to scare the horses and they got away [...] On the ridge just north of us, I saw blue-clad men running up a ravine, firing as they ran. The valley was dense with powder smoke. Long Hair's troops were trapped [...] The Cheyennes attacked [...] from the north, and Crow King from the south.

"After the battle the Indians took all the equipment and horses belonging to the soldiers. We did not know who the soldiers were until an interpreter told us that the men came from Ft. Lincoln in Dakota Territory. On the saddle blankets were the crossed saber insignia and the figure 7. The brave men who came to punish us that morning were defeated; but in the end the Indians lost. Over sixty Indians were killed, and they were brought back to the camp for scaffold burial. The Indians did not stage a victory dance that night. They were mourning for their own dead. The next day Sitting Bull's band packed our tents and started north to the Canadian line where we remained four years until Sitting Bull surrendered at Fort Buford."

That was an account by Moving Robe Woman, who fought against Custer's 7th Cavalry to avenge the death of One Hawk, her brother, in the Battle of the Little Big Horn.

Adapted from Frank Zahn's *Lakota Accounts of the Battle of Little Big Horn* (1931).

Merry Helm

Henry Wildfang

25 JUN

For Marine pilots young and old, the name Henry Wildfang is legendary. Henry Wildfang, nicknamed Bud, was born in Bismarck in 1916 and raised in Sterling, North Dakota. After graduation from high school, a stint in the Civilian Conservation Corps, and three years of college, Bud was accepted in the Navy Aviation program and began a thirty-seven-year career as a Marine Corps pilot.

Wildfang served in World War II, Korea, and Vietnam. He racked up an astounding 24,000 hours in the cockpit, qualifying in twenty-one different aircraft. Bud was awarded five Distinguished Flying Crosses, twenty-nine Air Medals, and the Purple Heart.

Wildfang's fifth Distinguished Flying Cross and his Purple Heart were earned on February 10, 1968. Bud was delivering fuel desperately needed by the 26th Marine regiment at the Khe Sahn combat base in Vietnam. Bud's C-130 Hercules Transport broke out of the overcast into a hail of hostile ground fire that shattered a portion of the right wing and set fire to the aircraft. Wildfang set down on the shell-pocked jungle strip and rolled the flaming plane into the edge of the jungle to keep the runway clear. Seven of the 10 crewmembers were killed, and Bud would forever carry burn scars on his hands and arms from trying to save his crewmates.

On August 31, 1977, Wildfang received the Gray Eagle Award from the Navy Air Corps. In part, the award states: "You, Henry Wildfang, are the first Gray Eagle recipient still on the squadron rolls and flying daily. Your flight hours exceed that of any other Navy or Marine Aviator on active duty. You are a legend in your own time. From Corsairs to Hercules. From Pusan to Khe Sanh. You have created a standard of dedication and service to Naval Aviation everywhere."

Bud retired from the Marines in 1978 and moved to Midwest City, Oklahoma where he enjoyed many years of retirement with his wife and family. In 2011 Bud was inducted into the Oklahoma Military Hall of Fame.

The Marines never forgot about Bud Wildfang. The award and trophy presented annually by the Marine Aviation Association to the premier Marine Aerial Refueler Transport came to be known as the "Henry Wildfang Award."

On this date in 2015, Henry "Bud" Wildfang passed away at the age of 99. He is interned in the North Dakota Veterans Cemetery south of Mandan.

Scott Nelson

26 JUN

Policeman Sneesby Shot

On this day in 1924, night policeman C.R. Sneesby of the Devils Lake Police Department died from a gunshot wound to the head. While patrolling outside the local post office the night before, Sneesby encountered a gang of four men who had broken into the basement of the post office using a crowbar. Panicked, the lookout shot Sneesby, and the rest of the gang dashed out of the building, piled into their Big Six Studebaker, and sped away into the night. Posses surrounded all the possible escape routes and eventually managed to capture the gang.

In their hurry, the clumsy bandits left behind a mountain of evidence. Two tanks, one full of oxygen and another full of acetylene, were found near the post office. Police deduced that the gang planned to cut through the steel door of the post office vault with a high temperature flame. A likely motive was difficult to discern, as the post office kept very little money in its vaults. Richer, easier targets were certainly available. The robbery, said investigators, was the work of amateurs — amateurs who proved deadly nonetheless.

Although Sneesby did not usually include the post office in his patrol rounds, an attempted robbery of the post office earlier that year had prompted the Devils Lake Police Department to include the building in the night patrol. Many people on the street heard the gunshot, but mistook the disturbance for the firecrackers that had been going off all evening. However, Sneesby was discovered in the back driveway of the post office shortly after the shooting by two men who drove past the scene. In the dim light of the flashlight, which still burned on the ground beside him, the men saw Sneesby lying on his back, still breathing, with his arms outstretched. Though he was rushed to the hospital, Sneesby died the next day.

Sneesby had only been a member of the Devils Lake police force a little over a year before losing his life in the line of duty. Sadly, when Police Officer Sneesby passed away, he left behind his wife and three children. If only Sneesby's trusty Airedale terrier watchdog, which usually accompanied him on his patrol, had been there to warn him of the danger lurking around the corner, he may have survived his encounter with the gang.

Carol Wilson

Comanche

27 JUN

In May of 1876, Lieutenant Colonel George Armstrong Custer led the men of the 7th U.S. Cavalry out of Fort Abraham Lincoln on an expedition intended to locate and rout tribes of Native Americans who were resisting their placement upon reservations. When Custer found these tribes encamped on the Little Bighorn River, he divided his forces into three groups and confronted them on June 25. When additional U.S. forces arrived two days later, this day, June 27, 1876, every man in the five companies under Custer's immediate command were dead. The lone survivors were a few horses, including Comanche, the former mount of Captain Myles W. Keogh. Although Comanche had been wounded in seven places, he was the only horse found wandering the battle-site that the cavalrymen believed could survive. The other horses had to be put down. As a result, Comanche became the sole survivor of Custer's company who fought in the Battle of the Little Bighorn.

Comanche began his cavalry career in April of 1868 when 1st Lieutenant Tom Custer purchased the horse along with forty-one other mustangs. The horse was soon sold to Captain Myles Keogh for $90 and received his name five months later after being wounded by a Comanche arrow during a skirmish in southwest Kansas. Following the death of Captain Keogh at the Battle of the Little Bighorn, Comanche returned to Fort Lincoln where he was nursed back to health by blacksmith Gustave Korn. The famous horse quickly became a favorite ride of the ladies at the fort. However, their constant rivalry over Comanche caused such a disturbance that the commanding officer of the 7th Cavalry, Colonel Samuel Sturgis, issued a statement decreeing that the horse was never to be ridden again and was to live out his days in comfort and ease as a living reminder of the Battle of the Little Bighorn.

From there on out Comanche lived a life fluctuating between beloved pet and downright nuisance. Although Comanche was honored as a war hero, he was something of an irritant. Accustomed to eating whiskey bran mash during his recuperation from wounds received at the Little Bighorn, Comanche degenerated into a drunk. Following his recovery, he hung around the fort's canteen on paydays, begging for beer from the soldiers. When not panhandling, or sleeping off his hangovers, Comanche was often found rooting through gardens and overturning garbage cans. Despite his behavior, the horse was treated as a valued member of the 7th Calvary until his passing away in 1891 at the age of twenty-nine. Following his death, Comanche was preserved by Kansas University taxidermist Lewis Lindsay Dyche. Apart from an appearance at the 1893 World's Fair in Chicago, Comanche has remained on display at the University of Kansas ever since.

Lane Sunwall

28 JUN

Angela Murray Gibson

Today is the birthday of filmmaker Angela Murray Gibson. Nobody is certain what year she was born, because she refused to reveal her age, and her tombstone reveals only the year she died – 1953. Best guess is that she was born in Scotland around 1878.

During the Roaring Twenties, American women gained independence and flourished as never before. Angela was one of those women. Her family immigrated when she was five, ultimately settling in Casselton. Angela was one of the first two women to graduate from what is now NDSU.

About that time, during production for a movie called *The Pride of the Clan*, actress Mary Pickford learned that Angela Gibson did performances that featured her Scottish heritage. Pickford arranged for Angela to come to Hollywood to work as an advisor. She ended up wearing one of Angela's Scottish costumes in the film.

Gibson absorbed a great deal by watching the day-to-day movie-making, and after the production wrapped, she went to Columbia University to study cinematography. She purchased a camera, but in an unusual move, she took her formal training not to Hollywood, but back to Casselton. She started the state's first movie studio. It was completely run and financed by women. Angela was the writer, director and actress, and her sister, Ruby, ran the business end. Her mother was recruited to crank the camera.

Movie clips reveal that Gibson didn't shy away from action. In one scene, she crawls out a second story window wearing a floor-length ruffled dress and slippery shoes. The scene cuts to the exterior, showing her slipping and edging down the roof.

Gibson started off with several documentaries – one about the life of a grain of wheat and another about a rodeo in Medora. Her earliest surviving feature film is called *That Ice Ticket*, a story about a young woman who, on a hot day, hangs out a sign offering ice to lure potential suitors. But her younger brother pulls a prank by hanging a smallpox sign over the ice sign. In the end, the heroine's true love risks his health to see her, and all is well.

When the depression arrived, costs of materials became so high that Gibson – like many others – had to give up her life as a filmmaker. Most of her films disappeared after that, but in 1976, the Centennial Commission discovered what remained and sought to restore the footage. Much of the film had been water damaged, but luckily Angela had transferred some of her footage onto what is known as "safety film," which survived in much better shape than the original.

Merry Helm

Dewey Dorman

29 JUN

On this date in 1911, Minot was planning for a spectacular Fourth of July, with fireworks, free vaudeville acts, a baseball game, a grand mask carnival on Main Street, a "sham battle" between Company D of Minot and Company E of Williston, and more.

One of the most talked-about attractions was an exhibition by local aviator Dewitt "Dewey" Dorman, who would take flight in his home-built fifty horsepower Bleriot monoplane. He had made his first flight on June 9, and he told reporters, "Yes, I am learning to fly and believe me, it is no easy task." He cited issues with weather, as well as simply learning how to deal with the ins and outs of a new machine, though he added, "I might say that I have mastered the details of the machine and I am positively going to fly at the races July 3, 4, and 5. I realize that I am taking chances every time that I fly, but I am willing to take them in order to satisfy the public. I have no doubt but that I will be able to make some very satisfactory flights."

However, a slight scandal rocked the event. It was reported that the Wright brothers might attempt to prevent Dewey from flying, claiming a patent on several of the devices used in his plane.

Dewey responded, "I do not believe that anyone can stop me from using this machine. Wright brothers claim a patent on practically everything that has been manufactured along the flying machine line, but I do not believe that they can make their claim hold in court." He said his monoplane was different than their machines, and was one of the few such planes in the United States.

Dewey did fly for part of the celebration, but it was not for long. Though the windy weather had not improved, he didn't want to disappoint the crowds of people there to see him. On his takeoff on July 4, the wind caught the machine and turned it over, breaking the propeller. He turned off the engine and escaped without injury, though the plane was no longer flightworthy.

Sarah Walker

30 JUN

Works Progress Administration

When Franklin D. Roosevelt assumed office in 1933, more than thirteen million Americans were out of work. But North Dakota was arguably the hardest hit of the forty-eight states. The depression was severe, but the droughts of 1934 and 1936 delivered the knockout punch. Wheat prices plummeted, prompting the value of farm land to dip from $22 per acre in 1930 to $12 in 1940. Historian Elwyn B. Robinson estimates that one third of North Dakota families lost their farms to foreclosure.

Many drifted into towns looking for work. Others left the state. The federal government provided $32 million in direct relief and farm aid for North Dakota between 1932 and 1935, but President Roosevelt felt that simply doling out relief payments would eventually lead to, "spiritual and moral disintegration." So, in an attempt to relieve the economic hardships, a series of national work programs were created.

The Works Progress Administration (the WPA) was developed in 1935 and would remain in operation until this date in 1943. Within two years of its establishment, the WPA had employed almost 53,000 North Dakotans. Much of the work in the state involved construction projects. From 1935 to 1943, the WPA built over 20,000 miles of highways and streets. It constructed over 700 new bridges and viaducts, and another 700 outdoor recreation facilities, like fairgrounds, pools and parks. 800 water wells were dug, and 39 sewage treatment plants were built. 500 new public buildings were erected, and 166 miles of sidewalks were laid by North Dakota WPA workers.

The WPA also operated numerous non-construction projects. Each county had a WPA sewing project, which employed more than 800 women. In one year alone, they produced over 800,000 garments to be distributed to North Dakota school children. A WPA mattress project in Minot produced over 43,000 mattresses.

The National Youth Administration, a program under the WPA, provided part-time employment in construction, research or library work for high-school and college students. Artists and other cultural workers were employed by the WPA Federal Arts Project, the Federal Music Project and the Federal Theatre Project. The Federal Writer's Project produced and published *The WPA Guidebook to North Dakota*. The Historical Records Survey documented biographical information on thousands of early North Dakota settlers. Today these documents provide a wealth of information for researchers and historians.

When the WPA officially ended in North Dakota, the Federal Government had spent a total of $266 million in the state. The program was intended to provide immediate help, but in the end, the WPA did much more – it lifted people's spirits while adding countless roads, parks, and artwork which made North Dakota a better place to live.

Kristina Campbell

Bismarck, North Dakota. State Capitol.
Credit: John Vachon, Farm Security Administration - Office of War Information Photograph Collection (Library of Congress), 1942.

JULY

JELLY

Garrison Dam Heartbreak

01 JUL

A heartbreaking deadline arrived on this date in 1953. Residents in towns along the Garrison Reservoir were required to evacuate by July 1 as the reservoir's rising waters swallowed up surrounding land.

The effects of the rising reservoir were devastating. Over 150,000 acres of river bottom land were lost, and towns such as Independence, Charging Eagle, Elbowoods and Sanish disappeared. Ninety percent of the area's population, mainly native people, had to relocate to land with soil less suited for their farming lifestyle.

Over 2,000 people of the Mandan, Hidatsa and Arikara tribes were heartbroken when their homes disappeared under what is now Lake Sakakawea. Driven to higher ground, many members of the Three Affiliated Tribes now live in Parshall, Mandaree, and New Town.

Holding back 7.7 trillion gallons of water, the Garrison Dam is one of the largest rolled earth dams on the planet. Flooding the upper Missouri River produced over 1,300 miles of shoreline, nearly 500 more miles than California's coastline. Lake Sakakawea was named in 1967 and covers 480 square miles of North Dakota.

For the people forced to abandon their homes and towns, the Garrison Dam represents a memory still painful to this day. While government compensation was given to those whose lands were lost, some things money couldn't replace. Bays are named now for towns that disappeared – such as Nishu Bay and the Van Hook Arm.

The Four Bears Bridge connecting Highway 23 with New Town is North Dakota's longest bridge and stands near the former town site of old Sanish. While constructing the new Four Bears Bridge in 2005, the waters were low, bringing remnants of old Sanish above the surface. Those old footings and foundations have since vanished again beneath the water.

Just 80 miles of the Missouri River flow freely in North Dakota out of 390. The Garrison and Oahe dams hold back much of the Big Muddy. While generating much hydroelectric power, the Garrison Dam will always have its largest impact on the people it forced from their homes.

Jack Dura

02 JUL

Freight Line Fugitive

Sheriffs and deputies from Fargo and Moorhead launched a large-scale manhunt on this date in 1923 after a robbery suspect killed a South Dakota sheriff and escaped near Moorhead. The suspect, Edwin Rust, was wanted on robbery charges in Brown County, South Dakota, and was being transported to Aberdeen by Sheriff Isaac Fulker.

Captured in East Grand Forks in June, Rust was placed in jail until he could be transferred to Aberdeen. On July 1, Sheriff Fulker arrived to transport the suspect. The two boarded the train, but Rust managed to kill Fulker and jump from the moving train. Sheriff Fulker left behind a wife and several children, and local Cass and Clay County authorities immediately formed a posse to capture the fugitive.

For weeks, Rust managed to elude authorities, despite the offer of a $500 reward. Then, on July 12, two men reported traveling with Rust on the train from Staples to Detroit, Minnesota – now known as Detroit Lakes. The Becker County Sheriff contacted Fargo with the news, and a large posse traveled to the small town of Detroit in hopes of catching Rust once and for all. For two weeks, the posse's search proved fruitless. Disheartened, the searchers returned to Fargo-Moorhead empty-handed. Two weeks later, Fargo's Sheriff Kraemer received word that Rust had been killed in a shoot-out with St. Paul police. Apparently, Rust had made his way to St. Paul and had taken up residence at a run-down guest house. He had dyed his blond hair black and had begun mugging locals to pay his way.

He was finally captured by police after he and a female accomplice stole a car. After being handcuffed and placed in the back of the police cruiser, Rust managed to free himself and jump from the car. He escaped down an alley, but was soon tracked by police to his rented room. A short gunfight ensued, and Rust was fatally shot. Only later did investigators realize that the dead criminal was, in fact, the wanted Edwin Rust; they also discovered that the young man had been on parole from Sacramento's Folsom Prison when he committed his crimes in Aberdeen.

Jayme L. Job

Mother's Pension Assistance

03 JUL

The problem of caring for the downtrodden poor has plagued civic government in North Dakota since territorial days. The essential question was how to care for widows, orphans and elderly persons in poverty who had no family members to properly provide for them.

In the time of the Progressive Era (1900-1917) state governments developed a new approach to caring for needy widows with young children at home. New legislation called the "Mother's Pension" law intended to help young widowed mothers preserve their homes, prevent the break-up of families, and lift children out of poverty, crime, and delinquency.

In that era, when death came to the father of a young family, the mother would be forced to work, often at low wages, and the children could be farmed out to relatives or other caregivers.

Mother's Pensions could be given to those moms who were the sole support of children, and the county would provide only enough money for food, clothing and shelter to keep the family together.

Lawmakers in Bismarck passed the Mother's Pension Law in February, 1915, authorizing counties to provide a monthly "payment of from $5 to $15 for needy mothers [who were] supporting children of a tender age" – defined as below fourteen. A county judge would decide which impoverished women were eligible.

It was on this date that the *Grand Forks Herald* reported that a woman in Jamestown, Mrs. J. Harris, had been granted the first Mother's Pension in North Dakota. Stutsman County provided her with $20 per month to care for her two children, the youngest being two years old, because she had been left penniless after the death of her husband. The county agreed to provide the aid for Mrs. Harris for twelve years, when the youngest would reach the age fourteen cutoff. However, it was stipulated that if Mrs. Harris re-married or moved out of the state, she would lose her Mother's Pension funds.

The law was challenged by Cass County officials in Fargo on grounds that judges lacked jurisdiction to decide who was eligible for aid, arguing that elected county commissioners should have the responsibility.

However, the N.D. Supreme Court ruled the law valid in January, 1917, because courts guarded minors' legal interests; and so Mother's Pensions aid for families became a vital child-support element within the county-welfare system.

Dr. Steve Hoffbeck

04 JUL

Independence Day

With many of North Dakota's young men and women already serving on the battlefields in Europe, the Fourth of July in 1917 promised to be a day of commemoration and consecration. For some, it was difficult to call it a day of celebration, but unlike Memorial Day, with the somber reflection that death may await loved ones serving overseas, the Fourth of July remained a celebration of patriotism, commemorating the battle for independence and democracy. According to the *Pioneer Express* from Pembina County, "It was observed as a day to be joyful of the memories of the past, proud of our history and progress, but thoughtful of the present and future."

The town of Pembina celebrated with an impressive parade. This included many floats with themes such as Liberty, the Conservation of Food, Law and Order, and Transportation. There were other war-related floats such as a Field Hospital, a Red Cross Ambulance, and even a naval theme represented by two large submarines complete with deck guns and radio antennas powered from beneath the waves by hidden automobiles. Young ladies flitted through the crowds pinning ribbons on lapels for those who contributed to the Red Cross.

The parade was followed by patriotic speeches, a ball game and picnics. Notably missing, however, were the fireworks, an otherwise grim reminder of the millions of shells falling on the battlefields overseas.

In Fargo, Island Park was the scene of a special flag raising with the Fargo Band playing the Star-Spangled Banner. That was followed by a day of patriotic speeches. A flag committee had been organized to hand out flags as people entered the park. A reading of the Declaration of Independence was followed by the audience singing "America." Here too, a ball game entertained the crowds, and the evening featured a patriotic program. As a special treat, free lemonade was supplied for the children.

At the Chautauqua in Tolley, North Dakota, Governor Fraizer spoke to more than fifteen thousand people, the largest crowd ever assembled at that event.

But as celebrations commenced across the state, war news continued to worsen. Battlefield casualties mounted, and National Guard units were entering the final stages of the organization as they readied for activation. North Dakota would soon be entering the war in a bigger way, with much more at stake.

Jim Davis

Immigrants Wanted

05 JUL

In 1907, President Theodore Roosevelt took note of a serious labor shortage across the West in general and the state in particular. Canada had made a systematic effort to attract new settlers to the western provinces, and the construction of 3,600 miles of Canadian railroads also required enormous numbers of laborers. The *Devils Lake Inter-Ocean* reported that the administration was taking steps to address the exodus of nearly 100,000 people to Canada the previous year. The newspaper acknowledged that the northern neighbor had outstripped the United States in competition for labor by offering high wages and free land.

The labor shortage was not a concern for the West alone. An article in the *New York Times* noted that concerns were growing as to how the labor shortage would affect the economy of the country as a whole. The railroads were advertising throughout the East for laborers, offering special inducements including transportation and higher wages. Labor was so scarce that mines in Utah paid Japanese immigrants an astonishing $170 per month. Western railroads were forced to purchase coal from Australia because of a shortage of miners. The increased expense was sure to drive up prices for freight, which would in turn drive up the cost of goods. Passenger travel would also become more expensive.

The Chinese Exclusion Act of 1882 is considered the first legislation by the United States to restrict immigration. The Immigration Act of 1907 further restricted immigration by banning "All idiots, imbeciles, feebleminded persons, epileptics, insane persons, and persons who have been insane within five years previous; persons who have had two or more attacks of insanity at any time previously; paupers; persons likely to become a public charge; professional beggars; persons afflicted with tuberculosis or with a loathsome or dangerous contagious disease; persons not comprehended within any of the foregoing excluded classes who are found to be and are certified by the examining surgeon as being mentally or physically defective, such mental or physical defect being of a nature which may affect the ability of such alien to earn a living."

Despite the restrictions, the *Devils Lake Inter-Ocean* was confident that in appointing an immigration commission, Roosevelt was taking steps to alleviate the labor shortage through immigration.

Carole Butcher

06 JUL

The Night of the Flying Saucers

If we were to read this headline in North Dakota today, it still might pique interest. Imagine it as the banner headline of the *Fargo Forum* in 1947. Typeset in all boldface, capital letters it read, "Report: 'Flying Saucer' Seen in N.D."

July 6 was a Sunday in 1947, an especially important day for newspapers. Fourth of July celebrations had come to an end. The Independence Day weekend had been a particularly peculiar one for some across the nation, as the lead paragraph stated:

"Those mysterious 'flying saucers' which observers have reported seeing in various parts of the nation in the past two weeks have been observed in North Dakota." Virgil Been of Elliott, in Ransom County, reported that he saw an object about the size and shape of a dinner plate, but green in color, above his mother's barn. Been, a U.S. Navy veteran, said the disc was also seen by his brother and mother as it passed overhead, about 30 to 40 feet, at a high rate of speed.

A man in Waterloo, Iowa had also reported seeing a similarly sized disc flying around 25 feet in the air. In the same week, people from across the country were daring to report their sightings of saucers and unexplained flying objects. The newspaper reported that the Army had a California-based fighter plane standing by and prepared to give chase, following the flying saucer reports from across the country.

U.S. citizens from Maine to Oregon reported the strange flying disks. An unidentified scientist from the Manhattan Project reportedly said the saucers were being used in experiments with atomic energy, but an official with the atomic bomb project said he knew nothing about it. The chairman of the atomic energy commission also claimed there was "no connection" with the nation's atomic project.

Hundreds, perhaps thousands, of people were said to be watching the night skies with cameras (and most likely, expectations) at the ready. Two days prior, two hundred persons were reported to have seen similar objects in Idaho. Hundreds claimed the same kind of sightings in Oregon, Washington and other western states.

From all the reported sightings, the paper announced, there were certain common characteristics. The disks were round or oval, flat, and flying in a peculiar undulating motion—all at terrific speed.

The front-page story ended with an ominous quote from the first reported observer, a man named Kenneth Arnold, that could have been lifted from a science fiction novel: "I don't believe it either," he said, "but I saw it."

Steve Stark

Band Camp

07 JUL

It was around this time in 1956 that the International High School Music Camp first began. The camp is still located between the U.S. and Canada in the International Peace Garden near Dunseith, North Dakota. Dr. Merton Utgaard was the camp's founder.

The camp began with humble beginnings. The first year, student housing stood in a field of dirt that quickly became mud on opening day, and it rained almost all week.

Fortunately, Dr. Utgaard wasn't ready to give up on his dream – which began with the founding of the International Peace Garden in 1928. Merton Utgaard, a young Eagle Scout, was among the 50,000 people who had gathered to witness the event.

Now jump forward to the summer of 1955; Dr. Utgaard is employed at Ball State University in Muncie, Indiana. He's gotten this idea in his head to start a band camp, but he can't settle on the location. After months of searching and "researching," he suddenly remembered that day on the U.S.-Canadian border and asks his graduate assistant, Marvin Field, "What happened to the International Peace Garden?"

What indeed? When Utgaard brought his idea to the Peace Gardens Board, it was decided that rustic buildings erected by Civilian Conservation Corps back in 1934 could be reformatted to suit the camp's need for barracks, rehearsal areas, and kitchen/dining spaces. From there, the idea took off. By early 1956, the newly formed "International High School Music Camp" was preparing to open, but Utgaard realized they had no money for promotion, postage, or stationary. Figuring they'd need $1,000 to launch the program, Utgaard and Marvin Field each borrowed $500 from their families and a local banker, and the plans moved forward.

The first session offered programs for band and baton twirling; 113 students enrolled, and that first week the Camp Band gave four performances for an International audience of nearly 10,000 spectators. Since then, the camp has dramatically developed. Approximately 2,500 students take part every year, and the offerings have grown to include a wide range of musical instruction and the creative arts. It's now one of the largest fine arts summer schools in the world. Students have come from all fifty states, every Canadian province, and from seventy other nations, and the summer staff includes some of the finest conductors and artist-teachers in the world.

Merry Helm

08 JUL

Cavalier County Rising

The original Cavalier County had been created in 1873 out of western Pembina County in northeastern North Dakota. Fur trader and postmaster Charles Cavileer was its namesake.

On this date in 1884, the modern Cavalier County began to take shape. Three energetic locals petitioned the governor of Dakota Territory for permission to organize the tract of land. Sixteen days later, the county officials were decided, with positions from sheriff to superintendent of schools. Ten months after organizing Cavalier County, over 5,000 people called it home. Today about 4,000 people reside there. Langdon is the county seat, with twelve cities dotting the county's map.

The county's history is a colorful one. A remnant of North Dakota's role in the Cold War stands north of Nekoma – the Stanley R. Mickelsen Safeguard Complex, colloquially known as Nixon's Pyramid. This missile defense facility was operational for four months before Congress deactivated the site in 1976. Built for over $6 billion, the base was bought for $500,000 in 2012 by a Hutterite colony in southeastern North Dakota. The base's concrete radar pyramid can be seen for miles around in a sea of wind turbines. These wind turbines help provide thirty percent of the nation's electricity from wind that comes from North Dakota. North Dakota is the top state for wind energy potential and is often called the "Saudi Arabia of Wind."

Cavalier County is also home to natural curiosities like the Pembina Gorge, North Dakota's deepest and longest unaltered river valley. The gorge is popular with hikers, canoeists and other outdoor enthusiasts.

The county also lies in the Prairie Pothole Region, a veritable paradise for half of North America's migratory waterfowl. Sloughs and wetlands provide key habitat for nesting ducks and geese.

In addition, Cavalier County holds one of North Dakota's four national natural landmarks. Rush Lake, a shallow, undisturbed lake, lies west of Wales on private land. It was designated in 1975. Three ports of entry into Canada are in the county: Maida, Hannah, and Sarles.

A quiet place on the prairie, Cavalier County has plenty of sites of interest -- for those who know where to look.

Jack Dura

Chicago's Savior

09 JUL

A Valley City man arrived in Chicago on this day in 1902 on a mission to save the city. Otto Faust left a wife, eight children, and a 1,400-acre farm after receiving a vision from God. Faust claimed that "he was told that Chicago was to be damned unless he came to the city and saved it."

Valuing "the salvation of the city more than his earthly possessions," Faust caught an early train out of Valley City. He carried on him only a small suitcase containing clothes, and in one hand a Bible. Upon his arrival to Chicago's Grand Central Depot, Faust walked up to the nearest police officer and said, "Please direct me to the house of the mayor of Chicago at once. I am here to save Chicago, and I want to have a conference with him before starting the work." The 'savior' was escorted to the local police department, where he spent the remainder of his visit singing hymns.

Jayme L. Job

10 JUL

Council of Defense Corporation

In the Special Session of 1918, the North Dakota Legislature created and funded the North Dakota Council of Defense. The Council was comprised of the governor, the attorney general, and twelve members selected by the governor. The Council of Defense was granted broad powers to oversee coal resources and agricultural production. The governor was granted additional power to authorize other actions necessary for the conduct of the war.

With Lynn Frazier as governor, the Non-Partisan League was firmly in control of state government. In an incredibly bold move, the Council, comprised completely of loyal members of the Nonpartisan League, met on this date and enacted the North Dakota Council of Defense Corporation. This private corporation issued one million shares of stock at one dollar per share, with the stockholders limited to the present members of the Council of Defense.

The aim of the corporation was quite simple. Issuing a seven-point declaration, its objective was to privatize and take over North Dakota's 2,200 grain elevators and warehouses and also several hundred creameries and cream stations. Under the control of the council, a board of trustees consisting of five to seven members chosen locally would oversee the operations. The former owners would be paid a rental fee based upon the actual assessed value of their business. In each community there would be a central point for weighing and grading the grain, which would be separated by type and grade and stored in the local elevators. The farmers would be paid for their grain plus any surplus profit, which would be prorated among them. There would be no dividends paid to the stockholders, but any proportionate expenses of the North Dakota Council of Defense Corporation would be covered. Creameries were to be operated in the same fashion.

The reaction was loud and swift. The following day outraged farmer-owned and independent elevator operators descended upon the council offices. But before the general public had time to react, the Council denied they had ever approved the takeover. There may have been some discussion, they stated, but nothing showed up in their minutes, and they claimed there was never any serious consideration of endorsing the idea. Although the Non-Partisan League never attempted to reactivate the corporation, their initial idea, on a much-reduced scale, surfaced in the next legislative session with a proposal for the North Dakota State Mill and Elevator.

Jim Davis

Division Day Banners

11 JUL

Creating North Dakota and South Dakota was no easy matter, with years of partisanship and multiple proposals tossed around for dividing Dakota Territory into states. One school of thought saw dividing Dakota into north and south as vital. About 500 delegates from the various counties convened in July of 1888 in Huron to hash out division of the territory.

By the end of the convention, most of the delegates supported division. Pro-divisionists penned a speech that condemned the "territorial condition," with increasing taxes, cramped industries and ruined interests. It read in part: "Rights are invaded, justice is denied, public improvements are held back, rightful political power is withheld, a voice in your own government is insolently refused." That sentiment referred to the inability of territory residents to choose state leaders. It was the President who selected the Territorial Governor, Territorial Secretary and Supreme Court Justices.

Attorneys, ministers, newspaper editors, farmers, and businessmen also attended the convention, participating in auxiliary committees to consider division. After much discussion, the convention adjourned after adopting a plan for a constitutional convention for North Dakota, and to take steps to also establish a state government for South Dakota.

In 1888, before a crowd at Huron's opera house, a group of women presented two white silk swallowtail banners to the convention representing North Dakota and South Dakota. North Dakota's banner depicted an oil painting of a young dark-haired woman holding a bundle of wheat. South Dakota's was a fair-haired woman holding a cornstalk.

Fargo businessman Waldo Potter accepted the North Dakota banner from Flora Gans, a clerk for an insurance company in Huron. Potter said the banner was "a gem of workmanship." Former Dakota Territorial Secretary George H. Hand thanked the women for the banners, and said, "We will bear them aloft until heaven's golden light shall kiss their folds, amidst the plaudits of a free and enfranchised people."

Today, the South Dakota State Historical Society displays the banners in Pierre. At its centennial, North Dakota wanted its banner back. Instead, the state received replicas of both banners.

Jack Dura

12 JUL

Charging Bear Adopts Captain Welsh

During the summer of 1913, an event near Fort Yates led to a full-page spread in the *Minneapolis Sunday Journal*, including photos and artwork. The story referred to Blackfeet/Hunkpapa Chief John Grass adopting Alfred Burton Welch, Captain in the U.S. Army, as his son.

North Dakota historian LaDonna Brave Bull Allard writes, "Adoption is one of our sacred seven rites of the Lakota/Dakotas Nation. We adopt all kinds of people young and old. If you lost a sister, you adopted another who reminds you of that sister or brother, grandmother, etc. […] We believe that you should never be alone in this world[…] It is our way."

Grass inherited his position as chief from his father, Chief Pezi. Grass fought at the Little Bighorn, and his war name was Mato Watakpe, or Charging Bear. When Charging Bear was younger, his father told him "not to fight the white man, but to help the white man, to give to him honor and respect, and then the white man would honor and respect him."

John Grass had mixed feelings about his people's struggle on the Standing Rock Reservation. "I like to see the old men dance," he said. "It is their custom, their bread, their life. They cannot change. I like to see the young people go to school and learn the white man's ways. I have tried to live up to my father's instruction and have set my feet in the paths of peace."

During a Bismarck banquet in the early 1900s, Grass spoke as a guest, through an interpreter, "of the burdens of his people, of their former prestige, of their depleted numbers and their lost and broken spirits."

One of the people in the audience that night was Captain A.B. Welch, who had grown up in South Dakota where he had daily contact with Native Americans. Welch quickly became an advocate for Grass's people, and over time the two men became close friends. Grass lost a son in 1910, and three years later, he decided to adopt Welch in memory of his late son. It was a great honor; the chief said it was the first time in history that any white man had been adopted into the Sioux nation using the full tribal ceremony.

The ceremony took place on June 12 near Fort Yates where Chief Pezi had once won a great battle. The warriors voted on whether Welch was worthy of this honor. One negative vote would have stopped the adoption, but Welch was accepted and was given his adoptive father's name, Mato Watakpe. With 500 in attendance, the ceremonies included speeches, converging of elders, drumming, dancing, and singing.

Charging Bear presented to Welch a specially made pipe, and Welch gave Charging Bear a gold watch. Welch also gave the tribe a barbecue, including two steers, 100 pounds of coffee, a wagonload of hard tack, and 100 pounds of tobacco.

Merry Helm

Emma Bates

13 JUL

Emma Bates was not a North Dakota native. However, North Dakota is perhaps where she made her biggest impact. Bates was born and raised on a New York farm and attended college in Pennsylvania but fell ill from overwork before she could graduate. After recovering, she held various positions in education before moving to North Dakota in 1887 to be an assistant to Professor John Ogden. In the years to come, she would be highly involved in education and in organizations such as the Women's Christian Temperance Union. She even served as editor-in-chief for a publication called *Western Womanhood*.

Due to her high skillset and involvement in the community, she became a candidate for Superintendent of Public Instruction. She spoke at the July 1894 Republican Party convention, receiving an enthusiastic response. An article she published in the July edition of *Western Womanhood* demonstrated her awareness of the issues surrounding education. She was highly concerned about reading, stating that "Most pupils of fifteen […] cannot read to enjoy." She believed reading would foster more independent thinkers.

She also expressed her objection to "cramming the mind with inexplicable facts," a sentiment that undoubtedly rang true with students and likely still does.

Bates' hard work paid off. She won the election for Superintendent of Public Instruction and went on to many achievements, from providing clean outhouses for schools to establishing a board to promote higher education. She died in 1921, and while she had no children of her own, no one can deny she was a mother to North Dakota education.

Lucid Thomas

14 JUL

The Peace Garden

The International Peace Garden straddles the U.S.–Canadian border between Boissevain, Manitoba and Dunseith, North Dakota. It was on this date in 1932 that the land was dedicated.

The idea for the Peace Garden began as the dream of a Canadian horticulturist, Dr. Henry J. Moore, a lecturer for the Ontario Department of Agriculture. He had an idea for a botanical garden celebrating the long and peaceful coexistence of the people of Canada and the United States.

Dr. Moore presented his idea for an "International Peace Garden" at the Association's next annual meeting, which was held in Toronto – the first time it was ever held outside the U.S. The Association liked the proposal and formed an international committee to find an appropriate site.

In North Dakota, a group calling itself the International Peace Picnic Association invited Dr. Moore and Ohio native Joseph Dunlop to visit the Turtle Mountains. They had organized specifically to promote the area as a location for the Peace Garden, and fortunately, Moore and Dunlop agreed that they had found the right spot.

Dr. Moore went up for an airplane ride over the area and later said, "What a sight greeted the eye! Those undulating hills rising out of the limitless prairies are filled with lakes and streams. On the south of the unrecognizable boundary, wheat fields everywhere; and on the north, the Manitoba Forest Preserve. What a place for a garden!"

During the next three years, gardeners and horticulturists converged on the site to shape the settings and construct the gardens. Dr. Moore determined it would be "not merely a memorial to the long period of peace which has been enjoyed by both countries, but as an example to the warring nations of the world that there is a better way to settle international differences than through recourse to bloody war, and as a memorial to international friendship that shall endure to all time."

An estimated crowd of as many as 70,000 people from Canada and the U.S. attended the dedication below a cairn with poles flying the flags of both countries. On it is written, "To God in his Glory we two nations dedicate this garden and pledge ourselves that as long as men shall live, we will not take up arms against one another."

A new feature is the 9/11 Memorial. Its plaque reads, "The International Peace Garden represents a unique and enduring symbol of the strength of our friendship as nations, our mutual respect and our shared desire for world peace. The events of September 11, 2001 failed to shake the foundation of our shared vision of peace and prosperity for all the world's people. This cairn, composed of steel remnants rescued from the devastation of the World Trade Center in New York, ensures the memory of this tragedy will not be lost and reminds us to cherish tolerance, understanding and freedom."

Merry Helm

The Only Recall-Elected Governor

15 JUL

The only North Dakota governor to be elected in a recall election died on this date in 1942. Ragnvald Nestos was governor from 1921 to 1925. He was born in Norway in 1877 and came to Buxton, North Dakota at age 16. He spoke no English at the time and lived with an aunt and uncle.

Nestos studied at Mayville Normal School and taught country school for a time. He later graduated from the universities of Wisconsin and North Dakota and then moved to Minot where he began a career in law in 1904. In 1910 Nestos was elected as a state representative. In this two-year term, he chaired the Tax Laws Committee. In 1912 he was elected state's attorney of Ward County.

Nestos' election into the governor's office came at a time of political upset. North Dakota Governor Lynn Frazier was ousted in his third term during political bitterness and economic depression – becoming the first U.S. governor to be recalled. While both candidates were Republicans, Frazier was a member of the socialist-leaning Non-Partisan League, while Nestos belonged to the Independent Voters Association, which was conservative and pro-business.

Nestos' term saw some firsts for the state. North Dakota began registering births and deaths to comply with the national standard. The state acquired a full-time health officer. Nestos also fought against illiteracy and championed education with his advocacy for libraries.

Outside of office, Nestos saw other successes. He helped Minot acquire a normal school and public library. He served on committees for the State Library Commission, the Young Men's Christian Association and the Boy Scouts of America. In 1942 Nestos was awarded the Silver Buffalo Award by the Boy Scouts for his service to scouting.

Governor Ragnvald Nestos never married, and he died in Minot on this date in 1942 following a stroke. He was 65. While elected during a dark time in North Dakota, the state's thirteenth governor left the office a little brighter than when he went in.

Jack Dura

16 JUL

Bismarck's Name

The trial of John H. Wishek, the former state senator and well-known banker and businessman from McIntosh County, began in Bismarck on July 9, 1918. Wishek, charged with sedition, faced several counts in the indictment including proliferation of pro-German propaganda and discouraging the sale of war bonds.

The trial's high profile sparked another rise in anti-German sentiment across the state. Almost daily authorities in Bismarck received letters demanding that the name of Bismarck be changed. Communications came from practically every state in the union and even from countries allied with the United States. Educators, politicians, preachers, soldiers and students questioned the appropriateness of the name of a noted German leader being used for the capital of an American state. Defenders stated that Prince Otto Von Bismarck was a truly great man who had in no way precipitated the war, and that the name was selected when the world was at peace. To change the name now would denote narrowness on the part of its citizens and would cost the city much in prestige. They also noted that it would cost a significant amount of money to reprint all the maps of the city, county, state and nation.

On this date in 1918, the name question had three Bismarck boys facing charges. Armed with brushes and yellow paint, it was their ambition to eliminate the name Bismarck from every location within the city. Under cover of darkness, they began with the Northern Pacific railway station and then proceeded to several locations, including the Bismarck Tribune, the Bismarck Shoe Hospital, and the Bismarck Commission. At each stop the offending moniker was obliterated. Once caught, city officials couldn't decide on charges, but eventually considered the adventure a boyish prank.

In an earlier editorial, the *Bismarck Tribune* itself had commented on anti-German sentiment. They noted that prior to the war, sauerkraut sold for $50 a barrel, but soon after the United States entered the war, it was difficult to sell at $14 a barrel, simply because it was a German specialty. The paper made the following proposal: "In the campaign to knock the German out of everything [...]may we not knock the high cost out of bread, meat, gasoline, clothes and shoes by giving them German names?" And they mused, "If we could do this, would it not be licking the Germans with German?"

Jim Davis

North Dakota Secedes From The U.S.

17 JUL

In 1934, controversial Governor William "Wild Bill" Langer was convicted of misappropriating federal resources for political reasons by promoting his political party, the Non-Partisan League, to federal workers in the state capital. This was a felony, and state law declared that no one could be Governor if convicted of a felony.

Lieutenant Governor Ole Olson believed that Langer's authority was removed at the moment of conviction. Langer asserted that he would remain governor until he exhausted the appeals process. Langer continued to perform the duties of governor, supported by his followers, while Olson and his party struggled to take control.

On this date in 1934, the Supreme Court of North Dakota decided that Langer was to be removed from office. Langer stubbornly refused, and barricaded himself and his most trusted supporters in the governor's offices.

At 10 o'clock that evening, Langer and 26 of his followers signed a declaration of independence, each declaring that they were present when the governor "declared martial law marking the Declaration of Independence for the State of North Dakota." An hour later, Langer issued Executive Order No. 10, calling out the National Guard and explicitly declaring martial law over the entire state of North Dakota.

By the morning of the 18th, however, tempers had cooled. Langer and his staff left the governor's office and departed the Capitol grounds. Ole Olson took his position as interim governor and withdrew the order of martial law, but did not make any mention of Langer's sedition. Two years later, with his conviction overturned, Langer was re-elected as Governor, then later elected to the United States Congress in 1940.

However, Congress refused to seat Langer due to his history of questionable ethics, and his declaration of independence was shown as evidence. Langer's response avoided the secessionist language, and he said it was simply "a nucleus for going out and putting up one great, big fight." Langer's true intentions on that evening in 1934 may not be known, but one might argue that for those few hours the State of North Dakota was briefly an independent nation due to "Wild Bill" Langer's struggle to stay in power.

Derek Dahlsad

18 JUL

Bismarck's Breweries

The town of Bismarck, by the very nature of things, was destined to become a bustling city. Bismarck's geography ensured its future, being located at the easiest, and narrowest, crossing of the mighty Missouri River. Bismarck was created by the Northern Pacific Railway, which brought newcomers to town after its tracks reached the crossing in 1873.

Consequently, Bismarck became a first-class frontier town in the 1870s, boasting five hotels, two drug stores, several general stores, three bakeries, plus forty more businesses, including harness shops and livery stables, and a gaggle of "Wild-West" saloons. Supplies for all those stores arrived by train until home-grown manufacturing began.

One of the first local suppliers was the Bismarck Brewery. Mr. H. Bose reportedly started it in 1873, but he never brewed anything. The Bismarck Brewery actually began in 1874, built by R. H. Girard. Girard & Company sold lager beer to local saloons at lower prices than the shipped-in bottled beers. Located on an acre of ground near the river, the brewery consisted of several wood-framed buildings, with a malt kiln, an ice house, and a cold cellar built of stone.

Girard operated it for several years, then sold it in 1876 to Jacob Kalberer, a Swiss immigrant, who rebranded the company as "Kalberer and Walter." On this date in 1877, the *Bismarck Tribune* published an advertisement, touting "Bismarck Brewery, Kalberer & Walter, Manufacturers of ALE AND BEER [with...] First Class Goods and Reasonable Prices."

They advertised heavily, because of intense competition. The Star Brewery, built in 1876, became a fierce rival because the owner, Judson E. Walker, hired a talented German brewer named August Boenicke, who had apprenticed in the Old Country and had worked in Cincinnati and San Francisco. But despite that hired gun, the competition was too much, and the Star Brewery closed in 1880, with Walker bankrupt. As for the Bismarck Brewery, it burned down in 1883.

The final chapter in Bismarck's brewing history came in 1884 when the nationally-famous Milwaukee Brewing Company built a magnificent new Bismarck Brewery– seven-stories-tall with solid brick walls.

This larger Bismarck Brewery opened in 1885, but then closed shortly thereafter, because the statewide prohibition of alcohol abolished *all* breweries in 1889, when North Dakota gained statehood.

The Bismarck Brewery buildings remained on the riverside, tall and empty, near the Liberty Memorial Bridge, until demolition in 1939.

Dr. Steve Hoffbeck

Native American WWI Heroes

19 JUL

North Dakota's history is filled with stories of brave soldiers and warriors. Throughout the spring and early summer of 1918, state newspapers were reporting stories of yet another—Charlie Rogers.

Rogers was a Sioux Indian from the Standing Rock Reservation. He entered into duty and served first in the 1st ND Regiment, then in the 18th US Infantry. It did not take long for this soldier to prove his bravery. "War whooping Indian chases 20 Germans" reported a headline in the *New Rockford Transcript* on this day in 1918. "Indian goes over the top," read another in the *Sioux County Pioneer* on June 27, 1918.

Although the stories were printed a few weeks apart, both came from the same source. Sergeant E.H. Tostevin, formerly of Mandan, wrote the North Dakota newspapers about Rogers' bravery in a battle. The letter, dated May 20, 1918, read: "Rogers leaped over the parapet swinging his old rifle over his head. He let out a yell that he had saved for years […] The Germans were pretty close before we mixed. Rogers, of course, had his gun loaded with five rounds, and his bayonet fixed. After swinging his gun around his head a couple of times, he brought it down to his shoulders and emptied his shells at the enemy, swung it again, yelled and jabbed and used the butt of his gun to smash the skull of another."

Tostevin and US and German soldiers looked on as Roger's fought his way through the oncoming enemies, whose actions seemed to be no match for the young Sioux. "Rogers' actions terrorized the Huns, and they beat it for their lives," wrote Tostevin. "I never saw a man move so fast in my life and I guess the Germans hadn't either."

Around the same time, the newspapers were reporting the brave actions of another young man, Joe Young Hawk, an Arikara from Elbowoods. In a battle at the Soissons front, Young Hawk was captured by five Germans. According to the papers, these five Germans were no match for him. He killed three of his captors with his bare hands by breaking their backs over his knees. Young Hawk was shot through both legs in this bout, but was still able to capture his other two captors and take them back to US lines. Major Welch of his division said this of Young Hawk, "I am terribly proud of him. He ought to have a medal, for really it took all kinds of nerve."

Young Hawk did receive that medal on his return back to the United States, but his bravery was not without consequence. Upon his return, Young Hawk began receiving treatment on his legs. He had three operations and each time, more of one leg was amputated. He also suffered injuries from being gassed. On June 23, 1923, Joe Young Hawk died from the wounds he suffered during his brave escape and capture of his captors.

Tessa Sandstrom

20 JUL

Circus Mishaps in Fargo

Barnum & Bailey's circus pulled into Fargo on this date in 1907, and it would soon experience a menagerie of mishaps. Early in the morning, the circus arrived from Ortonville, Minnesota, in four trains. Twenty tents were pitched at the show grounds near present-day Fargo North High School. The big top was 643 feet high and held 15,000 people. Horses, seals, elephants and camels comprised the exciting show, along with clowns, ski-sailers and Isabelle Butler's Dip of Death.

Unfortunately, excitement also came when a section of seating collapsed, hurling 300 people to the ground. Six people were slightly injured, including a Fargo judge who clung to a tent pole and scratched his chin as the seats fell. One woman's spine was injured severely enough that she sued the circus. A railroad agent was also injured, spraining his ankle. He settled with the show people to keep the issue out of court.

That was not all, however. A camel died from pneumonia the evening of the show. Worth $2,500, the animal was buried in the Fargo city dump on the edge of town. *Fargo Forum* reporters speculated its carcass would be a mystery to those excavating the land a hundred years in the future … 2007.

This wasn't the first time a visiting circus had encountered problems. An acrobat died from typhoid in 1905, and a camel was killed by an elephant in 1900. And in 1897, a circus was stranded in Fargo due to a lack of funds.

Despite all the extra excitement, Fargo continued to be a popular stop on the Midwestern show circuit for years afterward.

Jack Dura

An Explosion in Minot

21 JUL

A violent explosion rocked Minot on this day in 1947. People were thrown to the ground as far as two blocks away, and windows were shattered throughout a four-block radius.

The explosion occurred shortly before noon at the Westland Oil Company service station and bulk plant. It started with an undetermined detonation of gasoline holding tanks, which set off several more blasts nearby. Burning gasoline was hurled into the air, setting fire to nearby buildings. Ultimately, fire consumed four city blocks.

Lester Dahlen, manager of the Bridgeman Creamery next door to the Oil Company, "described the explosion as literally lifting the building into the air." Another witness claimed the explosion "resembled [his] idea of an atomic bomb." Owners of the Dakota Hide and Fur Company "thought a truck hit the front of [their] building." A Mandan Creamery employee "said she saw the flame bursting like a volcano from the burning tank." A farmer eighteen miles south of town said he saw the flames from his farmyard. Smoke from the disaster was visible up to 100 miles away.

Firemen were working with a low water supply due to a breakdown in one of the city's wells, and "city officials pleaded with residents of the city to be extremely careful in their consumption of water." Luckily, there was very little wind that day, and the defense strategy worked.

Hospitals readied themselves for patients at the first sounds of the explosion. Several people were rushed into the emergency rooms and treated for burns, many very serious. Those who were mortally wounded included employees of the surrounding businesses and one fireman – all suffering burns over 90-100% of their bodies.

In the following days, newspapers released eyewitness accounts citing a visible fuel leak as the cause of the disaster, but all reports were later retracted. Several hypotheses were set forward to explain the explosion, including crowded storage tanks and pumping negligence. But, R. J. Coughlin, president of Westland Oil Company, claimed the "pumps were 'dead' at the time of the explosion." He provided records of the week's transactions showing the storage tanks could each hold an additional 500 gallons of fuel. After finishing his own investigation, the president cited 'no explanation' for the explosion.

Government officials also launched an investigation, but after interviewing thirteen witnesses, Assistant State's Attorney B. A. Dickinson found "no cause established and no grounds for criminal prosecution." The explosion killed five people, destroyed nine businesses and caused nearly $1 million in damages. With no cause to point to, Deputy Fire Marshal H. R. Handtmann hoped it would at least increase public awareness concerning the need for caution at gas stations and bulk plants.

Merry Helm

22 JUL

The Water Level

A lack of rain and moisture for much of the month of July was a complaint for Jamestown on this date in 1901. There had not been a significant rainfall since the Fourth of July.

This trend was not to last, ending with a bang on the 24th, when a thunderstorm swept through. A farmer north of Jamestown, Theodore Gospodar, had an especially close encounter with the storm when he, his 18-year-old son, and his daughter, were caught in the elements while driving a wagon of hay.

As he lay on his back in the hay, the elder Gospodar was struck by lightning in the middle of his forehead. The strike "burned off a piece of the skin about the size of a silver dollar and singed the hair. His two elbows were hurt and the skin of both his legs reddened as if a hot iron had been applied. The left leg of his pants was stripped into shreds, and one ankle hurt." It took him fifteen minutes to regain consciousness.

In the meantime, Gospodar's daughter was left in a daze, and had a red mark on her leg. The son, also dazed, had pain in his elbows and feet, and his watch case had fused together. Yet the family otherwise seemed fine, though the front team of horses was killed. The hind team was bewildered but okay.

Despite this incident, the storm was just what the area required to refresh and address water issues, as a letter from resident Kate Faunce Chase in the First ward of the city pointed out in the *Jamestown Weekly* alert: "Will you kindly give a little space in your paper to the woes of those families in the First ward who are wholly dependent upon the city water supply? They cannot have a drop of fresh water during these warm days if the lawn faucets are left open farther downtown. That must be the reason, for during the recent rains there was enough water for household use at all times. We thirsty dwellers near the courthouse would much appreciate it, if our friends who live below us would kindly keep the faucets closed, excepting at the pumping hour."

Sarah Walker

Sally the Supreme Cow

23 JUL

Today, in 1951, one little cow from North Dakota was living as a normal cow lives. Sally the cow practiced the three m's—mooing, moving and being milked—and was relatively happy. By the next day, however, that one little cow had hit the big time.

Sally was an unassuming Guernsey on the Allen D. Meyer farm near West Fargo. But then she set a world record. And with her new honor, Sally began to hit papers across the state. Sally set the first world record in butterfat production by a North Dakota cow. She completed a year's production record as a senior 4-year-old with 16,439 pounds of 5.2 % fat milk, containing in it 846 pounds of butterfat.

The last world record set was 834 pounds of butterfat. The average for all cows milked in the state was 173 pounds, and in the U.S., the average was 200 pounds. She hit papers across the United States by the next day, where Meyer reported that her amazing feat was due to twice-daily milking, part of an official herd improvement registry test. He placed a value of $5,000 dollars on Sally. When he bought her three years prior, he paid $250 dollars for her.

Sally's roots traced back to "the famed O.K. Spires herd at Minot," papers reported, and she lived on a special diet of 3 to 5 pounds of beet pulp each day, as well as a 12-15 percent protein grain concentrate mixture and hay.

Meyer's treatment of Sally was not unlike the cows of the rest of the herd, and on average, he reported the milk's content to average out at about 485.4 pounds of butterfat. He also credited Leverne Neuschwander, who helped milk the cow twice a day, every day. Others whom he listed in the "production crew" were Clarence C. Olson, an NDAC extension dairyman who supervised Sally's output on behalf of the Guernsey club, and Dr. Glenn C. Holm, NDAC veterinarian who provided medical counsel.

It was a lot of excitement for one cow. Her picture even appeared in the paper. One thing was for certain, though: Meyer milked Sally for all she was worth.

And in the end, she proved that she really was worth the milking.

Sarah Walker

24 JUL

Intertribal Trade

When we think of international commerce, we often think of America's great cities like New York or Chicago, not the rolling hills and rugged badlands of North Dakota. However, for over thirteen hundred years, long before the great trading cities of our day, the Dakota prairies were home to some of the most extensive trading centers on the American continent.

As early as A.D. 350, there existed a highly developed network of trade throughout North America. Centrally positioned on the American continent, the Mandan, Hidatsa and Arikara villages located along the Missouri River served as two of the network's main trading centers. At these trading sites the Cree, Assiniboine, Cheyenne, Comanche, Teton, and Crow nations traded goods from around the continent. Long before the introduction of European commercial trading centers, or modern transportation methods, Native Americans of the upper plains traded for items originating from thousands of miles away; sea-shells from the Pacific Ocean, obsidian from Wyoming and conch shells from the Gulf Coast.

The intertribal trade was conducted at various times throughout the year. Both the Mandan and the Arikara conducted trade throughout the summer and into the fall. However, as some tribes traveled great distances to trade in the Dakotas, many carefully planned their arrival at the Mandan and Arikara villages.

Washington Matthews, an Army medical officer stationed at Fort Berthold in the 1860s, observed that when the Dakota tribes saw the dotted blazing star blooming on the prairie in the late summer, on a day much like today, "they knew that the corn was ripe, and went to the villages of the farming Native Americans to trade."

As with any system of international commerce, when the Native American traders arrived at the commerce centers they needed a measure of exchange, something by which everything traded could be compared. In the intertribal exchange of the nineteenth century, one standard of value was the buffalo-horse, a horse fast enough to run down an adult buffalo. For a single buffalo-horse, one could receive twelve spruce-poles to build a good skin-lodge, a few eagle tail feathers for a headdress, guns, a variety of European commodities, or even seashells from the coast.

By the 1860s this intertribal trade network was but a shadow of its former glory, and eventually disappeared completely. However, the resourcefulness and ingenuity of America's earliest commodity traders remain an important part of North Dakota's vibrant past.

Lane Sunwall

Mail Order Brides

25 JUL

In the early days of North Dakota, there were plenty of wide-open spaces. Settling this flat and untamed land did not come easy. Hard work, and a lot of it, was the order of the day. To survive in this new land, one needed a lot of grit, muscle and patience. These new settlers needed a spirit of survival; a dogged determination. And as many might tell you, they also needed women.

So where does a young male settler start looking for a wife, when there are no eligible young ladies within perhaps several hundred miles? One of the answers came in the form of the "mail order bride."

One particular account of a young farmer's experience with a mail-order-bride bears repeating.

On this occasion, a young farmer in a remote area of North Dakota ran an ad in an eastern newspaper, asking for a woman to come west for "the purpose of marriage." Soon a lady answered the ad and made arrangements to meet with the young farmer in a nearby city. Without thinking, the young farmer made the mistake of bringing along on the trip, one of his handsome brothers. Yep, you guessed it. Upon seeing his brother, the mail order bride forgot about the young man who wrote the ad and ran off with his older brother and got married.

End of story? Not quite. Although humiliated, the young farmer didn't give up. He placed another ad in the same newspaper. In time, another young lady from the east showed up. This arrangement seemingly turned out better for the young farmer: she was certainly someone he could see being his wife. Just days before the wedding, well, you guessed it again: she ran off with another of his brothers and they too got married.

Now one might suppose that by this time, the young man might have soured on all women. But in the true spirit of North Dakota determination, the young man didn't give up. The story turns out that after a while, and more importantly after all of his brothers were safely married, the young farmer finally managed to keep one of his own "mail order brides."

For this young farmer, survival on the North Dakota prairie did indeed require *dogged* determination.

Dave Seifert

26 JUL

Wobblies in Minot

In July of 1913, Jack Law and Jack Allen arrived in Minot, ND and set up headquarters across from the local Salvation Army. As organizers for the International Workers of the World, better known as the Wobblies, they had been invited into the community by J.M. Near of the *Iconoclast* – Minot's socialist newspaper. Near had been pushing for a group of local contractors to unionize.

Law and Allen immediately set about organizing what they referred to as the "wage slaves," urging the construction workers to go on strike and demand double pay. They used demonstrations, public speeches, and hymns rewritten into political songs to attract attention. To the patriotic cadences of "The Battle Hymn of the Republic," they sang "Solidarity forever, for the Union makes us strong."

Pro-business supporters in the community feared being forced to pay wages that would close them down. The Salvation Army opposed the violent and disruptive methods employed by the Wobblies. The general public viewed the Wobblies as anarchists, capable of violence. It was only a matter of time before confrontation would break out.

On August 10, the Minot city police arrested Jack Law and others who had gathered to hear him speak. Unbeknownst to the crowd, the city had quietly passed a ban on public speaking and blocking the street. As the police and fifty special officers hauled more and more of the crowd off to jail, other IWW workers continued to mount the soapbox until they too were hauled off to jail. The local socialists did not totally support IWW methods or views, but the Wobblies' Constitutional rights of free speech needed to be protected regardless. They too, joined the demonstrations. They too were hauled off to jail.

The city jail was small, so the socialists were kept inside the jail building. They sang socialist songs prompting the police to turn up the heat until both sides relented. The IWW workers were held in a hastily constructed bullpen outside the jail. They too sang late into the night. The fire department was called to hose them down but that failed to quell the singing, so the police brought in large rocks and sledgehammers. The IWW workers were told to reduce the rock in exchange for food and water. Most resisted.

News of the arrests spread quickly and IWW reinforcements from Michigan, Minnesota, and Montana poured daily off the trains. Public demonstrations continued as did the arrests. Eventually, the stockyard along the Great Northern had to be converted into a temporary jail to house the overflow. After two weeks, the city's resources had been stretched to the breaking point. In the end, the free speech demonstrations ended with a compromise. The prisoners would be released if they ended the street meetings. The local socialists, as a result of this incident, split into left and right wings which marked an end to their political power in Minot.

Christina Campbell

Bernell Rhone

27 JUL

On this date in 2002, Canterbury Park in the Twin Cities inducted horse trainer Bernell Rhone into its Hall of Fame. The press release stated, "An outstanding horseman and gentleman, Rhone scored his first victory at Canterbury with Green Meringue on July 3, 1985. Since then the North Dakota native has saddled winners in every racing season."

Bernell Rhone was born in April 1949 in Harvey. After high school, he earned his Master's degree in psychology from the University of Northern Colorado before switching to horse training. By his 10-year anniversary at Canterbury, Rhone's horses had 167 wins, earning over $1.2 million for the owners.

He trained many champions over the years and won the Canterbury Park training title in 1996. In August 2003, he set a Minnesota racing record when horses he saddled took first place in six of the nine races held on one day, including a 20-1 longshot.

In early summer 2004, one of Rhone's horses, One Smart Chick, was favored to win the Princess Elaine Stakes, but heavy rain the night before caused the race to be moved from turf to the main dirt track. One Smart Chick raced only on turf, so she was scratched.

But Rhone had another horse in that race: Pandorasconnection. Nobody thought the 13-to-1 long shot could win, not even her owner, who went boating on the St. Croix instead of attending the race. But when two other favored horses, Swasti and Nilini, also scratched, the outlook changed. Shortly before post time, Rhone told the St. Paul Pioneer Press, "That makes this a wide-open race. We have a shot if everything goes just right."

Jockey Juan Rivera said, "Bernell just told me to stay close to the (Number) 10 horse, because my filly doesn't have a big kick. Then she got in front and started (weaving). She didn't have any company and wasn't sure what to do."

Actually, Pandorasconnection had started on grass only once, so the familiar dirt track was to her advantage. She won handily, earning her surprised owner a purse of $24,000.

As people told Rhone what a good job he had done, he shook his head and said, "I'd rather be lucky than good."

Merry Helm

28 JUL

Labor Shortages

North Dakota is known for its low unemployment rate. A shortage of labor is not a new problem. On this date in 1900, the *Fargo Forum and Daily Republican* announced that farmers in the Red River Valley were finding it almost impossible to hire help. Farmers came into towns every day looking for laborers, but there were none to be found. Word had spread that it would be a poor harvest. As a result, the laborers who came from the south didn't want to take a chance on coming to North Dakota and finding no work. Instead, they went to Kansas where a bumper crop was expected. While it hadn't taken many people to plant the crop, the region needed thousands of workers for the reaping, threshing and hauling. But those hands were just not forthcoming.

The harvest was a time of movement. Laborers began their work in the south and gradually moved north. But the trains came to North Dakota without bringing a single laborer. The newspaper reported that there were fewer than 10% of the laborers required. Urgent appeals for harvest hands went unanswered. Ordinarily at that time of year, men looking for work lined the streets of every town. In 1900, they were nowhere to be found.

Fields that should have been harvested two weeks ago still sat unattended. Thousands of acres went in need of harvesting. Even though the yield was expected to be small – only six to eight bushels of wheat per acre – no farmer wanted to see the crop rot in the field. Farmer Thomas Nesbit contemplated plowing the crop under.

There didn't seem to be any immediate remedy for the problem. Some local businessmen proposed approaching the railroads and urging them to ship in laborers without charge. That was a solution they had resorted to several times over the past years. In the meantime, neighbors were expected to band together to harvest as much of the crop as possible.

Carole Butcher

West Fargo's Flyboy

29 JUL

It was on July 29, 1985 that astronaut-scientist Anthony England finally reached outer space. He was part of a seven man crew aboard the space shuttle Challenger, which orbited the planet 126 times in 7.94 days. Just six minutes after the shuttle was launched, one of Challenger's three main engines shut down. It was too late to abort the mission; instead the situation became an "abort to orbit" – the first time it ever happened. When the Challenger returned eight days later, the mission was considered a success.

Tony England was born in Indiana in 1942, but when he was ten, his family moved to West Fargo, which he calls his hometown. He grew up wanting to be a pilot, but his eyesight wasn't good enough, and he had to give up that dream. Instead, he studied math and science and went to MIT, where he majored in physics. When he discovered that he liked fieldwork, he brought geology into the mix and got his Ph.D. in geophysics.

England developed theories about how to predict the electrical properties of the moon and the planets, and it was this work that brought him to the attention of the National Academy of Sciences. The Academy wanted NASA to include scientists in their Apollo and Skylab space programs; Tony joined the Apollo program in 1967. Despite his eyesight, England was to become a pilot after all. He went to Air Force flight school, where he learned to fly jets.

England's first brush with space disasters came while he was working as a part of the support team for Apollo 13. England was there in the control room when the astronauts in the space capsule radioed, "Houston, we have a problem," and it was England who, with other engineers, scrambled to design the CO_2 scrubber, which they hoped would get the astronauts safely back to Earth. England was the one to talk the astronauts through the process of building their own scrubber in space. When the crew returned, their device was identical to the lab model the engineers had designed.

Tony was himself scheduled to fly to the moon on Apollo 19, but NASA canceled the program after Apollo 17. In 1972, England left NASA to work for the U.S. Geological Survey, for whom he led scientific expeditions to Antarctica and the Arctic. NASA tried to hire him back in 1976, but England was too busy and turned them down. Three years later, they asked him again, this time enticing him with another chance to go into space. He couldn't say no.

Tony's new role at NASA was as a member of the new space shuttle program. For the first three years, he flew shuttle simulators to help programmers and engineers perfect the computer navigation software. When he finally went up in the Challenger in 1985, his job as a mission specialist was to conduct many of the experiments in the on-board laboratory. England had only two chances to appreciate the view from space – once when his equipment needed to cool down and again on the last night of the mission when he could stay up late. The flight was during the annual Perseid meteor shower, and the Aurora Australis was in full view above Antarctica. He pinpointed West Fargo as the shuttle flew over North Dakota and was able to see automobile headlights outlining the highways below. Of the shooting stars zipping through the Aurora Australis, England said, "It was otherworldly. Definitely something to remember."

England left NASA in 1986 and went to work for the University of Michigan as a professor of electrical engineering while also conducting research in environmental remote sensing.

Merry Helm

Bertha Palmer

30 JUL

When Bertha Palmer arrived in North Dakota, was just two years old. She attended Devils Lake High School and after graduation she served in various educational roles; and she is most well-known for her time as State Superintendent of Public Instruction.

Bertha Palmer's first try for the office was unsuccessful, losing to Minnie Nielson in 1924. But in 1926 she ran again, securing a position on the nonpartisan ballot. Minnie Nielson didn't run again, but Bertha still had plenty of competition. Four others were on the ballot – all of them men.

After the primary the remaining candidates were Palmer and John Bjorlie. Palmer was working hard this campaign. On this date in 1926, she sent letters to supporters that detailed her calculations as to the number of votes needed for her to win. Her calculations paid off – when the results came in, she had beaten her opponent by over 4,000 votes.

After the election, she began utilizing the radio, giving fifteen-minute talks on different subjects. She liked the idea of radio being used to educate, so she even set up a Sunday radio show. The show had segments ranging from poetry to economics – an early foray into the realm of educational public broadcasting. Bertha Palmer, educator, broadcaster, and politician, served as Superintendent of Public Instruction until 1932.

Lucid Thomas

31 JUL

Elbowoods

For sixty years, Elbowoods, North Dakota was a hub along the Missouri River on the Fort Berthold Reservation. The town was located on a bend in the river and in the wooded bottoms, hence its name. The town site started to develop in 1889, and on this date in 1893, its post office was established.

Elbowoods shares a sad story with a number of other towns along the river – inundation by the rising waters of the reservoir created by the Garrison Dam in the 1950s. Other towns lost to Lake Sakakawea included Red Butte, Lucky Mound, Nishu, Beaver Creek, Independence, Shell Creek, and Charging Eagle.

Elbowoods had been home to reservation headquarters, some miles east of the mouth of the Little Missouri River and along State Highway Eight. A Catholic mission and school served the community and the first Four Bears Bridge over the Missouri River came to Elbowoods in 1934. The bridge's center span was later floated upriver and used in the second Four Bears Bridge to New Town.

New Town was created as a "new town" for residents of the communities lost to the lake. Located on the east river bluffs, New Town has become the new hub of activity for the Fort Berthold Reservation, and a busy spot in the Bakken oil field.

Elbowoods' post office closed in the spring of 1954 as the floodwater rose. Townsfolk moved buildings and even cemeteries as their community sank away.

After the Fort Laramie Treaty of 1851, the territorial lands of the Three Tribes exceeded more than twelve million acres. Various allotment acts and the 1910 Homestead Act greatly reduced the reservation, and with additional losses to the Garrison Dam flooding, only 4% of that original acreage remained.

Jack Dura

Chippewa Indian family with Red River oxcart
Credit: State Historical Society of North Dakota (A2472-2)

AUGUST

The Truth about Shiheke

01 AUG

On this date in 2003, *Sheheke, Mandan Indian Diplomat: The Story of White Coyote, Thomas Jefferson, and Lewis and Clark* was published. It was written by North Dakota historian Tracy Potter.

Sheheke is the Mandan chief who went east with Lewis and Clark to meet President Thomas Jefferson. In his book, Tracy Potter addresses some myths about the chief.

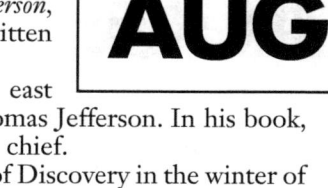

Sheheke and his people hosted the Corps of Discovery in the winter of 1804-05 and generously told them, "If we eat, you shall eat." He delivered on that promise by bringing them corn and taking Meriwether Lewis on a buffalo hunt. He helped Clark map the Yellowstone River in Montana and honored Lewis and Clark's request that the Mandan make peace with their neighbors, the Arikara. And despite the danger of being killed by the Sioux, Sheheke volunteered to go with Lewis and Clark to Washington to meet the president in 1806.

After that, the stories about Sheheke go astray. One version states that when he finally made it home in 1809, he lost rather than gained stature – that his stories of what he had seen out east were so wild that he was branded a liar. To be sure, his stories would have been hard to believe. While the Mandans had horses, they had never seen a wheel, let alone a carriage like the one Sheheke rode from Richmond to Washington.

He also told of ships large enough to cross the Atlantic Ocean, and buildings with marble floors, elaborate staircases, second and even third stories, architecture undreamed of by the people of the Mandan and Hidatsa villages. But it's not true that Sheheke lost stature because of his stories, as documented by English naturalist John Bradbury, who visited the Mandan two years after Sheheke's return from Washington. The Mandan chief told Bradbury that some of the young men now wanted to see the United States for themselves, and that he, Sheheke, was willing to lead the delegation. Unfortunately, it never happened. Neither did he ever return to St. Louis, as some claimed.

Stories of Sheheke's death are also misleading. Some have written that Arikara or Lakota Sioux Indians killed him in 1812. Others say he was killed by the Lakota 1832. But he was no longer alive in 1832. Actually, word came to Fort Manuel Lisa on October 2, 1812 that he had died in the single largest battle ever recorded between the Mandan and Hidatsa. Among the fourteen fatalities were Sheheke and his colleague, Little Crow, the war chief of his village.

Today, the Mandan and Hidatsa live in harmony, along with their old rivals, the Arikara, as the Three Affiliated Tribes of North Dakota.

Merry Helm

02 AUG

Duane Howard

Duane Howard was born in Devils Lake on this date in 1933. He married his childhood sweetheart, Orpha Hanson, in 1956. They made their home on the Howard Ranch in Minnewaukan until the rising waters of Devils Lake forced the couple to relocate to Sheyenne, North Dakota.

Howard was an all-around cowboy, competing at the highest level of pro rodeo. In her book, *My Heroes Have Always Been Cowboys*, North Dakota author Fran Armstrong talks about rodeo stars from the upper Great Plains. Of Howard, she writes, "As I listened to Duane talking about rodeo, I began to get a picture of who this man is. Not because he talks about himself. That's just about the last thing I could get out of him. He was always talking about other rodeo greats!"

One story Howard shared involved a rodeo trip to New York and fellow North Dakotan Tom Tescher. As Howard told it, "Tom was making (pancakes) for all of us [...] Lyle (Smith) came on over, and (Tom) invited Lyle to sit down and have some. Meanwhile, Tom put the sink stopper, which was just the right size, inside a pancake and gave it to Lyle. Lyle proceeded to butter it, put on the maple syrup and then cut it with a fork. Well, he sawed away with the fork, and then got the table knife out and really went to work! Tom and the rest of us were nearly choking with laughter [...] He gave Tom and the rest of us a few new names."

Duane had a stellar career. He placed at most of the bigger rodeos and won several big ones, including the National Final Rodeo in Dallas in 1961. One year, he was runner-up of the world, and another time he was third. "Guess the ones I enjoyed winning the most," he said, "were the old Madison Square Garden, where I won the Bull Riding in 1955, and winning the Bronc Riding at the Boston Garden in 1957."

In July 1961, Duane's horse fell with him at Cheyenne, Wyoming. He went into a coma and received his last rites, before he miraculously recovered. But his timing never returned, and his rodeo riding was pretty much over. He got into judging and he served on the board of the Professional Cowboys Rodeo Association. In 1998, Duane was inducted along with his friend Jim Tescher into the North Dakota Cowboy Hall of Fame. And in 2008 he was selected for the national Pro Rodeo Hall of Fame.

Duane Howard passed away in Sheyenne at the age of 82 in 2015.

Merry Helm

Grand Forks versus the Hobos

03 AUG

In 1897 it seems that bums and hobos might have been known for more than just hopping trains and sleeping under bridges, at least in Grand Forks!

On this date in 1897, the *Grand Forks Daily Herald* reported that a group of hobos took on the local Grand Forks baseball team, stating "a unique game of baseball was played yesterday at the local ball field." It seems the hobos were just hanging around waiting for the fall harvest to begin when according to the *Herald* they "demonstrated their ability to play ball with the same success that they dodge work."

The Grand Forks boys must have been looking for an easy win as they readied to take on the hobo team. Perhaps they thought differently after they heard the hobo's starting lineup: "Bowlegged Pete" was catching, the infield included "Shorty Swatts," "Peggy McNabb," "I. McCorker," and "Pie-Faced Charlie." In the outfield was "Lazy Red," "Hungry Jake," and "Bunty Spikes." On the mound for the hobos was "Milwaukee Mike."

Starting pitcher for the Grand Forks boys was a Mr. Hoar, who likely intended to make easy work of the hobo team.

After the Grand Forks boys scored a run in the first inning, Hoar started to give up a number of hits that "came more freely for the hobos than free lunches." So many in fact, he was taken out of the game and replaced by a man named Marshall.

Mr. Marshall had no better luck, and if it wasn't for some hot fielding by the Grand Forks boys, the game would have been a run-away for the hobos.

Quoting the article, the hobos' hurler, Milwaukee Mike, pitched with "as many graceful curves as a ballet dancer" while the Grand Forks team "punched more holes in the air than would fill a porous plaster." Whenever the local boys smashed what appeared to be a safe hit, a "weary Willy" stood waiting for it and it seemed first base looked "as far away as Alaska."

Despite the Grand Forks boys' seasoned efforts, and a tie going into the bottom of the last inning, they gave up a run to the hobo team and lost 3-2.

The hobo team would maybe have smiled with even more pride if they knew that fifty-eight years later, the Brooklyn Dodgers would win their only World Series as a Brooklyn team. Why the smiles? Because their nickname was: "The Bums."

Dave Seifert

04 AUG

Stutsman County Courthouse

Built in 1883, six years before North Dakota became a state, the Stutsman County Courthouse is the oldest of its kind in North Dakota. For almost a century the beautiful red brick structure was the center of both Stutsman County politics and law, only replaced by a new building in the early 1980s. A one-of-a-kind structure, the Jamestown landmark is listed on the National Register of Historic Places as an excellent example of the Gothic-Revival style of architecture.

The origins of the Stutsman County landmark trace back to Anton Klaus, the "father of Jamestown." An immigrant from Bruttig, Prussia, Klaus originally settled in Green Bay, Wisconsin in 1849 where he made his fortune in hotels, real estate, and shingles. Yet, following a major stock market crash in 1873, Klaus went bankrupt. And so, in 1874, the Prussian once again packed up his worldly possessions and followed thousands of other Americans into the West; eventually settling in Jamestown, Dakota Territory.

Klaus set to work, starting up a general store, buying real estate, building a brick factory and operating a hotel. In the process, Klaus once again assembled a fortune, which he liberally donated for public projects in his newly adopted home. The courthouse was one of his defining achievements. Anton Klaus donated not only the land for the new structure, but paid for the construction plans to build it, and he didn't get just anyone to design his hometown's new courthouse; he hired one of the country's most prominent architects, Henry C. Koch. Originally a topographic engineer for General Philip H. Sheridan during the Civil War, Henry Koch went on to design landmarks throughout the Midwest, including the Milwaukee City Hall, which at the time was one of the tallest buildings in the country. The Stutsman County Courthouse was Koch's only known building in North Dakota and construction was completed in 1883.

After a long and storied career, the Stutsman County Courthouse was acquired by the State Historical Society on this date in 1987. Despite the many years that have passed, as well as the development and modernization of its surroundings, the building still stands on the original site in downtown Jamestown– an enduring legacy of North Dakota's history and the civic pride of its people.

Lane Sunwall

UND's Fritz Pollard, Jr.

05 AUG

The Summer Olympics of 1936 in Berlin was a spectacle of Nazi hype in track-and-field. Adolf Hitler proclaimed his Aryan "Master Race" would defeat all others, but America's Jesse Owens won four gold medals, exposing the "Master Race" as a sham.

There was a side story in Berlin that summer that involved another black athlete. On this date, in 1936, Fritz Pollard, Jr., a University of North Dakota sophomore, went to the starting line in the 110-meter-high hurdles quarterfinal heat. It was a surprise that Pollard was *even there*, for Pollard had come "out of nowhere" to qualify for the U.S. team, finishing second in the Olympic Trials in New York, beating many highly-rated hurdlers. The only one who surpassed Pollard was Forrest Towns, the University of Georgia star, co-holder of the world-record. Pollard had finished second – beating USC's Roy Staley, also a world record holder.

Pollard had been a longshot, but he also faced another obstacle, having injured his leg during workouts on the cross-Atlantic voyage. He was not fully-recovered, but the concern soon dissolved as he won his heat handily in 14.7 seconds – knocking a German hurdler out of competition. Fellow-Americans Towns and Staley also won their heats.

The next day, August 6, brought the high-hurdles semifinals and finals. Both Pollard and Towns qualified in the semifinal races, but teammate Staley was eliminated.

Before an overflow-crowd of 105,000 spectators, with Hitler in attendance that day, UND's Fritz Pollard and the favorite, Forrest Towns, were in the 110-meter finals.

The starting-gun fired, and Pollard "flashed sensational speed," setting a torrid pace. Towns, a notoriously slow starter, trailed Pollard by a foot at the third hurdle, but Towns "really began to run," skimming over the next hurdles. For the first 80-meters, Pollard was leading the field. But, fatefully, Pollard's injured leg nicked the next-to-last hurdle, slowing Pollard for a heartbeat. In the blink-of-an-eye, the flawless Towns swiftly took the lead with a "finishing burst."

And so, America's Forrest Towns got gold, his 14.2 seconds setting an Olympic record, equaling the world-record. British hurdler Don Finlay edged past Pollard for silver, so UND's Fritz Pollard got bronze, though both finished with a time of 14.4, equaling the former Olympic record.

Fritz Pollard, Jr., (1915-2003), despite being hindered by a leg injury, brought home to North Dakota an Olympic bronze-medal, thereby doing his part to repudiate Hitler's malevolent and absurd race-theories.

Dr. Steve Hoffbeck

06 AUG

Traveling Jenny

Traveling Jenny was a cow on the Two Bar Ranch in Dunn County, part of a cattle herd owned by William Connolly. Many a time the Connolly cowhands had attempted to rope and brand Jenny, but she wasn't about to be caught.

Traveling Jenny was believed to be one of a number of super cows that roamed the range at that time. A cross between a Hereford and a buffalo, she had the heavy shoulders and chest of the buffalo and the white face of the Herefords. She was probably a product of free-range cattle mixing with stray buffalo from the National Park herd and she was as wild as the badlands she lived in. Her shaggy coat allowed her to withstand the severe cold of the open range and she preferred to sleep in the snow rather than the shelter of a barn or shed. She held the undisputed reputation of being the strongest, fleetest cow in the western part of the state and was always on the move, hence the name. She was the head of a herd of semi-wild cattle that mingled with the 700 head on the Connolly Ranch.

In April of 1936 the *Killdeer Herald* ran a story on Traveling Jenny, including a photograph taken by Leo Harris of Killdeer. The article retold the tales as to how no one had "been able to get within shouting distance of her" – a story was picked up by the press across the United States. Traveling Jenny was famous, so famous that a firm in Morrill, Nebraska offered Bill Connolly $300.00 for her, a lot of money in the Depression Era of the 1930s. So, on this date in 1935, he accepted the offer and announced that Jenny would be brought into Killdeer and shipped to Nebraska.

The months went by without any news on Traveling Jenny's arrival in Killdeer. In mid-October, twelve area ranches, including the Two Bar Connolly spread, combined their efforts into one spectacular cattle drive, rounding-up over 1,200 head. Fifty-three carloads of cattle were sent east, but there was no mention of the legendary animal, so we may never know if she took that fateful train ride south to Nebraska. Perhaps the elusive Jenny continued to live out her wandering life among the rugged buttes and rolling plains of the badlands.

So, if you happen to be driving out along the rugged hills of Dunn County some evening as the sun slowly sinks in the West, and you see a swirl of dust in the reddened sky, you might want to look a little closer. That could be Old Bill Connolly and the Two Bar hands still trying to put a rope on Traveling Jenny.

Jim Davis

American Soul

07 AUG

When Dakota Territory was settled, the United States encouraged the arrival of European immigrants. At a federal court hearing in 1918, Judge Charles Amidon, noted this in the sentencing of the Reverend John Fontana, pastor of the German Evangelical Lutheran Church of New Salem, who was convicted for violating the Espionage Act of 1917. The judge said, "We urged you to come, we welcomed you, we gave you opportunity, we gave you land, we conferred on you the diadem of American citizenship, and then we went away and left you. We have paid almost no attention to what you were doing."

But with the American Expeditionary Forces taking on increased front line causalities, Judge Amidon went on to note that the World War had thrown up a powerful searchlight that found "Little Germanies," "Little Austrias," "Little Italys," "Little Norways" and "Little Russias." He argued that these immigrants had cherished the American soil, but they had thrown a circle around themselves, and instead of keeping their oath of allegiance to support the United States Constitution, they continued to cherish and perpetuate everything foreign.

Rev. Fontana was sentenced to three years at the federal prison at Leavenworth, his offenses not very concrete—not buying war bonds and defending the attack on the *Lusitania*. Judge Amidon admonished him, stating, "Your body has been in America, but your life has been in Germany. You have influenced others under your ministry to do the same thing. A good many Germans have been before me, during the last month. They have lived in this country like yourself, 10, 20, 30, 40 years…but as I looked at them…[it] was written all over every one of them 'Made in Germany.' You promised you would bear true faith to the United States," he continued, "That meant that you would grow a new soul as soon as you could and put aside your German soul. It means that you will speak the American language, sing American songs, study American history and open your eyes through every avenue to influence American life. It means you will begin first of all to learn English, the language of your country, so there will be windows and doors through which American ideals may enter."

Judge Amidon felt a need to suppress the existence of these little "islands of foreignness," dealing with them in a firm hand. The business of making foreignness perpetual had to cease. If necessary, he declared they would cancel every certificate of naturalization in the United States. There was to be no more cherishing of foreign ideals. He reflected a common attitude of the times—that the day had arrived when every immigrant needed to grow an American soul.

Jim Davis

08 AUG — Atomic Bomb Project

Americans live in the dark shadow of nuclear weapons – bombs developed during World War II for fear that Nazi Germany might get them first. The idea of unleashing subatomic forces came from famous nuclear physicists, including Albert Einstein and Enrico Fermi.

When the U.S. decided to split uranium atoms and make bombs to win the war, there were thousands of people who worked within the top-secret Manhattan Project. Included were a number of North Dakotans, and two of those were from Fargo.

It was on this date, in 1945, that the *Fargo Forum* revealed the names of the two Fargoans who had participated. It was front-page news that George G. Maher (1919-2000) and Howard R. Kornberg (1918-1981) had been working at Oak Ridge, Tennessee, the facility that produced uranium for the thermonuclear weapons.

George Maher, a 1941 chemistry graduate of NDSU, worked as a chemist at Oak Ridge laboratory. His career started at the Atlas Powder Company, then he worked at a U.S. government dynamite plant, before becoming chief chemist at a Kentucky T-N-T facility.

Maher's father, Harry Maher, worked for the Fargo Veterans Bureau. When George began work at Oak Ridge, he could not tell his family what work he was doing. Only after the Hiroshima bomb exploded could he inform them fully of his whereabouts.

The other Fargoan was Howard Kornberg, a 1940 NDSU engineering graduate. Kornberg first worked for the American Bridge Company, and then went to Greenland to build an airbase. From 1943 to 1945, Kornberg helped construct the buildings at Oak Ridge.

Howard Kornberg never said anything about his work to his father, Howard G. Kornberg, who was general manager of the Fargo Foundry. The bomb project was a "hush-hush" affair, for the U.S. did not want the Russians or Germans to know about this closely-guarded secret.

After World War II ended, Kornberg worked in South Dakota and Mississippi. He died in 1981. Maher died in 2000. We have no record of what either man thought about the cruel and bitter legacies of atomic bombs – of a potentially unwinnable nuclear war that could kill two-billion people; or the proliferating "arms race" that brought perpetual anxiety. But, assuredly, each man knew that he had played a vital role in *ending* W.W. II – history's worst-ever war.

Dr. Steve Hoffbeck

The Woychik Girls

09 AUG

Clementsville, North Dakota, located in Stutsman County, got its start as a railroad station established by the Midland Continental Railroad. Situated in Rose Township, the town was approximately seven miles north of Spiritwood and about a mile west of the Barnes County border. Clementsville was named for an English stockholder with the railroad. However, the town never became very large. In 1917, the population was 57 residents, and three years later it hit 125. However, by 1940, only sixteen people lived there, and by the end of 1941, the post office was closed. By the 1950s, the *Valley City Times-Record* noted that Clementsville "does not appear either on the official North Dakota map or in the postal directory, nor is it listed in the census."

Yet people continued to stay on the land, including Marilyn and Marlys Woychik, the twin daughters of John and Cecilia Woychik. The girls, born on February 1, 1937, in Jamestown, would have composed 1/8 of Clementsville's population in 1940. Together with their parents, they would have made up a quarter of the town. These girls had a lot of talent, too. From the age of three, they were frequent singers at community programs.

On this date in 1952, the girls brought some limelight to the community. At the age of fifteen, they had gone to Chicago to audition for a television amateur hour. As a result, they appeared on WENR-TV. Marlys and Marilyn took first place that day.

At the time, the two girls were sophomores at St. John's Academy in Jamestown. Both would eventually marry and move away; yet they stayed involved with music for their entire lives.

Sarah Walker

10 AUG

What Lies Beneath?

Sixty-four years ago, the federal government anticipated a great series of floods to occur over the next few decades-floods that threatened to sweep away thousands of years of North Dakota history. Only these floods were not natural disasters. They were a planned part of federal water resource development programs. In 1945, the federal government began planning the construction of a series of dams that would provide flood control, hydroelectric power, irrigation, and recreation.

In addition to the hardships and loss experienced in the relocation of communities like Independence, Sanish, and Vanhook, it was also a shame to see many archaeological sites disappear. So, in the late summer of 1945, the Interagency Archaeological Salvage Program was created to evaluate the historic value of archaeological sites, and to remove and preserve items from these sites before the water rose.

Significant sites in North Dakota were included in the Missouri River Basin Project, a branch of the Archaeological Salvage Program River Basin Surveys. This project encompassed a vast array of sites extending from Missouri all the way to northern Montana. In North Dakota, water control projects like the Garrison Dam and the Oahe Dam threatened to submerge many historic sites like Ft. Stevenson, which disappeared under water when the gates of the Garrison Dam closed in 1953. Thankfully, the Smithsonian Institute came to the rescue of these sites, removing many of their treasures before they were lost forever.

On this date in 1966, the *Bismarck Tribune* reported that Smithsonian archeologists were excavating a prehistoric site near Cannonball. Since the start of the dig, the archaeologists had unearthed an entire house dating to prehistoric times. As the archaeologists sifted through the ruins, they slowly pieced together the story of the ancient people who lived there. These prehistoric inhabitants left behind three neat rows of rectangular houses that revealed a high level of community organization. Even the garbage, once discarded by the village people, revealed important information about their lives. These people were gardeners who raised such crops as corn and squash. The Cannonball site is just one of the many examples of the artifacts and history that were saved by the Interagency Archaeological Salvage Program.

It's ironic that the very dams created to control flooding in the Missouri River Basin nearly washed away many artifacts that held the key to North Dakota's prehistoric past. Today, the sites of old villages, forts, and houses lay deep beneath the still waters of man-made lakes, and no doubt these sites still hold a great many secrets left undiscovered by archaeologists.

Carol Wilson

Julien Monnet

11 AUG

Summer for some includes tennis. The 'thww-wwack' of a racket has echoed in North Dakota since the mid-1880s, when 'lawn tennis' infiltrated the region.

Grand Forks organized its tennis club in 1885, and by the first decade of the 1900s North Dakota had established state championships for individuals and doubles.

On this date in 1904, the *Grand Forks Herald* reported that Julien Charles Monnet, a lawyer from Cando, age 35, had won the singles championship at the state-wide tournament in Grand Forks' Town and Country Club tennis-grounds. Monnet defeated Theodore Elton in three straight sets. Monnet had also won the year before, when the 1903 championship was held in Fargo.

Mr. Monnet was a "wiry man," with "a tennis champion's body," standing five-feet-seven-inches tall and weighing 175 pounds. Born in Iowa in 1868, Monnet had been educated as a lawyer at the University of Iowa. He then came to North Dakota to practice law, first to Bathgate in 1893, then Langdon in 1895, and finally Cando in 1901.

Monnet was such a good tennis player that he was not only the state champion of North Dakota, but also became the singles champion of Iowa and Illinois during his prime years.

However, Julien Monnet's career in the legal profession surpassed even his tennis prowess. In 1905, shortly after winning his second North Dakota championship, he returned to the University of Iowa with his wife, Helen, and their three children. There he obtained a Master's degree in law, followed by further study at Harvard, earning a second law degree in 1908.

Following a short stint as a professor of law at George Washington University, Monnet accepted a call from the University of Oklahoma to establish a School of Law at its campus in Norman in 1909.

It was at the University of Oklahoma where Julien Monnet became a renowned figure. For thirty-two years he served as Dean of the Law School. The law building was named Monnet Hall in his honor.

J.C. Monnet retired from his university duties in 1941 and was swiftly inducted into Oklahoma's Hall of Fame. He died in 1961, at age 83. His North Dakota connections have been largely forgotten, but may his legacy as a tennis champion from Cando henceforth and evermore live on.

Dr. Steve Hoffbeck

12 AUG

Longest Serving Inmate

James LeRoy Iverson, North Dakota's longest serving inmate, was released from the Bismarck Penitentiary on this date in 2009. At seventy, Iverson had spent more than forty years behind the penitentiary's walls for killing two Grand Forks women in 1968. His release made national headlines, highlighting the growing number of elderly inmates within America's prisons

Iverson was convicted in 1969 for the killing Carol Mayers and Diane Bill, two employees of the Golden Hour Café in Grand Forks; Iverson, a local cab-driver, frequently drove Mayers to work. On the morning of November 27, 1968, both women failed to show up for the early shift at the café. Unable to reach either of the women, a manager sent someone to check on them.

The bodies of both women were discovered strangled at Carol Mayer's apartment. The apartment showed signs of a fierce struggle, so detectives first interviewed two men that lived in the apartment below. Information from that interview led them to Iverson, who admitted to knowing and driving the women on occasion. Detectives also noticed scratch marks up and down Iverson's hands, arms, and neck.

With a history of petty criminal charges, mostly related to burglary and home invasion, Iverson quickly became the number-one suspect. Search warrants on Iverson's car and home turned up blood-stained clothing and hair matching that of the victims. He was found guilty of both murders and sentenced to life in prison.

For forty years, Iverson watched the outskirts of Bismarck transform from empty fields into a vibrant shopping center with a busy expressway. While imprisoned, he joined Alcoholics Anonymous and took anger management classes. He went before the parole board and the victims' families nine times and was denied. Finally, in 2008, parole was granted during his tenth parole hearing. Shortly after his release, Iverson walked into a Wal-Mart and used a cell phone for the first time. He was amazed at the price of gas, which had gone up a fair bit; when Iverson had entered prison in 1969, gas was around fifteen cents a gallon.

Jayme L. Job

The Hell of High Water

13 AUG

On this date in 1993, the Red River Water Resources Council met on this date in Fargo to discuss the flood status of Devils Lake. North Dakota's largest natural lake started to swell after heavy rains in the spring, and was already up two and a half feet.

Major General David Sprynczynatyk, then North Dakota state engineer, gave a report on Devils Lake's flows with projections for the spring of 1994. In the two decades to follow, Devils Lake would not only grow, but increase seven times in volume.

As part of a closed basin, Devils Lake only drains naturally when its elevation reaches 1,458 feet. This event has happened twice in the last 4,000 years. The last overflow was less than 2,000 years ago. This overflow could be devastating for those downstream.

In 2011, Devils Lake reached a modern record of 1,454.3 feet. The flooding devoured roads, farmland, houses, and hundreds of thousands of trees. Despite the flooding, many farmers still pay taxes for their land, submerged or not.

Protection is in place on some parts of Devils lake. Outlets on the east and west release water into the Sheyenne. A control structure at Tolna was added in 2012 that protects those downstream from uncontrolled floodwater. The city of Minnewaukan has a levee in place.

Despite the immense flooding, Devils Lake is a fisherman's paradise. Walleye, bass and northern pike are common. Fishermen come from all fifty states and various foreign countries to fish North Dakota's largest natural lake.

Grahams Island State Park operates three campgrounds on the lake, with a beach, boat ramp, and a gathering space. Sully's Hill National Game Preserve offers hiking, wildlife and scenic views of the lake.

Through hell and high water, the residents around Devils Lake have adapted. Roadways have been raised or rerouted, causeways have been shored up and the lake continues to drive fishing and tourism.

Jack Dura

14 AUG

Henry Suto

On this date in 1945, President Harry Truman announced on national radio the unconditional surrender of Japan. His message, signaling the end of World War II, was met with wild jubilation across the country. But for one former North Dakotan, the news was bittersweet.

Henry Eiichi Suto was born in February of 1928 in Minot, North Dakota. His parents, first generation immigrants from Japan, operated a 24-hour café near the Minot railroad station. As Suto recalled, "about 50 Japanese people lived in Minot" and "it was a close community," meeting often for potlucks in the park. It was a happy time, but short-lived. When Suto's father and sister passed away in 1934, his mother packed up the remaining family and returned to Japan. Only seven years old and unfamiliar with the Japanese language, Suto worked hard to fit in. So, when he was approached by his teacher to sign up for the Japanese Army ten years later during World War II, he agreed. Like most soldiers fighting for Japan, Suto was certain of a Japanese victory. So when the Emperor admitted defeat in 1945, he was stunned. As he later remembered, it took a few days to accept the news.

After the war, Henry Suto worked for the American occupation force in Japan. He was impressed by MacArthur's work and appreciated the clean quarters and "American way of living." So when he later returned to the United States to live with his uncle's family in California, he found he easily fit back into American life. In an interview, Suto recalled, "While I was working on occupation forces, I think I had the feeling [of freedom] coming into my system or my heart, and so by the time I came here to the United States, the freedom of speech or freedom of whatever did not come as a surprise."

Within months of enrolling in school in California, the one-time Japanese soldier was drafted into the US Army to fight in the Korean War. Although trained to serve on the front lines as a Korean language interpreter, he was instead sent to Japan. Once discharged, Henry Suto returned to California, studied foreign trade and took a position with the Otagiri Company. The former North Dakotan with an unusual resume that included military service in both the Japanese and US Army passed away in 2008 at the age of 80.

Christina Sunwall

Ernest Steinbrueck

15 AUG

The State Historical Society of North Dakota was a fledgling organization in 1905. Although its roots went back to Statehood in 1889, the effort to save significant sites and artifacts was ill-defined and ill-financed. Several previous attempts to establish a statewide historical society, including one in 1895, had failed to gain public support, even though a room to house collections had been set up in the Capitol Building. By 1897, the organization had fallen into decay and much of North Dakota's early history was fading away or being exported to Eastern institutions.

In 1902, Dr. Orin G. Libby, a young history professor at UND, attempted to revitalize the organization. He contacted those who had pioneered the earlier efforts, and by 1903 a unified membership had been established with a new direction. With Clement Lounsberry as president and Libby acting as secretary, the State Historical Society of North Dakota was incorporated, and in 1905 it became sanctioned by the State Legislative Assembly. Realizing that a field operator was needed, Ernest Rheinhold Steinbrueck of Mandan was selected and was made the first Curator of Collections.

Steinbrueck was born in Dusseldorf on the Rhine in 1833, the son of a noted artist. After serving three years in the German navy, he married and the couple immigrated to America. He first settled in Ontario, but, after living briefly in Ohio, they came to Glen Ullin in 1883. Steinbrueck was well educated and had a long-standing interest in history, devoting himself particularly to the field of archeology. His occupation as a government surveyor heightened his interest in the area's past, particularly the history of the Mandan, Hidatsa and Arikara Indians of the Missouri River Valley.

On this date in 1905, E. R. Steinbrueck submitted his first report on the field operations of the State Historical Society of North Dakota. Even at seventy-two years of age, he had worked from April 15 to August 15 on village sites from the mouth of the Cannonball River to Fort Clark. More than 4,500 artifacts of the Native cultures had been identified in over thirty-one village sites, including seven sites he had found and explored during the season. Steinbrueck drew sketches and maps that are still in use today. Much of his time was donated, and most of his expenses were paid out of his own pocket. He continued his work for the Society until well into his seventies and died on January 25, 1918 at age 84. As a true pioneer *and* a pioneer in the field of archeology for the State of North Dakota, Steinbrueck not only helped preserve the state's past; he helped write its future.

Jim Davis

16 AUG
Strontium-90 Found in Cow's Milk

In 1957, Dr. Albert Schweitzer warned the world about the dangers of nuclear fallout from atomic-bomb testing. The humanitarian told of "radioactive particles" that "remained in the air" after nuclear-weapon explosions. Schweitzer said radioactive fallout drifted down to earth, "brought down by rain, snow, mist and dew little by little," and got into the human body through contaminated food and water.

The Nobel Peace Prize winner identified Strontium-90 as one of the chief radioactive dangers found in nuclear fallout. Strontium is an earth-metal that turns radioactive in atomic-bomb explosions. Strontium-90 does not exist naturally; it only exists in nuclear fallout. Its half-life of twenty-eight years makes it dangerous for forty years, with the potential for causing bone cancer and death.

On this date in 1966, a United Press International news story, entitled "Radioactive Milk Creates U.S. Puzzle," told of the lingering effects of Strontium-90 in cow's milk in North Dakota. It seems that radioactive dust containing Strontium-90 had drifted to the Northern Plains from above-ground nuclear testing in Nevada.

The Nevada Test Site, located northwest of Las Vegas, began nuclear-bomb tests in 1951, and scientists exploded nearly 100 nuclear bombs there through 1958. The government always made sure that the wind was blowing to the north or east, so that the fallout would not drift over Los Angeles or Las Vegas. This put North Dakota directly in the path of the radioactive dust.

In 1959, radioactivity was found in wheat and milk in the northern U.S. The fallout landed on grass in pastures, and cows ate the grass, concentrating Strontium-90 in cow's milk.

In 1961, the city of Mandan gained national notoriety for having a concentration of Strontium-90 in cow's-milk eight times higher than milk from Wisconsin or New York. An Atomic Energy Commission scientist thought that "more radioactive dust [had] fallen for some reason around Mandan, where the milk samples" came from.

Other news intensified Strontium-90 fears. Russia conducted numerous nuclear-bomb tests in 1961, causing the U.S. Public Health Service to advise parents to warn all children not to eat newly-fallen snow, which could hold radioactivity. Children thus became wary of eating either white snow or yellow snow.

Out of these swirls of controversy came the Nuclear Test Ban Treaty of 1963, prohibiting bomb testing in the atmosphere, underwater, or in outer space, reducing long-term fears of Strontium-90.

Dr. Steve Hoffbeck

JCR Mystery Man, Part One

17 AUG

It's hard to know where to begin with today's bizarre two-part story: perhaps with the disappearance of Jay Allen Caldwell from his father's ranch near Taylor, ND. His father was James Caldwell, a wheeler-dealer who made his first fortune during the Civil War. The elder Caldwell lost it all in the 1871 Chicago Fire – warehouses, stock, records, and proof of insurance.

Not yet thirty years old, Caldwell started over. In 1883, he moved to the Dickinson area with his mother, his first wife, and their two children, May and Jay. Caldwell became one of the wealthiest ranchers in Stark County – but bad luck seemed to follow wherever he went. His sister's children were burned to death in one of his sheds; an employee named Folly disappeared and was never heard from again; another employee was found dead in his bed; and the employee's wife drowned in the nearby Heart River. Mrs. Caldwell passed away as well.

All these events were overshadowed by the mysterious disappearance of Caldwell's 34-year-old son in 1907. Nobody knew if Jay was dead or alive, or if he had moved to another part of the country. But rumor suggested his relationship with his father bordered on violence.

About the same time Jay disappeared, a man was found wandering around a train depot in Waseca, MN. He had a dent above his left temple, was paralyzed on his right side, couldn't speak, and appeared to have amnesia. In his clothing, officials found the initials J. C. R., and he gained national interest as: "J. C. R. – Wandering Man of Mystery."

J. C. R. was placed with a Minnesota German family at first. He learned to walk with a cane, but when he showed no sign of regaining his memory or speech, he was transferred to the Rochester insane asylum. He was kindly-looking man with big brown eyes, and he quickly became a favorite among the staff. The *Newark Advocate* reported, "He has a winning smile, which illuminates his whole countenance, but his face in repose is pathetic."

Six years passed before J. C. R. again made national headlines; the Mayo brothers decided to operate to restore his memory. The nation held its breath, but the surgery didn't work. It did, however, put J. C. R. back in the public eye, and several months later, the Associated Press announced two of James Caldwell's sisters traveled from Chicago to Rochester to see J. C. R.

The *Oakland Tribune* reported, "J. C. R. recognized several names spoken by the women, selected the brand of the Cup and Saucer Ranch owned by [Jay] Caldwell's father, depicted by gesture how a friend of former years shot himself, and injected an eagerness in his pantomime [...] which he has not hitherto exhibited." But the women decided J. C. R. was about an inch too short to be their missing nephew.

Some months later, a nurse named Mrs. Pitkin got J. C. R. released by posing as his mother and, along with her attorney, took him to Dickinson. May Caldwell – Jay's only sibling – recognized him at once, and her descriptions of Jay's scars and markings matched those of J. C. R. James Caldwell, on the other hand, vehemently refused to recognize this man as his son.

The *Bismarck Tribune* reported, "[J. C. R.] visited the old Caldwell farm, in company with old friends, and points out the various landmarks as they are called off, counting off on his fingers accurate distances from place to place. He has also made a drawing of the old pasture fence, showing in what manner he was assaulted on Oct. 14, 1907. If, as believed by many people, the long-lost Jay Caldwell is the same person […] sensational developments may be looked for within a short time." Sensational developments indeed.

Merry Helm

JCR Mystery Man, Part Two

18 AUG

Yesterday we began a twisted tale that began when 34-year-old Jay Caldwell disappeared in the summer of 1907.

Certain people began to suspect J. C. R. was the long-lost Jay Caldwell. On this date in 1914, the *Bismarck Tribune* reported, "There has always been a mystery surrounding the sudden disappearance of Jay Allen Caldwell seven years ago. It was supposed that he was possessed of considerable personal and real estate property and that his father, James A. Caldwell [...] had quarreled with his son and possibly was responsible for his leaving."

The younger Caldwell's only sibling was an older sister – May Caldwell-Luff-Moran. The *Tribune* reported that when J. C. R. arrived in Dickinson, "[May] recognized her brother at once and embraced him most affectionately. The various scars and marks of identification on his body, which she had minutely described to the authorities, were plainly visible."

As many as 100 neighbors agreed the mystery man was indeed Jay Caldwell, but Caldwell Sr. vehemently refused to recognize the man as his son. In response, the neighbors chipped in to hire an attorney for the man they believed was Jay Caldwell, but Caldwell Sr. won the case. J. C. R. also lost an appeal. The case had a fatal flaw: J. C. R., Mystery Man, was found wandering in Waseca several months before Jay was ever reported missing. May still believed J. C. R. was her brother, however, and opened her home to him.

Just four months after winning the case brought by J. C. R., James Caldwell and his second wife were shot and killed by their hired man, a 27-year-old Russian named Mike Chumack. Chumack argued with the 74-year-old Caldwell over his wife's "companion" – a 14-year-old orphan girl. While window peeking into the girl's bedroom at night, Chumack had watched the old man sneak into the girl's room to molest her. Chumack said, however, that it was only when he brought up the topic of J. C. R. that the old man went for his gun. Chumack said he shot the couple in self-defense and then tried, unsuccessfully, to kill himself. This turned out to be not true, but that's a different story.

After the burial of the ranching couple, Caldwell's will was opened. He bequeathed $1,000 to each of his two sisters. His wife was to have received $15,000 and all of his property. The remainder of his fortune was to go into a 25-year trust for his missing son, should he ever return. To his daughter, May, he gave just $25.

The violent death of James Caldwell once again put J. C. R. in the national news, and in the summer of 1920, a St. Paul woman named Mrs. Blue positively identified him as her former husband, J. P. Harris. She said

Mr. Harris went fishing in the summer of 1907 and just never came back. Another woman, Mrs. Rose Harris, backed up Mrs. Blue's identification – Rose Harris was J. P. Harris' first wife; Mrs. Blue his second.

Most believed the J. C. R. mystery was finally solved. Mrs. Blue and her new husband took him back to their St. Paul home for the sake of Mrs. Blue's daughter – fathered by J. P. Harris before he disappeared.

Merry Helm

Presents from Bomb Bay

19 AUG

During the summer of 1944, Lt. Del Skjod of Mandan and his crew were sent deep into Germany to destroy a strategic target. Skjod was the pilot of a B-17G, flying with the 600th Squad of the 398th Bomb Group.

They had just finished their bomb run through a heavy field of flak, when shrapnel took out the crew's main oxygen supply. Del dove the plane down to a lower altitude, but this made them vulnerable to antiaircraft fire; they were sitting ducks for enemy fighters. So Skjod took them down to the deck – they would be hugging the ground all the way back to their home base.

Flying about 100 feet off the ground, Skjod took care to avoid populated areas, but at one point they came over a hill and found themselves flying directly over a German military base. Del remembered seeing a bunch of soldiers all lined up – whether they were in line for chow or to get new socks, Del didn't know, but when this B-17 came roaring over the tree tops, Del said the Germans scattered like scared rabbits!

Del told his gunners not to fire on anybody and, as far as he knew, nobody shot at them. Later, as they were following a telephone line, whenever he spotted a connecting box on one of the poles up ahead, he told his tail gunner to let loose with his twin fifties. Thinking they could perhaps disrupt communications, they took out every connector box they could.

Amazingly, they passed unscathed through the rest of Germany and then through occupied Holland. When they finally headed out over the northern English Channel, everyone breathed a sigh of relief.

Out on the water, they spotted a small Dutch fishing boat with two people aboard. As they passed over, the two men stood up and flashed victory signs at them. Del told his crew "Our mission isn't over yet." As he banked the plane into a wide curve, he had his crew put together a package of rationed cigarettes, hard candy, and German money from their escape kits. They attached the packet to a long streamer and placed it in a chute made for dropping propaganda leaflets.

As they came around, however, the fishermen were probably not quite as enthusiastic as they were at first. The only way the crew could drop the care package was through the bomb bay doors! Skjod and his men could never know what those Dutchmen thought as their large, 4-engine Fortress bore down on them with the bomb bay doors opening wide.

Del deftly brought the plane over the boat, and the drop was made. The tail gunner said the package nearly dropped right into the boat – it missed by just a couple feet. Del circled around again and saw the fishermen had retrieved the package and opened it. The Dutchman greeted them this time with broad smiles and enthusiastic waves.

You see, at this time of the war, occupied countries like Holland were suffering from extreme shortages and rationing – most of their produce was taken and shipped to Germany. With the money and the cigarettes Del and his crew dropped, these men could buy food.

While a bomber's job was normally to rain down death and destruction, Del said this little "bomb run" sure made him and his crew feel good.

Del Skjod passed away Christmas morning, 2003.

Merry Helm
Based on Scott Nelson's interview with Skjod.

Cloud Seeding

20 AUG

August in far western North Dakota brings to mind a vision of hot summer breezes, 90-degree temperatures, and dry prairie grasses. But due to the North Dakota Cloud Modification Project, farmers in the area aren't completely at the mercy of Mother Nature.

Six counties in western North Dakota – Bowman, McKenzie, Mountrail, Ward, Williams and part of Slope – participate in the Cloud Modification Project. This simply means that North Dakota pays $700,000 to help Mother Nature make more rain for her crops and earns $8 million dollars in increased agriculture. Cloud seeding can boost rainfall 4 to 10 percent. That certainly doesn't sound like a lot of extra rain to the average person, but to the farmer, that can mean an extra inch of water for his crop.

The birth of cloud seeding was in 1946, when scientists at General Electric discovered that silver iodide could make ice form. These days, Fargo-based Weather Modifications, Inc. still uses silver iodide to coax clouds to make rain. However, rain making has gone high-tech these days. The company's Cessna 300-A airplanes have remote sensing instruments that measure wind flow, liquid content in clouds, and precipitation droplets. This information, all fed into weather simulation models, can help direct the airplanes to the right cloud in the right place.

As scientists predict water shortages due to global warming, North Dakota, and other states such as Utah, Colorado and Texas, are looking at cloud seeding as a necessity. But not everyone agrees with cloud seeding. Bill Cotton, who studied weather modification as a grad student forty years ago, and is currently an atmospheric scientist at Colorado State University, claims repeated studies have not proved that cloud seeding works. He says a computer model used to analyze cloud seeding efforts in Colorado showed "not much difference" between seeding and not seeding.

North Dakota and clients around the world, like those in Morocco, Indonesia and Burkina Faso, continue to hire Fargo-based Weather Modifications, Inc. for its cloud seeding and precipitation enhancement. For some farmers in western North Dakota, cloud seeding is seen as the difference between seeing their plant seeds grow or fail.

Jill Whitcomb

21 AUG

Defining The Color Line

The famous leader of the early civil rights movement in the U.S., W.E.B. DuBois said: "The problem of the twentieth century is the problem of the color line."

The divisions in America that came from slavery continued long after human bondage ended with the Thirteenth Amendment to the Constitution. The color line dividing black and white was present in North Dakota underneath the surface appearance of total social equality, as early boosters of Dakota publicized the idea that all immigrants and ethnic groups would be welcomed.

For instance, regarding African-Americans, the *Bismarck Tribune*, in 1882, before statehood, publicly proclaimed: "There is no color line in this region. A man, no matter what his color, or previous condition of servitude, has the undisputed right here to take the free lands of Dakota, and work as hard as he sees fit, and make all the money he can. No one will deny him this privilege. A man is not sized up by his color in the Bismarck region, but by his worth."

The state Constitution of 1889 agreed, stating: "Every citizen [. . .] shall be free to obtain employment wherever possible," and anyone "maliciously interfering or hindering in any way a citizen from obtaining" employment would be "guilty of a misdemeanor."

Officially, there was not discrimination, but unofficially, the color line limited African-Americans to certain jobs and neighborhoods.

The color line became visible in an article in the *Grand Forks Herald* this week in 1908, showing how some businesses discriminated against certain customers: "In a large share of the restaurants, negroes are given to understand that they are not wanted as patrons" in Grand Forks, where the color line was "drawn rather closely."

Although there were no exclusionary signs on doors, an African-American could be discouraged from returning to a restaurant if the owner ordered the cook to put heaps of red pepper in his food – so much pepper that the meal became inedible. Another way was avoid printed menus and then charge a high price for the meal. And some restaurant-owners would pretend a customer was not there, and the person would "realize what he was up against" and leave.

Real life for North Dakota's African-Americans often called for using what was known as "black wisdom," knowing when to protest or when to endure unfair treatment while waiting decades for 1960s civil-rights-era advancements.

Dr. Steve Hoffbeck

Later Immigrants

22 AUG

Although most North Dakotans today are well aware of the role played by Scandinavian and even German settlers in the state's early history, few people are familiar with later ethnic immigrations, especially those that occurred at the turn of the nineteenth century. Between 1890 and 1910, immigration to the Great Plains changed dramatically, as changing political and social conditions in Eastern Europe led to an influx of Greeks, Italians, Czechs, and Poles to the state.

These later migrations were the result of several changes occurring in Eastern European countries. In Italy, southern Italians faced growing economic hardships and a scarcity of farmland as Italy witnessed a population boom. Land pressures combined with decades of drought to create poor conditions for the *contadini*, Italian farming peasants, and many became unemployed. In addition, an 1887 malaria outbreak wreaked havoc on the southern cities. From 1891 to 1910, over 30,000 Italian immigrants settled in the Great Plains, with nearly 1300 arriving in North Dakota to work on the railroad. Another group that traveled to the state seeking work on the railroad were Greeks, who founded Orthodox parishes in both Grand Forks and Minot. Jewish groups from Eastern Europe also began immigrating in large numbers at the turn of the century, mainly due to religious persecution from Russia. Six colonies of Jewish immigrants came to North Dakota between 1882 and 1910, most coming from the region that would later become Poland. Since they had been forbidden from owning land in much of Europe, the majority of the Jewish immigrants looked forward to homesteading as a way to earn land ownership.

On this date in 1912 the *Bismarck Tribune* published letters that the city's commercial club had received from prospective immigrants to the state. One letter came from an Italian man asking about the state's railroad; the man had heard that "the Northern Pacific railroad facilities were excellent" and stated that railroad lines in his own country were very poor. The second letter came from a Greek man hoping to bring a colony of immigrants to the city.

Although the diverse immigrations altered the state's landscape, the vast majority of immigrants continued to be of Scandinavian descent, and many of the newcomer groups left the state after work on the railroad declined and farming became more difficult. By 1920, only 400 of the 1300 Italian immigrants to the state remained.

Jayme L. Job

23 AUG

Anthrax Epizootic

Anthrax occurs naturally. The organism exists in the soil as a spore. A few anthrax cases are reported among livestock in North Dakota almost every year. Animals, domestic or wild, become infected by grazing on contaminated land or eating contaminated feed.

Anthrax in humans is associated with exposure to infected animals or contaminated animal products. The illness can manifest itself in various forms, including on the skin. Symptoms can present as quickly as two days or as slowly as two months.

The year 2000 was worst than most for anthrax in North Dakota. Until then, the state had quarantined an average of two farms a year, but in 2000, thirty-two farms had to be quarantined. It was declared an epizootic, or epidemic for animals. From July 6 to September 24, 157 animals died of anthrax on 31 farms. 62 people worked with the infected animals, but only one person showed any sign of contracting the disease. On this date, a 67-year-old North Dakotan who helped dispose of five diseased cows noticed a small bump on his left cheek. The lesion enlarged over the next two days, so he sought medical help. He showed no serious symptoms such as fever or malaise, but the bump surrounded by a purple ring was a signifying feature of skin anthrax. Luckily, it was easily treatable with antibiotics and the condition cleared up within two weeks.

Anthrax in people remains rare but persists as a concern for livestock producers. In 2005, more than 500 confirmed livestock deaths were reported in North Dakota with total losses estimated at more than 1,000. The dead animals included cattle, bison, horses, sheep, llamas and farmed deer and elk.

In 2016, the North Dakota state veterinarian issued a warning to vaccinate livestock, because the conditions were good for an anthrax outbreak.

Lucid Thomas

Chief Drags Wolf

24 AUG

The death of Hidatsa Chief Drags Wolf took place on this date in 1943. Only months before, he had vowed he would die before he watched his people's land destroyed by the Garrison Dam, and he was true to his word.

Drags Wolf was born in 1862 to Chief Crow Flies High and Peppermint Woman, who were members of the Water Buster Clan. Crow Flies High was a radical chief who – along with others on the Ft. Berthold Reservation – saw his people's quality of life collapsing. He refused to accept the traditional authority of the medicine bundle holders, and when Drags Wolf was about seven years old, Crow Flies High and Bobtail Bull led the Hushga band away from Like-A-Fishhook Village and went into self-imposed exile near Fort Buford. It wasn't until Drags Wolf was about thirty-two that his people were forced to return to the Ft. Berthold Reservation, where they settled primarily in the Shell Creek District.

Drags Wolf came of age while living in the traditional ways – hunting, trading and growing a few crops. When the band returned to Ft. Berthold, Drags Wolf was already a strong leader – one who many consider to be among the last great Hidatsa chiefs.

This was a time when Native American children were commonly being forced to attend distant boarding schools, where it was intended that they lose their traditional cultures. Yet Drags Wolf was able to convince the Bureau of Indian Affairs to start a day school right there at Shell Creek, so the children could stay in their own community while getting their education.

The following year, the U.S. Army Corps of Engineers held public hearings in a Ft. Berthold classroom to negotiate ways of dealing with the aftermath of opening the Garrison Dam floodgates. The Pick-Sloan Plan called for a series of five dams on the Upper Missouri that would prove disastrous for the reservation. The tribes' priceless river-bottom lands, as well as villages and homes, were about to be washed away forever, and tribal members were enraged.

Drags Wolf came to the meeting dressed in traditional regalia and war paint. When talking proved pointless, he said, "You'll never take me from this land alive!" Lt. General Pick was furious and called the people "belligerently uncooperative." As the Chief Engineer, Pick left the meeting with a "take it or leave it" attitude.

Drags Wolf left it. Just a few months later, he passed away with his land still firmly under his feet, and his body would later need to be exhumed and moved before the floodwaters advanced.

President Franklin Roosevelt once met Drags Wolf in Washington and later said, "This man Chief Drags Wolf is a wise old man if he only could speak English […] oh, what he could do for his people."

Merry Helm

25 AUG

Hellish Hail

In August of 1912, a ten-mile wide hailstorm swept from the northeast to the southwest, hitting the town of St. Thomas. A Towner County news story read, "Practically all of the windows in St. Thomas were broken by the hail stones... [which] measured about three inches and a half in diameter."

While baseball-size hail is fairly uncommon, there have been reports of stones much larger. In 1895, the *Milton Globe* reported on a hailstorm that hit Abercrombie. "Hail to the depth of six inches fell on the ground," the story read. The center of the storm was only about half a mile wide, [but] a number of farmers had their entire acreage of grain pounded out of existence."

Agatha Jerel Arms homesteaded with her husband near Wimbledon. She wrote of a storm that abruptly descended in July of 1905, "the temperature was very high and the air seemed to be charged with heat, but... about four o'clock it was considerably cooler," Arms wrote. "Many clouds were gathering in the northwest... in just a few minutes the breeze died down, and the whole sky turned black; the clouds were one solid blaze of electricity... the wind came up in gushers, and the air was filled with dust and dirt...Then... the rain came in torrents and the hail in chunks, some as large as a good-sized coconut... The storm lasted about ten minutes, and, from four to six miles wide, destroyed everything in its path... Gardens were plastered and grain fields were bare and black."

James Buttree was an adolescent when he moved to the Grand Forks area with his family in 1881. Later he wrote about the time his father and mother went to town and left the younger children with an aunt in her homesteader's shack. That night a storm came from the west. "That was an awful night... How that little shack hung to its foundations is a conundrum," Buttree wrote.

He continued, "The hail cut the tarpaper on the roof, and the [rain] water came through in a shower until it couldn't get away through the cracks between the floor boards ... [the] floor was a lake," he wrote. "The hail stones pounded the thin walls until it was almost impossible to make each other heard by shouting. The wind howled, and the lightning flashed constantly while the thunder pealed a terrific cannonade."

They later learned they weren't alone. "A mile away," Buttree added, "our neighbor in a more secure household sat in his window with a large field glass, and the continuous lightning enabled him to find us, and he watched us throughout the storm to ascertain if we survived safely."

Vilhjalmur Stefansson

26 AUG

A legendary Arctic explorer died today in 1962. He was Vilhjalmur Stefansson, born in 1879 to Icelandic immigrants in Manitoba. When he was two, the family moved to the Icelandic community of Mountain, in northeastern North Dakota, where Vilhjalmur lived for the remainder of his younger years.

Stefansson is said to have been a rugged boy who loved the outdoors and who only had occasional access to schooling. His father died when Vilhjalmur was just a boy, and to ease his mother's hardship, he moved in with his sister and helped a brother with his cattle and horses.

The early Icelandic settlers have become recognized for their strong quest for higher education, especially in the field of law. Stefansson enrolled at UND in 1898, where he shared a small draft house with another Icelander, Gudmundur Grimson.

Three years later, Stefansson was forced to leave UND for allegedly inciting a student protest. He transferred to the University of Iowa, and finished his degree. Since he was interested in learning about other cultures, Stefansson joined the Anglo-American Polar Expedition in 1906. He spent the next two years in the Arctic, spending the winter months with the native Inuit of Tuktoyyaktut.

Upon returning in 1908, Stefansson immediately went to New York's American Museum of Natural History to ask for funding to conduct a second expedition. With some financial help from the Canadian government, the Stefansson Anderson Expedition set out for northern Alaska to continue the study of the native cultures. Stefansson became particularly interested in a remote group of primitive Inuits during the next four years. The tribe had strong Caucasian features, and it was speculated they descended from Vikings.

Of one experience during this expedition, Stefansson wrote, "…the group was short of three things: ammunition, which we all knew was a necessity, and tea and tobacco, which the Eskimos believed were necessities. When we reached the mouth of the Horton on our way back to camp, we divided our party in two (and our) troubles began. It took us thirteen days to get to camp. We were delayed by blizzards, and found the hunting poor along the way. There was not enough food for the six of us," he went on. "We ate what we could, including the tongue of a beached bowhead whale. Four years dead, the carcass would have been hidden in the snow except that foxes had been digging into it… The pieces we ate were more like rubber than flesh."

The Stefansson Anderson Expedition concluded four years later, and arrangements were immediately made for another – the Canadian Arctic Expeditions – which took place from 1913 to 1918. Stefansson's findings were now being published in scientific journals and literary digests, and he also published a book titled, *My Life with the Eskimo*.

Merry Helm

27 AUG

True Sportsmen

There was a time in Dakota Territory, when the bounty of nature seemed limitless, with countless buffalo, ducks, and geese, along with endless grasslands and enough lignite-coal to last for centuries. Even fish, in rivers, streams and lakes, appeared to be over-abundant, as it was written in 1885, of Devils Lake – its "supply of extra fine fish is inexhaustible."

Well, the truth of the matter was that the buffalo were wiped out, the ducks and geese had to be protected, and even the grasslands were largely plowed up. And the waters, once teeming with fish, could be 'fished out' quite easily by taking too many "pike, pickerel" and perch with nets.

There had been multitudes of immigrants to Dakota who had been commercial fishermen in the old country, in Norway or Sweden, who knew how to use gill nets, and it was difficult to enforce state laws that allowed the taking of game fish only by hook and line, prohibiting spearing, seines, and nets.

Charles Cavileer, an old settler from Pembina, believed the fish should be better protected, for he witnessed "seining and netting" being conducted "night and day, Sunday included," and he saw people taking out "wagon loads" of fish.

R.W. Main of Cando, State Fish Commissioner, wrote about the decline of Gordon Lake and Jarvis Lake in the Turtle Mountain area, noting that anglers fishing legally with hook and line could catch from 200 to 300 fish in one day, while a man using an illegal gill net could take 900. The nets took the bigger fish, leaving undersized fish in a diminished fishery. Enforcement of the laws prohibiting netting became vital.

It was on this date, in 1914, that the *Wahpeton Times* reported that a man from Kindred, named Ole Swanson, had been arrested and charged with illegal fishing in the Sheyenne River. Swanson, a "well-known farmer, admitted his guilt and paid a fine of $10." Swanson had used a dip-net to take fish near the mill dam.

His neighbors had seen him netting and called the game warden. The *net result* of this case and other N.D. law-enforcement efforts in catching illegal fishermen was that the high ideals of conservation and sportsmanship prevailed.

Dr. Steve Hoffbeck

Sleep-talking Killer

28 AUG

During the early half of the twentieth century, migrant farm workers often spent the summer traveling north from Oklahoma to North Dakota, participating in the harvest of the nation's breadbasket as part of the Great Wheat Belt migration. Many of the workers 'rode the rails,' traveling illegally between destinations as hobos, by hopping train cars. Because of this, many of the workers saw much of the country, and the men often spent their evenings sharing stories of the places they'd been and the people they'd met. One such worker, however, shared a chilling story one night near Brocket, North Dakota that only his fellow bunk-mate could hear.

Lester Nathaniel Cash, a 31-year old transient harvest worker from Missouri, had hired on to work at the Oliver Stene farm in August of 1947. Stene's farm, located in Ramsey County, North Dakota, hired several temporary men each fall to help bring in the summer crops. Cash was hired on as a thresher and he lived with the rest of the farm's hired men in a bunkhouse.

Although quiet and reserved, Cash proved a good worker and got along with the others. However, one evening Cash began talking in his sleep, and his bunk-mate could hear every word. The Missouri thresher began telling the detailed story of how he killed a man in Sioux City, Iowa, four years earlier. Alarmed, and not exactly happy to be sleeping with a killer, the bunk-mate told his employer, Oliver Stene. Wary of alerting the authorities without additional proof, Stene told the threshers to keep an eye on Cash, and he also made sure his family members kept their distance from the possible murderer. Cash soon became aware of the additional scrutiny, however, and confronted Stene. Stene explained how Cash had been overheard while sleep-talking, and Cash flew into a fury, threatening to kill the other threshers, starting with the eavesdropping bunk-mate. Stene alerted the sheriff, and Cash was arrested on this date in 1947 and taken to Devils Lake, where he quickly earned the moniker "the Killer." Despite the nickname, however, no link was ever made by the FBI between Cash and any Iowa murder.

Jayme L. Job

29 AUG

Rural Post Offices

The early days of North Dakota saw a boom as the railroad and settlement both grew. Many towns we know today grew from the tiny communities plopped down by the railroad tracks.

One such town is Thorne, North Dakota, the rival of Dunseith south of the Turtle Mountains. The town's post office was established today in 1905, along with a string of other rural post offices in other towns in the state. Thorne grew along the Great Northern Railway, named after either a railroad man or as tribute to area's prairie roses. Thorne today is much smaller, just a tiny farming community with its railroad pulled up long ago.

Other post offices popping up on this day in 1905 included Lein, which really wasn't more than a farm post office for Lein Township in Burleigh County. Brothers Bernt and John Lein were postmasters after each other before the outpost closed in 1914. Mail then went to Driscoll.

Way up in Divide County, south of Noonan, another farm post office opened at Garfield the same day as Thorne and Lein. Postmaster Hattie Zimmerman oversaw mail duties for the post office on the extreme northwest edge of North Dakota. It closed after three years, mail sent to nearby Kermit, which later closed in 1943 with mail to Noonan. Noonan still operates its post office, but its population has been cut in half since 1990.

Other remnants of startup towns remain in North Dakota. The grain elevator of Rival, North Dakota still stands; Rival was supposed to be the rival of nearby Lignite, North Dakota, but it never grew. Rival lay along the Soo Line and Lignite on the Great Northern. A post office also existed in Rival, but it ended in 1909 after two years—one of many that came and went in establishing communities in North Dakota.

Jack Dura

Electric Cars

30 AUG

Automobiles changed life in America about as much as any invention of the 1900s. In a rural state like North Dakota, the long distances made automobiles a particularly welcome improvement over horse and buggy.

Early on, there were three types of autos available – powered by steam, electricity, or gasoline, and it was not immediately clear which system would triumph. Steam-powered autos, plagued by boiler explosions and corrosion, eventually fell by the wayside. Gasoline engines sputtered at first, being difficult to start, operate and maintain.

Electrics, shockingly enough, seemed poised to capture the market. On this date in 1915, the *Grand Forks Daily Herald* printed an advertisement for Detroit Electric cars that touted what it called the "obvious advantages" of going electric.

The ad touted Detroit Electric's finest features – that it ran clean with "no fumes or odors of gasoline about it." Its electric motor was "perfectly silent in operation."

Electric motors were simply designed – having no sparkplugs, carburetors, magnetos, oil-pans, or radiators to leak, fizzle, rust, or break. Electrics were simple to fix, rarely needing any attention at all. They started easily, needing no hand-cranking. And electrics rode smoother, without "explosions to jar and tire you and batter the mechanism."

The ad went on to tout the Detroit Electric's "wonderful simplicity," without a clutch, allowing everyone in the family, including "mother, wife, and daughter" to drive more "safely through even the most crowded streets… than…[with] a heavy, complicated gas car." Electrics, being so easily-drivable, also required no chauffeurs.

Improved batteries gave electrics "plenty of power and all the speed" needed in that era. The battery was sufficient for about 65 miles of driving, daily, enough for city drivers and many farmers.

Despite their advantages, electric autos never really caught on. North Dakotans didn't buy many. In 1911, the vast majority of the state's 7,220 licensed automobiles, according to historian Carl F.W. Larson, "were gasoline-fueled" – counting only about fourteen steamers and approximately "six electrics."

Gasoline-powered cars triumphed, due to electric starters and the superior horsepower. After all, electrics only cruised at 20 to 25 miles per hour.

By the late 1920s, electric automobiles practically vanished, with only the aforementioned Detroit Electric Car Company surviving.

And, as history revolves like a spinning wheel, electric-cars have recharged, only this time with dynamic brand names like Prius, Fusion, Leaf, Tesla, and Volt.

Dr. Steve Hoffbeck

31 AUG

Turkey Track Trouble

William Molash – better known as Turkey Track Bill – had a bad day on this date in 1912. It started off okay. In fact, he and a group of friends were partying it up pretty good.

Turkey Track had set up an illegal saloon, or blind pig, on Morris Carlson's deserted ranch a short distance from Shields, and among his customers that day were Mr. and Mrs. Guy Bolton and their 13-year-old son. According to the Minnewaukan paper, Turk and Bolton got into an argument of some kind. At some point, Bolton left for a while, and when he came back, he found his wife and Turkey Track in a second story room of the shack. The fight began again, and then it seems everybody moved on to Turkey Track's house, because Bolton wanted more beer. Turk was out, but he had a couple bottles of whiskey at home.

A man named Jacob Jaros happened to come along, about this time, looking for Turkey Track. He noticed people some eighty yards away by the river and was walking down the hill when he saw Bolton stand up. Jaros then heard a shot and saw gun-smoke rise from the grass below. When Mrs. Bolton screamed, Jaros turned around and headed to Shields for help.

At the coroner's inquest, Turkey Track said, "I was up at the house when the shooting happened, and I heard the shot and went back to where the whole bunch had been lying in the grass. Bolton was dying when I got there. No, I didn't shoot him, and what is more, I don't know who did. I am not worrying about the result of the case and only hope I get out in time to take in the fair."

Whether Turk got out in time for the fair isn't known, but we do know Mrs. Bolton's account of the killing was quite different than his. She said she and Turkey Track were sitting about eight feet apart and that her husband was standing behind her when she heard him say, "My God, don't shoot." She heard the shot and was turning toward him when he fell.

Mrs. Bolton said she didn't know if Turkey Track had a gun in his hand or not, but they were both terrified when they realized her husband was dead. They started for the house, weeping, and on the way up the hill, she said Turk put his revolver to his head and said, "Well, I'm done for now. I guess I'll kill myself." She grabbed his gun away, saying he'd done enough damage for one day.

Turkey Track stood trial for shooting Guy Bolton, but nobody witnessed who fired the gun, and the murder weapon couldn't be found. Suspecting Turk had thrown his revolver into the Cannonball, Constable Carlson searched the river until he found it. But, it was too late. Turkey Track Bill Molash had already been acquitted.

Merry Helm

Daughter of Gunnar Kvande, Williams County farmer, North Dakota
Credit: Russell Lee, Farm Security Administration - Office of War Information
Photograph Collection (Library of Congress), 1937.

SEPTEMBER

The Origin of Oakes

Oakes, North Dakota was founded on this date in 1886. Drawing its name from a Northern Pacific Railroad official, engineers platted the Dickey County town two weeks later, and four weeks after organizing, Oakes became a Northwestern Railroad station.

One month later, town lots went up for sale, ranging from less than $150 to more than $350. Seventy lots were sold that day, bringing in $13,000.

The Oakes' district representative was elected that November to the Territorial House of Representatives. The town's first preacher, schoolteacher and postmaster arrived that fall.

Eight months later, Oakes had three elevators and three hotels. The town incorporated as a city in 1888, and had a population of just under 400 by 1890. By 2000, over 1,900 people called the city home.

A prominent railroad town about a mile east of the James River on the drift prairie, Oakes is an agricultural magnet in southeastern North Dakota. Local crops include wheat, corn, soybeans and even honey. Livestock produced in the Oakes area varies, with cattle, buffalo and even emu.

Five sites in Oakes are included on the National Register of Historic Places. These include its post office, bank block, and an octagonal barn. A heritage museum and park were dedicated in the 1990s, giving a glimpse into Oakes' past with old buildings and historic displays.

Oakes is located in Dickey County, and the town holds nearly a third of the county's population. Despite its size, Oakes is not the county seat. That honor goes to Ellendale, founded in 1882, the same year Dickey County was organized.

Living by the slogan "Building the Future Together," Oakes bloomed, becoming one of just 33 of the state's 357 cities to have over 1,500 people.

Jack Dura

02 SEP

Gold!

On July 18, 1875, fifteen men left Bismarck, Dakota Territory, bound for the Black Hills. The men, led by H. N. Ross, were intent on proving the existence of large gold deposits in the hills, which Custer's expedition had reported the previous year.

Even though the Black Hills were granted to the Lakota tribes by the Treaty of Fort Laramie in 1868, the U.S. Government had commissioned General George Custer to launch an expedition into the hills in 1874 to investigate rumors of gold deposits. Custer and his men did indeed find gold, but they also came under attack by the Indians, who considered the area sacred.

When Ross's party of miners returned from the Black Hills in late August of 1875 with additional reports of gold, it set off a gold rush that put the small town of Bismarck on the map. On September 1, the *Bismarck Tribune* published an interview with Ross who claimed that each man in the party had discovered "paying dirt." Ross and the miners felt the U.S. Government would protect prospectors, despite the fact that they were breaking the 1868 treaty. The story was picked up nationally and run in papers across the country on this date in 1875. Within months, Bismarck was filled with prospectors hoping to reach the newly-formed town of Deadwood. A stagecoach service was set up to take the hopefuls all the way to the Black Hills.

In 1877, just as the miners had predicted, the U.S. Government seized the Black Hills from the Native Americans, opening the way for an even larger gold rush. Located at the end of the Northern Pacific line, Bismarck became a boom town. By 1877, the Northwest Express and Transportation Company was running daily stagecoaches from Bismarck along a 240-mile trail to Deadwood, with 175 men operating as many as twenty-six coaches and wagons at a time.

Bismarck merchants and traders made huge profits supplying miners, and the city's hotels were booked up for months. In 1879, however, the railroad reached Pierre, and by 1880, the business of the gold rush had moved south.

Jayme L. Job

Dick Grace

03 SEP

Surviving a plane crash is considered a miracle for any person, but imagine surviving forty-seven crashes in your lifetime! This was one of North Dakota pilot Dick Grace's greatest claims to fame. You might think that any pilot who crashed forty-seven times was clumsy, but not Dick Grace; crashing planes was his job.

After serving as a fighter pilot during WWI, Dick Grace returned home to begin a career as a barnstorming stunt pilot. During his early career as a daredevil, Grace was one of the first pilots to perform the death-defying act of jumping from one plane to another in mid-air. Little did he know, Grace was being watched with intense interest by Hollywood recruiters. In 1920, film actor Tom Mix approached Grace and asked him if he would be willing to crash a plane into the side of a barn in his new film *Eyes of the Forest*. Grace agreed, and thus he began an exciting career as a Hollywood stunt pilot. His spectacular crashes and stunts were featured in such films as *Hell's Angels*, *Wings*, and *Lilac Time*. He gained so much acclaim for his piloting skills that he even attracted the attention of Colonel General Ernst Udet, who tried to recruit him for the German Air Force before WWII. Grace adamantly refused the offer.

When the United States entered WWII in 1941, Dick Grace set aside his stunt career to fly as the oldest commissioned pilot in the Army Air Force at age forty-six. Despite his senior status, Grace refused all offers for desk jobs and promotions. He wanted to fly in combat where his daredevil skills would be most useful. "The only difference between crashing planes for a living and flying over Germany is that it is more dangerous to fly over Germany," said Grace. "When they shove clouds of flak up at you, they aren't kidding." But Grace was up to the task. Throughout the war, the North Dakota pilot flew approximately 70 missions, nearly twice the number of the average pilot. He received four purple hearts and the Distinguished Flying Cross for his service in both World Wars.

Even when he wasn't in combat or performing stunts in Hollywood, Grace made good use his time. On this date in 1928, the pilot began another exciting job crashing planes in experimental work for the Army and Navy. He was also a successful writer, penning such notable pieces as his autobiography - *Visibility Unlimited* - and "The Lost Squadron," a short story that he eventually sold to the RKO movie firm. In 1965, Grace's many battle and stunt-flying injuries finally caught up with him, and he died at sixty-seven. Dick Grace was an amazingly talented pilot, and although he suffered his fair share of broken bones - eighty-three to be exact - Lady Luck was certainly on his side.

Carol Wilson

04 SEP

Frances Densmore

In the summer of 1912, two peculiar figures trekked across the Ft. Berthold Reservation wearing high-collared dresses and heavy petticoats in the hot summer sun. Ms. Frances Densmore and her sister Margaret stuck out like a sore thumb as they hauled ungainly machinery such as a typewriter, a phonograph, and camera equipment across the natives' land. It was unusual for any woman of the time to travel to a reservation unescorted, but Frances Densmore was not a typical woman. She was an amateur anthropologist who traveled throughout the United States to gather wax cylinder recordings of Native American songs for the Smithsonian's Bureau of American Ethnology.

Ms. Densmore's interest in Native American music was sparked as a young child when she and her family lived across the Mississippi River from a tribe of Sioux in Red Wing, Minnesota. "We could hear the throb of the drum when they were dancing," wrote Densmore, "and sometimes we could see the flickering light of their campfire." Densmore went on to receive a formal education in piano and organ music at a conservatory, yet her fascination with Native American music never faded. At a time when Indians were considered strange and their music uncivilized, Densmore recognized the importance of music in understanding native culture. "Indian song, in my observation, is far from being a spontaneous outburst of melody," wrote Densmore. "On the contrary there is around it the dignity and control which pervade the whole life of the race."

On this date in 1912, Ms. Densmore was recording and preserving tribal songs of the Indians at the Ft. Berthold reservation. While at the reservation, she transcribed the phonograms into sheet music, and with the help of a native woman named Scattered Corn, she was also able to provide the English translations of the songs.

During her visits to North Dakota, Densmore recorded songs and interviews with such tribes as the Mandan, Hidatsa, and Teton Sioux. Some of Densmore's most important work came out of her research on the Dakota Sioux. For example, she managed to convince Sioux tribal members at the Standing Rock Reservation to talk on the phonograph about their sacred Sun Dance — a ceremony that had been outlawed by the U.S. government in 1882. Densmore's work is an early example of oral history recordings, an increasingly important part of historical preservation. Much of her North Dakota collection was donated to the State Historical Society, where it remains today.

Carol Wilson

Summertime Switchel

05 SEP

The burning question during the hot summertime weather in North Dakota's past was simply this: "How can we keep cool?"

For farmers, there was no getting around the sweaty work of haymaking or wheat harvesting with temperatures in the high 80s or low 90s. Whenever there was no breeze, common flies and horseflies buzzed around the haymakers and sweat ran freely down the workers' faces, causing them to pause frequently to wipe their brows with sleeves or handkerchiefs.

On the hottest days, farm manuals advised farmworkers to keep wet plantain leaves or wet prairie-weed leaves inside the headbands of their straw hats to prevent sunstroke or heat headaches. With dehydration an imminent danger, drinking plenty of water was essential, so farmers brought barrels of well water to the fields.

Some farmers even brought out large chunks of ice from their icehouse. The ice was kept in covered twelve-quart tin pails or earthenware jugs and sheltered under any available shade. The ice would slowly melt over six to ten hours, providing cold water for the entire day.

If a sweating worker got tired of plain water, farm families made flavored drinks that provided more energy. One of the best of these was a summertime concoction called "switchel," known for refreshing a harvest-worker's vitality on even the most sweltering of days. The basic switchel recipe called for one cup of maple syrup (or brown sugar), a cup of apple cider vinegar, and a half-cup of light molasses stirred together into a quart of cold water. After that, they mixed in a key flavor ingredient: one tablespoon of ground ginger. The spice contributed to the overall tonic effect that helped maintain the "proper amount of internal heat." Switchel thus quenched thirst and elevated blood-sugar levels, while the acid in the vinegar had a cooling effect and gave switchel some zip.

In 1913, the *Ward County Independent* newspaper asked the question: What had become of the "old brown jug ... set beneath the hayrack or [wheat]-shock at the end of the field?" Who remembered how to mix "switchel [...] in just the right proportions?"

Surprisingly, over 100 years later, switchel is making a comeback. Entrepreneurs are providing it through food co-ops and other stores, it can be found online, and you can even search up recipes to make your own—a healthy food to provide energy and electrolytes to help beat the heat.

Dr. Steve Hoffbeck

06 SEP

Tree-Tops Klingensmith

In the first week of September 1904, one of Fargo-Moorhead's most colorful characters was born. Florence Gunderson grew up in Clay County and was nine years old when she saw her first airplane. Florence's first airplane ride came during a fair in Fargo; she earned a free ride by distributing posters; as a passenger, she found the ride disappointing.

Florence had become Mrs. Charles Klingensmith by the time Charles Lindbergh made his historic flight across the Atlantic. Once more, Florence was lured by speed and adventure, and she took flying lessons. Her first solo flight was in 1928. Now, there was no turning back for "Tree-Tops Klingensmith." Her next adventure was parachuting from 1700 feet. It was a bad dive, and she was knocked unconscious, but only two weeks later, she made a more successful dive in Brainerd, followed by several in Bismarck.

In order to make a living, the state's first licensed female pilot set her sights on a new Monocouple. "I'll risk my neck, if you'll risk your money," she told potential investors, and on April 19, 1929, Klingensmith had a new plane christened "Miss Fargo." Tree-Tops performed her first major stunt in 1930. Cars lined roads almost two miles around Hector Airport as the 23-year-old made 143 continuous inside loops in one hour and 13 minutes – breaking the unofficial women's world record by almost 100 loops. Just a few months later, New York's Laura Ingalls made 980 loops, and the following summer, Tree-Tops met the challenge in Minneapolis, where 50,000 spectators watched her make 1,078 loops. As a racer, Tree-Tops collected the most coveted prize in women's aviation, the Amelia Earhart Trophy, at the 1932 Nationals. The following year, she was the first woman to compete in the $10,000 Phillips competition, featuring eight of the nation's best male pilots. She borrowed a bright red, lightweight, Gee Bee Sportster with a custom motor that tripled its horsepower.

The 100-mile race consisted of 12 laps around pylons. Florence was in 4th place after eight laps, averaging more than 200 mph. She was flying over the grandstands during her next pass when the fabric tore on one of the wings. She immediately veered off course, holding steady as she aimed for a plowed field to the south. Suddenly, the plane nosed into the earth from 350 feet up. Florence died instantly. Her parachute was found tangled in the fuselage, leading many to believe she tried to bail out.

The crash was shown to be from structural failure and not pilot error, yet Florence's death soon became an excuse to bar women from competing against men. When officials prohibited them from entering the Bendix Air Race at the 1934 Nationals, the women protested. Amelia Earhart herself protested by refusing to fly actress Mary Pickford to Cleveland to open the air races. Instead, the women held their own air meet in Ohio.

It's pretty safe to say Tree-Tops would have been proud of them.

Merry Helm

Typist to Treasurer

07 SEP

Bernice Muriel Asbridge faced many obstacles on her road to success. She was born in Arena, North Dakota on this date in 1919. She graduated from Bismarck High in 1937 during the Great Depression and hired on as a bookkeeper for a department store, where she worked until she married Donald Asbridge during World War II. Donald trained with the 9th Infantry Division and would go on to fight in Germany.

Bernice traveled with him from army base to army base, serving as a clerk-typist at each new stop. In 1943, she gave birth to her first daughter, Donna, but because of the demands of base life, baby Donna was raised by grandparents until Bernice and Donald returned in 1945.

That same year, Bernice went to work for the county auditor, again as a clerk-typist. In 1950, she gave birth to a son, Darold. It was a time when only 12% of mothers with children under six were working outside the home. In 1948, she was promoted to machine bookkeeper, putting her in a good position to help support her family.

Tragically, in August of 1952, her husband Donald suffered a cerebral hemorrhage, which paralyzed the right side of his body and left him without speech and unable to work. This left Bernice as the sole provider. Her hard work led to a promotion in 1955 to second deputy auditor. And, when the county auditor retired in 1958, she ran for the position and held it for ten years.

The next step for Bernice was a run for state treasurer. At the 1968 September primaries in Fargo, she was given the Republican nod, making her the only woman on the Republican state ticket. She went on to lead a solid campaign, resulting in her election on November 5. The following year, Bernice was elected as chair of the North Dakota State Investment Board, and she served in that position until 1972.

Bernice Muriel Asbridge had overcome hardships and social boundaries, helping pave the way for the many women who would follow into public office.

Lucid Thomas
Drawing upon the book *Important Voices* by Susan E. Wefald.

08 SEP

The University of North Dakota

The University of North Dakota was founded six years before North Dakota became a state. In 1883, the Territorial Legislature passed a bill that called for locating the university in Grand Forks. The University included only a few acres of land. Two miles outside Grand Forks, the new campus was surrounded by farms and fields.

The first classes were held on this date in 1884 with eight students. The first building was Old Main, which housed all the offices, classrooms, and the library. More buildings were eventually added to accommodate the growing enrollment.

In 1918, the University suspended classes as the campus became a temporary army base. Soldiers trained there before being shipped to Europe. During the Depression, students received free housing in exchange for manual labor. Students lived in railroad cabooses that they called "Camp Depression." They worked around the campus, doing housekeeping, yard work, and minor construction. Meals were not included, but many Grand Forks citizens regularly invited students to their homes for meals. Enrollment grew to over 3,000 after World War II. New housing and new academic buildings were added.

The 1960s and 70s saw many student protests. The largest protest involved 1,200 students upset over the shooting at Kent State in 1969. By 1975, enrollment reached 8,500. The John D. Odegard School of Aerospace Sciences was added in the 1970s. In 1997, much of the school year was cancelled because of the Red River Flood.

Enrollment currently stands at over 15,000. The campus spreads over 548 acres. It is a far cry from the few acres and one building that started the school. Students can pursue studies in more than 200 academic fields including the humanities, business, law, engineering, education, and medicine.

The state's oldest university continues to grow in the twenty-first century. The Ralph Engelstad Arena opened in 2001 – the site of men's and women's hockey games. The Alerus Center also opened that year for the football team. In 2004 the Betty Engelstad Sioux Center opened. The Betty hosts volleyball and basketball. Other additions include a Wellness Center, a parking garage, the Energy and Environmental Research Center, and new housing.

UND's economic contribution to North Dakota continues to be enormous. It is estimated at $1.3 billion per year and the school is the second largest employer in the state after the Air Force.

Carole Butcher

Prohibition Problems in Minot

09 SEP

Local and Federal law enforcement officers had their work cut out for them during the Prohibition Era (1920-1933). The nation was divided over Prohibition; some believed the law could reform all Americans, while others saw nothing wrong with making, selling, or drinking liquor.

Rumrunners, bootleggers, and moonshiners abounded. The money involved in illegal liquor operations flowed so freely that the profits corrupted some government officials, who protected criminals. Such was the case in Minot with its proliferation of illicit "speakeasies" – saloons located in what was called "High Third" street on the west side of the downtown area. Numerous liquor establishments operated there before, during, and after Prohibition. Minot was a railroad city known as a "rough" town.

On this date in 1931, corruption charges came forth against City Commissioner "Nap" (Napoleon) LaFleur, who was in charge of the Minot police department. Five local citizens petitioned Governor George F. Shafer to suspend LaFleur for failing to "properly enforce the liquor laws." The petition informed the governor that Commissioner LaFleur had said publicly that "the citizens of Minot who desired, could manufacture and sell intoxicating liquors" and that bootleggers could make and sell "beer for the purpose of making a living." The complaint alleged that Commissioner LaFleur was assisting local bootleggers and that LaFleur had instructed local police to refrain from interfering with the moonshiners, many of whom were unemployed in those first years of the Great Depression. It was well known in Minot that Commissioner Nap LaFleur had been selling beer-making equipment and other bootlegging appliances in his hardware store. Governor Shafer acted on the petition, ordering a hearing in Minot on October 8. The prosecutor there, P.M. Clark of Mohall, however, recommended that the case be dismissed. At a final hearing before the governor, in Bismarck, on November 4, lawyers from both sides failed to show up, and the controversy fizzled out.

Prohibition itself dissolved soon thereafter. When Franklin Roosevelt took office in 1933, Congress repealed the controversial act. In the depths of the Great Depression, all levels of government legalized alcohol in order to tax it. North Dakota's state government expected to realize $125 to 150 million annually in liquor revenues.

Perhaps it came as no surprise that some Minot saloonkeepers continued selling illegal alcohol to evade licensing fees and taxes even after Prohibition's repeal.

Jacob Clauson and Dr. Steve Hoffbeck

10 SEP

Make Way for New Town

On this date in 1950, a groundbreaking ceremony was held at the town site of New Town, North Dakota. A furrow of earth was cut on the future Main Street for the town, which was being created out of the certainty that the Garrison Reservoir would flood other towns along the Missouri River.

About 900 residents of Sanish and Van Hook had to relocate, and they decided to join together as one town. But what to call it? The name Sanhook was proposed, as was Vanish, an ironic name for the town replacing those lost under the dam's waters. The new town was eventually named just that: New Town. No vote or proposal was ever held for the name.

At the time of the groundbreaking, the U.S. Army Corps of Engineers was appraising properties that would be lost in Sanish and Van Hook. Surveyors were also working to reroute the railroad and Highway 23. Studies were also underway for the construction of a new bridge south of Sanish.

As the townsite of New Town began to take shape, the site was platted and lots were sold. Land for a school was presented as gift to the school district, and each church congregation was also given a free lot.

New Town's first election was in 1951, with the decision to dissolve the governments of Sanish and Van Hook on the ballot. Both towns approved the measure. Another election weeks later transferred both towns' assets to New Town. By this time, New Town was just one building on Main Street, but homes and businesses would come within the year. The first business was a bar, followed by a lumber company.

Today, New Town is a growing city of over 2,300 people on a major route for the state's oil industry. A casino, historic sites and water recreation draw visitors, and despite its heartbreaking origin, New Town today is a bigger city on the state's biggest lake.

Jack Dura

Patriot Day

11 SEP

Any adult alive on September 11, 2001 probably remembers where they were when the Twin Towers fell. New York City may seem very far away from North Dakota, but North Dakotans were directly affected by the event. A mother lost her daughter; a police officer from North Dakota reported for duty on his day off and spent the next week working at Ground Zero. Many North Dakotans went to war in the aftermath. It may seem overwhelming when one tries to contemplate over 3,000 people who died that day, but each person has a story. Each victim left behind family and friends who continue to feel pain and anguish over their loss.

But sometimes good things come out of terrible events. Jenette Nelson watched the attacks from her living room in North Dakota. She knew her daughter Ann was on the 104th floor of the north tower. It was painful to watch the coverage and to learn that Ann did not survive. When her belongings arrived home, they included her laptop.

Jenette said it was five years before she could bring herself to open the computer. When she finally did, she found Ann's bucket list. It included activities such as scuba diving at the Great Barrier Reef and volunteering for charity. One item caught Jenette's attention: Ann wanted to build a home in North Dakota.

An organization, New York Says Thank You, heard of the bucket list. New York Says Thank You travels the country after disasters, like tornadoes, hurricanes, and fires to help the communities affected rebuild. It seeks to do for the rest of the country what people did for New York after 9/11. The group consists of New York City firefighters, ground zero workers, and the families of victims.

In 2012, more than 500 volunteers traveled to North Dakota. They worked to build an 11,000 square foot ski lodge in Bottineau. The building was designed to accommodate disabled children. It would also welcome injured veterans.

The North Dakota project was the first that honored a 9/11 victim. The building is called Annie's House. Jenette says the project is a comfort, and an item on Ann's bucket list to cross off.

Carole Butcher

12 SEP

Cowboys in Dickinson

In 1871, the spot that would someday become Dickinson started off as a Northern Pacific Railroad survey site. Nine years later, the railroad finally arrived and the site was named Pleasant Valley Siding. The next year, it was renamed for Wells Stoughton Dickinson, a land agent and politician from New York. Dickinson's brother, Horace, lived in the area and watched over the town as his brother's namesake developed and flourished. A post office was established, and Dickinson next became the county seat, and then in 1900 officially became a city.

On this date in 1932, Dickinson was in preparations for its Jubilee celebration. As they prepared for parades, plays depicting the old days, and throngs of visitors, the Dickinson Daily Press printed biographies and memories of pioneers connected with the area. One such man was Guy Dickinson, the son of Horace Dickinson.

Although Guy was born in New York, he grew up in North Dakota, and for the sake of the jubilee, he willingly reminisced over the good old days of a true wild west.

For example, Guy remembered that every fall, when the cowboys in the area came in "off the range," they went to the McNair's barber shop, but not for a haircut. They would shoot up the place! After first getting into the proper holiday spirit, they would shoot "the mirrors and the bottles of hair tonic and other tonsorial preparations ... leaving the shop completely demolished, [they would] take the barber on a spree of four or five days, and when properly sobered, they would return and inquire the amount of damage and what would be required to replace the broken equipment." This went on until the sheriff insisted that guns must be "hung up upon visits to the city," cutting down a bit on the recurring new decorations.

Guy Dickinson wasn't the only one who remembered bullets flying. Mrs. Catherine Ray moved to the area with her husband in 1883. "According to Mrs. Ray, life in Dickinson in the early days contained plenty of thrills to relieve the monotony for the women of that period. [She remembered] one experience when she and another lady were walking down the street and a band of cowboys rode by punctuating the atmosphere with their pistols. One of them wheeled his horse around and rode shooting into the door of a nearby saloon, returning after he had properly ventilated the building."

Sarah Walker

North Dakota School for the Deaf

13 SEP

On September 10, 1890, the North Dakota School for the Deaf was founded in Devils Lake. Only one student made an appearance on that first day of class, but by the end of the year, twenty-three pupils were enrolled. The original school was housed in an old frame building provided by the citizens of Devils Lake, but by 1893, a new building designed by deaf architect, Olof Hanson, was opened on eighteen acres of land donated by the Great Northern railroad. North Dakota's School for the Deaf acted as a boarding school where students learned to communicate through a "combined system" of sign language, finger spelling, speech, and writing. Students also learned practical trades such as shoemaking, carpentry, sewing, and printing, which would help them find a job and earn a living in the future. The school is still open today serving the deaf children of North Dakota.

Carol Wilson

14 SEP

Chief Rain-in-the-Face

The noted Hunkpapa Lakota warrior, Rain-in-the-Face, died at his home on the Standing Rock Reservation in North Dakota on this date in 1905. His name was one that oftentimes carried terror with it, and he was among the Indigenous leaders who defeated Lt. Colonel George Armstrong Custer and the U.S. 7th Cavalry Regiment at the 1876 Battle of the Little Big Horn.

Born near the fork of the Cheyenne River around 1835, he once said to Charles A. Eastman that he had to work for his reputation. Rain-in-the-Face loved to fight and play games. He took pride in being a tough opponent. When he was about ten years old, Rain-in-the-Face got into a fight with a Cheyenne boy older than him. He got the best of the boy but was hit hard in the face several times. His face was spattered with blood and streaked where the paint had washed away, as if from rain. It was that incident that earned him his name.

Rain-in-the-Face first fought against the whites in the summer of 1866 when he participated in a raid on Fort Totten. He painted the usual eclipse of the sun on his face—half black and half red. Hohay, the Assiniboine leader of the raid, challenged Rain-in-the-Face and his friend Wapaypay to ride right through the fort. The dare was accomplished without injury to either.

In 1868, he fought the U.S. Army at the Fetterman massacre near Fort Phil Kearney in Montana and was on the warpath during the Black Hills War near the Tongue River. When Rain-in-the-Face returned to the Standing Rock Reservation, he was betrayed by some of the Indigenous peoples and captured by Tom Custer, George's brother. He was taken to Fort Abraham Lincoln and imprisoned. Eventually freed by a sympathetic soldier, he returned to the reservation.

It was this humiliating imprisonment for which Rain-in-the-Face swore vengeance on Tom Custer, boasting that one day he would cut out his heart. Rain-in-the-Face then fled to the Powder River and, in the spring of 1876, joined the Sioux under Sitting Bull, traveling with them to the Little Big Horn River in early June.

Some say that Rain-in-the-Face was involved in the death of George Custer. He would only say, "some say I killed the Chief, and others that I cut out the heart of his brother [Tom Custer] because he had caused me to be imprisoned. In that fight, the excitement was so great that we scarcely recognized our near neighbors. Everything was done like lightning". This feat was further popularized by American poet Henry Wadsworth Longfellow in "The Revenge of Rain in the Face."

On this date in 1905, Rain-in-the-Face died of a lengthy illness at his Standing Rock Reservation home.

Cathy A. Langemo

Wintering

15 SEP

There are many historic sites operated by the State Historical Society of North Dakota. The state owns fifty-seven sites, to which access varies. There are some sites that never open to visitors.

For a number of the sites, the summer season opens May 16. Visitors can learn about a historic site's early settlers from its interpretive centers. Those centers, such as the Gingras Trading Post and Fort Abercrombie, close during the winter, though the grounds remain open year-round. Standing plaques at historic sites help inform visitors in the off-season.

Many state historic sites lie off the beaten track. The Standing Rock site in Ransom County sits on the county's highest point, and it is located a half-mile up a loose gravel road. A turtle effigy in Mercer County is not only well isolated from nearby roads, but its exact location is somewhat of a secret. Grant County's Medicine Rock is both a drive south of Elgin and a walk along a farm field to see the sacred Native American site described in Lewis and Clark's journals. Some sites are totally inaccessible to the general public. They might be on private land or sacred to Native Americans.

For the most part, North Dakota's historic sites are easily found, and each tells a story. Visitors can follow the camps and battles of the Sully and Sibley campaigns. The Corps of Discovery's time in the state is marked by sites at the Mandan villages and near the spot of their winter camp by Washburn.

History is always unfolding in North Dakota, and the State Historical Society is still acquiring sites. For instance, Lawrence Welk's boyhood home near Strasburg was a recent purchase. While numerous interpretive centers close during the winter, visitors are still able to walk the sites' grounds and reflect upon the past.

Jack Dura

16 SEP

The First U.S. Peacetime Draft Law

On this date in 1940, President Franklin Roosevelt signed the Selective Service and Training Act. War had been raging in Europe since 1939. The German military machine held much of Europe and was assaulting Great Britain.

The draft law came over a year before the U.S. entered the war after Japan attacked Pearl Harbor in December, 1941. Thus, North Dakota, along with all other states, sent their young and eligible men to draft offices to sign up for potential service in a war that had not yet touched the U.S. The law required all healthful men between the ages of 21 and 35 to register for inclusion in the draft. Nationally, 16.5 million young men were in the pool for military training. Some men were exempted – ministers, theological students and government officials, plus those who had dependents and those working in vital industries.

Astute observers noted that those with health problems that would hinder military performance would be rejected. Men with flat feet, heart problems, poor vision, or bunions would not be taken by the draft. Nor would those with tuberculosis, ingrown toenails or enlarged tonsils.

The draft law passed despite the opposition of North Dakota Senator Gerald P. Nye. He believed it had been a mistake for the U.S. to get into the First World War, and Nye did not want us to get involved in another European war.

Senator Nye criticized FDR for having a "thoughtless" foreign policy. Nye charged that it was impossible to measure our "defense needs without a definitely known foreign policy." Nye said the FDR administration was raising "hysteria" concerning a possible threat from Germany. During the draft debates, Secretary of War Henry Stimson said there was "a very grave danger of a direct attack on this country by Hitler." Nye pointed out that Germany lacked sufficient ships to transport and supply enough soldiers to successfully invade.

Senator Nye feared that FDR, seeking an unprecedented third term, was becoming a dictator. This peacetime militarization was "mimicking Hitler to stop a fear of Hitler," and FDR was "blasting our own democracy."

Nye's warnings went unheeded, and North Dakotans submitted to the draft. In Burleigh County alone, over 2,500 registered their names.

Christina Perleberg and Dr. Steve Hoffbeck

Call me Ishmael

17 SEP

On this date in 1932, a whale travelled through North Dakota. This whale was not swimming across the great grass sea, though; he crossed by train. He was said to be the world's largest embalmed whale—not a claim many would contest—and he was called "Colossus." The whale was around 58 feet long and weighed over 72 tons. It took approximately 3200 gallons of a special embalming fluid to preserve him. Colossus could be viewed on the Northern Pacific tracks in a specially constructed, glass-sided steel car made just for him.

Colossus was captured in December of 1931, 60 miles off the coast of Catalina Island in the Pacific Ocean. He was harpooned by men of the Pacific Whaling Co. and battled with them for eight hours.

The embalmed whale travelled with a crew of men, including Captain David Barnett, who was later advertised as "one of the most famous whaling masters now living, having spent 56 of his 72 years on whaling vessels, and what he doesn't know about whales, just isn't worth knowing." Barnett would go to schools and give presentations, often lecturing in biology classes.

Despite Barnett's boasts, his mastery of cetaceans seems suspect from the prospective of contemporary science. The *Minot Daily News* quoted him as saying that whales seemed to have "no reasoning power […] no sense of smell and very poor eyesight. Only its hearing is keen."

Not only was the whale and his crew there; Barnett was accompanied by a 13-foot octopus, some starfish, "blubber," a harpoon gun and whale bone, among other "unusual features."

This exhibit stopped for two days in Bismarck near the Northern Pacific Depot, and in Minot for three days on the Great Northern right-of-way near the International Harvester building.

The whale would travel the United States for several years following, changing crew hands and locations. Newspapers heralded his appearances, and one even reported: "Colossus is travelling on his transcontinental tour in a style that would flatter a movie star."

It was a whale of an exhibit. Though one must wonder about how it smelled…

Sarah Walker

18 SEP

Book Burning in Drake

When the janitor of the Drake Public School tossed a pile of books into the building's furnace in 1973, he did not do so as a symbolic act or a political statement. The school always burned its waste, and the thirty-two copies of Kurt Vonnegut's *Slaughterhouse Five* were not being used by the students. But what the janitor did not realize was that those few insignificant books would become the fuel for a great controversy.

It all began when a new English teacher in Drake's public school, Bruce Severly added three books to his students' reading list: James Dickey's *Deliverance*, Kurt Vonnegut's *Slaughterhouse Five*, and an anthology of short stories by such authors as Steinbeck, Hemingway, and Faulkner. When one student pointed out the offensive four-letter words in the books, some parents were furious and brought the issue before the school board. Members of the board unanimously voted to remove the books from the reading list, and the unused reading materials were disposed of in the furnace without another thought. Yet in that seemingly unimportant act, the people of Drake earned themselves an infamous reputation as "book-burners." Nothing could prepare them for the storm of outrage that waited beyond the town limits.

It wasn't long after the alleged "book burning" that newspaper and television reporters flocked to Drake to get the scoop on this controversial story. Much to the dismay of its citizens, the tiny North Dakota town was thrust into the spotlight. Letters and phone calls poured into the school board and Bruce Severy's home. It seemed as though the whole nation wanted to put in their two cents worth. The Drake school board was mercilessly compared to Nazis, fascists, and the book-burning characters of Ray Bradbury's novel, *Fahrenheit 451*.

Naturally, the citizens of Drake were upset by the negative press and the intrusion on their everyday lives. "This was not meant to be nationwide," said disgruntled resident, Ida Kemper. "It was for our little town. We have our standards and we will stick to them. The others can do what they want." The little town of Drake is still remembered in histories of censorship and book-burning today. But whether or not they deserve this mark of infamy is debatable. As school board member, Mel Alme pointed out, "If the book hadn't been burned, if it had just been put away, none of this would have happened."

Carol Wilson

Tex Hall

19 SEP

Yesterday was the birthday of Tex Hall, who was born in 1956 on the family's cattle ranch near Mandaree. He was one of eight children and is of Mandan and Arikara ancestry. His Native name, Ihbudah Hishi, means Red Tipped Arrow.

During Hall's early childhood, his grandfather served as chairman of the Tribal Council for the Mandan, Hidatsa, and Arika – now called the Three Affiliated Tribes. Hall remembers his grandfather telling him, "Pay attention and learn as much as you can, because someday you may have to lead your people."

Hall's father, Leland, also sat on the Tribal Council. Like many others on the Ft. Berthold Reservation, Leland struggled to support his large family. Hall and his brothers each had just two sets of overalls, one for school and one for farm work. Believing education was vitally important, Leland urged his children to study hard and "compete with the non-Indians in their own arena." Hall graduated from high school in a time when only 40% of Native Americans got their diplomas. Only 8% were getting college degrees when he graduated from the University of Mary, in Bismarck, but he didn't stop there. He earned a Master's degree in educational administration from USD. He began teaching school and coaching basketball and eventually became principal and then superintendent in Mandaree. In 1995, he was named North Dakota Indian Educator of the Year.

Like his father and grandfather before him, Hall eventually won a seat on the Tribal Council. Then, in 1998, he became the first sitting council member to be elected chairman of the Three Affiliated Tribes. He was re-elected four years later. Hall was elected President of the National Congress of American Indians in 2001. It was the first time in history that anybody from his tribe, or from the state of North Dakota, has been elected to this position. Chairman Hall presented his 2005 "State of the Indian Nations Address" before the National Press Club in Washington, D.C. In his address, he expressed concern that federal spending on healthcare for Native Americans is 1/3 less per capita than for Medicaid recipients, and that even federal prisoners receive better healthcare. He points out their death rate from flu and pneumonia is 71% higher than the national rate; diabetes is 249% higher; and tuberculosis is 533% higher. Among many other issues, Hall is also troubled about "jurisdictional confusion." As it stands, tribes don't have legal jurisdiction over non-Tribal members who commit crimes on reservations. If a non-Tribal member commits rape or murder on tribal lands, tribal police can't legally detain them.

Chairman Hall was recently inducted into the ND Sports College Hall of Fame, not only for his excellence as a high school basketball player, but also for establishing Tex Hall Basketball Camps in the U.S. and Canada.

Merry Helm

20 SEP

Old Shady

Blakely Durant was an unlikely celebrity. The humble and quiet black man had been born into the antebellum south in 1826, near Natchez, Mississippi. The son of former slaves, Blakely moved with his family first to Texas, then north to Cincinnati, hoping to escape the dangers of the south. Even in Cincinnati, there were no schools open to African Americans, and Durant continued to face discrimination. He eventually grew up, got married, and moved to a farm in Mercer County, Ohio. When the Civil War broke out, Durant volunteered for the 71st Ohio Infantry, under the command of General William Sherman.

Durant was made a cook, which he excelled at; he was frequently asked to cater dinners for the Union officers. One evening, General Sherman and some other officers heard Durant playing his old guitar and singing a tune. The song had been written by an Ohio schoolteacher in 1861, and was known locally as "The Day of Jubilee." The first few lines of the song went:

Yah, yah, yah, come laugh with me,
De white folks say Old Shady am free,
I spec' de year of Jubilee am a-comin'...
Then away, then away, I can't stay...for I am goin' home.

The Union officers believed Durant wrote the song, and began calling the cook Old Shady. Durant traveled with Sherman to Shiloh, and all the way to Vicksburg. He was often asked to sing for the officers and their wives. When the cook lost his guitar while retrieving the regimental colors during the Battle of Pittsburgh Landing, several of the officers bought him a brand new one. In 1888, Sherman wrote a sketch of Old Shady in his published memoirs, claiming that his singing often brought tears to the eyes of many Union officers.

After the war, Durant moved with his wife and children to Grand Forks, North Dakota. Sherman later wrote that he believed Durant had moved as far north as possible for safety reasons, without leaving the United States he had fought for. In Grand Forks, Durant was a local celebrity, known widely as Sherman's "singing cook." Sherman even came to visit him, and Durant traveled to St. Louis to attend the General's funeral. Old Shady passed away in Grand Forks on this date in 1894, and his obituary appeared as far away as the *New York Times*.

Jayme L. Job

Potatoes Save the Day

21 SEP

How did North Dakotans endure those Depression years from 1929 through 1940? This story tells one of those ways.

In the autumn of 1931, a terrible drought had wiped out crops and pastures in northwestern North Dakota and northeastern Montana. Farmers and ranchers there had become destitute. Over 6,000 families were in trouble, and 30,000 people needed help. The Red Cross led a major effort to get food, funds, and clothing to the drought-stricken region.

In 1931, a newspaper story in the *Bismarck Tribune* reported on the relief effort. North Dakota's Red Cross director, R.A. Shepard, worked with Governor George F. Shafer to arrange aid for the families. He announced that potatoes would be the centerpiece.

Accordingly, the Red River Valley Potato Growers Association appealed to its members to send potatoes for hungry people out West. The farmers were very willing to help. It was harvest season, and the potato-growers were having their own troubles because prices for potatoes had fallen so low that it did not even pay to pick the potatoes because hiring the workers cost more than the potatoes were worth.

Rather than have the potatoes rot in the ground, growers donated their crop to the relief effort. To dig the potatoes, school administrators agreed to release children for two days so that the youngsters could help with the harvest.

The job got done. Young people picked hundreds of tons of potatoes, the farmers hauled the harvest to railway stations, and the four railroads operating in North Dakota shipped the carloads free-of-charge to the drought area.

Eventually, more than 150 carloads of potatoes arrived in northwestern North Dakota and northeastern Montana in what was called a marvelous "self-help program."

And so, the school children who picked the potatoes learned that hard work could help feed hungry families—a heart-warming story of Red River Valley potatoes helping save the day in 1931.

Dr. Steve Hoffbeck

22 SEP

Rough Justice

"Take that! You will ruin no other man's child!"

Those words echoed through the air after a pistol-shot in the front yard of Michael Murphy's house in Grand Forks. The bullet hit Charles Link and he fell, dead. Link, a 25-year-old housepainter, had criminally assaulted Michael Murphy's six-year-old daughter, and, when Murphy found out, he avenged the crime.

It was on this date in 1893 when the *Grand Forks Herald* related the details of the child molester's death. The crime had occurred four weeks earlier, and the villain threatened death to the girl if she told anyone.

The perpetrator came back one evening, but the little girl ran away and informed her mother. When Michael Murphy arrived home, he learned the terrible facts. He got a clear description of the wrongdoer from neighbors on Reeves Drive who had seen him lurking.

After a sleepless night, Murphy started out at daylight to find the man and quickly ascertained that it was Charles Link, the housepainter. Murphy met with police chief Patrick Hennessey, and both went to Link's hotel room.

Link tried to escape, but they brought him to Reeves Drive, where neighbors identified the criminal. Inside Murphy's house, the evidence of Link's guilt was made complete by the reactions of Murphy's child and the badman himself.

Murphy instructed Officer Hennessey to see that Link did not escape. As the policeman escorted Link out the front door, Murphy followed. After several steps, Murphy pulled out his pistol and shot Link dead, for doing "wrong against his child."

Murphy surrendered himself immediately. The coroner's jury ruled "the killing justifiable," but Murphy was tried for homicide for taking "rough justice" on his own.

At the trial, Murphy's lawyers used the "temporary insanity" defense. Murphy periodically suffered from epileptic seizures that had begun at age nine after his skull had been fractured when a mule kicked him in the head. Doctors testified that Murphy killed Link during epileptic mania brought on by the wickedness of the crime.

The jury found Murphy "not guilty."

Murphy, a banker and devout Catholic, made deep penance. He later became Grand Forks' mayor, serving from 1910 to 1914. He lived to age 72, dying at his home in 1930. The echoes of the gunshot and tragedies of September, 1893 faded from history, but never stopped reverberating within the consciousness of the Murphy family.

Dr. Steve Hoffbeck

Honest John Burke

23 SEP

John Burke launched his senate campaign on this date in 1916 by speaking before a small crowd in Fargo. Burke was considered one of President Wilson's most ardent Democratic supporters and was extremely well-known to North Dakotans; from 1907 until 1913, he had served three terms as the state's tenth Governor.

Burke was born in Harper, Iowa, to a family of Irish immigrants in 1859. After obtaining a law degree from the University of Iowa in 1886, he set up his practice first in Des Moines, and later in Henning, Minnesota. In August of 1888, he became a resident of Dakota Territory, when he moved to Devils Lake to become a partner at the law firm of Henry Middaugh. Middaugh had been impressed with the young lawyer's powerful oratory, a skill that would also endear him to future political constituents. While working in Rolette County, he met and married a St. John schoolteacher by the name of Mary Kane.

Burke's first political race came in 1890, during an election for the North Dakota House of Representatives. He won the race with a large popular vote, and later won a seat in the North Dakota Senate. Although he received the Democratic nominations for State Attorney General, a district judgeship, and a seat in the U.S. Congress during the 1890s, he was defeated in each race by the state's Republican majority. In 1906, facing a divided Republican party, Burke succeeded in a bid for North Dakota Governor. Passionate and enthusiastic, Burke's stirring oratory secured his election and re-election during three terms.

In 1913, President Wilson appointed Burke U.S. Treasurer, and three years later, Burke ran for the U.S. Senate. His campaign platform centered on free-trade policies and isolationism, advocating the position that the U.S. should avoid entering the Great War at all costs. On the evening of September 21, he told Fargoans that the Wilson administration was fighting to keep America out of the war. After a short-lived campaign, Burke lost the election to incumbent Porter McCumber. However, Wilson won reelection and Burke was reappointed to the treasury, where he served until 1921. His integrity in office earned him the nickname "Honest John," and since 1963, a statue of him has stood in Statuary Hall in the U.S. Capitol building in Washington, D.C.

Jayme L. Job

24 SEP

Rabbi Benjamin Papermaster

In 1891, the city of Grand Forks consisted primarily of Scandinavian immigrants. But with the growth of the city, more immigrants came from Eastern Europe and Russia, seeking a better life. The city's Jewish community grew, expanding to sixty families.

One week before Passover in 1891, Rabbi Benjamin Papermaster arrived in Grand Forks. Coming from his hometown of Kovno, Lithuania, Rabbi Papermaster organized the local Jewish community into 'The Congregation of the Children of Israel' or B'nai Israel.

With a Rabbi and an official congregation, the Jewish community now needed a place of worship. Grand Forks Postmaster and local politician, William Budge, donated a piece of land to the Jewish community. A synagogue was built at the corner of Second Avenue South and Girard Street, at the cost of $3,000. That corner of Grand Forks, along with surrounding neighborhoods, consisted mainly of Jewish homeowners. On Rosh Hashanah in 1892, the first services were held in the new temple.

Rabbi Papermaster created a tightly knit Jewish community in Grand Forks. Members of the synagogue who started as peddlers now had become local jewelers, clothiers and grocers. They drew others to the synagogue, due to Rabbi Papermaster's drive to help those in need. As the only rabbi in the Red River Valley, Rabbi Papermaster was called upon to prepare kosher meats, provide Matzo and supplies for Passover, and bring prayer books for area Jews. His duties extended to performing weddings and the occasional bris, as his responsibilities were to every Jewish community in North Dakota that didn't have their own rabbi.

The Jewish community thrived due to the leadership of Rabbi Papermaster. High Holy Days drew Jews from all over the state to the synagogue in Grand Forks. The 300-seat temple was standing-room-only for the services, with every inch of floor space used for extra chairs.

Rabbi Papermaster passed away on September 24, 1931. Rabbis came from Devils Lake, Minot, and Williston to mourn the death of the much-loved Rabbi. Members of the Jewish communities from Winnipeg and St. Cloud, Minnesota arrived for the funeral as well. Protestant church leaders from Grand Forks, along with Mayor E. A. Fladland paid their respects to the rabbi. The B'nai Israel Synagogue in Grand Forks is still going strong.

Jill Whitcomb

The End of Johnny Benson

25 SEP

Poor Johnny Benson had led a turbulent, dramatic life that was filled with heartache and jail sentences. To many, Johnny was merely a criminal. To others, he was a hopeless romantic who was prone to bad luck. Much of Johnny's misfortune began with his marriage to Marvel, a woman prone to partying and fraternizing, but whom Johnny loved anyway. His misfortune only grew worse when in 1939 he was sentenced to four years of jail for armed robbery.

The time in jail proved difficult for Johnny, but it only grew worse with word of Marvel's continued partying, despite her promises of faithfulness and good behavior. "Oh what a poor sap I was to fall for the same old line," he wrote to Marvel. "Fooled me just as completely as though I hadn't had five and a half years of bitter experience already. I'm still a weakling, why does it always take me so long to catch on? [I'm just] under your spell, I guess."

Despite his remorse and disappointment, Johnny must have fallen for the "same old line again" and returned to Marvel after being released early from jail. He was returned again after violating parole. Marvel did help in his second release by saying his behavior was a result of her own poor behavior. While Marvel worked on his release, both she and Johnny promised a new start with each other. But, it would not be a start for the better.

According to federal agents, Johnny, Marvel and their children often traveled together when he delivered liquor. On August 10, 1946, Marvel and the children acted as a screen between Johnny and federal agents as he made for an escape. He shot one of the agents in the hip and though the agent recovered, it was this shooting that led the agents to set a trap in Sanish and wait patiently for the desperado, whom they believed would come to visit his mother.

The agents were right. On September 25, 1946, Johnny crept into the sleeping town at about 3:30 in the morning. When the agents identified themselves, Johnny tried to flee and was shot down in the alley. According to the *Minot Daily News*, Johnny held an envelope filled with money and a note for his mother and family. The note told of his intention to flee across the seas and asked his mother to use the money to pay off debts owed.

The *Minot Daily* referred to Johnny as a "fugitive desperado," but the *Sanish Sentinel* and Sanish residents looked more remorsefully on the shooting. "People in this community have watched the case with interest," reported the Sentinel. "[They] are truly sorry that the young man they had known came to this end."

Tessa Sandstrom

26 SEP

Prairie Pothole Birds

North Dakota's skies teem with life when waterfowl migration begins in September. Half of North America's waterfowl flock to the state where the Prairie Pothole Region is a jewel for ducks, geese, and other birds. This week marks the start of the hunting season for ducks, geese, coots and mergansers for North Dakota residents. The non-resident opener is October 1.

Dozens of national wildlife refuges attract waterfowl to North Dakota, including Lake Ilo near Killdeer, Chase Lake north of Medina, and Long Lake near Linton. The rich Prairie Pothole Region blankets much of the state east of the Missouri River, and it extends into Montana, Minnesota, South Dakota, Iowa, and Canada, though the district is shrinking in size.

Wetlands and grasslands have been lost to agriculture and drainage, and the Prairie Pothole Region is considered the most endangered breeding habitat for waterfowl in the U.S. Only half the original wetlands remain after cropland conversion, and only a fraction of that is protected.

Federal, state, and private ownership conserve a number of wetlands in North Dakota, saving stopovers in places like Lake Tewaukon where snow geese gather in spring, and Chase Lake, a haven for pelicans. Breeding ducks neared five million birds just a few years ago, but just over three million ducks fly the state's skies today as drier weather and cropland conversion continues.

But looking to the state's skies this fall one is still apt to see a diverse collection of birds roaming our central flyway — blue-winged teal, giant Canada geese, and if you're lucky, maybe you'll even see an endangered whooping crane. Just three-hundred exist in the wild, and they too will be on their way south through North Dakota.

Jack Dura

Bungled Train Robbery

27 SEP

This date in 1897 was an inglorious day for a young group of would-be train robbers. The previous night at about midnight, westbound Train No. 1 was late in arriving in Fargo. The *Bismarck Tribune* reported: "The delay was due to the special request of a number of highwaymen and was unavoidable under the circumstances, as the highwaymen were temporarily masters of the situation. It was a surprising event, considering the locality, as it has always been supposed that the holdup line was a good deal farther west."

Engineer Hooker was just a few miles east of Moorhead when he noticed a man on the mail car. A few minutes later he was confronted with two revolvers and, as the *Tribune* put it, "requested to be very good and very obedient in his handling of the engine. Within a few minutes other masked men appeared with Conductor Corcoran and his brakeman, who were also left on the engine, under guard, with an injunction to behave themselves."

The robbers seemed to know what they were doing. They unhitched the passenger cars and what they thought was the baggage car, all of which coasted to a stop in the distance. Then they took charge of the engine, the mail car and what they thought was the "express car," in which would be a safe filled with money.

A distance down the tracks, the train was brought to a halt, and all the trainmen were put under guard. "[It] is stated," reads the story, "that one helper who was asleep when the raid began was forced to stand out on the grade during the time the men were at work inside, attired in his night dress, and [wondering] what the wild waves were about."

The robbers started first with the mail car – "to make their selections of property." The story reads, "They took a number of loose registers, opened a number of letters looking for money, and left them torn and scattered about the floor of the car, and made away with what valuables they ran across. But their work was very incomplete, for they left a dozen registered pouches on the rack, all of them filled with registered letters and parcels – a valuable haul, had they secured it.

"The conductor of the train was also relieved of $25 in cash but was allowed to keep his watch. The other trainmen contributed as liberally as they were able, and the engine and car were allowed to proceed to Fargo, where it was discovered that they were short the balance of the train."

The story went on to say an engine was sent out to retrieve the missing cars, including the passenger coaches. "Some of the passengers were well heeled," the story reports. "It is said that one man had $6,000, and another $1,000, all of which will be grief to the robbers when they learn of it. There were three or four of the robbers, and when the stop was made to rifle the mail car, one of the men exclaimed: 'Where in [heck] is the express car,' showing that they had intended to cut that off and go through it also."

"The men are said to have been young, cool headed and apparently adept at the business, although their rifling of the mail car, overlooking the articles of real value, and failing to land the boodle in the express car would indicate that they were a cheap brand of highway robbers."

Investigators found the robbers left behind twenty sticks of dynamite – doubtless for use in blowing up the safe in the missing express car. "It was a solid piece of work," the *Tribune* reported, "but as far as a successful looting of the train is concerned, it was much of a fiasco."

Merry Helm

Rats!

28 SEP

Rats were not native to America, but came from the Old World on ships about 1775. These gray rats, officially known as Norway rats (*Rattus norvegicus*), arrived in Dakota on the early Missouri River steamboats. The rats found food and cover near trading posts and Native American villages. As towns sprung up in the 1890s, rats moved in by hitching rides aboard freight trains and steamboats.

The first rat reported in Grand Forks was killed in the Robertson Lumber Yard in June of 1900, and "it was regarded as a great curiosity," and the oldest residents said it was the "only one ever seen in the city."

These house-rats were sly and cunning, entering basements through cracks in stone foundations and burrowing into cellars, coming out at night to forage for scraps of food. Some rats lived in stables and carriage houses, eating from garbage piles and devouring leftover oats scattered by the horses.

It was on this date in 1905 that the *Grand Forks Herald* published an article telling of a man who had been bitten by a rat in his hotel room. Supposedly, the rat bit him on a "tender part of his body," and he called the police to help him locate a physician to cauterize his wound.

The stealthy rodents proliferated and infiltrated businesses, restaurants, and warehouses, causing so much "damage all over the city," that the Commercial Club formed a "Committee On Rats" in the spring of 1908.

Businessman George H. Wilder told the Rat Committee that he had declared a "war on the rats" threatening his store, and urged the city to devise an overall plan to get rid of the pests. And so the committee paid $1,000 to bring a rat exterminator to town to kill the rats with traps and poison.

The city also advised citizens to buy sealed garbage cans and to clean up stables and carriage-houses. New houses featured rat-proof, solid-concrete foundations; and cement sidewalks replaced the old boardwalks, which had harbored rats.

The Grand Forks Mercantile Company put a want-ad in the newspaper for "good, live cats" and paid 25 cents for each cat hired to patrol their buildings for rats.

In the end, the city cleaned itself up and won the war of extermination against the rat population.

Dr. Steve Hoffbeck

29 SEP

Land Spill

On this date in 2013 Steve Jensen discovered America's worst on-land oil spill. It was in his wheat field near Tioga, North Dakota. Crude oil poured out of the ground, emptying over 20,000 barrels onto seven acres of the Jensens' 1,800-acre farm.

The spill's source was a leaking underground pipeline. Tesoro guessed that the cause was a lightning strike. Eleven days after Jensen's discovery, the state notified the public about the spill. It posed no threat to groundwater or nearby lakes and streams, but it was estimated that the clean-up of over 860 thousand gallons of oil would take up to eighteen months. Contamination from the spill spread as deep as thirty to fifty feet. Eight acres of the wheat field were cordoned off – the size of over seven football fields. Cleaning the earth required a thermal desorption unit, which removed hydrocarbons from the soil.

Assembled in May 2014, the 130-ton, 50-foot tall machine could process over 1,000 tons of contaminated soil a day. A 16-member crew began working 24/7. As the project manager told the *Bismarck Tribune*, they'd even work through winter at "full speed ahead."

A year and a half after the spill, the North Dakota Health Department estimated that there was still more than two years to go on the cleanup, and the initial $4 million cost estimate had grown to $20 million.

One good bit of news was that Tesoro was able to recover several thousand barrels of oil. The company even promised the Jensens the honor of levering the first scoop of clean soil back into their field as the project neared completion.

Jack Dura

Creepy Karpis

30 SEP

Alvin "Creepy" Karpis got his nickname for his crooked, sinister smile. While in the Kansas State Penitentiary for stealing a car, Karpis fell in with members of the Ma Barker Gang, a family of brutal bank robbers known for their bloody heists. When Karpis was released from jail in 1931, he teamed up with the Barker Gang and headed north.

Hiding out in St. Paul, Minnesota, the Karpis-Barker gang staged a number of daylight bank robberies around the Midwest. On this date in 1932, Alvin Karpis, Freddie and "Doc" Barker, Karpis' old partner Larry De Vol, and Jess Doyle walked into the Citizen's National Bank in Wahpeton, North Dakota, with machine guns drawn.

A cashier tried to hit the burglar alarm, but was caught and beaten by one of the robbers. The gang roughed up the bank manager until he gave them about $7,000. The robbers then took two hostages, bank stenographer Ruth Whipps and customer Doris Stock, as human shields in case there was a gunfight.

As they headed out the back door, a man saw the robbers escape and ran to a nearby store to raise the alarm. The people of Wahpeton quickly formed a posse and pursued the Karpis-Barker Gang. A small firefight broke out when the posse caught up with the robbers, and the poor hostages received the only injuries in the battle. Miss Whipps was hit by shotgun pellets and Miss Stock was shot in the leg. The robbers escaped, but they had to figure out what to do with a car full of bullet holes and two injured hostages.

The injured ladies were dropped off at a farmhouse about twenty miles east of Wahpeton and were picked up by the pursuing posse and taken to the hospital; both survived the ordeal. Karpis and his gang then stopped at a farm and offered to buy the farmer's car. The farmer saw the bullet holes in the gang's car, and Karpis admitted they had just robbed the bank. This sympathetic farmer said, "All the banks ever do is foreclose on us farmers," so he sold them the car and the Karpis-Barker gang made a clean getaway.

The gang continued robbing banks and kidnapping people for ransom until Ma and Freddy Barker were shot by the FBI in 1935. Public Enemy Number One, "Creepy" Karpis, was arrested in 1936.

Derek Dahlsad

Six-man football, Wildrose, Williams County, North Dakota. High schools have fallen off so much in attendance that many smaller towns play with six men instead of eleven
Credit: Russell Lee, Farm Security Administration - Office of War Information Photograph Collection (Library of Congress), 1937.

OCTOBER

The Williams Constitution

01 OCT

"An act to provide for the division of Dakota into two States and to enable the people of North Dakota, South Dakota, Montana, and Washington to form constitutions and State governments and to be admitted into the Union on an equal footing with the original States." Thus read the Enabling Act of 1889, which set into motion the final division of Dakota Territory into two separate states as well as the creation of Montana and Washington.

Although the Enabling Act of 1889 set the ball rolling towards North Dakota statehood, the northern half of Dakota Territory had far to go before it could place its own star upon the flag. It still had to approve a state constitution. The North Dakota Constitutional Convention took place throughout the summer of 1889, and like so many other official assemblies, it was a messy affair. Cities and townships fought for the placement of government institutions in their communities. Jamestown vied with Bismarck for the permanent capital but settled for the state hospital. Mayville, Fargo, and Grand Forks each competed for their pick of new state educational institutions. And somewhere in the regional jockeying the main articles of the constitution managed to be brought to a vote. On July 20, 1889, an early draft of the North Dakota Constitution was first introduced under the less than auspicious title of "File Number 106."

File Number 106, also known as the Williams Constitution, contained many of the provisions integrated into the final constitution passed by the convention. It laid out the rights of the population, made clear who was eligible to vote, and set out the duties of the executive, legislative, and judicial branches.

The origin of the Williams Constitution was not initially known. Rumors were circulated by the *New York Times* that William Evarts, former Secretary of State and notable Senator from New York was paid $500 by a number of Burleigh County cattle barons to draft the document. Only later was it revealed that the Williams Constitution, the source for a large portion of the final constitution, was actually written by Professor James Bradley Thayer of the Harvard School of Law. His work was not at the request of cattle interests, but the finance chairman of the Northern Pacific Railway. One may find it peculiar that the author of such an important document would initially remain nameless. However, as the document was written by an East Coast professor, with help from a Wall Street lawyer and at the behest of one of the heads of the largest railroad interest in the territory, the backers of the Williams Constitution felt that should the document's background be known its prominent association with out-of-state interests would hurt its chances to pass.

Despite its out-of-state origin many aspects of the Williams Constitution were adopted in the final draft of the Constitution of North Dakota which was approved on this day, October 1, 1889.

Lane Sunwall

02 OCT

The First Casualty

Joseph Jordan - a Sioux man of the Standing Rock Reservation - enlisted in Company I, Second Infantry of the North Dakota National Guard on July 22, 1917. He served overseas from December 15, 1917 to January 3, 1919 and was wounded during battle. According to General Order 5, issued from the First Infantry Brigade at Selters, Germany, he showed gallant conduct and self-sacrificing spirit during numerous battles in France and Germany. He was cited for his courage and awarded a Silver Star.

War does not discriminate; it feeds upon both the fears of the soldiers who brazenly face death, and also upon the families who worry about their safety. These are the individuals who remain behind, the family members and friends, who whose daily lives are burdened with the fear of never casting their eyes on their loved one again.

On the night before the departure to Camp Greene, North Carolina, Joseph Jordan's eighteen-year-old wife joined him in Bismarck. She spent the night weeping and begging him to allow her to accompany him to Camp Greene, but that was not possible. He repeatedly assured her that he would be fine, and she would have to remain behind.

As the train left the station on this date in 1917, the lifeless body of Private Jordan's wife lay in a mortuary but a few hundred yards from the tracks. Unable to overcome the grief of seeing her husband off to war, the young woman, in the early morning hours, came into the bedroom and cried out that she had taken poison. As she slumped onto the bed, a bottle of carbolic acid fell from her hands and clattered on the floor. Her husband rushed her to the hospital, but nothing could be done, and she died within the hour. Her remains would be returned home to the reservation where she had lived, escorted by her family. In the eyes of many, she was Bismarck's first victim of the Great War.

Only four hours after the death of his wife, Private Joseph Jordan boarded the train, bound for Camp Greene and eventually the battlefields of Europe. For this bereaved husband and soldier, his greatest battle was fought long before he faced the enemy guns on the battlefields of France.

Jim Davis

American Crystal Sugar

03 OCT

Whether it's granular or powder, brown or white, sugar remains a staple in households across the country. For many North Dakotans, that sugar is often bought from the grocery store in little five-pound blue and white bags with the words "Crystal Sugar" neatly printed across the face. While we often associate our sugar with sugarcane, a commodity grown in the tropics, the sugar we buy from "Crystal Sugar" is produced right here in Midwest using our own homegrown beets.

While knowledge of the nutritional and medicinal value of its predecessor dates back to ancient Egypt, the first modern sugar beets weren't developed until the mid-eighteenth century. In 1747 Prussian chemist, Andreas Marggraf, found that sugar crystals retrieved from crushed beet roots were entirely identical in their properties to sugar crystals from sugarcane. Marggraf's student, Karl Achard, further expanded on his research and developed beets with a higher sugar content as well as the process by which to extract it. These discoveries may have gone unheralded but for the Napoleonic War and a British blockade of Western Europe. Denied access to sugarcane from the West Indies, the French expanded the Prussians' work; breeding beets with an even higher sugar content. After Napoleon's fall and the return of imported sugarcane, the French sugar beet industry declined; but its viability had been clearly demonstrated time and again.

After some delay, American farmers and businessmen exported the plant to the United States, and in 1879 E. H. Dyer constructed the first commercially successful sugar beet factory in Alvarado, California. One company, American Beet, quickly established itself as a leader in the sugar beet industry.

While American Beet produced tons of fine grade sugar, its name conjured images of the unpleasant purple root vegetables consumed as a child. Perhaps with this in mind, seventy-five years ago this day, American Beet re-christened themselves the American Crystal Sugar Company. Crystal Sugar experienced rapid growth through the following decades; establishing additional processing plants in North Dakota and Minnesota. In 1973, the Red River Valley Sugarbeet Growers Association purchased American Crystal Sugar and moved its corporate headquarters from Denver to Minnesota. While the organization centralized its operations on the Red River Valley, it expanded its beet processing capacity – building or buying factories and expanding its technological capabilities.

Today, American Crystal Sugar is the nation's largest beet sugar refiner; producing not only sugar but also molasses, livestock food pellets, sugar beet seeds and sugar beet pulp. Their factories produce roughly 15% of America's highest quality sugar in Drayton and Hillsboro, North Dakota; Crookston, East Grand Forks and Moorhead, Minnesota; and a recently acquired factory in Sidney, Montana, which operates under the name of Sidney Sugars Incorporated.

Lane Sunwall

04 OCT

An Innocent Bystander

Whiskey and cards don't mix. On this date in 1894, The *Fargo Forum* reported a scuffle that resulted in the near death of Andrew Ness, an innocent bystander who was seriously wounded in French Joe's gambling joint on Front Street in Fargo.

The trouble all originated with "Gambler" John Hogan and Abram "Debs" Morris. Morris and the innocent bystander Ness were seated in a small room at French Joe's, trying to get up a game of cards.

Morris had no money, and called out to Hogan to come in from another room and "stake him." Hogan refused to lend Morris any money, and one angry word led to another. According to the news account, both men were under the influence of liquor. Before long, Morris had Hogan by the throat and started pushing him backwards.

At this point, Hogan drew a revolver. Morris, seeing the weapon, quickly dodged just as Hogan pulled the trigger. The bullet struck Andrew Ness, who was sitting innocently at the table. Ness sank to the floor with a groan.

Hogan, upon seeing what he had done, dropped the revolver and quickly rushed to the wounded Ness lying on the floor. He tore away Ness' clothes to see what damage the bullet had done. Morris, not content to let the quarrel drop, again grabbed Hogan by the throat. By now, the crowd that had gathered to witness the affray separated the two men before more damage could be done.

Fargo Police Officer Gowland arrived and placed both Morris and Hogan under arrest. Hogan, seeming penitent, yelled, "I did the shooting—it was all an accident—I'm responsible for it and am willing to stand by it."

Both men were quickly locked in the city jail.

The innocent victim, Andrew Ness, was placed on a cot in the corner of the room. Drs. Wear and Campbell, who attended Ness, reported that the bullet glanced off a rib, and entered the liver. Although the wound was serious, they were hopeful he would recover.

Dave Seifert

Red Wing Creek Crater

05 OCT

More than two hundred million years ago – but probably not on this date – a meteorite slammed into what is now McKenzie County, leaving behind a crater five miles across.

Many people confuse meteors with shooting stars. Generally, a shooting star is the size of a grain of sand. A meteor, on the other hand, is large enough to survive its fiery trip through the atmosphere and to reach the earth's surface – at which point it becomes a meteorite. Meteors of this size are often asteroids or comets or fragments from a comet's tail.

The Red Wing Creek crater near Williston is believed by many scientists to be connected to a group of at least five massive comet fragments that bombarded the earth within hours of each other during the Triassic Period some 240 million years ago.

The largest crater formed by these collisions – the Manicouagan in Quebec – is 62 miles across. Some of the others in the group are in Manitoba, France, and the Ukraine. The craters are now located very far apart from each other, but at the time of impact, the planet's continents were still primarily one land mass, so the five locations were much closer together and all in a pretty-much straight line.

When large meteors like these collide with the earth, the damage can be spectacular. Shock waves roll over the earth's surface, through its fragile crust and into its mantel and core. Trillions of tons of debris can be sent into the atmosphere. Dust and debris from cosmic collisions and explosions can remain in the atmosphere for months and sometimes even years. Around the year A.D. 535, for example, Earth was wrapped in a swarm of atmospheric debris that produced two years of continuous winter. During those two years of darkness, it snowed in the summer, areas that were typically drought-stricken experienced constant flooding, crops failed, and famine decimated Italy, China and the Middle East.

When the Red Wing Creek grouping landed, the impact of the comet fragments was nothing short of catastrophic. In fact, it's believed these collisions caused history's third largest mass extinction, affecting approximately 80% of the planet's species and bringing the Triassic Period to a close.

Many millions of years later, a massive meteor also hit Mexico, forming a crater more than 100 miles across. This one is believed to have caused the mass extinction of the dinosaurs at the end of the Cretaceous Period.

Despite the fact that North Dakota's Red Wing Crater is more than five miles across, it unfortunately has filled in over the millennia and can't be seen from either land or air. Unlike craters formed by volcanoes that leave a rim above ground level, the Red Wing Crater, as well as the Newporte – a smaller one in Renville County – are both below ground level and were accidental discoveries recently made by oil drillers.

Merry Helm

06 OCT

Turtle Mountain Forest Reserve

When settlers began arriving in the Turtle Mountains in the 1880s, they discovered the only densely wooded area for miles. The Turtle Mountain forest was a ready source for building materials, fence posts, and fuel. As the railroad moved into the area, there was a demand for wood as rail ties. At first, the supply seemed endless. But as early as the 1890s, it became clear that the widespread logging would soon leave the area bare of trees.

On this date in 1897, the *Grand Forks Herald* announced that Colonel Clement Lounsberry had been ordered to report on a proposed forest reserve. Lounsberry was special agent of the General Land Office. The proposed forest reserve would cover over 100,000 acres of the Turtle Mountains, extending from Bellecourt to Bottineau, a distance of 36 miles. Lounsberry was tasked with investigating the area and reporting on the feasibility of placing the area off limits to logging and settlement.

The land had been withdrawn from the market in 1892, but the government paid little attention to the area. Settlers disregarded the residency prohibition, making homes there and using large amounts of timber. As a result, extensive areas were nearly stripped of their trees. The *Grand Forks Herald* indicated that many North Dakotans opposed the suggestion for a forest reserve, as had the 1893 state legislature. The new attention being paid to the Turtle Mountains was not welcome by those who lived there. They were afraid they would be forced off what they considered to be their land. The scrutiny also resulted in legal action against some of the settlers. The newspaper reported that the U.S. District Court in Fargo was preparing to hear over one hundred cases of timber trespass.

The land in the Turtle Mountain Forest Reserve was set aside, but without funding. However, in 1906, the North Dakota Forest Service was established, and the new agency was able to take responsibility for managing the reserve.

Today, the Turtle Mountains offer a spectacular recreation area that straddles the American-Canadian border. Popular activities include camping, fishing, and horseback riding. It is our good fortune that our ancestors were farsighted enough to save it.

Carole Butcher

Dakota Student Becomes Journalism Legend

07 OCT

On October 7, 1996, journalism legend Edward K. Thompson died in New York City. Thompson was born in 1907 and grew up in St. Thomas, ND, where his father had a dry goods store and, later, a banking business. Thompson's mother was an art lover, and she shared with her son her enthusiasm for artists and fine paintings. The family traveled a lot, including a trip to Europe, so Thompson grew up with a wider view of the world than many of his peers.

Thompson finished high school at age 15 and moved to Grand Forks to attend UND. As editor of the *Dakota Student* during his senior year, Thompson got in trouble with UND officials. The local Ku Klux Klan controlled the Grand Forks school board and City Council during that period, and Thompson had published a story from one of his writers that criticized Wesley Ambrose – Presbyterian pastor and leader of the local KKK.

After graduation, Thompson began his journalism career as editor of Carrington's *Foster County Independent*. Two months later, he moved to Fargo, where he became the night editor of the *Fargo Forum*. A few months after that, he moved again, this time to Wisconsin, where he worked as a reporter for the *Milwaukee Journal*.

Eventually, Thompson moved into the arena that would define his legendary career; he became the newspaper's picture editor. The position allowed his love of art to flourish, and he was, in fact, credited with being the first journalist to use large-scale photos in newspapers.

Thompson's gift for finding "just the right photo" came to the attention of Henry Luce, the owner of *Time* magazine. It so happened that Luce's missionary father had raised him with tales of Teddy Roosevelt and his adventures in western North Dakota. Luce wanted to start a national picture magazine, and North Dakotan Edward Thompson quickly rose to the top of his list. In 1937, Luce offered Thompson a hefty raise, and Thompson accepted. Their creation was to become a smash hit – a luxurious publication called *Life*.

Thompson served in the Army during World War II, during which he edited a highly regarded magazine for the air force. By 1944, he was in charge of German Air Force intelligence. Afterwards, he returned to *Life* magazine, where he stayed until retiring in 1968.

Thompson was far from finished. For two years, he served as special assistant to the Secretary of State for Far Eastern Affairs. Then, he went back into the magazine business, founding *The Smithsonian*, one of the largest monthly magazines in the United States.

Thompson retired – again – in 1980, at age 72. As he reflected on his accomplishments, he began another project; he wrote a book called *A Love Affair with Life & Smithsonian*. And here's another little something, Thompson's son grew up to become editor of *Readers Digest*.

Merry Helm

08 OCT

Great Pumpkin Festival

In the 1880s, the question was asked: "How large will pumpkins grow in Dakota?" The answer was "pretty big." The man behind the large-pumpkin question was Joseph Barth, manager of the St. Paul One Price Clothing store in Bismarck.

Barth was promoting a pumpkin-growing contest that would also promote the clothing store. In the month of May 1886, Barth sent a free packet of pumpkin seeds to each farmer in the Bismarck area, along with a brochure for the store.

Store manager Barth offered $100 in prizes. The gardener who grew the largest pumpkin would win a "$25 Suit of Clothes." The second-largest pumpkin would get a $20 "suit of clothes" and the third-largest would win a $15 suit. Additionally, a $10 suit would go to winners in four other categories: "longest pumpkin," "smallest pumpkin," "nearest-square pumpkin," and "oddest-shaped pumpkin."

Hundreds of farmers answered the call, though many feared that early-summer dry weather might shrivel the vines. Thankfully, timely rains fell, and pumpkin patches yielded a marvelous crop for the contest.

In 1886, the *Bismarck Tribune* reported that the store-sponsored pumpkin festival was a Grand Success. Farmers and families had traveled to Bismarck for a grand get-together in the local armory. Over 700 people came for a magnificent banquet and for the awarding of prizes.

The largest pumpkin belonged to Fred Hollembaek of Bismarck, who won the $25 suit of clothes. "Longest pumpkin" honors went to John Allen of Conkling (near Washburn). He got a suit worth $10. John Hitchcock from Burnt Creek had the "smallest matured pumpkin," winning him a $10 suit. The "nearest square pumpkin," grown by B.F. Gage of Bismarck, was also good for a $10 suit, as was the "oddest shape" winner, the award going to John Gragniror of Buchanan in Stutsman County.

The banquet was a feast of pumpkins made from the pumpkins entered in the contest. The main course was pumpkin griddle cakes, accompanied by baked pumpkin, pumpkin pudding, and pumpkin pickles, along with pumpkin sauce, pumpkin jelly, pumpkin meringue, pumpkin chocolate cake, and pumpkin jelly cake. The finale, of course, was a plenteous serving of pumpkin pie for all 700 people in attendance.

Altogether, it was "Some Pumpkins," as country-folks used to say, at Bismarck's fabulous Pumpkin Festival in 1886.

Dr. Steve Hoffbeck

McNair Escapes Again

09 OCT

Infamous escape artist and murderer Richard Lee McNair escaped, along with two other inmates, from the North Dakota State Penitentiary in Bismarck on this date in 1992. The escape was the second of three.

In 1988, McNair pleaded guilty to the murder of Minneapolis truck driver Jerome Theis and the attempted murder of Richard Kitzman of Minot. Born and raised in Oklahoma, McNair - a sergeant with the U.S. Air Force - had been stationed at the Minot Air Force Base. On a November night in 1987, he attempted to burglarize the Farmer's Union grain elevator on the outskirts of Minot. During the burglary, he was surprised by Kitzman, the operator of the elevator. After shooting Kitzman five times, he rushed outside and fatally shot Theis between the eyes as he waited for his semi to load. Miraculously, Kitzman survived the attack and was able to provide testimony that resulted in McNair's capture. The murderer was sentenced to two terms of life in prison at the Bismarck State Penitentiary.

He initially escaped from the Minot municipal police station in 1988, shortly after being arrested. Then, in 1991, he and a cohort of prisoners planned another elaborate escape. However, one of the prisoners tipped off a guard and the group was placed in isolation. Afterward, McNair became a model prisoner and even participated in a youth crime prevention program.

Then on October 9, 1992, McNair and two other inmates went to the prison's education room to watch a screening of *The Ten Commandments*. As McNair expected, no other inmates showed up for the film. As guards only patrolled the exterior halls, the three men had the room to themselves. They removed some ceiling tiles and crawled into a large air duct. From there they made their way outside, shimmied up a fencepost, landed on the roof of the visitor's room, and dropped fifteen feet to freedom.

The first prisoner was captured within three hours, and the second two days later. McNair, though, would not be captured for another nine months. He made his way across the country, burglarizing from Arizona to West Virginia, and posing as a journalist. He was caught in Grand Island, Nebraska, in July of 1993 and extradited back to North Dakota.

Deemed a problematic prisoner, McNair was moved to a federal prison in Louisiana. There, he hid himself in a shrink-wrapped pallet of repaired mail bags. When a forklift took the pallet out of the prison, he cut himself free, and spent another year and a half on the run, before being recaptured in 2007.

Jayme L. Job

10 OCT

Casselton Corn Show

Casselton was in the midst of its first state Corn Show on this day in 1913. Businessmen of the city planned the show to highlight the agriculture of the state, especially the growing and manufacturing of the several varieties of corn harvested in North Dakota. The city raised $1,500 to fund the event and invested several months of preparation into throwing the show together. The show featured a 25-man band from Fargo, dozens of business booths featuring North Dakota products, hot-air balloon rides, carnival rides, a homemaker's tent, several agricultural exhibits and demonstrations, nightly dances and daily parades, a motorcycle race, and a football game between Fargo and Casselton.

E. B. Klein, a prominent Casselton businessman, was in charge of the show's decorating committee that covered the city in yellow, green, and white streamers. A gigantic arch made of corn and fodder was erected on the city's main street, bearing the words "Corn is King" on one side, and "Welcome" on the other. The arch was over 25 feet high, and 38 feet long. Casselton's main street was transformed into 'Corn Row,' and featured product and machinery exhibits, corn displays, and entertainment pavilions. President Worst of the North Dakota Agricultural College opened the show with an informative presentation on crop rotation. Worst was considered one of the foremost agricultural experts in the nation at the time, and his speech was thoroughly enjoyed by the audience. North Dakota Governor Hanna closed the show with a second anticipated address.

Cash prizes were awarded in several categories to the show's agricultural exhibitors. The coveted prize of 'Corn King' was awarded to Knute Tideman of Kindred for his gross yield of 109 bushels. His brother, Oscar, took second in the contest. A large number of Cass county schoolchildren also participated in the festivities; the North Dakota Better Farming Association created a separate judging category for the children to enter their produce in. The kids were also involved in a school parade on the last day of the show, and came in large numbers to see the juggling and ball-rolling sponsored by the show. All in all, the three-day event was a smashing success, both in terms of involvement and attendance.

Jayme L. Job

Kodak from Nodak

11 OCT

On this date in 1881, a homesteader living in Hunter, North Dakota, took out a patent for camera film that would forever change the world of photography. The inventor, David Henderson Houston, was to become a major player in the Kodak empire.

Houston, the son of a tenant farmer, was born on June 14, 1841 in Auchterarder, Scotland, the same year his family emigrated to the United States. In 1879, Houston came to Dakota Territory looking for land and bought 400 acres near Hunter, 30 miles northwest of Fargo. There, he continued inventing and came up with an improved design for a disc plow and also helped develop Blue Stem Seed Wheat. But his main interest continued to be photography.

It was his business relationship with George Eastman that encouraged Houston to further improve photography equipment. Eastman, who was a high school dropout, had great vision. He bought 21 camera patents from Houston, including the invention that made them famous – a portable camera. Up until then, people had to rely on professional photographers. For this new hand-held camera, Eastman paid Houston $5000, as well as monthly royalties for the rest of his life.

Houston then came up with another idea that would take the portable camera to a new level. In 1881, he received patent #248,179 for Photographic Apparatus described as "a camera whose inner end has a receptacle containing a roll of sensitized paper or any other suitable tissue, such as gelatine or any more durable material that may be discovered, and an empty reel, upon which the sensitized band is wound as rapidly as it has been acted upon by the light." Film on a roll.

By melding the portable camera with roll film, the first Kodak camera was soon introduced with the slogan, "You Press the Button, We Do the Rest." Interestingly, Houston is said to have come up with the name Kodak by playing with an abbreviation of where he lived—northern Dakota or Nodak. Eastman later stated, "I knew a trade name must be short, vigorous, incapable of being misspelled to an extent that will destroy its identity, and, in order to satisfy the trademark laws, it must mean nothing."

The new camera, which sold for $25, made it possible for any amateur to take good snapshots. It was small, lightweight and came loaded with a roll of film long enough for 100 exposures. Once the roll was used up, the entire camera would be sent in so that the film could be processed and the camera reloaded with a new roll at a total cost of $10; the lucrative business of film developing had begun.

Eastman Kodak flourished, and Houston died a rich man May 6, 1906. His house was later moved to Bonanzaville, in West Fargo, where it's available for tours.

Merry Helm

12 OCT

Bread Week

North Dakota is well-known for its wheat production. In 2012 alone, North Dakota farmers harvested 7,760,000 acres of wheat; only Kansas had more acreage. Measured in bushels, North Dakota's total wheat harvest was 339 million bushels! Now, that's a lot of work—and a lot of wheat which will soon be a lot of flour!

Wheat has long been an important crop for the state. On this date in 1937, it was reported that Governor Langer reflected on this when he effectively told North Dakotans to eat cake…and whatever other pastries and breads they could. All of these goodies were preferably to be made with homegrown wheat flour. It was all in celebration of "Bread Week," which Langer proclaimed from the 11th to the 17th of October.

His proclamation read, "Throughout the ages bread has been known as the staff of life. It continues today as one of our most important foods, being widely recognized as a basic part of a well-balanced diet. Wheat farmers, wheat millers and bakers of North Dakota represent a highly important part of the industrial life of our state […] In order that the people of North Dakota may be well informed of the true place of baked wheat foods in the diet and may join in recognizing bread as important to our physical and industrial welfare, I, William Langer, governor of North Dakota, do hereby proclaim the week […] as North Dakota Bread week and call upon all good citizens to join in its observance."

Grocers, bakers, farmers and millers were set to put this proclamation into effect, and various special displays of breads and other flour-based foods, made with North Dakota wheat, of course, were set up around the state in honor of the week.

If nothing else, the governor's proclamation provided a perfect excuse to serve breads, rolls, cakes, pies, scones, cookies, donuts, and all of the flour-based treats one could imagine.

Sarah Walker

The Belgian Hare Department

13 OCT

North Dakota is a major agricultural state, but while people might think of sugar beets, wheat or soybeans, they rarely think of rabbits. However, North Dakota has a history of commercial rabbit production for food and fur. Rabbit was common menu fare until the increase in beef consumption in the 1960s.

One of the most popular rabbits in the early part of the century was the Belgian hare, bred to closely resemble the wild hare. It was first bred in Belgium by crossing domestic and wild hares. The breed was shown for the first time in the United States in 1877. They quickly became very popular, and Belgian Hare Breeding Clubs were formed.

On this date in 1900, a column appeared in the *Fargo Forum and Daily Republican* called "The Belgian Hare Department." This was during a period known as the "Belgian Hare Boom." Rabbits were selling for spectacular prices, some of them for as much as $500 to $1,000. In his column, author W.F. Cushing countered rumors of a decline of the rabbit industry and impending disaster. There had been reports of breeders in California simply turning their rabbits loose in the wild. But Cushing said his California correspondent reported that such was not the case. Cushing acknowledged that there were badly bred rabbits being promoted as the genuine Belgian hare, and these were worth very little, but he asserted that the true Belgian hare was a highly successful breed, and the business was growing every day.

However, by 1917, the breed began to fall out of favor. Belgian hare expert James Blyth explained, "Belgian hares are naturally very athletic, and attempts to turn them into a meat rabbit were unsuccessful." The Flemish Giant, a very large animal, became the meat rabbit of choice. While a Belgian hare averages eight pounds, a Flemish Giant averages fifteen pounds.

It is difficult to determine the scope of the modern rabbit industry in North Dakota. The domestic rabbit is not considered livestock by the United States Department of Agriculture. Because of this, the value of the rabbit industry is unknown, and no one can say how many rabbits are raised each year in North Dakota. Many commercial breeders across the world still raise Belgian hares.

Carole Butcher

14 OCT

The Boom

The oil boom has brought more people, more houses, and more jobs to North Dakota. Many people would say the boom has been a good thing. However, as time progresses, more people are coming forward with complaints about the side effects, including workplace risks.

The death of Dustin Payne is just one of many examples. Payne was a 28-year-old former Marine from Hazel Green, Alabama. He came to North Dakota after his time overseas.

On October 6, 2014, Payne was welding a water tank when there was an explosion. An ambulance was dispatched and rushed Payne to the hospital. Unfortunately, he died five days later. It was later found that the water tank had not been cleaned of oil residue, causing the explosion. He left behind many loving friends and family, all of which had good things to say about him, such as his laugh and smile. The following week his body was flown back to Huntsville, Alabama where it was met by fellow Marines. The company was given a $70,000 fine for Payne's death, and another $27,200 for other violations.

But amidst the tragedy, there is some light to this story. Payne left behind his family, but they were not left behind by others. Days after his death a Facebook page sprang up dedicated to his memory, including a donation page for the family. Then the Fubar, a restaurant in downtown Huntsville, waived its cover charge for one night and had all profits donated to the family.

So, while this story may remind us of many risks associated with jobs in the oil patch, it also reminds us how great people can be when others are suffering.

Lucid Thomas

Fools' Gold

15 OCT

Herbert Chaffee became president of the Amenia and Sharon Land Company bonanza farm near Amenia, North Dakota, when his father passed away in 1892. The Chaffees believed the welfare of their workers was key to the success of the bonanza farms, but this benevolence was vulnerable to abuse.

In October 1909, a California gold miner named John Armstrong arrived at the farm in need of Chaffee's help. The old miner said he had $40,000 of gold bullion as collateral if Chaffee would consider lending him money. The gold was in Minneapolis, and Armstrong invited Chaffee to see the gold for himself.

Armstrong, Herbert Chaffee, and Chaffee's son Eben arrived in Minneapolis on this date in 1909. Eben Chaffee took shavings from the gold bars for analysis by a gold assayer. Armstrong claimed a jeweler had given him the name of assayer W. H. Harper, who happened to be living at the nearby Rogers Hotel.

Chaffee and his son met Mr. Harper and gave him the shavings from the miner's bullion. Harper's tests showed the metal was pure gold.

Chaffee cashed a $25,000 check, worth over half a million in today's dollars, and gave Armstrong the loan in crisp hundred-dollar bills. The trio then went to dinner, but as they ate, the younger Chaffee became suspicious. He excused himself and went to find Harper, the assayer.

Armstrong, realizing the jig was up, and also left the table, saying he'd be right back. Young Chaffee found that Harper had checked out immediately after the gold was tested. The Chaffees rushed back to their hotel and found Armstrong's room empty.

The whole process had been a scam from the beginning. Chaffee took the supposed gold to another assayer's office and found it to be $15 worth of brass.

Two years later, a man was arrested in California for performing the same scam on a woman in Ohio. Chaffee's son traveled west and identified the man as none other than John Armstrong.

A few days before Armstrong's extradition to Minnesota, a drowned body found in San Pedro Bay California was identified as Armstrong. However, the police thought the scammer was much too smart to have taken his own life, and they believed Armstrong faked his death to get away with Herbert Chaffee's twenty-five grand.

Derek Dahlsad

16 OCT

Germans Left Behind

Around this date in the late 1880s, German Russians were being drafted into the military to fight their German kinsman. This marked the beginning of the second mass migration of Germans – this time from Russia to the United States, with a very large number of them settling in central and southwestern North Dakota.

The choice to stay or go wasn't an easy one. Germans had created thriving farms and businesses in separate communities that allowed them to retain their culture and language. Even as they became more and more threatened, many were reluctant to leave. By the 1920s, the ones who stayed behind were considered enemies of the state, and their lives became a living hell.

Michael Miller, a Germans from Russia bibliographer, has been communicating with a number of Germans who remained behind. In one letter, Lena Dyck wrote, "1929 to 1930 was a difficult time for us. Stalin gained power after Lenin's death. There were terrible conditions, people were deported, everything was left behind. Whoever had a good economical farm was evacuated. We were also on this list, although my sister could not go; dad was also sick, no mercy. At night during a cold winter, about 1,930 [of us] were put on cattle trains destined for the far cold north, deep into the woods. I, with other children, was allowed to go back, but where to? I earned my living with strangers, was not allowed to attend school as an enemy."

Johann Schauer, who remained in Russia said in a 1993 letter to relatives "Until the beginning of the Second World War we lived in Neudorf, Odessa. I was drafted into the Red Russia Army. (I) was wounded...and was two years in a POW camp in Germany. After that they made me a [Russian] translator in the German Army, and I was always close to the front... then I became a soldier in the German Army and fought to the end of the war [...] I had to fight against the Russians in Russia."

When Johann tried to find his parents after the war, they were no longer in Odessa. In 1944, they had been allowed to leave their farm but had to leave everything behind except what would fit into their horse-drawn wagon. They made it to Poland, but the following year, the Russians sent them to a Siberian slave-labor camp, the tragic fate of thousands of German Russians. Johann found them there, but he ended up getting arrested and jailed for five years for having served in the German army. In 1988, Johann and his family were finally able to move to Germany, but ironically, they were unwelcome.

For many years, Germans from Russian weren't allowed to communicate with Americans, but as that ban has lifted, more and more German Russians are connecting with distant family members here in North Dakota.

Merry Helm

Galvanized Yankees

17 OCT

By 1863, as Civil War casualties mounted, the Union faced a seemingly endless struggle to find new recruits. Caught between draft riots in the North and an increasing demand for more troops, President Abraham Lincoln approved a plan in early 1864 to seek volunteers from among Confederate prisoners of war. By summer, nearly 1,800 Confederate prisoners had taken an oath of allegiance to the United States and enlisted in Federal military service. For renouncing their Confederate allegiance, their peers derogatorily referred to them as "Galvanized Yankees".

Equally unimpressed with the Galvanized Yankees was General Ulysses S. Grant. Opposed to enlisting prisoners for military service, Grant doubted the reliability of these former Confederates. So when Major General John Pope pleaded for more troops on the Western frontier to protect steamboat travelers and traders from increasing Native American hostilities, General Grant sent the only soldiers he was willing to spare: the six new "galvanized" regiments of U.S. Volunteers.

In late summer of 1864, 600 men of the First U.S. Volunteer Infantry Regiment boarded a steamboat in St. Louis headed for their new home at Fort Rice in Dakota Territory. The Missouri River was low that year, requiring the regiment to march the final 270 miles. Lacking tents and wagons, the men dodged rain and hail carrying the meager supplies they had been issued. Marching on only salt pork, hardtack and coffee, four men died of chronic diarrhea before reaching their new post. The regiment finally arrived at Fort Rice on this day, October 17, 1864.

The Dakota post was a difficult assignment. One soldier compared it to Siberian exile. Winter temperatures hovered around 30 degrees below zero. Malnutrition and scurvy were often fatal companions. Eleven percent of the command did not survive the winter. The charge to establish peace on the upper Missouri was also a tall order for the 23-year-old commander, Colonel Charles Dimon. Although he did make some allies, attacks by Lakota, Cheyenne and Yanktonai parties cost the regiment another fifteen men.

Fortunately, the soldiers found a few distractions. Among the fort's supplies, the Quartermaster discovered a small printing press from Fort Union. Two enterprising soldiers secured permission to publish a newspaper. The *Frontier Scout* contained articles ranging from serious military matters to light-hearted stories, including one about a bear nicknamed Grizzly who nearly begged the post out of sugar.

The long-awaited orders to leave the rough and tumble Fort Rice finally arrived on October 6, 1865. Three days later, the Galvanized Yankees of the First U.S. Volunteers boarded their steamboat and happily said goodbye to their temporary Dakota home. In the final *Frontier Scout* editorial, Captain Enoch Adams wrote to his men, "We are the first fruits of a re-united people. We are a link between the North and the South—let us prove that it is a golden link, and of no baser metal."

Christina Sunwall

18 OCT

Lutheran Brethren High School

This is a story about a high school, called Hillcrest Academy. The school began in Wahpeton, moved to Grand Forks, and, eventually, moved again – to Fergus Falls, Minnesota.

In 1903, the Lutheran Brethren Church established a bible school in Wahpeton, renting a classroom at the Wahpeton high school. The school's main goal was to train missionaries and send them forth.

Quickly outgrowing this cramped space, the church people built a boarding school in Wahpeton in 1904. Later, influential members in the national church wanted to add a high school, which they did in 1916. The response was enthusiastic, and the school got so many students that it began running out of dormitory space.

Consequently, school-administrators searched for a larger building, and found one in Grand Forks, the Aaker's Business College building. On this date, in 1918, the *Grand Forks Herald* reported the transfer of the school to Grand Forks, a distance of 120 miles.

The school had planned to begin Fall classes on October 10th, but on October 9th, the City Health Officer, Dr. Henry O'Keefe, issued a citywide quarantine – because the worldwide influenza epidemic had hit North Dakota. O'Keefe closed every public-gathering-place – theaters, schools, and churches – for seven weeks.

Churches had no worship services; movie theaters showed no films; libraries were locked; billiard rooms were abandoned; and school hallways stood empty.

The quarantine ended November 24, so, finally, the Lutheran school held its first day of classes at the new location in Grand Forks.

This Lutheran-school thrived in the early 1920s, but the onset of the Great Depression caused severe financial stress. The school met its obligations, through thrift, extreme belt-tightening, and faithful teachers who worked for miniscule wages. Distressed, but ever hopeful, the school sold its Grand Forks building in 1935 and moved to Fergus Falls, 139 miles southeast, where they got a bargain-price on a bankrupted college's building. Four-and-one-half stories tall, the magnificent red-brick building was a godsend.

The high school eventually got its own name, Hillcrest Lutheran Academy, in 1948. The academy reached its centennial-year in 2016, recalling its lengthy history – its genesis in Wahpeton; its 1918 transfer to Grand Forks; and its continuing development on the crest of a hill in Fergus Falls.

Wahpeton is just 28 miles from Fergus Falls. So, in reality, historic Hillcrest Academy moved only a short distance from its original North Dakota location.

Dr. Steve Hoffbeck

Edward Curtis

19 OCT

When Edward Curtis died on this date in 1952, he left behind a massive body of work – twenty volumes of photographs attempting to capture a way of life that had largely ceased to exist.

Curtis was born in Wisconsin in 1868 but grew up near Cordova, MN. When he was 21, he moved with his father to Washington Territory, where he eventually owned a photography studio. Sometime during the mid-1890s, he began photographing Native Americans digging for clams and mussels on the tidal flats of Puget Sound.

Later, he became an official photographer for the 1899 Harriman Expedition, during which he documented indigenous people in Alaska. The experience greatly increased Curtis' personal interest in Native cultures, and he began visiting tribal communities in Montana and Arizona to document what he termed "a vanishing race."

In 1904, Teddy Roosevelt hired Curtis to photograph his children and then later hired him to photograph a family wedding. The president also wrote a letter of recommendation to J. P. Morgan, who, two years later, agreed to finance Curtis' North American Indian Project. Curtis described it as an effort "to form a comprehensive and permanent record of all the important tribes of the United States and Alaska that still retain to a considerable degree their [...] customs and traditions."

To capture his "vision," Curtis hired people to pose for him and removed any semblance of modernity (for example clocks) from the scenes. He also had tribal members reenact scenes such as war parties, even though those days were over and tribes were now starving on reservations. University of California professor Gerald Vizenor writes, "Curtis was motivated [...] to pursue a photographic record of the last natives, and he did so with romantic, pictorial images that ran against the popular notions" of Native American life.

Curtis thus softened the image of American Indians then held by the public and was simultaneously criticized for recreating history and presenting it as "real." On occasion, for example, he asked tribal members to stage ceremonies out of context and out of season, not realizing the spiritual significance of what he was asking. In an effort to comply, his subjects sometimes faked their way through these sessions to hide their spirituality from the public, which in turn assumed the images were authentic.

The vast body of work Curtis created is simply astounding. He spent 30 years visiting and photographing more than 80 tribes across the U.S. and Canada. Working alone or with various assistants, he took more than 40,000 pictures, published 20 volumes of work, recorded more than 10,000 examples of Native speech and music, and much more.

Merry Helm

20 OCT

Most Decorated Soldier

As an infantryman, Woodrow Wilson Keeble of Wahpeton became the state's most decorated soldier. He fought with the North Dakota 164th in WWII and as a marksman and expert with a Browning Automatic Rifle, he had one of the military's most dangerous jobs – yet he survived more than five years of ground fighting in that war.

When the Korean War erupted, Keeble reenlisted, telling a friend, "Someone has to teach those kids how to fight." Attached to the 19th Infantry Regiment of the 24th Division, he was near Kumsong, North Korea, when Operation Nomad began on Oct. 13, 1951. The army's objectives were a series of very steep, barren mountains covered with loose stone and rubble. The weather was brutally cold, and with the enemy entrenched high above, soldiers fighting their way up these ridges were sitting ducks.

Keeble was with the 1st platoon of George Company when it joined the fray on the 15th. According to records, he was wounded that day, treated and returned to action. On the 17th, he was hit again, treated and again returned to action. On the 18th, his actions earned him a Silver Star. But, his actions on this date – October 20 – went far beyond the call of duty.

Keeble and his men were in a support position behind the 2nd platoon, which got pinned down by three nests of machine guns and two trenches of riflemen. Keeble left his own platoon and crawled to the one that was pinned down – and minutes later, they saw him heading up the mountain on his own. The official record reads: "…hugging the ground, he crawled forward alone until he was in close proximity to one of the hostile machine-gun emplacements. Ignoring the vicious stream of fire, which the enemy crew trained on him, he activated a grenade and, throwing it with great accuracy, successfully destroyed the position.

"Continuing his one-man assault, he moved to the second enemy position and destroyed it with another grenade. Despite the fact that the hostile troops were now directing their entire firepower against him and unleashing a shower of grenades in a fanatic attempt to stop his advance, he moved forward against the third hostile emplacement.

"Stunned by an enemy concussion grenade, he hesitated only long enough to regain his senses, then renewed his assault and skillfully neutralized the remaining enemy position with exceptionally accurate rifle fire. As his comrades moved forward to join him, he continued to direct deadly accurate fire against nearby enemy trenches, inflicting extremely heavy casualties on the foe. Inspired by his courageous example, the friendly troops swept the enemy from the hill and secured the important objective…"

When the 2nd platoon reached the top, they found Keeble had taken out 9 enemy machine-gunners and 7 riflemen. 1st Sgt Joe Sagami wrote, "As often seen in movies but seldom seen on the actual place of combat, Sgt. Keeble refused evacuation [even though he] had fragmentation wounds in his chest, both arms, left thigh, right calf, knee and right thigh."

Overall casualties were extremely high during this operation, and with no replacements available, the army returned Keeble to duty within the week. Sagami said his wounds were bleeding through his bandages, he was badly limping, and he was so weak he could hardly raise his weapon.

Master Sergeant Keeble's fellow soldiers twice recommended him for the Medal of Honor for what he did that day, but both times the paperwork was lost. Although a Distinguished Service Cross was eventually awarded to Keeble, his family is seeking to have it overturned in favor of the Medal of Honor he so richly deserved. Keeble died in 1982, in part due to complications from his war injuries.

Merry Helm

21 OCT

Fargo's Red-Light District

Liquor and prostitution appear to go hand in hand, especially when the liquor is illegal. In the early twentieth century, most of the residents of Fargo who were prone to imbibe the spirits of the vine did so by crossing the bridge to Moorhead where wine and liquor were legal. But if they were looking for a little more warmth than alcohol could provide alone, then their footsteps may have veered to the seedier side of Fargo, to a place called "the Hollow." This was located at the foot of First Avenue North where, in a variety of establishments, the world's oldest profession was practiced.

A woman by the name of Corrine Holmes recently had been issued an injunction, restraining her from conducting an immoral house in the Hollow, but she countered that she was in the hotel business. In fact, she was in the process of building a hotel that charged two dollars per day and there was nothing illegal going on. Nonetheless, she was under the watchful eye of the Enforcement League, an unofficial group of citizens dedicated to enforcing North Dakota's constitutionally mandated prohibition law.

So, Fargo's red-light district carried a double vice in the eyes of the League and other organizations such as the Women's Christian Temperance Union, which supported the efforts to eradicate this menace to society. These efforts were directed by Andrew Johnson, one of the prime movers against the immoral houses, and a zealous leader of the Enforcement League in Fargo.

At 3:15 a.m. on this date in 1904, a terrific explosion rattled the windows across the city and echoed throughout the valley. As the dust settled, an uninjured Corrine Holmes viewed the damage. Although the blast was significant, the two and a half story building, with a thick foundation, was minimally damaged. The dynamite had been poorly placed under a small addition that took most of the force, and this section was reduced to kindling. A thirty-foot length of fuse, which burned at one foot per minute, had allowed the perpetrator to be long gone by the time of the explosion.

Corrine Holmes vowed to continue her hotel business and offered a $500 reward. The cowardly act actually aroused sympathy for Miss Holmes and suspicion was cast on the Enforcement League. Eventually, National Prohibition would be enacted, and liquor and prostitution would go even deeper underground; But until then, the Hollow wasn't necessarily a place for the sleepy.

Jim Davis

Camp Buell

22 OCT

It was on this day in 1962 that the State Historical Society of North Dakota acquired a small, unimposing parcel of land just south of Milnor, North Dakota, known as Camp Buell. Today, it's little more than a quiet piece of prairie, but for one day on July 3, 1863, the little speck of land was the bustling overnight stopping point for General Henry Sibley and his army as they worked their way across the upper plains following the US-Dakota Conflict of 1862.

In the spring of 1863, General Sibley's Army, consisting mostly of infantry, left Fort Pope for the plains of northern Dakota Territory. As the US forces struggled through the unending prairie, they camped every evening to regroup and rest after the day's grueling march. While each encampment was different, the forces attempted to strategically locate themselves near a good supply of water, not only for refreshment, but for survival in the hot dry climate. The summer of 1863 was particularly brutal. The countryside, suffering under a protracted drought, was a nightmare of choking dust, unbearable heat, and maddening dryness. While eastern Dakota Territory was normally filled with small freshwater ponds, years of scarce rainfall had made most water sources little more than brackish mud puddles; forcing the men to either strain large quantities of algae from their water or dig wells to locate something suitable for drinking.

The water at Camp Buell was no different; like so many other campsites, its only water source was a fetid lake. But that day's march had been grueling. The pack animals had given out and a number of men had fallen to the prairie grass alongside the trail. Too weak to continue, they had to be carried to the campsite in the Army's ambulance. When the men finally arrived at the camp they didn't care about the condition of the water. The soldiers were ready to drink about anything. They simply scraped the algae from the top of their water pots and gulped down what they could.

Today, little remains of Camp Buell or the other overnight campsites from that bitter 1863 campaign. Nonetheless, their retention plays an important role in the preservation of North Dakota's past. Sibley's expedition and its tragic outcome represent an important chapter in the late nineteenth century struggle between the United States and the American Indian population of the Upper Plains. While sites like Camp Buell are perhaps not as popular as Fort Abraham Lincoln or Fort Union, their quiet dignity, set among North Dakota's expansive plains, provide a timeless memento of the state's early past, and a haunting reminder of the trials and hardships faced by those who fought on both sides in the struggle for America's Upper Plains.

Lane Sunwall

23 OCT

Flu-Flues and Putters

It was not your typical match play in golf. Rather than taking on another team of golfers, Ray Anderson and Alex Olson would be playing against two archers instead; the first doubles match of archery golf was played in Grand Forks in 1924.

Archery golf was not common in North Dakota, but the sport was introduced to Grand Forks when Anderson and Olson took on archers C.D. Curtis and Martin Maier. The first match play had been played a year before by Olson and Curtis. Curtis beat the 19-year-old golf champion by ten strokes, but Olson gave Curtis a challenge in their rematch in July, losing only by two strokes.

But how exactly did archers compete with golfers on a golf course? Archery golf had evolved from field archery, where athletes walk about a field and shoot at targets of varying distance. The sport was adapted to golf rules, where the archer "tees" off, and plays the length of the hole, until finally finishing the hole by hitting or dislodging a tennis ball that is propped up ten centimeters from the ground. Archers receive penalty strokes for hitting bunkers, the rough, or losing arrows.

Like golfers and their clubs, archers are equipped with a number of arrows for various distances. Carbon arrows are used for long distances, while aluminum arrows are used for shorter fairway shots. Arrows fitted with a "judo point" were equivalent to wedges in getting close to the hole without the arrow skipping past the target, and special "Flu-flu" arrows were used for short distance shots. A blunt point would be used to hit the tennis ball.

Match plays between an archer and a golfer were common in Europe, especially the United Kingdom, and on the east coast. According to the *Grand Forks Herald*, however, "Matches of this kind are new to the northwest and probably the only ones ever held off the east coast."

Though the sport was new, the singles matches between Curtis and Olson had attracted much attention, and now, the two were pairing up with partners for what the *Herald* reported as possibly the only doubles match ever played in the sport. The match took place at the Lincoln Park golf course. According to the *Herald*, "The match was played one point to the hole, low ball alone counting." The competition was close over the nine holes played. The first hole was halved by the archers and golfers. The archers gained the lead after winning the second and third holes. The teams halved the next three holes, and the golfers gained one on the seventh. The eighth hole was halved again, but the archers held onto their lead and were victorious over the golfers after winning the ninth hole.

Tessa Sandstrom

First Beer License in North Dakota

24 OCT

For North Dakota, Prohibition came hand-in-hand with statehood in 1889. Although the ban on alcohol was extremely unpopular with the majority of citizens in the state, the Woman's Christian Temperance Union and ministerial associations managed to thwart any efforts to amend the Constitution and repeal the laws. Bootleggers and "blind piggers" became folk heroes, and bathtub gin became commonplace. Prosecuting violators was difficult, and people like Frank "Shoot to Kill" Watkins worked for the Enforcement League in an attempt to stop the flow of illegal booze.

With the initiation of the Volstead Act, prohibition became a national issue in 1920, so North Dakota was not alone in its fight against alcohol. But nationally, the law proved to be very unpopular and hard to enforce. It was so difficult to obtain a conviction that the States Attorney for Ward County decided to prosecute only the more serious infringements.

By the early 1930s, it was evident that Prohibition was a failure, and Congress passed a series of laws modifying the Volstead Act, eventually eliminating it by the end of 1933. Following the national trend, the citizens of North Dakota passed an initiated measure by a large margin on November 8, 1932. This repealed Section 217, Article 20 of the state's Constitution, effectively ending prohibition.

The 1933 Legislature passed Senate Bill 263 allowing the sale of beer by municipalities. However, that wasn't enough. Another initiated measure, which passed by almost sixty thousand votes on September 22, 1933, provided for the licensing of on-sale beer establishments.

On this date in 1933, Frank Zappas of Jamestown obtained the first beer license ever issued in the State of North Dakota. A special ceremony was conducted in the office of Governor William Langer with newly appointed State Beer Commissioner Owen T. Owen officiating.

Frank Zappas, a Greek immigrant, was the proprietor of the Palace of Sweets, a confectionary store he established in 1917. He was one of the leaders in the movement to abolish prohibition in North Dakota, and seeing the possibility of success, he remodeled his store into the Palace Café. The cafe boasted horseshoe shaped booths and a private balcony for the celebration of special events.

It may be looked upon with a bit of irony that the second beer license was issued to the Gladstone Hotel, which was also located in Jamestown. Forty-four years earlier, almost to the day, Jamestown was serving as the center of the Prohibition movement when the official news came that North Dakota would enter the country as a dry state.

Jim Davis

25 OCT

1918 Flu Epidemic

The 1918 outbreak of influenza was devastating–killing 20 to 30 million people. As with the plague in the Middle Ages, people grasped at straws, trying to understand where the disease came from and why it was so potent. The country had certainly seen flu epidemics before, but unlike previous strains, the 1918 variety didn't settle for typical high-risk individuals, such as the elderly and those in weakened conditions. On the contrary, the 1918 flu was killing mainly healthy robust men and women in their twenties and thirties.

A "sanitary scientist" featured in a Towner newspaper article published this week theorized that World War I soldiers, who had dug miles and miles of trenches across central Europe, had unwittingly unearthed tainted remains of plague victims. Since embalming and disinfecting were unknown to Europeans during the Middle Ages, he postulated that the germs were still viable and waiting to be released into the air. With so much earth blown apart by ammunition blasts, the theory of the unleashed human remains seemed as valid as any other of the time.

Whatever the cause, it was clearly airborne, and within seven days, every state in the Union had been infected. Then it spread across the Atlantic. By April, French troops and civilians were infected. By mid-April, it showed up in the Far East. By May, the virus had spread throughout Africa and South America.

In North Dakota, schools and colleges closed their doors for a month or more during the worst part of the epidemic. A 1918 editorial in the North Dakota Agricultural College newspaper encouraged students to cheer up, because after more than a month of no studies or social functions, they were once again able to open the school; meanwhile UND was still closed because of the epidemic.

One story from those times is of Matt Barlett, who homesteaded with his brother, Allison, near Minot in 1908. All went well until the winter of 1918-1919, when the epidemic hit. Allison died, and Matt was taken to a hospital. He sent a message to relatives in Wisconsin asking for help taking care of the ranch and stock. Two volunteered—Charlie and George Bartlett—but both became ill as soon they arrived. Charlie started for home, but was taken off the train at Eau Claire, Wisconsin, where he died. George was nursed by a neighbor and recovered. Matt also recovered, but ended up giving up his ranch.

Fortunately, the 1918 flu peaked within two to three weeks after showing up, leaving as quickly as it arrived. And thankfully, the 1918 strain ran its course that year and has never resurfaced.

Merry Helm

Cheers to Grand Forks!

26 OCT

Few people would guess that Grand Forks came into being because of a keg of beer, but supposedly it's true. Traders were the first Europeans to visit the Red River Valley when they came to trade manufactured goods with Native Americans in exchange for pelts and furs. Known as Les Grande Fourches, a fork created by the joining of the Red River and the Red Lake River became a rendezvous point as early as the 1740s.

In 1811, farmers established Selkirk Colony at present-day Winnipeg, but to survive the winters, they depended on imported food and equipment. Ships from England tried to supply them by coming south from Hudson Bay via the Hayes River, but the short summers didn't cooperate. The next step was to try to get goods that came north on the Mississippi River from New Orleans to St. Paul. To transport goods from St. Paul, Métis people created oxcart trains, but these were so slow, they could complete only two trips per summer.

In 1858, St. Paul businessmen offered $1000 to anyone who could successfully travel from St. Paul to Winnipeg by steamboat. In 1859, Anson Northrup beat out the competition by coming up the Minnesota River to Crow Wing, MN, where he dismantled his boat. He then hauled it overland to the banks of the Red River, where he put it back together again. He then launched it and successfully navigated the Red River to arrive at Fort Garry.

Meanwhile, traders were still conducting business at Les Grande Fourches, which was now on the mail route that ran between Fort Garry and Fort Abercrombie near Wahpeton. Being a halfway point, the government established a post office on the fork in 1870. The new steamboat business kicked into high gear, and passengers started traveling the river. Seeing a lucrative venture, railroad tycoon James J. Hill partnered with a steamboat captain, Alexander Griggs, to form the Red River Transportation Line. Griggs had proved himself a capable man who, at fifteen, had honed his sailing skills on the Mississippi River to earn his pilot's license when he was only nineteen.

Roughly 130 years ago, Alexander Griggs was participating in a flatboat race on the Red River to Fort Garry. When his crew spotted a keg of beer that had accidentally fallen off another boat, they snagged it and ended up getting so drunk that Griggs had to tie up at the forks to spend the night. He intended to finish the journey to Winnipeg the following day, but morning brought them a rude surprise. During the night, the temperature had plummeted, and their boat was frozen in place. According to the story, the men had to build a shelter for the winter, and with time on his hands, Griggs surveyed the land and became convinced the site would be ideal for a new town.

So it was that on this date, in 1875, Alexander Griggs platted his town and has ever since been known as the "Father of Grand Forks." If that doesn't deserve a toast, I don't know what does.

Merry Helm

27 OCT

Henry Gayton

During this week in 1974, Larry J. Sprunk sat down with Henry Gayton. Larry was working with the Oral History Project. From 1974 to 1977, he and Robert Carlson traversed the state, driving almost 80,000 miles and conducting 1,214 interviews. The goal was to record North Dakota history from those who lived it – to hear stories from all parts of the state and all walks of life.

Henry Gayton was one of the interviewees. Born in 1902, Henry was raised near Selfridge. But at the age of 6 or 7, Henry left home for the Catholic boarding school at Fort Yates. There wasn't any other option. As he said, "Either you went to the Catholic boarding school or you didn't go."

The school at Fort Yates was one of many Indian boarding schools. Some were run by the federal government. Others were mission schools, some of which received federal funding. The goal of these schools was to assimilate Native Americans into mainstream American culture. The schools shared similar programs with a focus on the English language, farming and a strict military-type regimen.

Henry remembered the typical schedule. The students would wake up around 5 or 6 in the morning, pray, eat breakfast, do housework, go to church and pray again before bed. Henry recalled, "You don't have a chance to play. You're praying all the time. Then the ol' sister'd be walkin' around, you know, and she'd be listenin'. You're not prayin' and, boy, up goes your ear."

Students were also punished if they were caught speaking their native language. And they were stuck at school, away from their families, September through June. There was no running away either. As Henry said, "Police were right there, you know."

However, in the 1930s most of these schools were closed. A report revealed that the students were poorly taught and poorly treated. Unfortunately, the end of the schools didn't result in equal education for Native Americans. Into the 1960s, many teachers still believed their role was to "civilize," not educate.

But perhaps even a poor education was an education. Henry admitted "I went through high school, but doggone I thought I was too smart. Now I realize I shoulda went on to school, kept on a goin'. It's too late."

Alyssa Boge

Ragnvold Nestos

28 OCT

North Dakota has the distinction of having had the first governor to ever be recalled, but the person who took away his job in the recall election is little known today. On this date in 1921, Ragnvold Nestos, an immigrant bachelor from Norway, became the thirteenth governor of North Dakota.

Nestos was born in a mountainous region of Norway in 1877, the oldest of ten children. Because Ragnvold was in charge of herding the cattle, and because their farm was so isolated, he rarely had the chance to attend school, averaging only about three months of school a year. When he immigrated to the United States at age 16, his education was equivalent to a fifth grade in American schools, and he could neither speak or understand English.

He traveled to America on a small boat called The Prince, using money borrowed from his uncle, who lived in Buxton, North Dakota. The trip from Liverpool to Philadelphia took thirteen days, and when he arrived, he had 85 cents in cash, and a stash of hard tack and butter. Unfortunately, the container smashed and covered his only good suit in butter; but the hard tack was still intact enough to last until he reached Buxton.

In his memoirs, Nestos recalled "In November 1893, I started in the first grade in the Buxton public schools. I worked for my board, doing chores during the week and working in my uncle's harness shop on Saturdays."

Within four years, Nestos advanced enough to be able to attend Mayville Normal School, followed by UND Law School. He became adept at debating and public speaking, and after starting a law practice in Minot, he got interested in politics, first getting elected as a state legislator. By 1916, Nestos had started making a name for himself and narrowly missed being elected to the U.S. Senate. Four years later, he was endorsed by the independents to run for governor, but his friend and colleague, Bill Langer, joined the Non-Partisan League and beat him. The following year, a delegate convention of the Independent Voters' Association met in Devils Lake to consider the state's political future.

Nestos recalled, "After nearly two days of debate, we decided to recall the Governor, the Attorney General, and the Commissioner of Agriculture and Labor. I was selected by unanimous vote to make the race for the governorship against the man who then occupied the office, Lynn J. Frazier. "A long and bitter campaign followed, and on October 28, 1921... I won by a majority of 4,102. On November 23, 1921, the newly elected officials were inaugurated, the first to be elected in a recall election." In June 1922, Nestos won the Republican nomination for governor and was reelected for another term.

Thus it was that a shepherd boy – with almost no education, with no English skills, and only eighty-five cents in the pocket of his buttery suit – rose to fill the highest office in North Dakota.

Merry Helm

29 OCT

Rodeo Six Pack

In October of 2009, North Dakota rodeo stars Joe Chase and Tom Tescher were inducted into the National Cowboy and Western Heritage Museum's Rodeo Historical Society. The two were national rodeo legends, joining 1957 National Saddle Bronc Champion Alvin Nelson and nationally-known saddle bronc and bull riding champion Duane Howard, who were also inducted.

The four were part of the famous North Dakota "Six Pack" dominating rodeo across the country in the 1950s and '60s, along with Dean Armstrong and Jim Tescher.

Tom Tescher was a tough, ranch-raised kid who grew up dreaming of being a bronc rider like his older brothers Alvin and Jim. The son of Matt and Antoinette Tescher of Sentinel Butte, he began rodeoing in the Medora arena in 1943. In 1948 and 1950, he won the North Dakota Saddle Bronc Riding Championship at Sanish.

Over the years, Tom won at most of the country's biggest rodeos, ranking in the top ten of saddle bronc riders from 1955 through 1958 and qualifying for the 1959 and 1960 National Finals Rodeo. Tom and his brother Jim established "The Home on The Range Champions Ride" at Sentinel Butte in 1957.

The other North Dakota inductee, Joe Chase, was a Fort Berthold Mandan/Hidatsa Indian. He visited the pay window at some of the nation's biggest rodeos. Some said that watching Joe on top of a bronc was like watching poetry in motion.

Born in 1933 to Joseph Sr. and Anna Fredericks Chase of Elbowoods, Joe credited his older brother Emanuel in getting him started in rodeo. At age 16, Joe won his first title, the 1949 North Dakota Saddle Bronc Riding Championship at Sanish. He led the Hardin Simmons University of Abilene, Texas, to two national championships.

Joe became the first North Dakotan to win national college titles, including the national saddle bronc title in 1952 and 1953. He participated in bull riding and bull dogging and was runner-up all-around cowboy. After graduating, he traveled the circuit with the famous "Six Pack."

Joe qualified and won on some of the toughest bucking stock in the U.S. and Canada, including on Whiz Bang, Figure Four, War Paint and Snake. He qualified in saddle bronc for the National Finals Rodeos in 1960 and '61. Injury forced his retirement from rodeo in 1962.

Cathy A. Langemo

Sad Tale of a Soiled Dove

30 OCT

They were called soiled doves, fallen angels, and scarlet women. In the early days of statehood, these monikers referred to the women who plied the trade of prostitution. During the waning years of the nineteenth century that trade was prosperous, conflicted, and deadly in the streets of Fargo.

On this date in 1895, the *Fargo Forum and Daily Republican* newspaper reported a sad tale of struggle for one of its fallen women. Readers of a story entitled "Wanted to Die" were moved by the tale of Viola Lyons, described as "a tall, slender blonde who would be attractive except for the mark of dissipation on her face."

Viola had fallen on bad times that would become even harsher. Abandoned by her husband, who left her to join the Salvation Army, Viola - out of desperate necessity - became a working girl at one of Fargo's numerous brothels.

Following a quarrel with the house madam, she was forced to leave that house of ill repute. Circumstances soon found her drinking whiskey in the company of a soldier at a saloon in neighboring Moorhead, Minnesota. Events transpired that led the agonized Viola into taking a debilitating dose of laudanum, a dangerous narcotic that was popular throughout the frontier West.

Although she was aided from her narcotic stupor by a physician, she was expelled from Moorhead, back into Fargo, only to be arrested and thrown in the city jail. Behind bars and in a despondent state, Viola attempted to slit her wrists with a pen knife. When the jailers discovered the bleeding prisoner, they confiscated the knife, and it was reported that she "threw herself on the hard bench of the cell with a wail of despair and began to cry as though her heart would break."

Historian Carroll Engelhardt notes that the *Fargo Forum* account was typical of others that were sympathetic to the plight of the many women who were victims of faithless men and economic circumstances. So-called 'purity campaigns' across the country were reflected in the Fargo Moorhead area, and well-intentioned community reformers campaigned to improve the lives of prostitutes and fight prejudices against them as "irrevocably fallen."

Ernest efforts were undertaken to provide the girls with homes, employment and religious instruction. Other noble efforts continued throughout the cities and nation as prostitution sadly emerged as a national issue into the Progressive Era. Yet, prostitution on the prairie remained a seemingly intractable element of a growing state.

Steve Stark

31 OCT

A Haunting in Bismarck

When the National Historic Preservation Act was created in 1966, it preserved many older buildings that come with interesting histories, superstitions, and, this being Halloween, things that go bump in the night.

The Former Governors' Mansion in Bismarck is a large, Victorian mansion built in 1884. Some have claimed to hear ghostly footsteps on the stairs, and doors closing on their own. Skeptics noted that those who resided in the house frequently complained about it being drafty, and, it was also noted that older, non-insulated structures often creak and groan. But spiritualists have attributed these manifestations to the ghost of Governor Frank Briggs, who died in the master bedroom in 1898. Did he have unfinished business?

In the Historic District of downtown Bismarck, some occupants of the buildings between Main and Thayer Avenues along Fourth Street have occasionally reported feeling a presence, especially in the KFYR and Bismarck Tribune buildings. Perhaps it was not the events within the buildings themselves, but the ground upon which they are built. Populated with saloons, brothels, and gambling houses in the 1870s, this area was known as Bloody Fourth and was at the epicenter of a violent period in the history of Bismarck. Gamblers, soldiers, and prospectors played the odds, and many were buried on the large knoll at the upper end of Fourth Street in Bismarck's first cemetery. However, the notorious element soon moved on and this area became quiet and respectable. Maybe some remained, at least in spirit.

In the early morning hours in late August of 1883, two policemen sitting on a bench at the south end of Fourth Street noticed a figure of a woman dressed in white approaching them. As she neared the center of the street she suddenly vanished. Not a sound was heard, nor a footprint could be found in the dust of the street. A few nights later, several men, including a reporter for the *Bismarck Tribune*, stood spellbound as the figure of a man emerged from the shadows and, without the sound of footsteps, proceeded northward towards the cemetery. It then returned, only to vanish among the shadows of the buildings that occupied the ground where ten years earlier Dave Mullen had been gunned down in the doorway of his saloon by members the 7th Cavalry seeking vengeance. Could it be that Mullen desired to converse with his former patrons whose souls were bound to the cemetery to the north, having then returned to protect his property from the ghosts of the 7th Cavalry?

Jim Davis

Era Bell Thompson in class, Driscoll, N.D.
Credit: State Historical Society of North Dakota (00032-BL-39-09)

NOVEMBER

Era Bell Thompson

01 NOV

On this date in 1945, the first issue of *Ebony* magazine was published. Now, one doesn't typically associate Black culture with early North Dakota, but one of the state's most noted celebrities started out on a farm near Driscoll.

Era Bell's family moved to North Dakota in 1914 when she was nine years old. She and her three brothers were excited about the move, because they expected cowboys and Indians. But the most they got was her Uncle James, who had homesteaded here seven years before.

A few days later, Era was led into a 4-room schoolhouse full of people, including Era's red-haired teacher, who had never before seen a black person. The experience was agonizing, with classmates laughing at her, trying to touch her hair and staring at her light-colored palms. After some time, Era made friends, but she felt completely out of place.

Three years later when Era's mother died, the family moved to Bismarck, where her father got a job working for Governor Lynn Frazier as a private messenger. Even in this larger town, there were only two black students, and again, a hush fell over the schoolyard when Era showed up for school. Now in seventh grade, Era learned to loathe Friday afternoons when boy-girl games were played. Worse, one of her textbooks informed that all black people were "thick-skulled." And on the days that slavery was discussed, Era cut class. But Era soon distinguished herself as a gifted runner, and the track became one of the few places she fit in. However, on the bus she learned to sit in aisle seats so onlookers wouldn't gawk at her.

After high school, Era enrolled at UND, but the YWCA refused her a room, the streetcar would pass her by when she tried to board, and job positions were suddenly filled when she applied. She finally found a job working for a Jewish family in the part of Grand Forks known as Little Jerusalem.

In college, she fell back on what she had learned from her experiences in Driscoll and Bismarck. She survived the prejudice and made friends. She also pursued her love of running, breaking five UND women's track records – in dashes, broad jump and hurdles – and tied two national records. She began writing for the campus paper, showing herself to have a substantial wit and talent.

When her dad died, Era went back to Mandan to run a used furniture store so she could pay off his debts. A white pastor and his family took her in as their foster child and helped her get her college degree, and from there, she went to Chicago. Despite her college degree, she found very little opportunity for a good job, so in 1946, she wrote her life story, titled *American Daughter*. Because of the success of her autobiography, *Ebony* hired Era Bell Thompson as an associate editor. By 1964, she became the international editor of the prestigious magazine.

Merry Helm

02 NOV

Happy Birthday

Today marks the birthday of the great state of North Dakota. We entered the Union in 1889 along with South Dakota. The states were entered alphabetically, so North Dakota became the 39th state, with South Dakota at number 40.

It was on this day in 1947 that the Spruce Goose made its first and only flight. Howard Hughes – business man, movie producer, multi-millionaire, aviator, and recluse – designed the single hull flying boat to hold 750 troops during wartime. The plane contained eight 3,000 horsepower engines and wings that were twenty feet longer than a football field. Due to rationing of steel and aluminum during World War II, the Spruce Goose was constructed using the "Duramold" process – thin wood pieces laminated to each other using heat and wood glues. The end product was lighter and stronger than aluminum. The Spruce Goose made its maiden voyage, with Howard Hughes at the controls, across the harbor in Long Beach, California. It was shortly after the voyage that Hughes placed the Spruce Goose in "hibernation" for 33 years, until his death in 1976. 2004 saw the release of *The Aviator*, a film about the life of Hughes, his love of aircraft, and his eventual mental illness. The Spruce Goose currently makes its home at an aviation museum in McMinnville, Oregon.

Other birthdays on this important day include French Queen Marie Antoinette, frontiersman Daniel Boone, America's 29th President – Warren G. Harding, and movie tough-guy Burt Lancaster.

On the political scene, it was November 2, 1948, that Harry Truman beat Thomas Dewey. Despite predictions from pollster George Gallup and the *Chicago Tribune* declaring, "Dewey beats Truman," Truman won the presidency by 3.5 percentage points. Georgia's Jimmy Carter beat Gerald Ford for the Presidency on this day in 1976. And President Ronald Reagan signed a bill on November 2, 1983, establishing Martin Luther King, Jr. Day as a federal holiday.

Sesame Street's own Cookie Monster also shares his birthday with North Dakota as well. Voiced by Frank Oz, Cookie Monster is well known to Sesame Street viewers as the googly-eyed blue furry monster who loves cookies. However, because chocolate and oils can damage the fur of a Muppet, Cookie Monster rarely eats actual cookies while filming. Fat-free oatmeal cookies are sometimes used, but most often rice cakes are painted to resemble his infamous chocolate chip cookies. Cookie Monster doesn't seem to mind.

As today marks North Dakota's birthday, we encourage you to celebrate by exploring our grand state, or by simply enjoying a delicious piece of birthday cake. Or, if you prefer, a rice cake painted to resemble a cookie.

Jill Whitcomb

North Dakota's First Year

03 NOV

On this date in 1890, one full year had elapsed since the creation of the states of North and South Dakota. On November 4, 1889, Governor John Miller issued a proclamation requesting all duly elected legislators to meet on Tuesday, November 19 to elect two senators for the United States Congress and attend to the duties of setting up the laws for the new government. On the first ballot, Gilbert A. Pierce was elected the first US Senator, but it took nine more ballots before Lyman Casey won a clear majority to become the second Senator. They would join Henry Clay Hansbrough who had been elected as the first congressman in the general election.

The newly created state Constitution outlined the rights of the citizens of North Dakota, but it was the duty of the legislature to define these rights and set up a civil and penal code. For this purpose, the legislature was granted one hundred and twenty days instead of the sixty days allotted for a regular session. The legislators began the task of sorting through 239 senate bills and 357 house bills. They would use the full 120 days and adjourn on March 18, 1890.

With the Farmer's Alliance in control, much of the session was involved with farmer related legislation. Several years of drought had farmers eager to set interest rates on loans and limit the ability of banks to foreclosure on farmland. Another large block of time was spent limiting the power of the railroads and granting regulatory authority to the Board of Railroad Commissioners.

On February 3, 1890, Senate Bill 167 was introduced to move the Louisiana Lottery from Louisiana, where it was no longer sanctioned, to North Dakota. Money flowed freely into the hands of those who would support the bill, and more was offered if it was passed. The Lottery Company offered the state $150,000 annually along with 250 thousand bushels of seed wheat for impoverished farmers. In the end, the House indefinitely postponed a vote on the bill, defeating it by inaction.

The legislature authorized the construction of the Agricultural College, among other institutions, but no funds were appropriated and funding was left to the cities where they were located. Women's Suffrage was ignored. The Prohibition Law passed on December 19, 1889, with attempts to lessen the fines and eliminate jail time moderately successful.

It would take several more sessions to correct various omissions and errors in the new laws, but overall the new Ship of State was afloat. Popular pontificator Dennis Hannifin, the so-called Squatter Governor, and, incidentally, now a teetotaler, was pleased.

Jim Davis

04 NOV

King John Satterlund

Washburn, the oldest city in McLean County, was founded on this date in 1882. The man responsible was John Satterlund, who, by the time he died, was known across the state as "King John."

Satterlund immigrated with his parents from Carlstadt, Sweden, when he was eighteen. He was smart, well-educated, and a risk-taker. The family settled in Minnesota, but John headed west, ahead of the railroad, when he was twenty-two. He established his first homestead fifteen miles north of Bismarck, at a spot called Dry Point, and then headed north to Canada to help build the railroad between Port Arthur and Fort Williams. When he returned four years later, he bought a large chunk of land in Burleigh County and got serious about farming and ranching. But it didn't appear to satisfy him.

He soon speculated on property farther north and planned out the city of Washburn. He became one of the first commissioners for Burleigh County and then set his sights on breaking away to form McLean County, with Washburn as the county seat. Satterlund served as the new county's first sheriff and was also a U.S. Marshal for four years.

Continuing his trail blazing, Satterlund opened a roller mill in Washburn, and the Merchants Hotel in Bismarck. He established the first Bismarck-Washburn stage line and, with his long-time friend Louis Peterson, brought in the first telephone service between the two towns. Satterlund was also the editor and publisher of his own newspaper, the *Washburn Leader*, and was the receiver in the Bismarck land office for twelve years. And if that's not enough, he owned his own coalmine – the well-known Black Diamond. On the home front, he and his wife, Charlotte, raised five children.

Eventually, Satterlund got into politics. He was twice elected to the state legislature and soon concentrated on getting handpicked men into office. One of his good friends was a U.S. senator from Wisconsin – C. C. Washburn – for whom his town was named. In fact, it was Washburn who was able to give King John the one thing he didn't have – a railroad line into town.

A 1930 obituary gives us a hint that King John was, of course, not perfect. He had a daughter living nearby, yet he was living alone in the Grand Pacific Hotel in Bismarck. Charlotte was gone – having moved to California to live with another daughter.

"There have been many instances of misused authority in the summing up of Satterlund's life," the obituary reads, "but the good that might be said of him far outweighed the balance. He was the product of an era when [bosses were] good for the country […] He was of the old school, a real man, and McLean county regrets his passing."

Merry Helm

Blanchard Fire

05 NOV

The thriving town of Blanchard was completely wiped out on this day in 1908, as an enormous fire ravaged the community in the early morning hours. The fire spread quickly, consuming the entire business section within a few short hours. Several residences were also destroyed, leaving many people homeless and possessing only the pajamas on their backs.

Located in Traill County, along the North Dakota-Minnesota border, the small town of Blanchard was considered a boom town, with a rapidly growing population approaching four hundred. Although four hundred does not sound like a boom town today, in 1908, Blanchard was one of the quickest growing communities in the state.

Around 5 o'clock that fateful morning, the fire began in the city's Woodman's Hall. The exact cause of the fire is unknown, but it was believed to have started very small, as the first residents on the scene believed it would be confined to the Hall. Then a powerful wind began to blow, and the small fire quickly grew. The townspeople were unable to control its spread. The city, being rather young, had not yet established any type of fire department.

The fire on that November 5 spelled the beginning of the end for the growing town. Perhaps because the town had expanded so quickly, the city had not bothered to take out fire insurance. Additionally, fewer than half of the city's residents and businessmen were insured. Consequently, the city was unable to rebuild much of what was lost. The total damages amounted to over $50,000 and included the city's post office and community hall. The majority of the residents were forced to move elsewhere – even those who had insurance – because of the lack of services and employment. Today, the population of the town is around eighty individuals, or about a fifth the number recorded during the 1900 census.

Jayme L. Job

06 NOV

Homebrew

Innovation has always been important in the success of any business, but this was particularly true in the moonshine business of the 1920s in North Dakota. Federal and State Prohibition officers scoured the countryside looking for any sign of stills and even sniffed the air for the telltale smell of fermenting mash.

On this date in 1923, officers raided the Nels A. Hanson farm near Hankinson but failed to find a still. It was known to them that Mr. Hanson was considered one of the leading bootleggers of his community and that his product was considered to be above reproach, but they could never locate the still that he used to brew his mash. After some discussion, Mr. Hanson was convinced to take them to it, so he led the way to his pig sty. He moved the pigs from one pen to another and then he began scraping away the pig litter in the first pen. Using a hammer, he proceeded to open a trapdoor where a small ladder extended to the basement under the sty. The basement was lined in tar-paper protecting six barrels of mash and a 15 gallon still. The barrels were covered in old blankets to keep out the seepage from above. It was believed that he used the still at night to prevent detection of the smoke and the pig sty masked the smell of the mash. The close proximity of the pigs also opted for a quick turnaround time for disposing of the cooked mash.

Most stills in North Dakota were mom and pop operations, or at least mom knew that pop had one. For some people, making moonshine was the only way of saving the farm due to the depressed farm economy. They were not major operations run by a crime syndicate. In fact, those who operated the stills were often considered local folk heroes. Homebrew was everywhere, but nonetheless it was illegal, and violators were prosecuted with varied results. It is interesting to note that public sentiment so much favored homebrew that by 1932, the Ward County States Attorney was convinced that he could no longer get a conviction where homebrew was involved so he refused to prosecute any additional violations.

As for Nels Hanson, he received 90 days in jail and a $200.00 fine but received high praise from the Federal prohibition agents for masking both the sight and the smell of his still in such an innovative way. He was, in a sense, a real North Dakota entrepreneur.

Lane Sunwall

Apocalypse

07 NOV

By the end of October in 1918, the people of North Dakota held an apocalyptic view of unfolding events. The whirlwind pace of an incredibly violent year had eclipsed anything ever witnessed before. Editor F.W. Wardwell of the *Pioneer Express* at Pembina said, "It takes blood to make people understand what war means and what war is. We do not recognize the war demon until he comes near enough to see his red garments."

By mid-October, the casualty lists were swollen with the names of local heroes when just as suddenly, in the cities and towns across the state, pestilence, in the form of the Spanish flu was taking its toll, adding to the misery. Death was on most doorsteps.

Famine was the final member of the Four Horsemen of the Apocalypse, as mentioned in a book by that name, which was becoming popular at the time. While not manifesting in the state, rationing and food shortages had become a part of everyday life. To add to the turmoil, in many parts of the state, vigilante law dealt with slackers and seditionists as an intolerance of German ethnicity greatly strained communities. Meanwhile, as huge forest fires in northern Minnesota killed hundreds of people and destroyed complete towns, clouds of smoke rolled through the state, casting an eerie gloom.

But if it is always the darkest before the dawn, news from the battlefield and the home front was beginning to indicate that the end of the war was in sight. After battlefield deaths had risen with the latest push, they now declined with the Germans driven back and Austria surrendering unconditionally. On the home front, flu death likewise had peaked and communities were beginning to allow social gatherings. Meanwhile, a bountiful harvest had lessened the food shortages, but there was much work to be done, as it would be months before conditions in Europe would allow the return of most troops.

In 1918, the war-weary population of North Dakota was preparing to launch the United War Work Campaign on November 11. The major welfare organizations had combined their fund drives into one major effort to promote the welfare of the soldiers in France and in training camps across the nation. Nationally, $250,000,000 was the goal, with North Dakota's share being slightly over $1,000,000. Peace was in sight, but the war effort carried on.

Jim Davis

08 NOV

Aloha Eagles

Today is the birthday of Aloha Pearl Taylor Brown Eagles, who was born in 1916 in Duluth. She grew up in Crosby, MN, trained as a nurse, and graduated from Hibbing Junior College in 1936. Aloha and her husband, Donald, moved to Fargo in 1942, where they raised two sons. In 1967, she campaigned as a Republican for District 21 and was elected to the North Dakota Legislative Assembly. She served eighteen years, until 1985.

Eagles represents another example of how the North Dakota Republican and Democrat platforms exchanged places during the 20th Century. As a Republican, Eagles introduced House Bill 319, which called for legalized abortion in cases of rape, incest, or if the mother's health was in danger. The bill also allowed for abortion if the unborn child had serious physical or mental defects.

This was in 1969, four years before the Roe vs. Wade decision. Because of her views, Eagles became the target of death threats and hate mail. State troopers were temporarily assigned to protect her. The bill failed in the House by a vote of 52-42. When she introduced a similar bill in 1971, it was defeated by an even wider margin of 85-15.

In 1973, Eagles introduced a resolution to ratify the Equal Rights Amendment for women; the ERA was originally presented to Congress fifty years earlier by Susan B. Anthony's nephew. His bill got stuck in the Judiciary Committee, which was chaired by a strong opponent of the amendment. But in 1970, it finally went before Congress. That August, it was approved.

The ERA had to be ratified by three-fourths of the states. Within four years, 33 of the required 38 states had approved it. In North Dakota, Aloha Eagles' push for ratification failed by one vote, but women representing several organizations launched an immense lobbying and informational campaign. Their efforts resulted in the amendment being ratified in 1975.

It was almost three years before another state ratified the ERA. The deadline was moved from early 1979 to mid-1982, but no other states stepped up; the bill died just three states short of ratification. Aloha Eagles was named North Dakota Woman of the Year in 1973, and Woman of the Year in Government in Fargo in 1976. That same year, UND presented her with their Law Woman's Award. Eagles died in 1992, at age 75.

Merry Helm

Jim Jam Jems

09 NOV

Sometimes the truth hurts, and even offends, but that didn't stop Sam Clark and C.H. Crockard, publishers of *Jim Jam Jems*. As the magazine's forward warned, "Here in the confines of this little booklet [...] we intend to write just whatever we damn please and say just as much."

The publication was widely read, but in 1912, Clark and Crockard were indicted by a federal grand jury in Fargo for sending "obscene and immoral" reading matter in interstate mail. Meanwhile, news dealers throughout the state and in Minneapolis and St. Paul were also being arrested for selling the publication. *Jim Jam Jems*, however, continued "selling like hot-cakes," and Clark and Crockard continued publishing while fighting the charges. They insisted the publication was in no way obscene and had even helped bring several people to justice. Their mission, they said, "was the cleaning up of some of the filthiness existing in the country." For them, the magazine was just political and social commentary that often skewered church or political officials. To the state, however, the publication was obscene.

One of the articles considered most lewd was titled "Chicken-chasing." This article made the point that young women were vulnerable due to a lack of laws to protect them. The article said in part:

> In most states, the age of consent is fixed by statute at 14 to 16 years. [...] Can you imagine a little girl 14 or even 16 years of age as the legal custodian to her person [...] of sufficient age to dispose of their virtue to the first brute that happens along? [...] [T]he men who make the laws and the men who are supposed to enforce them are too often 'chicken-chasers' themselves, and it seems that it is a hard matter to change the existing conditions.

For the next five years, Clark and Crockard contended the charges, and the trials often flopped back and forth between guilty and not guilty. The legal battle finally ended December 1917 with a conclusion of guilty.

Jim Jam Jems continued to circulate, however, and Clark and Crockard retained their colorful voice in later issues. Clark later moved to Minneapolis and began taking on other endeavors. He spent less time on the publication, and the August 1929 issue was the last of *Jim Jam Jems*.

Tessa Sandstrom

10 NOV

Riders of the Wooden Wings

These men could fly a hundred feet across the plains of North Dakota, and all they needed to do so was a steep slope, a proper landing place, and their two wooden skis. Through the 1920s and 30s, these ski jumpers were North Dakota heroes, and many helped North Dakota, a state with no mountains and few hills, turn into a ski jumping center. Determined to continue participating in the sport they loved, many of these men built ski jumping slides throughout the state, and on this day in 1932, one of the most prominent jumpers of North Dakota was in the process of building one in Minot.

Casper Oimoen, the repeating National Champion and future two-time Olympian, set about establishing ski jumping as a major sport in Minot. Casper helped found the Minot Winter Sports Club with the goal to "create, develop, encourage, and maintain interest in all winter sports." With their club founded, Casper and the five other men who formed the first team of Minot Ski Riders set about building a ski jumping slide. With the financial help of Minot Chamber of Commerce, the Minot Winter Sports Club began building the 225-foot-long slide on the highest bluff in Minot, now commonly known as North Hill. The slide was completed and dedicated on January 1, 1933.

Prior to its completion, Casper had brought fellow Olympians and ski jumping champions from across the country to Minot as a possible site for tournaments sanctioned by the Central Ski Association, a division of the National Ski Association. Many of those visitors returned to compete at the dedication tournament held on February 5. When the tournament began, it appeared to be an instant success. A crowd of 4,000 gathered on the terraced spectators' hill to watch the jumpers perform their leaps. Among the athletes were Casper and his Olympian teammates Guttorm Paulsen of Chicago and Pedar Falstad of Devil's Lake. The much-anticipated event was cut short, however, when a north wind brought in an unexpected blizzard. The tournament was postponed until March 5, but the Minot Winter Sports Club promised even more noted athletes, including the entire 1932 Olympic team. When the tournament was finally held, it was a great success. Thirty-five contestants showed to participate, and Casper, the home-town hero, won the first Minot tournament. Paulsen finished second, and the Devil's Lake favorite, Falstad, finished third.

The Minot slide remained in operation through the next few years. The "riders of the wooden wings" could build their imitation hills for jumping the plains of North Dakota, but they could not divert the harsh North Dakota weather. According to Casper's daughter, Sonja Oimoen Stalions, "Winter blizzards became co-conspirators with wind to thwart the optimism which once characterized Minot's early-day ski sport spirit." The slide eventually blew down and the lumber was reused for other recreation programs, and no more did spectators gather to watch the "riders of the wooden wings" jump the broad North Dakota plains.

Tessa Sandstrom

Dr. Agnes Hoeger

11 NOV

Good Samaritan homes exemplify the best of "North Dakota Nice." In 1922, the Reverend August Hoeger saw the need for such a facility and opened the first in Arthur, North Dakota. His daughter, Agnes, was impressed by her father's example, and when she graduated from high school at fifteen, she entered college to prepare for work as a medical missionary. After ten years of study, she was ready. Dr. Agnes Hoeger traveled by land and sea for fifty-one days, then stepped off a ship in Madang, New Guinea on this date in 1935, beginning thirty years of medical work in that country.

But Agnes's first visit was cut short when she had to accompany an ill co-worker back to the States. Rather than return to New Guinea immediately, she fulfilled numerous speaking requests and studied tropical medicine in London. When she returned to Madang, she found the hospital now had electricity, allowing for lights in surgery and an x-ray machine.

With WWII looming in August 1940, Agnes was transferred to nearby Finschafen, with hopes the village would be ignored by both the Japanese and Allies. But by February 1942, all missionaries were evacuated. Walking eighty miles at night through dangerous mountain jungles, they avoided detection by Japanese bombers.

Unable to return to New Guinea during the war, she came home and was commissioned to the U.S. Army Medical Corps in Peru. In New Guinea, she had helped eradicate yaws, a tropical infection. In Peru she educated the people to decrease hookworm and malaria.

In 1946, she finally returned to New Guinea for a full term, rebuilding and "making do" with the remnants of war. She was particularly heartened when natives became Christians and ceased their clan wars.

On furlough in the 1950s, Agnes gave speeches and earned a Master's Degree in public health, then returned to New Guinea for one last term. In 1965, she returned home to care for her aging parents while serving as director of medical services at a Good Samaritan home. She earned her seventh post-secondary degree, then traveled the country by bus, teaching record-keeping to Good Samaritan personnel.

At 72, Agnes technically retired, but she went on to serve with the Peace Corps in Tonga. Back in the States, she continued speaking and doing Good Samaritan medical records work. She made one last move to Good Samaritan home in Kissimmee, Florida, where she died at the age of 82.

Karen Horsley

12 NOV

Ken Bischke

The winter of 1949 is one that many people around the Minot area would not soon forget. Record snowfall and cold temperatures were the norm that winter. Of course, the high winds only added misery to the 10 to 25 below zero temperatures. Local and area bulldozers, along with the North Dakota National Guard, tried in vain to unplug the eight-foot drifts covering Highway 83.

Those in the rural areas of Ward County were particularly at risk. Before long, calls began coming in to the Red Cross. The head of the Red Cross was Dr. Devine, who quickly contacted Ken Bischke for help.

Bischke, born in Max, North Dakota, was a Navy pilot during WWII. His flying expertise was needed again; this time not for war, but to help his friends and neighbors survive this life-threatening winter. Without hesitation, Ken quickly got on board and was ready to fly. His first mission was delivering hay to the stranded cattle. Using a DC-3, Ken would fly low over the drop zone and hay bales were pushed out the door.

Next, he began making milk runs. Ken delivered empty milk cans to the dairy farmers and returned with full ones for the children in Minot. He could only carry four full cans in one load, so his trips were numerous.

Bread was also in short supply during this bitterly cold winter. The Sweetheart Bakery packed Ken's small plane with seventy-five loaves of bread. Barely able to lift off, Ken delivered the bread, and then flew off to Stanley for mail.

Many area farmers were without phones. Ken would drop a foot-long spike with a colored streamer over remote farmsteads. The spike contained the message that he would fly over again in two hours. If an emergency existed at the farm, they were to stamp out a code in the snow, and Ken would then land his plane and take care of their needs.

Ken saved many lives during the winter of 1949. He flew over sixty missions, picking up stranded travelers, helping fly doctors to deliver babies, and transporting food, medicine, and fuel.

Ken Bischke will be long remembered as a selfless man who when needed, came to the aid of his neighbors.

Dave Seifert

Johanna Kildahl

13 NOV

It was in the late-summer of 1883 that fifteen-year-old Johanna Kildahl arrived in the Mauvais Coulee Valley, near Lake Alice, about twenty miles north of Devils Lake. She traveled from Minnesota with her brother, Andrew, to meet the rest of her family who had homesteaded on the land in the spring of the year.

After a week of traveling in a prairie schooner behind a team of oxen, Johanna stepped off the covered wagon into a billowing sea of prairie-grass. She smiled happily at her new home, a small framed house and a tent.

Johanna immediately fell in love with the Dakota scenery. She later recalled the virgin prairie as rich with water, grass, ducks, geese, and prairie chickens, in beautiful sunsets, sunrises, mirages, and glorious northern lights – "a garden of the gods."

Coming from a land where trees were endless, her family was among the first to plant the many groves of box elder and cottonwood trees on the slopes around the Mauvais Coulee Valley.

It took five years before Johanna Kildahl had a town nearby, with Maza established in 1888. It was during this week in 1893, when the *Grand Forks Herald* noted that Maza was expanding by adding a Methodist church to its cluster of buildings along the Great Northern branch-line to St. John.

Homesteading for the Kildahl family was not always beautiful and breathtaking, except perhaps in memory. Johanna wrote that the weather was harsher during those times, for winters were "longer and more severe; blizzards more frequent and of longer duration." Frost came earlier in the fall and later in the spring. Thankfully, their sod house provided a cozy comfort for it was "warm in winter, [and] cool in summer."

Despite the hardships, Johanna described her pioneering days as a time "to feel befriended by the 'peace of the morning, the light of the sunset and the happiness of the sky'; to find time to think, to pray, and to give thanks. These were the days of real neighborliness, accommodation, cooperation and friendliness. There were no locks on doors and nothing was ever disturbed or taken."

Johanna's recollections still resonate within today's North Dakotans, for they carry the experiences of many ancestors who settled on these rolling prairies. Johanna and the Kildahl family's experience was not one of a kind, but it was admirable, once for all.

Michelle Holien

14 NOV

Women's Suffrage

Women's suffrage is a story older than North Dakota's statehood, dating back to territorial times. It was a political and progressive issue viewed as important to some, but a joke to others. Only men could decide.

Perhaps the first milestone was in 1883 when women of Dakota Territory were allowed to vote in school elections. In 1889, women also gained the right to vote for the state superintendent of public instruction. North Dakota's legislature nearly passed a women's suffrage bill in 1893, but it lost in a bitter drama on the last day of the session.

Suffragists in North Dakota had a leader in Elizabeth Preston Anderson. As President of North Dakota's Women's Christian Temperance Union, she closely followed events in the legislature. Without her records, history may have forgotten the failed 1893 women's suffrage bill.

In the early 1880s, there was no organized group in the state promoting women's suffrage. But a meeting in Grand Forks in the spring of 1888 set the wheels in motion. A crowded convention was held at the Grand Forks County Courthouse. Those in attendance heard lectures and letters of support from men and women alike. More public meetings followed and other clubs formed around the state.

In 1895, North Dakota's first statewide suffrage convention was held. It was called to order by local suffragist Dr. Cora Smith Eaton— the first woman doctor in North Dakota. The convention heard letters from Susan B. Anthony, North Dakota Senator Henry Hansbrough, and others. Anthony's letter outlined how to organize support for suffrage on the local level.

Other conventions followed, with meetings in Fargo, Larimore, Devils Lake, Hillsboro, and Lakota. The women's suffrage movement snowballed in the early twentieth century. Every legislative session from 1901 to 1911 included a bill about women's suffrage. None were made law.

In 1914, North Dakota voters - all men - voted on a referred measure for women's suffrage. It failed, getting about 45% of the vote. In 1916, North Dakota's Non-Partisan League took up the challenge as a champion of women's suffrage. The effort would eventually grant women the right to vote for presidential electors, county officials, township officers and most city officials. Full suffrage finally came in 1919 with passage of the Nineteenth Amendment to the U.S. Constitution.

Jack Dura

Mr. Muskrat

15 NOV

What is a muskrat? Native to North America, muskrats are aquatic animals that live near bodies of water. In some areas of the United States, they are known as "Swamp Bunnies," though they do not resemble a bunny. Like a cross between a beaver and a rat, the muskrat is larger and heavier than a normal rat and lacks the flat tail of a beaver. If asked today, many North Dakotans could describe the creature as one they had seen along rivers and streams.

On this day in 1922, one family described the muskrat as their very own family pet. It seems that George L. Hutchins, whose family lived near Hamilton, North Dakota, came across a muskrat while he was out driving late one night. The muskrat appeared in the road and ran forward into the headlights, as if bewildered.

Hutchins stopped the car, got out, and struck the little animal over its head with the car's auto crank, knocking it out cold. He tossed it into the back of his car and continued on his way. When he got back to his house, Hutchins said the muskrat had revived. It was walking around, happy as a muskrat.

Hutchins took the muskrat into the house, where his family grew to love it. They fed the muskrat milk and crackers and vegetables, and they filled their bathtub full of water for it to play in. The muskrat swam around in their tub and tried to dive into it. It stayed tame, following members of the Hutchins family around.

The family dog did not like the muskrat as much as its owners seemed to. However, according to the *Minot Daily News*, "in an encounter between the two, the dog came out second-best."

The muskrat did not try to escape, and except for that first encounter with the auto crank, the Hutchins reported no need to restrain it. Mr. and Mrs. Hutchins even said that when they drove their car to town with the muskrat between them in the front seat, it sat there, happy, not moving, not trying to escape.

After a few days, the Hutchins family returned the tamed muskrat to the wild. They left it near the Tongue River in the woods. As they drove away, it sat by a tree, "taking a farewell look at them."

On a side note, striking any animal over the head and removing it from its habitat is generally frowned upon. This author suggests that with the advancements of technology, those seeking a new or even exotic pet try searching their computer rather than using the same technique. Yet, in that time, one happy little muskrat joined a family for a short time only, easily tamed by a rap on the head.

Sarah Walker

16 NOV

Horses for Europe

"One man's trash is another man's treasure," is a saying that was especially true following World War II. Since tractors took over for horses in the fields, many farmers were left with horses they couldn't get rid of. According to the *Mandan Pioneer*, North Dakota farmers had found an outlet for their extra burden.

In 1946, North Dakota was in the process of gathering horses from across the state to ship to Europe. There had been some discussion over butchering the horses for meat to send to starving Europeans, but the horses were to be put to better use. The United Nations Relief and Rehabilitation Agency purchased thousands of horses across the state, primarily eastern North Dakota, and was shipping them to Europe to replace those that had been killed, starved, or butchered during the war. The UNRRA hoped the animals could be used in an effort to rebuild the European agricultural economy.

The plan seemed to be a blessing to both Europeans and Americans. According to Leo J. Murphy, the manager of the Jamestown sales yard, most farmers were glad to sell off their horses. "The animals were a detriment because of the feed they consumed as compared to the amount of farm work they did," he said. "North Dakota farmers can spare these horses because tractors have replaced them."

The first shipment was in June when 600 horses were shipped from Jamestown. Afterward, 4,200 horses were shipped, and another 1,600 horses were gathered in Jamestown and throughout Stutsman County. They awaited trains that would ship them to ports in Savannah, Georgia, Portland, Maine, and Newport News, Virginia. From there the horses would be shipped to Europe. According to the *Pioneer*, 6,000 horses were to be shipped by the end of the month.

The horses did not just go anywhere. Different types of horses would be sent to countries where they would be most useful. Smaller horses, for example, were sent to Greece, while larger ones were en route for Poland, and if receiving one horse wasn't enough, some farmers could expect a two-for-one deal. According to the *Pioneer*, "Everybody concerned denies it, but the evidence of the eye indicates that some of the mares are going to become mothers." By the time the horses arrived at their destinations, Christmas might indeed be coming early for the European farmers.

Tessa Sandstrom

The Butterfly Guy

17 NOV

For Emil Krauth, chronic insomnia was first his curse and then his blessing. He was born around 1872 in the German village of Eberbach. As a child, he became fascinated with the stone entrance to a local cemetery. Carved into the stone were butterflies, which, his pastor explained, represented the Resurrection of Christ; the butterfly begins as a caterpillar that retreats into a cocoon and then emerges beautifully transformed.

Emil suffered from poor health as a child. He left Eberbach to study art in Karlsruhe, Germany, while continuing to seek answers at the University Clinic of Heidelberg. His physicians finally told him his only hope was to go to a land with an arid climate.

Krauth chose New York, where several of his siblings lived. But once there, he found himself plagued by a new problem: he couldn't sleep. Becoming more and more anxious, he thought he was losing his sanity. His doctors thought he might improve if he lived in the open country. They suggested North Dakota, much to the dismay of his brothers and sisters. They told him no man of education and culture could be happy in "a land of ice and snow, bare and void, neglected by nature, and fit only for coyotes and cowboys."

Emil followed his doctors' advice, however, and arrived in central North Dakota in October 1907. He was pleasantly surprised to find he loved the open prairie and its incomparable sunsets. He dabbled in farming and then went into business selling real estate and insurance in Hebron.

Fresh air and sunshine improved his health, but insomnia still had him worrying about his sanity. One summer evening, he sat on his porch looking for a diversion, when he noticed a large "silk-spinner" moth circling the porch light. It brought to mind the stone-carvings outside the Eberbach cemetery, and his boyhood fascination with butterflies was re-awakened. He ordered a book on butterflies, made a net, and began to ramble the Hebron hills looking for specimens. After each excursion, he used his butterfly text to identify his trophies and then carefully mounted them.

As Krauth's collection grew, so did his zest for life. His friends teased him, saying there would soon be no more butterflies or moths to discover. People generally agreed there couldn't be more than thirty or forty species on the North Dakota prairie, but Krauth made an accidental discovery. One evening, darkness caught up to him as he walked home, and, to his surprise, he found there were more moths and butterflies out at night than during the day.

With his insomnia now working to his advantage, Krauth spent many hours bagging night fliers, and his collection continued to grow. He bought more books on butterflies, subscribed to entomology magazines, and wrote letters to other collectors. He also started raising his own specimens and learned about their growth habits. Soon he was trading for moths and butterflies native to Asia, Africa, South America, and Europe. He also began to travel and was the first to discover the Parnassus butterfly east of the Rocky Mountains. In the Black Hills, he discovered a new species of butterfly that has since been named in his honor: *Colias christina krauthii*. The original specimen is now in the American Museum of Natural History.

Krauth died on this date in 1941, leaving a mounted collection of more than 10,000 specimens – the largest private collection in the nation. After his death, part of his collection went to the State Historical Society of North Dakota, and the other went to a Hebron attorney. Having found his passion, Emil Krauth happily admitted he lived his life "chasing butterflies instead of dollars." Even at night.

Dave Seifert

The 1937 Bakers' Strike

18 NOV

Across the ages, many people have gone on strike for different reasons and seeking different outcomes. In November of 1937, the General Motors plant in Michigan was going through its third sit-down strike. North Dakota also had a simultaneous labor disagreement in Grand Forks: a bakers' strike. And these bakers were definitely standing up.

The strike began on a Sunday, and before the week was over, problems had escalated as eighteen men were arrested. Throughout this time, five baking firms - Blacks, Chicago Bakery, Colton-Wilder, Franks and Eddy's - were trying to keep going in the midst of strike by "concentrating their baking operations" at the Eddy plant. The employers of these firms had taken to doing "the actual baking" themselves in an effort to ramp up production.

On this date, the picketers for the strike stopped trucks from delivering bread. The picketers, reported to be mostly transported Fargo men, kept two trucks of the American Railway Express Co. from taking out any loads, and then later stopped a Hiller Transfer Co. truck from taking out its second load.

By noon, officials from the five baking firms announced that they would not be attempting any more bread deliveries until their drivers were granted some protection against "picket violence," and all bread deliveries in the city were stopped. Representatives from Minneapolis had come in to help with negotiations that evening, and members from the newly organized Associated Industries of Greater Grand Forks met with police to ask for more police protection for the bakery delivery trucks. The eighteen picketers were charged with conspiracy to prevent the performance of a lawful act.

The strike was still not completely settled until the next day. George Cox, manager of Cox's bakery, met with a non-union group and had already signed a working contract, and others were continuing to negotiate, and an uneasy peace was restored.

Things cooled down after that, though those picketers had to wait untill December 14 to find out what would happen to them. Their case was dismissed, and they were discharged from custody at the request of the complainants of the action. The bakers had returned to work and folks had bread on their tables once more.

Sarah Walker

19 NOV

Bicycle, North Dakota

A number of communities have come and gone in McKenzie County, where Watford City sits at pretty much the heart of everything. A century ago, however, many towns dotted the prairie in that largest county in the state.

One example is Bicycle, North Dakota. The name was Anglicized from nearby Beicegel Creek. Bicycle was located about six miles northwest of Grassy Butte, and in this week during 1916, the post office was established. Anne Fane was Bicycle's postmaster before the site moved west six miles to the home of Reuben Lyon, who took over from Mrs. Fane. Louis Elstrand and Frances Cook were later postmasters. The original Bicycle sat at the entrance to Scairt Woman Road along County Road 50.

The place didn't last long. The little post office closed on Halloween in 1935 with mail service switching to Grassy Butte. Other McKenzie County towns met similar fates. Charbonneau, North Dakota, declined in the 1950s and '60s after its school and post office closed. Schafer began to die when the railroad went around the one-time county seat. Rawson dissolved its government in the early 2000s. And Juniper, at the mouth of Cherry Creek on the Little Missouri River, was platted, but no structures were ever built. Even the county seat saw changes as it was hosted by Alexander and Schafer before winding up in Watford City, which was located on the Great Northern Railroad line.

At the time of Bicycle's beginnings, Watford City was barely three years old. A hundred years later, the boomtown could barely keep up with its population, which grew to over 7,500 people.

Jack Dura

Lewis and Clark Move In

20 NOV

On this date in 1804, the Lewis and Clark Expedition moved into their winter camp on the upper Missouri River, fourteen miles west of where Washburn now stands. One of President Jefferson's missions was to make contact with Native American tribes along the way, and to tell the Knife River Indians, in particular, that "their late fathers, the Spaniards," had surrendered their territory and that "Henceforward, we become [your] fathers and friends."

In honor of their friendly new neighbors, the expedition's winter camp was named Fort Mandan. Construction of the fort began November 3 and required two weeks of intense work in very cold weather. By the time they were done, more than a foot of snow was on the ground and ice was floating in the river.

Jefferson chose 29-year-old Captain Meriwether Lewis to lead the expedition, describing him as "brave, prudent, habituated to the woods, & familiar with Indian manners and character. He is not regularly educated, but he possesses a great mass of accurate observation on all the subjects of nature which present themselves here, & will therefore readily select those only in his new route which shall be new."

A collapsible boat was being constructed for the journey, but it was about a month behind schedule. So it was that two days before the delayed start date of August 31, Lewis received word from his 33-year-old friend, William Clark – a straight-talking, six-foot redhead – who agreed to go along on the expedition. The eternal link of Lewis and Clark possibly wouldn't have happened if the boat-builder had finished his job on time. Clark was a war veteran, like Lewis, and was comfortable with roughing it. The original Corps of Discovery consisted of forty strong. Their cargo included scientific tools, arms, camping equipment, medicine, food and twenty gallons of whiskey. They also had twenty-one bales of presents for the Indians, including tools, brass kettles, needles, and fishhooks.

One member of the expedition who isn't readily known was Seaman, a black Newfoundlander dog that Lewis had purchased in Pittsburgh. Seaman made the entire 8,000-mile trip to the Pacific Ocean and back and had to endure the same cold, the same bad food, the same danger, and the same mosquitoes, ticks, and fleas as the rest of the crew. The Indians were impressed with Seaman in the same way that Lewis and Clark were when they first saw antelope and buffalo. People offered to trade fur pelts for him, but Lewis wouldn't give him up. Then, one night, Seaman was kidnapped.

In his book, *Undaunted Courage*, Stephen Ambrose writes, "In the evening, three Indians stole Seaman, which sent Lewis into a rage. He called three men and snapped out orders to follow and find those thieves, and 'if they made the least resistance or difficulty in surrendering Seaman, to fire on them.' When the thieves realized they were being pursued, they let Seaman go and fled."

Merry Helm

21 NOV

Illegal German School

Issues such as segregation, racism, and religious differences often don't make headlines in North Dakota, but they have existed in different forms during the state's history. One high-profile case erupted in the town of Expansion, a tiny port on the Missouri River that never got beyond a population of 75.

This area in Mercer County had a large population of prosperous German families whose children entered public school unable to speak English. The parents felt this disadvantage was a large problem for their youngsters. These families were predominantly Evangelical Lutheran, and they desired more religious instruction for their children, as well.

Sometime in 1915, a number of German Lutheran farmers decided they needed to have their own school. They organized, adopted resolutions and petitioned Mercer County Superintendent of Schools Thomas to approve their plan. They already had a church building, so they began to remodel it to include a school. They set a curriculum that offered all the same classes as the public school, but also added some religion-based courses. They ordered textbooks with money from their own pockets and hired a graduate from Concordia College in Moorhead to be the instructor.

At some point in early 1916, Superintendent Thomas decided to oppose the school, because the children were being taught English through the use of the German language. He said English had to be taught from within the English language. The farmers resisted, saying they were in charge of their children's well-being, not the government. They wanted their kids to have the best education they could, based on their own unique needs.

Superintendent Thomas responded by ordering the parochial school closed. Invoking the compulsory education law, he declared all the German children had to immediately enroll in the public school. The challenge was too much for the Germans, and they refused. At least two were arrested. In March 1916, the *Bismarck Daily Tribune* reported, "Jacob Haffner was arrested, charged with refusing to send his children to school. Superintendent Thomas claimed the parochial school was not provided for by law. Haffner was taken before a justice at Stanton and fined. This case has been appealed to the district court on the grounds that the parent, not the state, is keeper of his child."

Three days later, State Superintendent E. J. Taylor sided with the county superintendent. Sullivan and Sullivan, the high-profile Mandan attorneys were representing Haffner, as well as Fred Pfenning, who was arrested on a similar charge. A Stanton newspaper reported their cases were to go before the state Supreme Court, and on this date in 1916, Sullivan and Sullivan succeeded in getting Judge Nuessle to order State Superintendent Taylor to show just cause for why he didn't approve the school's curriculum. Unfortunately, records of what ultimately happened no longer exist.

Merry Helm

The Noble Experiment

22 NOV

In 1906, the *Hope Pioneer* reported on a meeting of the local Women's Christian Temperance Union. The purpose of the organization was to educate about the dangers of alcohol and drugs and to promote prohibition. During its heyday, the organization played an important part in North Dakota history, expanding its concerns to include women's suffrage, labor laws, and prison reform.

Susan B. Anthony organized the WCTU in 1874 because men would not allow women to participate in Christian Temperance Meetings. The guys even adding "men" to the name of their group made it clear that women were not welcome.

Jamestown hosted the state's first WCTU convention in 1890. The meeting drew a huge crowd, largely because the keynote speaker was Susan B. Anthony. The organization quickly caught on across the state.

Prohibition has a long history in North Dakota. In 1887, the territorial legislature gave communities the right to enforce prohibition on a local level. When the vote on the state constitution was held, an amendment approving prohibition passed on a narrow vote. The saloons closed on July 1, 1890. North Dakota became a dry state, but illegal alcohol remained readily available.

As part of its effort, the WCTU urged members to erect public drinking fountains. The hope was that men would take advantage of the free water instead of going into the secretive illegal saloons for stronger drink. One of the remaining WCTU fountains can be found in Park River.

The North Dakota chapters also supported the goal of national prohibition. This was accomplished when the 18th Amendment was passed in 1919. As prohibition became a nationwide reality, the membership of the WCTU began to decline.

After prohibition was repealed in 1933, North Dakota also began to relax liquor laws by allowing beer sales. Hard liquor followed in 1936. The "noble experiment" was officially a failure.

The WCTU is still active today, opposing the use of alcohol, tobacco, and illegal drugs. It operates a publishing house and offers programs to schools, but the membership is just a sliver of its peak in 1931.

Carole Butcher

23 NOV

The 10 Commandments of Farming

William C. Palmer's life was steeped in agriculture. He came from a farming family in Wisconsin, where he was born and raised. For a few years in the midst of his college career, he was in charge of the sub-station of the Minnesota Agricultural College and Experiment Station at Lynd, Minnesota. When he graduated in 1903, he had earned four college degrees—one, of course, in science and agriculture. Before and after that time, he engaged in soil management investigation for the US Bureau of Soil under O. C. Gregg, a man known as "The father of Farmers Institute work."

In 1910, Palmer joined the staff of the North Dakota Agriculture College in Fargo, now NDSU. That year, the college launched extension work, and Palmer helped organize it. He started the college press service, which was made up of farm information stories distributed to the dailies and weeklies of the state. In addition, he was in charge of the college's film and slide service on agricultural topics and publicity.

For thirty-five years, he worked at the NDAC. Finally, he retired in 1945, after spending almost fifty years in agricultural extension and research work. So, William Palmer knew something about his agriculture.

Therefore, when he sent out some rules of farming in pamphlet form to newspapers across the state, people paid attention. So, here are William Palmer's Ten Commandments of Farming, as printed in the *Munich Herald* on this date in 1910:

> Commandment I: Thou shalt plow deep.
> Commandment II: Thou shalt keep the surface loose and level, and the lower soil compact.
> Commandment III: Thou shalt add organic matter to the soil.
> Commandment IV: Thou shalt summer fallow when rainfall is less than 15 inches.
> Commandment V: Thou shalt grow corn or a cultivated crop every two to five years.
> Commandment VI: Thou shalt grow clover, alfalfa or some leguminous crop every few years.
> Commandment VII: Thou shalt grow early maturing crops.
> Commandment VIII: Thou shalt keep down the weeds.
> Commandment IX: Thou shalt keep stock.
> Commandment X: Thou shalt plant trees.

You may be wondering what this all means. The rules to live by were: diversified farming, crop rotation, and soil conservation. Hallelujah! Palmer's commandments continue to help farmers reap what they have sown.

Sarah Walker

Sunrise Ranch Lighthouse

24 NOV

Seventeen miles southwest of Mandan, nestled in the bottomlands of the Heart River, is a ranch called the Sunrise. It started as a 160-acre homestead, filed in 1883, by a Swedish immigrant named Magnus Nelson. Two years ago, the Nelson Sunrise Ranch was inducted into the North Dakota Cowboy Hall of Fame in the ranching category.

Since Magnus' day, the Sunrise has since grown to 8,000 acres, with only 10 percent under cultivation. Used primarily for raising cattle, this native prairie-land is still wild and rugged enough to be called, by some, the "Little Badlands."

The Sunrise has been passed down through the family to Magnus' grandson, Clifford, who says, "When Grandpa came here, there was literally nothing here. They talked about the Indians traveling through and coming right into the house. The main thing they wanted was fresh bread. They'd get two or three loaves, and then they'd be on their way. They never bothered anybody. I suppose they had corn bread, but this was [yeasted] bread made from wheat flour."

Eighteen years after staking his claim, Magnus Nelson did something rather unusual, but fitting to the ranch's name. It was 1901 and people still traveled by horseback or in horse-drawn buggies and wagons. Out there in those isolated hills, it was easy to get lost after dark, and that made for some dangerous conditions, especially in the winter. Ranch land also lacked fences that people further east could often use to guide themselves to safety.

Magnus did a sensible thing—he built a sandstone lighthouse on a bluff overlooking his spread. When winter storms threatened, he or one of his family members would climb to the top of the hill and light a lamp in the lighthouse as a beacon of safety. It worked—several times, endangered wagons or riders would take refuge in the Nelson home, where they found food, warmth, and hospitality. The Nelsons further used their unique lighthouse for entertaining visitors—especially for those who liked to play cards. Magnus died in 1913. By then, he had expanded his original claim into a 1600-acre operation. Five years later, Nelson's son, Adolph, obtained full ownership, and in 1942, Adolph, in turn, expanded the ranch by purchasing a piece of land known as "Chata Wakpa" or "Big Heart" in Indian terminology.

For a while, the ranch was made available to area folks for camping, and it also was used for rodeos. In 1961, Adolph's son, Clifford took over the operation, which he still runs with his wife, Norma. By 1983, the homestead's centennial, Magnus Nelson's stone lighthouse had deteriorated. Because of its high, exposed location, it had been hit by lightning on more than one occasion, and it was not in the greatest shape. But the original sandstones were still on the site, so family members rebuilt the structure and added a new roof in time for the hundred-year celebration.

Merry Helm

25 NOV

Scrap Drives

Devils Lake announced that it had surpassed its collection goals during a recent scrap metal drive on this date in 1942. Scrap drives, in which people collected and salvaged all manners of things, became a common feature of the home front during World War II.

In September of 1942, the U.S. Government issued a challenge to local communities to pull together and complete an intensive drive. North Dakota State salvage director, E. E. Campion, called on everyone to help meet the challenge, but especially targeted the state's businessmen. Government officials believed that businessmen were in a strong position to aid the drives, given their resources and influence. Campion asked the state's roughly 20,000 businessmen to look through damaged, discarded, and used merchandise as a potential source of material. The director claimed he was "sure that if the merchant knew that the old stove laying broken up and useless would make ten 4" shells, that the abandoned radiator will make seventeen .30 caliber rifles, and that the leaky wash pail will make three bayonets, he would collect every bit of savagable scrap in his shop or store room and start it on its way to becoming valuable war material."

In Fargo, citizens heaped up scrap material into an enormous pile stretching along two blocks of Broadway in October. Not to be outdone, residents of Devils Lake set a goal to collect 895 tons. By November, they announced that not only had they surpassed their goal, but had actually more than tripled it, delivering 3,024 tons of metal for donation. Officials admitted that the donation was only achieved by sacrificing the Civil-War era cannon that had been placed in the Ramsey County fairgrounds and the large metal capstan from the historic steamboat, the Minnie H. This ship had been the flagship of Captain Edward Heerman and had ferried locals between the north and south shores of Devils Lake from 1883 until 1908. The ship's anchor and other metal relics that survived the War's scrap drives are on display today at the Pioneer Daughter's Museum in Fort Totten.

In October, even without the final tallies and donations, the government announced that the drive had accumulated enough scrap metal to build fifty-two first-line battleships, with North Dakota donating 13,559 tons to the cause. By November, the state's donation was equivalent to nearly sixty pounds of metal for each North Dakota resident!

Jayme L. Job

Ralph Engelstad

26 NOV

On November 26, 2002, UND benefactor Ralph Engelstad quietly passed away after a battle with lung cancer. Engelstad was born in 1930, the grandson of a Norwegian immigrant who farmed potatoes near Thief River Falls, MN. The year Engelstad graduated from high school, Ben Gustafson, a future dean at UND, encouraged him to enroll at UND and try out for its fledgling hockey team. Ralph ended up as the team's goalie and graduated in 1954 with a business degree. He had two mottos: "The harder I work, the luckier I get," and, "No dream comes true until you wake up and go to work."

In 1959, Engelstad moved to Las Vegas, where he had secured government contracts to build Federal Housing Authority homes. There, he invested in 145 acres of barren land north of town. In 1967, he sold the land to Howard Hughes for what is now the Las Vegas Air Terminal. Engelstad used the profits to buy the Flamingo Capri Motel, which he replaced with the hugely successful Imperial Palace. Ralph and his wife, Betty, were once listed in Business Week as among of America's fifty most generous philanthropists. The most notable example of their financial support was their donation of the $104 million Ralph Engelstad Arena in Grand Forks. Engelstad also purchased the George S. Patton Papers and donated them to the Elwyn B. Robinson Special Collections portion of the Chester Fritz Library.

Engelstad was a complicated man whose sense of compassion was contradictory. He was the first casino owner to include an on-site medical center for his Imperial Palace employees, 13% of whom had some form of disability. For his humanitarianism, Engelstad received special recognition from President George H.W. Bush. At the opposite end of the spectrum, Engelstad was accused of bigotry several times. In 2000, UND officials were responding to Native American staff and students who felt degraded by the school's mascot, the "Fighting Sioux." Engelstad threatened to turn off the heat and pull his funding for the half-completed hockey arena unless the Sioux logo remained. His ultimatum led UND's board of directors to unanimously vote to keep the mascot. Ten years earlier, he had also been enmeshed in a high-profile situation in Las Vegas. Engelstad owned the third largest antique car collection in the world, including cars owned by Italian dictator Benito Mussolini and three infamous Nazis: Adolf Hitler, Herman Goring, and Heinrich Himmler. His interest in these cars spilled over into an extensive collection of Axis and Nazi memorabilia housed in the Imperial's "war room." It included swastika banners, uniforms, propaganda posters, weapons, and a portrait of Hitler reading, "To Ralphie from Adolf."

In 1986 and 1988, Engelstad held parties in the war room on Hitler's birthday, and the resulting scandal ended with the state of Nevada demanding $1.5 million for harming the state's reputation. Engelstad insisted the parties were tongue-in-cheek, but he paid the fine so that he could retain his gaming license.

Merry Helm

27 NOV

Rural Telephone Administration

In May of 1935, the Rural Electrification Administration—better known by its initials REA—came into being to provide electricity for farms and small communities. Besides bringing the benefits of electricity to make farms more productive and add modern conveniences to farm homes, electricity to power radios also reduced the feeling of isolation for farm families. Telephone service, widely available in populated areas, wasn't available due to the high cost of rural development.

In the early months of 1949, Congress was working on legislation to provide rural telephone service modeled after the success of the REA. While farmers and farm organizations applauded the rural telephone bill, private telephone companies such as Bell Telephone strongly opposed it, calling it socialism. The House passed the bill on July 13, 1949, but it dragged on in the Senate. Farmers, encouraged by farm organizations, began writing thousands of letters to Congress. In early November of 1949, the law passed and was quickly signed by President Harry Truman who made $25 million available for low-interest loans. The first Rural Telephone Administration loan in North Dakota was given to Abercrombie for a quarter of a million dollars.

The REA became involved after a significant advancement in emerging technology by Western Electric. Known as the side carrier telephone system, it transformed REA power lines into telephone lines. The telephone signal could be carried by the power line using a converter between phones and the electrical wiring. It was cheap, easy to install, and required little maintenance.

During this week in 1950, a report was published on the progress of providing rural telephone service. While seventeen applications for loans by REAs, totaling slightly over $1 million were made in North Dakota, private companies were also attempting to obtain their share of the market. Over the year-long period since the bill was passed, Bell Telephone expanded services across the state. Buildings and lines were established in Williston, Minot, Crosby, Max, Rutland, Litchville, and other areas as they worked to complete an estimated $25,000,000 development program. Many rural areas decided it was easier and faster to have Bell Telephone provide the service. In the long run, RTAs were not as widely distributed as REAs, but the 1949 legislation was instrumental in bringing rural telephone service to North Dakota by energizing the competition. Now farmers had one more thing besides the rooster to wake them up—the ringing of a telephone.

Jim Davis

The Angel of the Prairies

28 NOV

Anna Shatswell was born in Vienna, Austria, on this date in 1875. She immigrated with her family to New Ulm, MN, when she was thirteen.

Shatswell wanted to pursue a career in nursing, so she studied in San Francisco and practiced in St. Paul before coming to Devils Lake in 1906. There, she was among the state's earliest pioneer nurses. As she described it, she worked in a "little hospital on the prairie with a staff of one doctor and two nurses."

In an interview with the *Williston Herald* in 1967, Shatswell claimed, "nursing on the prairie involved a lot of ingenuity and perseverance, because hospitals were few and far between."

As one of the state's earliest nurses, Anna spent many years traveling great distances in harsh weather to reach sick patients.

"I went wherever the doctors needed me, and I shook the snow out of my clothes many a time—it was an ordeal, but it was rewarding, too," she said.

Anna remembered traveling to treat an abundance of stricken patients during the 1918 flu pandemic. One victim from the Fort Buford area told her fretful family, "if Nurse Shatswell comes, I will live; if not, I will die, that's all." Thankfully, Anna arrived, and the girl did indeed live. "I brought her right out of it," Anna said.

Anna and her sister staked a homestead claim in Divide County and built a farm together. Anna then opened a six-bed maternity hospital in Crosby. During her 60-year career as a registered nurse, she said she "delivered most of the babies from Minot to Crosby and as far south as Williston." She said she kept track of the number of babies she delivered until it got as high as 1000, when she quit counting.

It was in Divide County that Shatswell became widely known as the Angel of the Prairies. "I didn't make much money," she said, "but I didn't charge folks when they had no money, because they had to provide food and clothes for the little ones running around."

Anna broke her leg and was confined to a wheelchair when she was in her eighties. Unable to walk, the nurse was forced into retirement after sixty years of service. But she remained lively and energetic, and she took pride in her ability to remain up-to-date, saying, "I have to keep up with what's going on in the world, or I might get old, you know."

When several of her friends suggested she might do better living in a nursing home, Anna quickly disagreed. She said she wanted to be around her books and papers and to laugh and "say foolish things." She felt being surrounded by only the elderly would keep her from staying young.

Anna's grown 'babies' continued to visit her well into her nineties, often bringing their families. "The rewards of a lifetime spent nursing are manifold," she said.

Merry Helm

29 NOV

Hero Turns Outlaw

Today's story is about a veteran who came home a war hero. But unlike others, Verne Miller took a drastically wrong turn. Verne Miller, who served with the ND National Guard in WWI, was clean cut, tall, and blond with chiseled features. When he came home, he became a policeman and was then elected sheriff. But, in July 1922, he was found to have embezzled some $6,000 from the South Dakota county that employed him.

The law caught up with Miller in St. Paul the day after Halloween. The fugitive sheriff gave up without incident and pled not guilty. But when the case went to trail, he approached the bench and pled guilty. He was fined $5200 and sentenced from two to ten years in the South Dakota State pen.

After eighteen months, Miller was released and worked as a farmhand for $70 a month until the terms of his parole were met.

Miller was soon indicted for violating prohibition laws, and in June 1925, he turned himself in. But as soon as his father and uncle posted bail for him, he skipped town. The next summer, he met Vi Mathis, who had recently divorced her husband who was in prison for first-degree murder. Vi was a working at a carnival in Brainerd, MN, when a belligerent customer started bothering her. Miller came to the rescue, and the two were soon inseparable.

A year later it was rumored Verne Miller was the driver of a getaway car when a bank was robbed by six men back in Huron. Miller was by now hooked up with one of Al Capone's guys as a bootlegger. He and Vi were running liquor between Chicago and St. Paul and delivering to hotels and speakeasies across the Dakotas.

Things went well for the pair until February 1928, when Miller was involved in a brawl in which two patrolmen were shot and wounded at the Cotton Club in Minneapolis. Miller's partners, Kid Cann and Bob Kennedy, were indicted but let go due to lack of witnesses.

A few months later, Miller was also indicted for shooting a prohibition agent, so he and Vi skipped town. They landed in Montreal, where they opened several casinos with a New Jersey mobster. Miller's crime network quickly expanded. When he and Vi came back to the States during the Depression, Miller soon became part of what the FBI dubbed the Holden-Keating gang, which included Harvey Bailey, the leader, Tommy Holden, Francis "Jimmy" Keating and accomplices Machine Gun Kelly and Frank "Jelly" Nash.

Soon after, Miller and his gang robbed a bank in Willmar, MN, getting away with $140,000. But one gang member was killed, and two locals were wounded. During their investigation officials soon came across three dead or dying Kansas City men, Sammy Stein, Mike Rusick, and Frank "Weanie" Coleman. All were shot with a .45-caliber machine gun.

Machine Gun Kelly said the killer was Verne Miller, who was soon running with the likes of Pretty Boy Floyd.

For the next three years, Verne and Vi lived the high-life, robbing banks across the country. Murder was commonplace in their world, and it was inevitable Verne would die badly. Yesterday was the anniversary of his death in 1933. He was found dead on the outskirts of Detroit, nude, beaten, and trussed-up.

Merry Helm

30 NOV

Fort Sauerkraut

The Dakota Territory Indian Wars ostensibly ended when Sitting Bull surrendered his people at Ft. Buford in 1875. Tribes were confined to reservations with poor land where wild game had been hunted to near extinction. The government promised them rations and supplies, but graft and corruption was so rampant in the Bureau of Indian Affairs that if these items actually made it to the reservations, they were poor-quality leftovers.

By 1890, nationwide starvation on reservations set the stage for a major Indian uprising. A Paiute named Wovoka proclaimed the People could find salvation in something called the Ghost Dance, and Indian delegates from Dakota Territory journeyed to learn more. The movement was primarily peaceful and promised a Messiah and a return of the buffalo through songs, dances, and visions. Some, however, saw it as a call to overthrow all whites and take back their lands.

Journalists sounded an alarm when the Ghost Dance movement reached Standing Rock that fall. Standing Rock Agent James McLaughlin assured settlers that things were well under control and told them the newspaper stories were based on rumors. Nonetheless, by November 15, those rumors had Mandan residents in a widespread panic. Women and children fled across the river to Bismarck, and volunteer militias sprang up. As the news spread to surrounding towns, officials found themselves trying to protect friendly tribes from violence.

In *The Indian Scare of 1890*, Father Louis Pfaller wrote, "One of the most unique of the stories coming out of the scare was that of Hebron and its famous 'Fort Sauerkraut.' As soon as the telegraph warnings reached Hebron on November 17, young men jumped on their horses and rode madly over the prairie to warn the settlers. All night long," Pfaller wrote, "wagons rattled over the rough terrain toward Hebron. One man was in such haste that he had gone several miles before he discovered that his family had bounced out of the wagon."

Fort Sauerkraut was on a hilltop overlooking the town and was constructed almost entirely of sod. The fort's first line of defense was a series of wires strung to trip enemies advancing under cover of darkness. Inside this was a five-strand barbed wire fence, followed by rifle pits, which connected to underground tunnels that led to the interior of the fort. The 7-foot sod walls surrounding the fort stretched several hundred feet across. Inside these walls was a sod house about 100 feet long and 8 feet deep; this was to house the women and children during an attack.

The rumored uprising never took place. The Ghost Dance movement was officially and tragically quelled at the Wounded Knee Massacre less than a month later.

Volunteers with the Hebron Business Club rebuilt Fort Sauerkraut in August 2004.

Merry Helm

Richardton, North Dakota. Boys playing in the snow
Credit: John Vachon, Farm Security Administration - Office of War Information
Photograph Collection (Library of Congress), 1942

DECEMBER

Inmate School

01 DEC

Inmates at the Bismarck prison made the news in December 1914, but not because they were causing trouble. Rather, they had decided they needed more education.

The *Bismarck Daily Tribune* reported, "prisoners at the State Penitentiary took the initiative in the matter of attempting to secure a school in which they could improve their time in the evening by studying such subjects as spelling, writing, arithmetic and the like [... They asked] Warden Talcott to allow them to hold such a school, [and] the warden took the matter up with the state board of control." Every board member supported the idea, particularly J. W. Jackson.

The article continues, "Six of the inmates who have been better educated than the average expressed their willingness to act as teachers, and classes were formed, about 60 prisoners enrolling, and an average of 45 or so attending each class night.

"The matter was taken up with the state superintendent's office, and Superintendent Taylor and his deputy have co-operated (sic) in every way possible. Last week, Mr. Jackson, [Supt. Taylor and his deputy], and W.L. Gross of the commercial department of the high school went out to the penitentiary and visited the classes while at work.

"All were pleased with the spirit of the men in the classes," the story went on, "and as a result of this visit, Mr. Gross has been secured to supervise the school work done at the penitentiary hereafter. He will be assisted by the inmate teachers. Books have been secured.

"The classes meet regularly three nights a week for two-hour periods, and into these hours a great deal of work is crowded. One difficulty in carrying on the work as it now is done is the influx of new prisoners, every week, or perhaps more often at this time. These new prisoners, if they enter into the school work, are backward, and the whole class must review for their benefit."

Indeed, new prisoners were a continuous problem. Two years later, the *Tribune* reported a steady rise in the number of new inmates. In 1916, the prison population reached its highest number to that date: 296. Prisoners were described as coming from a wide array of religious faiths. In addition to religions commonly expected in North Dakota, there were Dunkards, Mormons, Free Thinkers, Jewish Orthodox, and many more. The *Tribune* reported, "The occupation most commonly represented was that of common laborer [...] 48 of the inmates styled themselves farmers; 12, cooks, and 10, teamster.

However, hopes remained high and the *Bismarck Daily Tribune* concluded that, "The inmates seem to be learning things from the start, judging from their papers, and the plan is a good one."

Merry Helm

02 DEC

The Mysteries of Lutefisk

There is a powerful Norwegian-American heritage in North Dakota. In fact, North Dakota has been recognized as the most "Norwegian" state in the U.S., having, in 1990, 29.6 percent of its population identifying as "primarily or secondarily Norwegian."

Along with this proud heritage comes lutefisk, the target of much derision. Lutefisk, as defined by historian Art Lee in his book *Leftover Lutefisk*, is a "uniquely prepared fish eaten by Scandinavians in general and Norwegians in particular." The word comes from the "Norwegian words *lute* (meaning to wash in a lye-and-water solution) and *fisk* (fish)."

Prior to the days of refrigeration, Norwegians preserved codfish by drying it in the sun, and, after being stored for any length of time, the fish became very hard. To soften the fish, Scandinavians soaked it in lye-water, and then carefully washed off the lye. Lye is a chemical used to make soap and unclog drains, but strangely-enough, it's also used to make pretzels shiny brown, to cure olives for eating, and to put a gleam on bagels.

After rinsing off the lye, cooks plunge lutefisk into boiling water to cook it into a gelatinous state, then serve it with oceans of melted-butter and plenty of salt.

When Norwegians immigrated to N.D. in the 1870s and onward, they brought the lutefisk tradition along with them.

It was on this date, in 1912, that a Grand Forks grocery-store advertised "Lutefisk [...] fresh soaked" for 5 cents a pound. December brought the "lutefisk season" for the local Norwegians, who could buy either the dry fish ready for preparation, or the soaked fish, ready to serve in a short time.

The dried fish had to be softened-up, and its preparation took about three weeks. This was considered an art. It had to be saturated in fresh water for four days; then immersed in lye-water for four days, and finally, drenched for four more days in freshwater, being sure to change the water daily, to extract all the lye. Then came the cooking; and it was wise to open kitchen doors and windows, using a "good breeze and electric fan" to air it out. Even with good ventilation, the kitchen smelled of lutefisk for two weeks.

Why do people still eat lutefisk? Well, it is traditional and truly Norwegian.

Non-Norwegians hold their noses, wondering, and exclaim: Uff-Da!

Dr. Steve Hoffbeck

Dakota the Dinosaur

03 DEC

North Dakota is no stranger to dinosaurs; the state has a fascination with them. Fourteen dinosaurs are on display at the Dickinson Dinosaur Museum, including a 37-foot tyrannosaurus rex. In June 2014, "Discover the Dinosaurs" presented an exhibit of animated dinosaurs at the Bismarck Civic Center. It proved to be very popular. The Hell Creek Formation in North Dakota is well known for dinosaur discoveries. Fossils can be seen in museums all across the state. But the most spectacular North Dakota dinosaur was only recently put on display.

Paleontology student Tyler Lyson came across the remains of a dinosaur on his family's property in 1999. There was no indication the remains were anything special, but for several years, Lyson continued to investigate the site. He ended up discovering not only the bones of a dinosaur, but also fossilized soft tissue, which is extremely rare.

Noted British paleontologist Phillip Manning teamed up with Lyson. They excavated the site in 2006 and revealed an extraordinary 67-million-year-old duckbill dinosaur mummy. The presence of the soft tissue allowed scientists to estimate the size and speed of the dinosaur. They concluded that it was 35 feet long, weighed 3 ½ tons, and could run 28 miles per hour. A CAT scan showed that it had much more powerful hind legs than scientists previously believed.

On this date in 2007, Manning and Tyson formally unveiled Dakota the Dinosaur. It is the best-preserved dinosaur found in a century. Although it has been described as a mummy because of the soft tissue, the entire dinosaur had long since been turned to stone. The remains were found near what had been a river, but scientists do not know how Dakota died.

Scientists have agreed that Dakota the Dinosaur has altered their understandings. Only a few pieces of dinosaur skin have been found, and most of them are very small. Scientists believe the scales on Dakota are evidence of camouflage coloring. The dinosaur also had a padded palms and hooves on its feet. Dakota is on display at the State Historical Society of North Dakota and serves as a cornerstone of the museum's expansion.

Carole Butcher

04 DEC

The State versus Mary Wright

In 1908, Mary Wright was a topic of conversation throughout North Dakota. In August of that year, she was arrested and held in jail at Devils Lake where she was accused of killing her 16-year-old stepdaughter, Beulah Cox. Authorities originally theorized that Wright was jealous of the girl and put poison in her food. Wright and her stepdaughter boarded on the farm where they worked. Many witnesses testified to the many arguments between the two.

A preliminary hearing had been held in September. The courtroom was crowded with spectators eager to get a glimpse of the accused. The *Evening Times* of Grand Forks described the case as "the most interesting that has been brought before the courts in this state in some time."

Wright sat "like a statue," showing no emotion as the hearing began. Two friends of Beulah occupied front row seats. They, too, were a center of attention. The first witness was a friend of Beulah's who had been with her the night before she died. Annie Wonderlich testified that Beulah had told her of being beaten and threatened by Wright. Beulah had even said she was afraid that Wright was going to poison her.

The next witness was Henry Miller, who was courting Annie Wonderlich. He spent the evening with Annie and Beulah at Annie's house, then walked Beulah home at 1:30 in the morning. He testified that Beulah told him of the harsh treatment she received from Wright. He said he heard Wright threaten to kill Beulah. Another boarder in the house confirmed Miller's statement that Wright and Beulah had a contentious relationship. He testified that he frequently heard Wright and Beulah arguing. He was eating a meal when Wright came to him and told him that Beulah was dead in her bed. Other witnesses reinforced the testimony about the stormy relationship.

The theory of Beulah's death changed during the trial. The prosecution put forth the argument that Mrs. Wright was furious that the girl had gone out at night and stayed out late. Wright was accused of losing her temper and choking the girl to death, then putting carbolic acid on her lips to make it look like the girl had committed suicide.

In February 1909, a jury found Mary Wright guilty of manslaughter. She was sentenced to five years in the penitentiary.

Carole Butcher

Patricide on the Prairie

05 DEC

On the evening of April 28, 1930, officials were in Anamoose, 60 miles southeast of Minot, investigating North Dakota's fourth killing in six weeks. That afternoon, 66-year-old Theodore Kummer had been shot in the head while taking a nap. Kummer's 21-year-old daughter, Anna, confessed and said her mother was working outside in the garden when she killed her father.

Mrs. Kummer and her son, John, said their sympathies laid entirely with Anna. Speaking through an interpreter, Marie, who was German-Russian, said, "It was either to be him, Anna or myself."

Neighbors confirmed Theodore was "a tyrant." Anna's brother John told authorities his dad was a heavy drinker, and he mistreated his family even when he was sober. Their brother, Emil, he said, had a crippled arm from a beating his father gave him as a boy.

The night before the killing, Kummer threatened his wife with a knife, and Anna locked her mother in a room to prevent her from getting killed. The next day, Anna and her mom were walking home from the grocery store when Mrs. Kummer said she was going to leave her husband because she "could not stand it any longer."

Anna was charged with first-degree murder and imprisoned in Towner under a $10,000 bond. It didn't matter what the amount was, however. Anna said she didn't want to "obtain her liberty." It appeared the relative peace and calm of the jail was comforting to her.

The trial began in early December. Minot defense attorney F. J. Funke entered a plea of not guilty by reason of temporary insanity. Jacob Kummer, a son from a previous marriage, testified he had never seen his father show brutality to either Marie or Anna. Anna was the youngest child, and Jacob said his father favored her when she was little. "She was his pet," he said.

Lena Johnson testified she was in a rented room in the house when she heard the fatal shot. Afterward, Anna came back and opened her door, telling her not to be afraid – she had just shot her father. "I had to do it to save my mother's life and my own," she said.

On December 5, 1930 Anna, who was described by neighbors as a "bright girl," listened to her attorney present evidence to show she was insane, with the mental age of "eight years and two months." The *Bismarck Tribune* reported, "Her mother has described her as appearing to be 'without sense' immediately after the shooting; her sister has expressed the belief she was insane at a time shortly after the shooting; a psychologist placed her mentality as that of a child; and a physician this forenoon was positive she was insane at the time of the shooting."

The verdict came in four days later. Anna was found guilty of second-degree murder and sentenced to eighteen years in prison.

Merry Helm

06 DEC

The Secrets of Bob Watson

Today's story is from the *Mandan Daily Pioneer* in December 1926.

"'Bob Watson,' 22, hotel clerk, pick and shovel cement worker, nifty swain of local young ladies, former miner, rodeo rider, today joined HER husband, Glen A. Halling on a farm near Price, N.D. Her masquerade locally, as a young man, came to an end after more than a year's residence when Chief of Police Nels H. Romer, of Mandan, and Chief Martinson, of Bismarck, called in a Red Cross nurse and others in Bismarck last evening to settle their suspicions on the matter of sex.

The story explained, "'B' had cashed a check on a Mandan bank with a Bismarck grocer. Funds were insufficient. Bob was arrested but released on making good the amount and payment of a fine when arraigned before Justice Harry Crane in Bismarck.

"'Yes, I'm just an ordinary girl,' she admitted. 'Why I've been wearing men's clothes and working as a man for years,' she told Chief of Police Romer.

"In September 1925, Bob secured a job as a night clerk at the Nigey hotel here, holding it for six months," the story went on. "She, rather he, had a high voice but got by. She rustled huge chunks of ice and did a man's work. [An argument] over a telephone bill ended the job.

"Then Bob got a place with a gang of laborers tearing out old cement sidewalks, paving and areas at the Mandan federal building. [But] hustling heavy wheelbarrow loads of refuse proved too much for her.

"My name was Dorothy Foster. I'm 22 years old. I was born and raised at Townsend, Montana. And I was married at Anaconda, Montana in 1923 to Glen A Halling," Bob explained. "Glen and I worked together in the copper mines at Butte and Anaconda. Sure, I've been wearing men's clothes ever since I was a little girl. I like 'em," she told the police.

The story goes on to say, "And then she exhibited clippings telling of prizes won riding the bucking horses and steers at rodeos in Butte and Anaconda. Pictures of the 'boy wonder' were carried by the papers of the two cities. Her masquerade was perfect.

"'I can't afford to wear girl's clothes. They cost too much,' Bob, or rather Dorothy, declared as she buttoned the natty college boy coat, shuffled her oxford shod foot whose ankle was encased in snappy checked socks, and clapped a neat fedora over her genuine man's haircut.

"'Afraid you'll have to,' said the minions of the law.

"Dorothy has gone to join her husband who is working the Wetzstein Brothers farm, near Price, on shares. Between jobs in Mandan, between dances and her masquerades, she has cooked for him, helped with farm work. But she isn't keen on farm life," the story read.

"I've had a lot of fun out of life anyway," she said.

Merry Helm

Camp Depression

07 DEC

Students are always looking for cheap accommodations, but in the 1930s, the University of North Dakota took this stereotype to a whole new level. On this day in 1933, the *Leader* reported that university officials had established a new innovative dormitory for students struggling through the Depression. "Conceived by the university officials as one means of beating the depression," said the *Leader*, "the most unique dormitory in the United States is made up of six cabooses that have been joined together and remodeled."

That's right, UND bought six cabooses to use for dormitories. Officials joined four of the cabooses together to be used as sleeping quarters, while one served as the kitchen and washroom, and the sixth was the study hall. Thirty students shared the new quarters, and each paid only $2 a week for the accommodation. The cheap and unique dormitories were attracting so many students that the university bought two more cabooses to accommodate incoming students.

The new dormitories were known as "Camp Depression" by the students who lived there, but the atmosphere was anything but depressing. The students living there worked together and combined their resources to keep Camp Depression a comfortable place to live and study, and UND was still providing quality instruction and curricula. Despite the damaging effects of the Depression, UND and its students were still flourishing. "Entering its second half century of educational service," reported the *Leader* "the University of North Dakota today ranks among the finest of American schools. The institution enjoys a Class A rating, the highest accorded any university."

Apart from cheap accommodations and education, the university also offered students a means of making income and paying for their education. For those already housed in Camp Depression, it was a requirement to work on campus for four hours a week to help pay room and board, but the university also employed 219 other students under the Civil Works Administration. Men and women worked on several projects on campus, including the preparation of the two new cabooses for Camp Depression, painting and repairing other campus buildings, replacing the sewer line on campus, and helping professors with various projects, including O.G. Libby's preservation of pioneer biographies. Overall, the work helped many students remain either partially or entirely self-supporting.

The University of North Dakota was definitely working to help students pursue an education throughout the 1930s, and Camp Depression was among one of its greatest ideas. The *Leader* reported that the university's efforts had set a new model for universities, arguing that the school "typifies a growing feeling that the true college is not necessarily a collection of ornate buildings with marble corridors [...] Coming through the depression years with an excellent record, the University of North Dakota looks forward to even better days in 1934."

Tessa Sandstrom

08 DEC

Fort Pembina

Long after the Dakota Uprising, citizens of Minnesota were still afraid of Indian attacks. The Minnesota Legislature petitioned Congress for protection against incursions by the Sioux. On this date in 1869, Major General Winfield Scott Hancock recommended the establishment of a fort at Pembina in the Dakota Territory, located only two miles south of the Canadian border. As late as 1823, the United States and Canada had both considered Pembina as Canadian. That changed when Major Stephen H. Long's survey of the 49th parallel showed that Pembina was definitely in United States.

Pembina was already an important settlement by 1869. It was established by the French as a fur trading post, and later it became involved with the bison trade. In 1851, the United States chose Pembina as the site for the first post office in present-day North Dakota. According to the 1860 census, Pembina was the most populous settlement in the future state. A mixed group of citizens inhabited the town, including Indians, Americans, immigrants, and Métis people. The settlement was associated throughout its history with French Canada, the Hudson's Bay Company, the Red River Colony, and the Red River ox cart trains.

General Scott located the fort a mile and a half south of the settlement, just above the mouth of the Pembina River. The Fort was completed on July 8, 1870. It was originally called Fort Thomas in honor of Major General George H. Thomas, who died on March 28, 1870, but that September it was renamed Fort Pembina. It reached a maximum garrison strength of 200 men in 1878. By 1890, only twenty-three men were stationed there.

The War Department began abandonment procedures in 1891. A fire extensively damaged the Fort on May 27, 1895, and it was officially abandoned on August 16, 1895, with the last soldiers leaving in September. The fort was later sold at public auction.

Carole Butcher

World's Tallest Structure

09 DEC

In early December 1966, the North Dakota Board of Higher Education accepted title to the KTHI-TV tower from the Pembina Broadcasting Co. The move put the gigantic tower into the hands of the state and allowed UND and NDSU to add a powerful antenna for broadcasting educational television programming.

The KTHI tower was the tallest, man-made, land-based structure in the world. The only structure that was higher is the water-supported Petronius Platform in the Gulf of Mexico. The North Dakota tower was completed in 1963 about three miles west of Blanchard, southwest of Hillsboro. It now transmits for KVLY, an NBC affiliate in Fargo.

The tower held the record for highest man-made structure for eleven years until, in 1974, a radio tower in Poland surpassed it by 57 feet. When the Polish tower collapsed in 1991, the KVLY mast again hit the top of the list.

A crew of eleven men assembled the tower in thirty-three working days. The cost was half a million dollars and its broadcast area is roughly 30,000 square miles—an area about the size of Hawaii, the District of Columbia, Massachusetts, New Jersey, and Connecticut put together, with a thousand square miles left over.

The original call letters of KTHI were specifically chosen for H-I, referring to the height of the mast, which is 2,063 feet tall. Once it was completed, the Federal Aviation Administration imposed a limit on further construction of this height; no structure in the United States can now legally exceed the KVLY tower's height.

There are many interesting facts and figures about this structure. It's taller than the Washington Monument, Eiffel Tower, and the Great Pyramid *combined*. It contains two million feet of steel, guy wire strands and elevator cable, and the structure, along with its guy anchors, takes up 160 acres of space.

Here's some more trivia for you. If a hunter at the base of the tower shot a .45 caliber pistol at a goose flying near the top, he would have to lead the goose by more than the length of a football field. If the tower had its base at the bottom of the Royal Gorge in Colorado, the antenna would still be 563 feet above the upper rim. In a 70 mile-per-hour wind, the beacon light on top sways approximately ten feet. If a 20-second commercial started at the same moment a baseball was dropped from the top, the commercial would end nearly four seconds before the ball hit the ground. If an ironworker on the antenna dropped his wrench, it would be traveling 250 miles per hour when it hit the ground.

To get to the top, workers can either use a service elevator or a ladder —one might guess the elevator would be more popular. Once they're up there, however, the transmission signals are so strong they can hurt the fillings in their teeth.

Merry Helm

10 DEC

The Line of Duty

Law enforcement is and always has been a dangerous occupation. Everyday, our police and other law enforcement officials put their life on the line. On this date in 1911, Sheriff George F. Moody of Wahpeton became another name in a long list of officers killed in the line of duty.

Jake Steffes was renting an old farm seven miles west of Wahpeton. After he came home, he saw a stranger inside his house and tried to get him to leave. The stranger refused and Steffes quickly rode off to Wahpeton in search of the sheriff.

Steffes, Sheriff Moody, and a deputy soon returned along with the driver of the team to the farmstead. The stranger was still inside the house. Angry words between Sheriff Moody and the stranger ensued. The stranger claimed to be a Pinkerton Agent by the name of Weldemeir. Sheriff Moody then said, "If that's so, then come on out."

As soon as he appeared on the porch, the stranger leveled his rifle at the sheriff and pulled the trigger. At almost the same time, the sheriff also managed to fire a shot, which grazed the stranger's hand. Sheriff Moody took one more step toward the intruder and fell dead to the ground.

Jake Steffes quickly jumped on his buggy and tried to leave the scene, only to be overtaken by the murderer. He pushed Steffes off the buggy, stole his rifle, and took off heading south.

Posses were immediately rounded up and the pursuit was on. They picked up his trail south of town, and followed him into and through Elma Township. Eventually, he was spotted by a group looking for him south and east of Vernon.

The posse eventually killed the fugitive's horse, and then began chasing him on foot across a field, firing shots back and forth. The chase went on for another four miles before they had the outlaw surrounded. The fugitive was eventually shot by a member of the posse from Hankinson.

The murderer's identity is still shrouded in mystery. It is likely he was Charles Moline, an escaped insane convict who had killed his father in Pierce County.

Dave Seifert

Threshing Tragedy

11 DEC

A headline in the *Larimore Pioneer* simply stated, "A Horrible Story." What followed was a gruesome accounting of an event that began with an accident but grew into a tale of revenge and murder. On this date, a threshing crew was operating near Portland on the Goose River in Traill County. As was usual on the threshing crew, when the bundles were brought in, the worker known as the band cutter would slice open the bundles. Another member of the crew—known as the feeder—would pitch the bundle into an open chute that lead to the rotating blades on the cylinder of the threshing machine. On this occasion, however, the band cutter accidently cut the hand of the feeder, who angrily snatched the knife and sliced open the abdomen of the band cutter. The band cutter, knowing he only had moments to live, grabbed his murderer and hurled him into the cylinder of the threshing machine where he was mangled beyond recognition. The band cutter died only a moment later.

The details of the event were reported to the editor of the *Larimore Pioneer* by a man who had supposedly come from the area, so it was very believable—but there were a few problems. In following up on the information, the editor of the *Pioneer* learned that although the event had supposedly taken place near Portland on this date, the people of Portland knew nothing of it. When further investigated, it was revealed that the same story had appeared in the *Bismarck Tribune* and the *St. Paul Pioneer Press* a few months earlier.

The actual truth as to when and where the tragedy took place was never learned. However, there was a different tale being told, which was given enough credibility that it had evolved into a poem written by Cecil E. Selwyn—an old-time resident of Manitoba. In this version, credited with happening in Cavalier County, the feeder on the threshing machine had cast a thirteen-year-old band cutter into the cylinder, and as a consequence, the other members of the crew hanged him. Lynching was a crime, so there would be a need to hide the facts to protect the crew. Although cloaked in secrecy, eventually—through guilt or loose talk—elements of the event had surfaced. However, the tale had *supposedly* happened over in the next county.

Jim Davis

12 DEC

White Bread Blues

Owners of North Dakota's grain milling businesses were in an uproar during this period in 1908. Bleached flour had just been outlawed through the efforts of Professor E. F. Ladd, a scientist at the North Dakota Agricultural College who became one of the nation's foremost crusaders for the pure food and drug laws.

In November 1908, the *Bismarck Daily Tribune* reported: "At 10 o'clock Monday evening the case of the Russell-Miller Milling Company [and others] vs. E. F. Ladd, as food commissioner of North Dakota, was submitted to [District Judge Charles Pollock], after arguments covering 12 hours... [The plaintiffs] summed up, making a strong plea for their petition to throttle Commissioner Ladd in opposing the bleached flour process."

"[The defendant held] that the bleaching process is a fraud in that the consuming public is not aware of what has been done to the flour and that it is injurious to the public health, the court was asked to place its official ban on the process.

"The outcome of this action will decide the fate of the Alsop process for bleaching" the story read. "At the present time there is not a mill in the country that is without one of these devices, and it is the Alsop people who are fighting for their existence."

The story also revealed the millers were paying their expert witnesses from between $50 a day to a lump sum of $1,000 to testify for them. On Ladd's side, however, no witnesses were paid. The article stated: "the testimony of Professor E. F. Ladd was by far the most striking, impressive and sensational in the case. The results he has accomplished in his experiments has not been approached by the experts on the opposing side... Arrayed as he is against the millers of the entire country, it is conceded that he has put up a good fight."

To understand why the case was so dramatic, we remember the American homemaker of the day. White bread was still relatively new. As a paper from Fort Wayne, IN, put it, "the market will hardly buy anything but "bleached" flour because the housewife will have nothing else."

But, Professor Ladd warned, live animals exposed to the nitrites in bleached flour died sudden and violent deaths. On November 7, 1908, a story from the *Fargo Forum* read, "That an alcohol made from bleached flour contains a poison that was strong enough to kill rabbits and did kill a number of them that were used in a series of experiments, was the startling testimony that was given by [Professor Ladd today]. On the other hand, that it was not the alcohol that killed, but was a poison left in the flour by the bleaching process, was also proved by the professor."

"Professor Ladd did not make these experiments himself," the story read, "as he did not want it said that he had mixed up some sort of dope."

Indeed, the experiments were carried out by two professors from the NDAC—a Professor Smith and Dr. Van Es, who did post mortem exams.

Their test results showed rabbits injected with the alcohol from bleached flour quickly collapsed or went into convulsions. Five of the six subjects died within hours—the sixth was given a second dose the next day and died within fifteen minutes. On the other hand, three rabbits injected with alcohol from non-bleached flour had no trouble.

Meanwhile, the brouhaha was also taking place before the Dept of Agriculture in Washington. On December 10, Secretary Wilson sustained Professor Ladd's findings that "flour beached with nitrogen peroxide is an adulterated product under the law and it cannot legally be sold."

Merry Helm

13 DEC

A Small State After All

It has often been said that ties run close in North Dakota. It's the biggest small town in the world—or so it seems.

On this date in 1968, the *Minot Daily News* published a story that illustrated that point in an unexpected way. Mark Marsall, a former resident of Mandan, who was then living in California, met Robert E. Larson, of Minot, while in Mexico, out in the Pacific Ocean—when Larson saved Marsall's life.

Larson was in Mexico on a business trip with college friend Steve Bergren, from Chicago, who was fluent in Spanish and would serve as translator. On the night they arrived, they were relaxing around the hotel pool when a woman ran up to them and asked if they could swim. The two men could definitely swim—they had taken and passed a diving course while at Stanford. When they said they could, the woman told them that two men were drowning in the ocean.

According to reports, Marsall and his teenage son Joe had been caught in a stiff undertow, or rip current. Responding to the Marsall's cries for help, Larson and his friend quickly swam to the two men. They found Marsall, but not his son—Marsall had told his son Joe to take off for the shore, to save his own life. Marsall, meanwhile, was almost on his last breath. Larson towed him back to the coast while Bergren stayed behind to look for Joe. Towing a person with one arm while swimming for two was difficult for Larson. However, after about ten minutes, Marsall was sufficiently rested to hold onto Larson's swim trunks, making it easier for them to get to shore.

Marsall's son Joe made it back safely, too. Bergren gave up his search and came in, so all four were accounted for and safe, and Bergren and Larson were heroes.

Water incidents and resultant injury and death can occur almost anywhere, but perhaps it's not a danger most North Dakotans are mindful of, living as they do in a land-locked region. But in this instance, meeting an old North Dakota neighbor was more than a lucky break—it was a saving grace.

Sarah Walker

I Want to Believe

14 DEC

This week in 1948, Lieutenant George F. Gorman wrote a letter referring to an incident known as the Gorman Dogfight, one of the early "classics" of Ufology.

On October 1, 1948, Lieutenant Gorman was returning from a cross-country flight with his squadron of North Dakota Air National Guard. When the pilots got to Hector airport in Fargo, Gorman decided to log some night-flying time. As he was preparing to land, the control tower advised him that a Piper Cub was in the air. Gorman saw the Piper 500 feet below, but then the taillight of another plane flashed by on the right. The tower insisted there weren't any other planes in the sky, so Gorman told them he wanted to investigate and took off after the moving light.

He closed to within about 1,000 yards to take a good look, later saying, "It was about six to eight inches in diameter, clear white, and completely round without fuzz at the edges. It was blinking on and off. As I approached, however, the light suddenly became steady and pulled into a sharp left bank. I thought it was making a pass at the tower. I dived after it and brought my manifold pressure up to sixty inches, but I couldn't catch up with the thing. It started gaining altitude and again made a left bank," he said. "Suddenly it made a sharp right turn and we headed straight at each other. Just when we were about to collide, I guess I got scared."

Gorman said he cut sharply toward the light, which was once more coming at him. When it again appeared that they'd collide, the object shot straight up in a steep climb-out, disappearing overhead. Gorman again went after it, but his plane went into a power stall, and the object disappeared. Gorman was so shook up that he had a hard time landing his plane, even though he was a veteran pilot and flight instructor.

The official explanation the Air Force gave was that the light was merely a lit weather balloon. But Gorman's story wouldn't die. In April 1952, *Life* magazine did a story on UFOs, claiming to offer "some scientific evidence that there is a real case for interplanetary saucers."

The article went on to describe the Gorman Dogfight: "For 27 hair-raising minutes, Gorman pursued the light through a series of intricate maneuvers. He said it was... going faster than his F-51 (300-400 mph). It made no sound and left no exhaust trail. After Gorman landed, the light having suddenly flashed away in the upper air, he found support for his story—the chief of the control tower had followed the fantastic "combat" with binoculars.

That's right. Both men in the control tower saw the whole thing, as did the two men in the Piper Cub. The Gorman Dogfight has now become one of the most noted UFO encounters in Project Blue Book, the Air Force's official record and denial of such things.

Merry Helm

15 DEC

Capitol Custodian

North Dakota government is staffed with various public officials created by constitutional or legislative processes, and these positions are normally filled by appointment, election or personal application, with selection made through a supervising committee. Seldom does the Legislature create a position and actually name the individual to assume it.

The Board of Administration was created to oversee maintenance of a number of public buildings, and this included the janitors at the State Capitol Building. William A. Laist Jr. was one of these janitors. Born in Germany in 1866, Mr. Laist came to the United States in 1885 and began working at the Capitol in 1893. Most often referred to as Billy, Mr. Laist was an exceedingly popular figure on the Capitol Grounds and, on March 8, 1929 the North Dakota Legislature passed Senate Bill #128.

This Bill created the position of Custodian of the Capitol Buildings whose duties were to oversee the persons employed as janitors and distribute supplies. This individual would serve as an official guide and would also act as the Capitol Grounds law enforcement officer with powers equal to that of a sheriff. To that end, he would be supplied with an appropriate insignia and uniform with an annual salary of $2,000 a year. But in an unusual move, Section 3 of Senate Bill 128 actually named William Laist to the position and what was even more significant—he was granted the job for life. He could only be removed for lack of good behavior and then only by the governor.

After the Capitol fire in 1930, Billy Laist went on to assume his duties in the new Capitol Building. In 1933, when salary cuts were being enforced on state workers, Billy's pay was set in law and could not be decreased, so he voluntarily took a 20% pay cut, an act that required an Attorney General's opinion to accomplish.

On this day, in 1936, William Laist Jr. succumbed to cancer having served forty-three years at his post. He had witnessed the rise and fall of the Non-Partisan League, the burning of the old Capitol Building, the construction of the new one, and the tumultuous years of the mid 1930s during the Langer Administration. Honorary pallbearers included then current Governor Welford and two former governors, all of the Supreme County Justices, the Attorney General, the Secretary of State and the entire Board of Administration, as well as numerous other public officials and friends. Billy had served under a total of seventeen governors but he said the secret to his success was that he never mixed in political scraps of any kind.

Jim Davis

Murder and Lynching

16 DEC

It was about four o'clock in the morning, on this date in 1913, when about sixty men smashed in the doors of the Williston jail, overpowered the sheriff, and dragged Cleve Culbertson from his cell.

It had begun two months earlier when a man calling himself Maurice (not Cleve) Culbertson showed up in Ray asking for directions to the Dillon farm north of town. Culbertson reached the Dillon home that afternoon and asked for work. Mr. Dillon told him he wasn't hiring but invited him to stay for supper.

After the meal, Culbertson followed Dillon to the barn and shot him four times. Mrs. Dillon came running and Culbertson killed her with a shot to the chest. He then killed their 12-year-old daughter in her bed. Dillon managed to crawl from the barn to the road, where a neighbor discovered him. Dillon was able to convey that Culbertson might actually be Loren Marsh, Mrs. Dillon's first husband who had abused and deserted her. Meanwhile, Culbertson walked the six miles back to Ray, not realizing Mr. Dillon was still alive.

Culbertson registered at the hotel in Ray. During the night, he snuck to the front desk, ripped the page with his signature from the hotel registry and left. The next day he was found hiding in a freight train's coal tender. The train crew knew about the murder and handed Culbertson over to authorities.

Culbertson said he was in Williston at the time of the crime, but when brought before Dillon, the dying man gave a positive ID. So did his neighbors and the hotel clerk. Then, Dillon's mother-in-law added a confusing twist, saying he was not Loren Marsh, her daughter's first husband, making the motive a mystery.

The courthouse during the Williston trial was standing room only. The defense argued insanity, but Culbertson was convicted of first-degree murder and sentenced to life. The prosecutor, Usher Burdick, warned Sheriff Erickson to move Culbertson to Bismarck, but it didn't happen. Four nights later, a mob battered down the door.

Culbertson was dragged screaming and yelling a mile through the streets behind two cars. He pleaded for mercy all the way. At a bridge over the river Culbertson was strung up, and his body was found riddled with bullets. Witnesses said they recognized none of the mob members.

Some feel that Burdick acted wisely, letting things die down, and never arresting anyone.

Merry Helm

17 DEC

An Arthur of All Trades

Arthur Wellesley Kelley was born in New Brunswick on December 17, 1832. Forty years and one week later, he became the first postmaster of Jamestown, of which he was the first settler. And the first merchant. And owner of the first general store.

Kelley's first view of what would become Jamestown was on May 9, 1872. He had been in a partnership dealing in the hay and wood business at Fort Totten for five years. Now he wanted to strike out on his own. He had heard the railroad was approaching the James River valley and decided to have a look.

Kelley liked what he saw and went back to Fort Totten for his merchandise and livestock. When he returned to the valley a month later, graders were at work, track-layers were approaching, and the military arrived to create Fort Seward while Kelley created a tent store.

When Kelley felt his little store was well enough established, he left it with a temporary manager and went back to Fort Totten to get his wife, Frances, and their two children—Horatio, 12, and Jennie, 6. They were the first children in the new little village called Jamestown.

The Kelleys lived in a tent for six months until their one-room log cabin was built. The town now consisted of many other businesses operating in tents—three hotels, several saloons, and three general stores were all located on the west bank of the river where the Anne Carlsen school now stands. By Christmas, Kelley was named postmaster, and he distributed the mail from his store.

When Fort Seward closed five years later, Kelley salvaged timbers from one of the buildings and built an impressive new building called the Capital House. Arthur and Frances sold peanut butter, kerosene, and vinegar in bulk. Apples and crackers were sold from barrels, and sugar, flour and coffee beans were sold in 100-pound sacks. They also sold 5 and 10-pound pails of syrup. Out front on the sidewalk, the Kelleys encouraged farm trade by selling hay bales.

Kelley was the town's first notary public, which led to yet another of his firsts; he officiated over the town's first marriage ceremony: a wedding between a soldier named Gillespie and a Miss Bowden.

Jennie later talked about how she and her brother loved running on the prairie. They grew up with the town and went to school with the military kids. She also talked about their Native American neighbors and said there was a friendliness between them and the early white settlers. On one occasion, Mrs. Kelley came in to the house to find her husband sitting on the floor smoking a pipe of peace with eleven Indian visitors.

Frances died in 1908, and Arthur followed fourteen days later. Their children and grandchildren carried on in their place, with Arthur Kelley II running a grocery store in the tradition of his grandparents until 1936.

Merry Helm

Dickinson Clay Products Company

18 DEC

Shortly before the turn of the twentieth century, a UND biology professor and his brother purchased an old brick plant near Dickinson and turned it into one of the state's premier brick plants.

Producing high-quality fire brick and face brick, the Dickinson Fire and Pressed Brick Company employed up to thirty men, but it was seasonal work since the brickyard was unable to operate during the winter months. In 1934, to keep the men employed year-round, art pottery was introduced to the plant. Soon, art pottery production surpassed brick production. In keeping with the changes, on this date in 1934, the company's name changed to Dickinson Clay Products Company.

The trade name of the pottery, Dickota, included the first four letters of the city, Dickinson, combined with the last three letters of the state. Retail sales of Dickota Pottery spread quickly from Dickinson to Bismarck and eventually throughout the Midwest, especially after the addition of Charles Grantier.

A UND graduate and former student of Margaret Kelly Cable, Charles G. Grantier, joined the company as a designer shortly after its reorganization. Using the abundant native clay found nearby, Grantier found inspiration for his designs in the surrounding region, evidenced by work ranging from a small buffalo figure promoting North Dakota to a tipi-shaped incense burner and mountain sheep bookends. Another popular motif created by Grantier was called "Sundog." A familiar sight on the frigid plains of a North Dakota winter, Grantier captured the natural phenomenon on clay ashtrays and bowls with rainbow-like lines radiating toward the sun near the horizon. But the pieces designed by Grantier and produced in the largest quantities were souvenir commercial wares, such as an ashtray produced for the Lewis and Clark Hotel depicting an image of Red Tomahawk, the same Native American profiled on the state highway signs.

The Dickinson Clay Plant attracted other notable North Dakota artists as well. UND's Margaret Kelly Cable spent several weeks at the plant designing dinnerware known as Dickota Cableware. Laura Taylor, known for her Rosemeade pottery, also designed an ashtray with a lounging lion while conducting classes in Dickinson.

Although Dickota Pottery proved the economic viability of using western North Dakota's clay in commercial pottery, its success was short-lived. The worsening economic conditions of the Great Depression forced the plant to close its doors in November of 1937.

While working for the Dickinson Clay Products Company, Charles Grantier penned these lines for a 1936 advertising brochure:

Clods of clay—too long
you've lain awaiting
the potter's hand.
You're destined now to
Please the eyes of
men throughout the
land.

Your gorgeous hues of
Reds and blues
Of tans and buffs and
creams,
Are truly those the
Potters choose
To weave in many
themes.

Tis "Dickota" I shall
name this ware
From which these clays
have come,
And shape the clay
with gentle care
As the potter's wheel is
spun.

Christina Sunwall

The Whiskey Runners

19 DEC

Five hundred quarts of nine-year-old whiskey were carried from the jailhouse to the Stutsman County Courthouse this week in 1922. Sheriff Dana Wright had seized the liquor from smugglers in 1921, during the first year of Prohibition, and the whiskey had been stored in the jail as evidence. At the orders of the court, Sheriff Wright smashed every whiskey bottle at the courthouse window, in full view of an audience gathered on the grounds below. This spectacle warned rum-runners that any liquor smuggled through North Dakota would not make it out.

The long unguarded border between North Dakota and Canada, with its flat land and numerous road crossings, was an ideal location for smugglers to connect Canadian liquor warehouses to speakeasies in the United States. A quart of whiskey could be bought for $3.50 in Canada and sold for $20 in the States. Rum-runners loaded bottles of liquor into sacks to save space and crammed them into the biggest cars they could find. A decoy car usually led the way, sniffing out hidden roadblocks. Drivers were hired with a promise of a thousand dollars, almost a year's salary, as payment for three trips across the border. Unfortunately, most drivers were caught before the third run.

Jail was often the second stop for captured runners, after a visit to the hospital to fix bullet wounds and broken bones. The rum-running business was incredibly dangerous for both drivers and police. A routine traffic stop in Minot turned into a shoot-out at point-blank range between a police officer and a smuggler. A Sioux Falls driver, whose wife thought he was a travelling auto-parts salesman, died in a shootout with Bottineau County sheriffs. As the smugglers increased their firepower to defend their whiskey cargo, the sheriffs upgraded to Thompson and Browning machine guns. Women drivers were even used, in hopes of discouraging the police from returning fire. Even if the smugglers made it through without a shoot-out, their high-speed escape down rough dirt roads often ended in a crash.

Mortal risk and a tightening of Canadian laws slowed the stream of cars carrying liquor into North Dakota, but the smuggling still continued until the end of Prohibition in 1933.

As for Dana Wright, the Stutsman County Sheriff, he changed jobs when his term ran out in 1927, but he didn't leave the fight. With Prohibition still in effect, he headed north, becoming a customs agent at St. John in Rolette County, watching for those rum-runners sneaking across the border.

Derek Dahlsad

20 DEC

The Non-Swearing Knights of America

Robert C. Wynn, founder of the Non-Swearing Knights of America, announced to the *Grand Forks Herald* on this date in 1908 that the organization would build its headquarters in Minot.

Born in Ohio in 1855, Wynn came to North Dakota in 1900 from Indiana while employed with the Great Northern Railroad. He worked on the Granville-Sherwood line until his retirement in 1933.

The Knights started in 1885 after three railway men witnessed a freight train crew shouting curses within hearing distance of the women's restroom at the Des Moines rail station. The three men, including Wynn, were horrified at the scene and vowed to refrain from swearing the rest of their lives. Wynn claimed that it was never the intention of the group to spread outside of these three railroad men, but soon others heard of the vow and wished to follow suit. In 1914, North Dakota Governor Louis B. Hannah affixed the title of Colonel to Wynn, which he retained for the rest of his life.

Colonel Wynn became nationally recognized for founding the organization. He ran his anti-profanity campaign from his train, which he called the "Sunshine Limited." The group's membership peaked at nearly 7,000 members from every state in the Union. Shucks.

Jayme L. Job and Jim Davis

Dr. Anne Carlsen

21 DEC

On this day in 2002, North Dakota lost a passionate teacher and visionary—Dr. Anne Carlsen. She leaves behind the Anne Carlsen Center for Children in Jamestown as her lasting legacy.

Carlsen was born to Danish immigrants in Wisconsin in 1915. She was missing her forearms and lower legs, but early on, her family recognized her quick wit and keen mind. Her father told her, "Anne, two arms and two legs missing aren't as important as one head that's present. The best way to make that head help is to get it educated."

So at age eight, Anne went to school. Carlsen learned how to write and feed herself without hands. With the help of a kiddie car, she learned to walk and run. She even learned how to swim, play baseball, and other games her friends played. She did so well that four years later she graduated from eighth grade by the time she turned twelve.

During high school, Carlsen underwent a long hospital stay for surgery and physical therapy, learning to use artificial legs. Still, she graduated by age sixteen. She wanted to teach, so she went on to the University of Minnesota, graduating *cum laude* in 1936. But despite her obvious talents, Anne met with a host of obstacles when she tried to get a job. Finally, in 1938, she was hired by the Good Samaritan School for Crippled Children in Fargo.

She remembered, "I bought myself a new dress and hat and a Greyhound bus ticket and headed west to Fargo. I had never been to North Dakota. I was offered $25 a month, plus room and board. I thought I was at the peak of my career."

Three years later, the school was moved to Jamestown. Anne blossomed as a teacher, and after getting her master's and doctoral degrees, she became the school's administrator in 1950. For the next 31 years, she dedicated herself to making sure handicapped children and adults were not treated as second-class citizens.

"It's gratifying," she once said, "to see those who've become successful by universal standards, as teachers, physicists, homemakers [...] But others whose handicaps are so severe that they can't be employed are successes, too. If they do the best they can and contribute whatever they're able, they're really doing as well or better in life than most non-handicapped people."

In 1958, Eisenhower awarded Carlsen the President's Trophy for Handicapped American of the Year. In 1971, she was a guest on *The Today Show*, and in 1983, President Reagan appointed her to serve as vice chairperson of the Committee on Employment of the Physically Handicapped.

"Handicapped children and adults are no longer second-class citizens," she later wrote. "If I have helped in any way to bring this about, then my work here at Jamestown has had a purpose."

Merry Helm

22 DEC

Fargo Orphan

A heartwarming story was reported by the Cass County Juvenile Court Commissioner in his annual report in 1922. Too often, the Commissioner's reports were filled with heartbreak rather than happy endings. However, for one small boy, the Christmas of 1922 proved to be the happiest in his young memory, as he reunited with his lost family. The story of "Billy" became known in Fargo as early as 1919. Although Billy was not the boy's real name, it became the pseudonym that the papers chose to call him.

Billy began his life in Wisconsin. His was an unhappy family, and his father left his mother destitute shortly after the boy's birth. Her choice to marry had led to the estrangement of her own family, and so the woman and her infant son were alone in the world. They lived in poverty and hunger until the mother succumbed to illness and passed away. Billy, then only a toddler, was placed in a Wisconsin orphanage until authorities learned that the boy's father was alive, remarried, and living in Moorhead, Minnesota. They quickly sent Billy to live with his father. The second wife, however, was unaware of the first wife or son, and soon left the man. Billy's father blamed the boy for his misfortune and began to beat him. Finally, he was told to leave the home. Not knowing where to go or who he could possibly turn to, Billy crawled inside a Fargo sewer pipe to take refuge from the cold. One night, his sobs attracted the attention of a nearby resident. Freezing, bloodstained, dirty, and hungry, nine-year old Billy was coaxed out of the pipe, and he became a ward of the county court. For three years after, Billy lived in two foster homes.

One day at school, a flash came across Billy's face—while listening to children discuss upcoming plans for Christmas, Billy had suddenly remembered his mother's maiden name, a name he had forgotten. Within days, his maternal uncle and grandmother were found living on a farm outside of Eau Claire, Wisconsin. The Juvenile Court Commissioner placed Billy on the next train out of Fargo, and the boy reached his new home in time to celebrate Christmas with his own family. As for the Commissioner, he was glad to report that Fargo's famous orphan had finally found a home.

Jayme L. Job

Delivering Presents

23 DEC

James Grassick started his career as a physician in Buxton in 1885. Each year, he put together handsome booklets for his friends for Christmas. In one of these, he wrote of a special Christmas Eve he experienced back in the horse and buggy days. It was after nightfall when the good doctor was called to attend a woman in labor in a remote settler's home.

"The wind was blowing briskly, the air crisp, the sledding heavy and the snow falling thickly. But our good Doctor," he wrote, "was used to such conditions, they were in the line of his calling. He had faced storms before…"

However, Dr. Grassick soon found the trip tough going. "It was now quite dark," he wrote, "the stars were hid, and all sense of direction was gone except what could be learned from the wind… The snow, charged with icy particles came down more thickly," he wrote, "the biting wind increased in velocity, the cold became more intense and our traveler was beginning to feel its effects…"

When Grassick felt himself giving up, he let up on the reins, and his horses instinctively moved toward safety. Finally, they stopped in the shelter of a haystack, and the doctor looked around to get his bearings. When the snow lifted for a few seconds, he made out the dim outline of a sod shanty and made a dash for it. It turned out to be the home of his patient.

Inside, two small children, Betty and Bobbie thought he was Santa Claus and were disappointed he wasn't bearing presents. Grassick comforted them and went in to see their mother. "As midnight approached," he wrote, "it became evident that a visit from Santa was a certainty and just as the clock struck twelve a terrific swirl of the wind made the rafters creak and the pane of the little window rattle; but these sounds were only the prattle of tiny feet as Santa's coursers mounted the roof on their way to the chimney…"

"And within," he continued, "stood Grandma with her outstretched apron ready to receive the parcel as she had often done before. She evidently was not disappointed for in the fullness of her heart she cried out excitedly, 'Look here! What is this?'" A boy and a girl.

Grandma had clothing for only one baby, so Dr. Grassick spread his heavy coonskin coat before the fire and wrapped the newborn twins in it.

"The sun came up without a fleck to mar its brightness," Grassick wrote, "a million diamond points sparkling in its course. Soon the news of Santa's storm journey, and of the gifts he had left for Betty and Bobbie, were known in the settlement, and they were not long wanting in clothes for the two infants, for the good ladies of the neighborhood soon provided the needful. And the Doctor's coat was thus released from its mission of Christmas helpfulness."

Merry Helm

24 DEC

Christmas Creatures

An interesting Christmas tradition of the Germans from Russia is recounted in the book *Ethnic Heritage in North Dakota*. Authors Kas and Ida Greff wrote, "As early as two weeks before Christmas the Belznickl would gather his chains, rattling and roaring at the window just to be sure we wouldn't forget he was coming. Now if anything can keep you from misbehaving, the Belznickl could. After all, he could drag you away on Christmas Eve."

The Greffs wrote that the Belznickl would finally show his face on Christmas Eve after dinner. "His rattling and growling would keep on for an hour or two," they wrote. "When he let up for a few minutes, we would worry that he had skipped our home and gone somewhere else. He and the Kristkindl did, after all, leave gifts and treats and we certainly didn't want to miss that. Usually preceding the actual entrance of the Kristkindl and Belznickl, we would furiously say prayer after prayer.

"Finally the Belznickl came in with the Kristkindl behind," they continued. The Belznickl "was a furry thing that crawled on all fours, rattled his chain, and grabbed anyone or anything that got in his way. [He wanted] to get the bad kids and drag them away. Often he had to be held back by Mom or an older brother or sister. We'd pile on the bed, many times 10 or more of us kids. He'd make a grab for us and we'd run.

"The Belznickl was really our father but we didn't know that. We were so scared we didn't even recognize the big bear-like robe that we used on the bed. Later Mother would remind us 'the Belznickl will get you' if we weren't good.

"Our first reaction to the Kristkindl was always what a beautiful angel she was," they continued. "She was a neighbor woman dressed as an angel and would ask if we'd been good. She reminded us to say our prayers, and this was usually followed by an Our Father and a Hail Mary. The Belznickl in this whole process would try to grab our legs in order to take us away. A great havoc was created with prayers being said amid screams of agony and peals of laughter. After the children received their gifts the awesome duo would leave and the evening settled down. Gifts were opened, songs were sung, and stomachs were filled with Christmas treats."

Merry Helm

Fargo's Christmas Tree

25 DEC

The Northern Pacific Railroad founded Fargo in 1871. On the other side of the river, another town was growing at the same time—Moorhead. Minnesota was already organized, and there were concerns of how the Dakota Territory was going to develop for its people. However, land in Moorhead was extremely expensive, so many people had moved to the Fargo side of the river.

J. L. Sharp wrote about those first years, saying, "In the summer of 1872, it may be said there was a lively time here at Moorhead, as a notorious lot of characters had arrived with the railroad. Among these were Shang, Jack O'Neil, Dave Mullen and also the noted Edward Smith and Sallie O'Neil.

"These people were industrious in their various pursuits, and many queer things were done. Gambling and shooting were prominent pastimes for the people. A shooting match before and after breakfast was not an unusual occurrence. The public was one day brought as eye and ear witness of a shooting 'duet' by Dave Mullen and Ed Smith. Neither party was greatly injured, however.

"Jack O'Neil had been several times shot in the head but had escaped with his life. Sallie, his better half, one day after a drunken row threatened to kill him with a butcher knife, chasing him round and round the tent; but from this attack he also escaped and went to Bismarck, where Fatty Hall ended his thrilling career by shooting him 'amidships.'"

It's not surprising, therefore, that we look at what happened the following year in Fargo. It was 1873, and the town's citizens decided to celebrate their second year with a community Christmas celebration. There weren't a lot of pine trees in the area—in fact probably none—so they ordered a Christmas tree from Brainerd, Minnesota.

The tree arrived by train, and the boxcar was sidetracked in front of the Headquarters Hotel. But the following morning, it was discovered that the tree had been stolen during the night. A snowfall the night before had covered all footprints, so there wasn't clear evidence of who would do such a thing, but it didn't take long for the Fargo to suspect Moorhead.

Fargoans held a protest meeting, and the Moorhead suspects were hanged in effigy from the NP Bridge that linked the two cities. Then, the following night, the tree was mysteriously and anonymously returned.

Perhaps it was the Christmas spirit, but Fargo folks felt bad. So in appreciation for the tree being returned, they held a mock funeral. They draped a locomotive and boxcar in black and proceeded with great stateliness to the bridge. The effigies from the previous night were then cut down and given a ceremonious burial in a snowdrift.

Merry Helm

26 DEC

Polyphon

Player organs and pianos were fairly common near the end of the nineteenth century. They used volumes of air to create musical notes or open valves, causing a note to be struck with a hammer. In the late 1890s, the saloon in Knox obtained an interesting musical device to attract customers but, unlike the others, this device produced music with a plucking motion, much like what happens in a music box.

It was known as a Polyphon and was operated by a large, flat, metal, record-like disk just under twenty-four inches in diameter. In the disk were small rectangular holes with the punched-out area protruding from the opposite side of the disk. The disk was mounted over a set of combs whose eighty-three teeth produced notes similar to a piano keyboard. As the disk was rotated over the combs, each protruding part of the disk plucked a specific part of the comb thus creating the musical notes, which were amplified by a soundboard. The whole device was powered by a spring-wound gearbox.

This instrument had been constructed by the Regina Music Box Company of New York and the model installed in the Knox saloon also included a snare drum, bass drum, and cymbals. According to Russell Reid, superintendent of the State Historical Society, this may have been the first jukebox introduced into North Dakota.

The Polyphon was later sold to Theron Delameter, editor of the *Knox Advocate*, who operated a theater on the second floor above the print shop. The Polyphon was used between acts in theatrical productions. When the print shop closed, the building's second floor became a storage place for old crates. The jukebox slowly deteriorated until it was rediscovered by Theron's son, Lyman, who donated it to the State Historical Society of North Dakota.

On this date in 1950, music from the Polyphon was echoing through the halls of the Liberty Memorial Building on the Capitol Grounds. F. L. Harrington of the Historical Society had nearly completed the restoration of the device. He had hand-crafted approximately seventy parts and spent three months working on it, and it was once again able to play the twelve disks that were donated with it. The disks included such songs as "Come Take a Trip in My Air Ship," "Meet me at the Fountain," and the not to be forgotten, "Please Come and Play in My Yard."

Jim Davis

Avalanche to X-Ray

27 DEC

The names of North Dakota's newspapers have been quite varied throughout history. There have been celestial names such as the *Churches Ferry Sun*, the *Hannah Moon*, the *Aneta Star*, and *Burnstad Comet*. There have been progressive-sounding names such as the *Saint John Leader*, the *Halliday Booster*, and the *Prairie Promoter* out of Cooperstown. There have been simply conventional names such as the *Haynes Gazette*, the *Inkster Review*, the *Hunter Times*, or the *Landsford Journal*. There have also been unconventional names such as the *Hamilton X-Ray*, the *Alice Avalanche*, the *Fargo Blade*, the *Pink Paper* out of Bathgate, or the *Loco Weed* out of Schafer.

Over 1,421 different newspaper titles have been identified in the nearly 150-year publishing history of the state. In 1897, North Dakota had 126 newspapers, and only six years later that grew to 227. By 1919, a person living in ND could subscribe to 327 different newspapers published across the state.

There were interesting names such as the *Donnybrook Mirror*, the *Gascoyne Pennant*, the *Grand Forks Plaindealer*, the *Devils Lake Inter Ocean*, the *Pioneer-Arrow* out of Fort Yates, or the *Crystal Call*. To soar above the rest of its competition you could even find the *Crosby Eagle*. The first newspaper published in the state was the *Frontier Scout*, which began in 1864 at Fort Union.

On this date in 1888, the new proprietors of the *Dakota Blizzard* out of Casselton found the name of the newspaper intolerable and were determined to change it. They reasoned:

"There is neither wit nor sense in the name. Upon taking possession of the office, the present proprietors inherited it, just as some unfortunates inherit from their ancestors, idiocy or lunacy. They cannot get rid of the curse entailed upon them by the bad conduct of their progenitors, but this heritage of a christening by wild-eyed lunacy—or a mild form of idiocy—we can dump into the waste basket and give to the paper a reputable and meaningful name to begin the new year…, relieving the strain upon our long-suffering subscribers."

The new name chosen to replace the title of *Dakota Blizzard* was the *North Dakota Republican*. This name would last only five years before being replaced by the *Casseltonian*. One wonders what these editors would have thought of a new newspaper that began publishing in Casselton in 1898 with the unconventional name of *The Eye*.

Jim Davis

28 DEC

Noodles by Leonardo

Durum wheat from North Dakota makes some of the world's greatest pasta and noodles, but for decades, those oodles of noodles were made outside the state. In fact, on this date in 1911, the *Grand Forks Herald* touted the quality of the "Minnesota" brand of macaroni and spaghetti that was so good that even little children would "want it three times a day."

It took a long time, but, in 1980, the first exclusively-pasta plant in North Dakota, located in Cando, became a reality. The name of the facility was Noodles by Leonardo, an "integrated durum mill and pasta plant," located right in the heart of durum-wheat country.

The man behind the noodle-factory was Leonard Gasparre, who hailed from St. Paul, Minnesota. Gasparre had set his eyes on Towner County where durum was said to grow best, located in the middle of the "Durum Triangle," named for the region around Cando which produced about 80 percent of the nation's durum wheat. The Noodles by Leonardo plant broke ground in 1979, and began production of macaroni, egg noodles, and spaghetti in 1980, bringing 150 new jobs to Cando while increasing the city's tax base.

The 1980s became a time of prosperity and economic stability for Cando, and the pasta plant employed 300 workers by 1993. The facility soon exceeded its capacity, so management opened a second pasta plant in Devils Lake in 1992.

Noodles by Leonardo endured until Leonard Gasparre died in 2011 at the age of 83. After selling the Devils Lake factory, his family consolidated operations to Cando facility. Soon there was talk about selling the Cando plant as well. It seemed as though the end of the pasta-making era in Cando had arrived. Fortunately for Cando, Jim and Bruce Gibbens, with some other investors, saw the opportunity that lay at hand and purchased the facility.

Today the plant goes by the name of Cando Pasta LLC and though it doesn't employ as many people as it had in the 1990s, its revival was a victory for the town of Cando. Rather than send durum wheat out of state, Dakota pasta-makers in Cando make boxes and boxes of elbow-noodles, rotini, deluxe shells, medium shells, and penne rigate, or, we might say, a whole "lotsa pasta."

Michelle Holien

First White Baby Born in North Dakota

29 DEC

In June of 1806, a 26-year-old Scottish man signed on to work for the Hudson's Bay Company in Canada. John Fubbister was from the parish of St. Andrews in the Orkney Islands and soon became known around Fort Albany as The Orkney Lad.

Working as an agent, Fubbister paddled his canoe up-river to deliver supplies to remote fur-trading outposts. He was small, but he worked hard under harsh conditions, and within a year he earned a pay raise for performing his duties "willingly and well."

In 1807, Fubbister was assigned to a brigade under the command of Hugh Heney. That summer, they canoed and portaged 1,800 miles from Fort Albany to the Red River near Pembina.

What nobody knew was that John Fubbister was actually a woman named Isabel Gunn. The other thing they didn't know was that – during the trek – she was four months pregnant.

Back in Scotland, Isabel had an affair with a man named John Scarth, from Firth. When Scarth signed on with the Hudson's Bay Company, Isabel did, too. Some say she didn't want to be separated from Scarth. Others believe it was because she was poor and had only two other options: get married or be a domestic servant. Whichever the case, women weren't allowed in the company, so she disguised herself as a man.

Isabel and Scarth kept their affair hidden for a year, but then she became pregnant. She kept on working, though, and by fall, the colder weather allowed bulkier clothing to hide her condition.

Isabel went into labor on December 29, 1807. The head of the Pembina post at that time was Alexander Henry. Presenting herself as John Fubbister, Isabel went to Henry's house and asked him to let her sit by his fire, because she wasn't feeling well. Henry was puzzled by the Orkney Lad's behavior but agreed and went upstairs to his room.

In his journal, Mr. Henry later wrote, "I returned to my room, where I had not been long before he sent one of my own people, requesting the favour of speaking with me. Accordingly, I stepped down to him, and was much surprised to find him extended on the hearth, uttering dreadful lamentations; he stretched out his hands towards me, and in piteous tones begged me to be kind to a poor, helpless, abandoned wretch, who was not of the sex I had supposed, but an unfortunate Orkney girl, pregnant and actually in childbirth."

Isabel Gunn had not only made history by being the first European woman in Canada, but also by giving birth to the first white child born in North Dakota.

Isabel and her baby, James, were sent back to Albany in the spring, but the only work she could get there was as a nurse and washerwoman. In 1809, she sailed back to Orkney where, it is said, she died a pauper in 1861 at the age of 90.

Merry Helm

30 DEC

Some Dark Mystery

Truth is stranger than fiction, as confirmed in today's story, which appeared in the *Bismarck Tribune* on this date in 1878. "Not long ago," the story read, "a trance medium arrived in Bismarck, and the coterie of spiritualists of the city have been quietly conversing with the spirits of the departed, through the gifted medium, until they unhesitatingly declare that better mediumistic powers have never before been developed."

The reporter was impressed enough to ask for a private sitting with the medium. The story says he had no particular person he wanted to contact when the séance began, but he didn't have to wait long before the spirit of Mrs. Noonan appeared. She had died at Fort Lincoln less than two months earlier.

Mrs. Noonan did laundry for the 7th Cavalry and also acted as a midwife for the surrounding territory during her years at the fort. She married a man named Clifford in 1869, then James Nash two years later, and then Corporal John Noonan two years after that.

On November 4, Mrs. Noonan died after a two-week illness. Before she died, she asked to see a priest and told a fellow laundress she wanted to be buried in the clothes she was wearing at the time of her death. After her death, however, the laundresses thought it was indecent to just put her in her coffin as she was; they decided to bathe her and bury her in a nicer dress. What they discovered set off a string of events that made national headlines. Mrs. Noonan was a man.

The *Bismarck Tribune* wrestled with a way to report the story. The Corporal and his wife had been married five years, during which Mrs. Noonan had worn fine fashions at the fort's festivities and gatherings. A reporter wrote, "[Corp. Noonan] will probably swear when he hears the sad news. The deceased was in the habit of shaving every day, and in that way kept down a heavy beard. He was a Mexican with coarse voice and masculine looks all over. The secret of the unnatural union… may be clothed in some dark mystery."

Meanwhile, Corp. Noonan was out in the field with the 7th Cavalry. When they returned and learned what the women had discovered, Noonan was not only grief-stricken, his fellow soldiers ostracized him. Noonan soon deserted. A *Tribune* reporter found him in the stables of the lower garrison. "I dare not say that the medical officers were wrong," Noonan said, "but I know that I am right, and I know that my wife was a woman. There is some terrible mystery about this thing that I can't understand." Two days later, Noonan shot himself through the heart.

At the Bismarck séance a month later, the reporter said Mrs. Noonan's apparition told him her real name was Joseph Drummond; he had become a woman to hide a terrible crime committed in Washington D.C. fifteen years earlier.

Merry Helm

Justice James Morris

31 DEC

For the fifty people who have served as North Dakota Supreme Court justices, December 31st is often their last day in office. On this date in 1964, one of the state's longest serving justices retired; James Morris served on the court for nearly 30 years.

He was born in a sod house near Bordulac, North Dakota in 1893 and practiced law in Carrington in the 1920s after serving in World War I. He worked as a city and states attorney in Foster County before his appointment to assistant attorney general and eventually attorney general in 1928. He also practiced law in Jamestown before his election to the North Dakota Supreme Court in 1934.

Morris was reelected in 1944 and 1954. In 1947, he took a year's absence to serve as a judge at the war crimes trials in Nuremberg, Germany, appointed by President Harry Truman. Morris felt "especially fortunate to be assigned" to the task, which he considered a milestone for international jurisprudence. He presided over a trial for twenty-three officials of a manufacturing company that provided chemicals and ammunition for Adolf Hitler's final solution.

All of the officials were charged with offenses that included crimes against peace, plundering property, and murdering civilians. In the end, the four-member tribunal found various defendants guilty for a smattering of crimes with sentences prosecutors found "light enough to please a chicken thief." Prison terms for those convicted ranged from a year and a half to eight years.

Morris later summarized the verdicts and sentences as mixed, with judges unable to agree on who was guilty or whether the defendants had the freedom to exercise choice in the crimes. Another judge on the panel dissented in a 114-page opinion filed months after the trial.

As for Morris, his fellow judges thought he was more worried about looming Russian communism rather than Nazi war crimes, but ultimately, Morris's work did indeed help convict several defendants, a process that helped further international human rights law. He died in Bismarck in 1980.

Jack Dura

CPSIA information can be obtained
at www.ICGtesting.com
Printed in the USA
LVHW050804261221
707138LV00021B/2301

9 781732 841055